CONTENTS

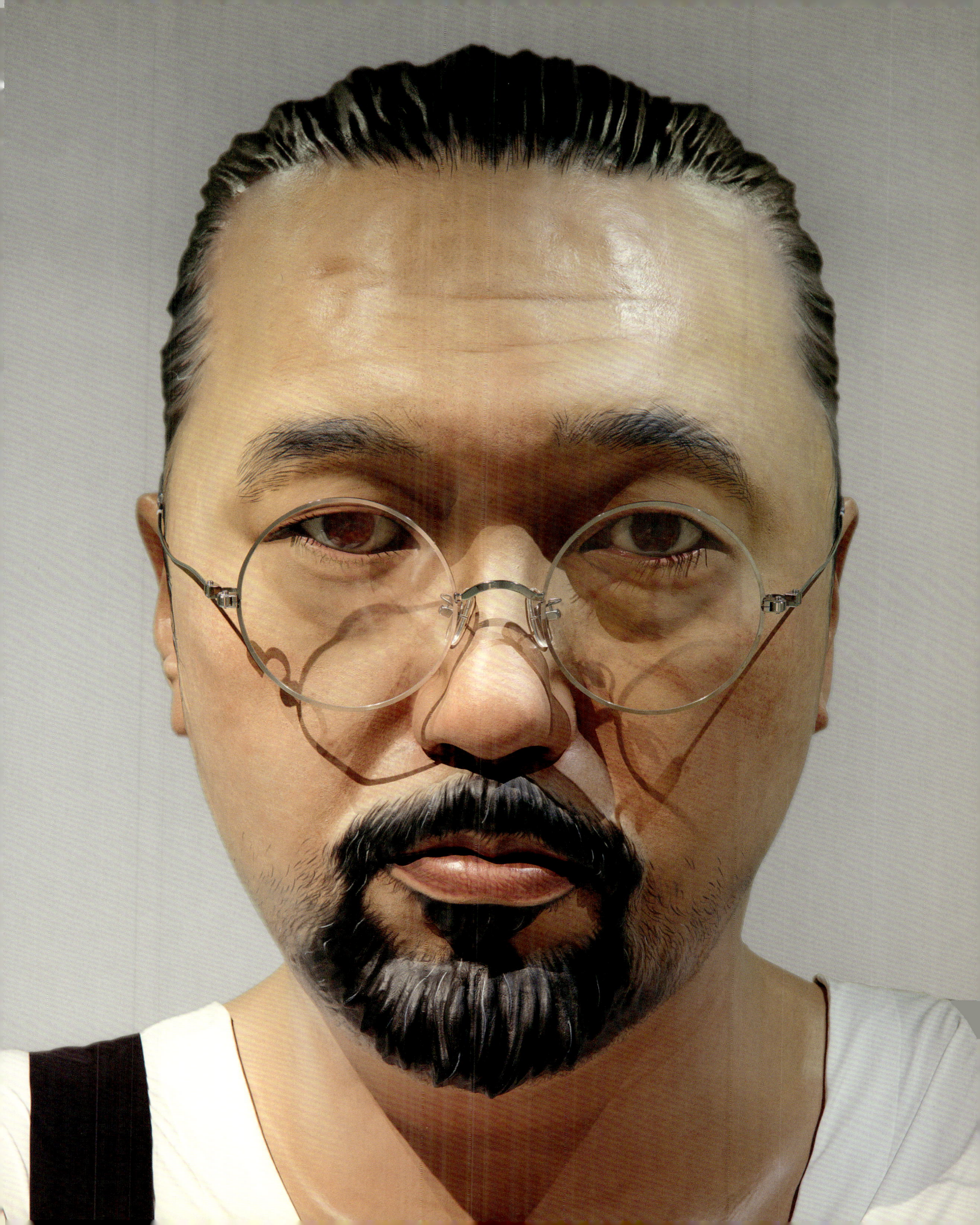

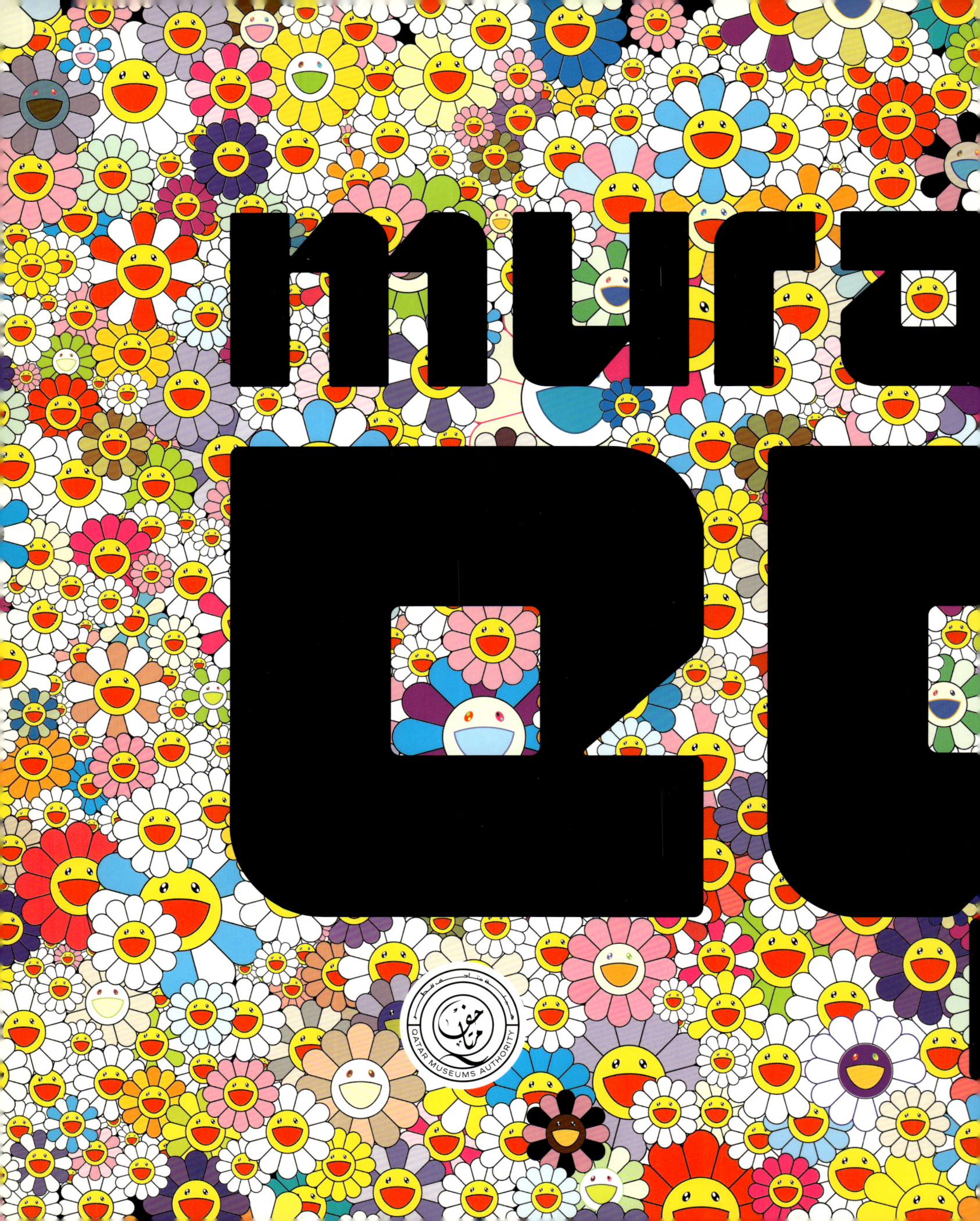

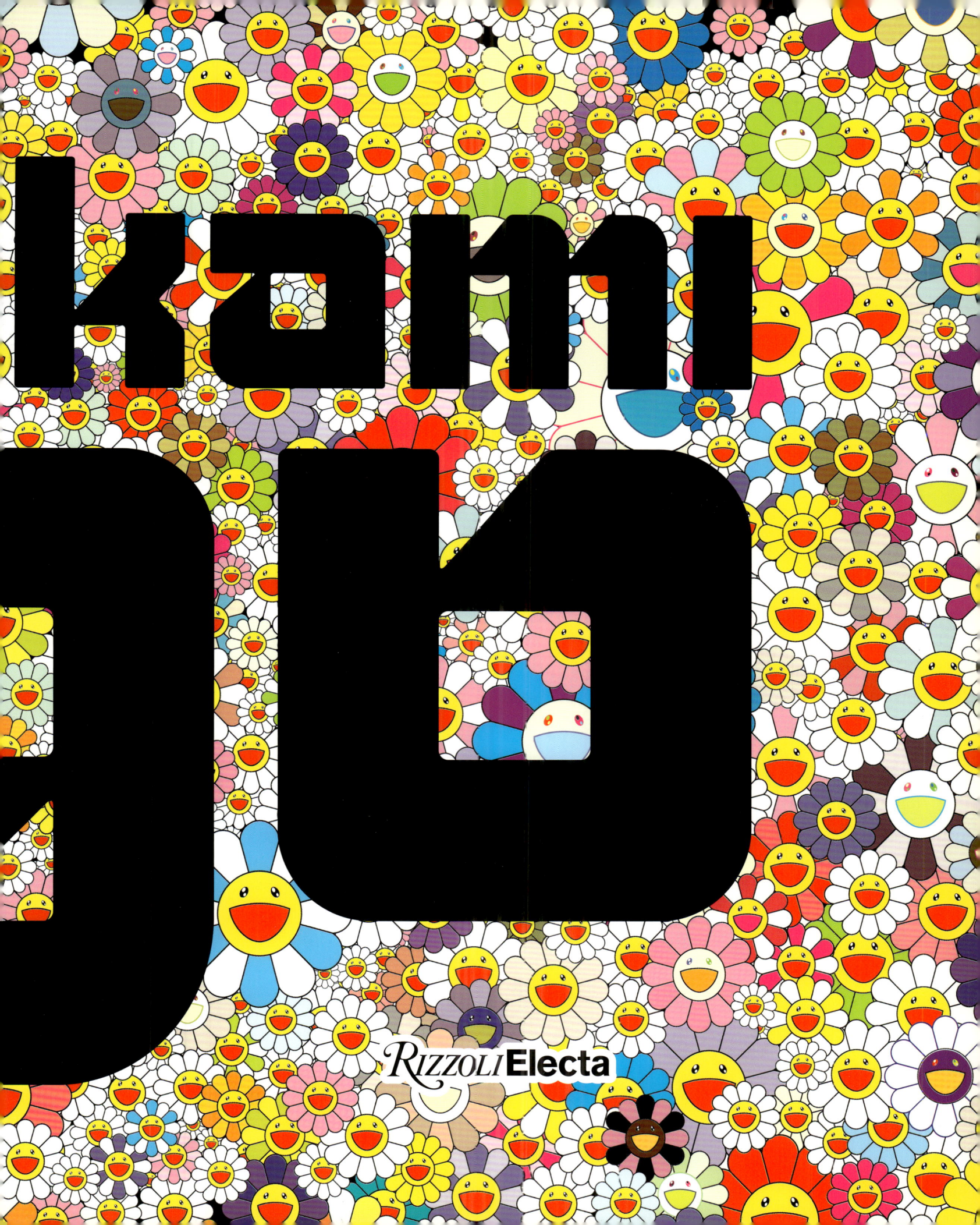

"MURAKAMI—EGO" IS A SELF-PORTRAIT.

For a long time, I have been making a portrait of Japan, the picture of a nation and a culture. Today that picture has exploded. "Murakami—Ego" is the portrait of my many identities.

People seem to really need a depiction of the artist's face. Just look at magazines: They always want to put the artist's face somewhere. That's why I started making self-portraits. I paint the surface of things. My ego is pure surface. That's my self-portrait.

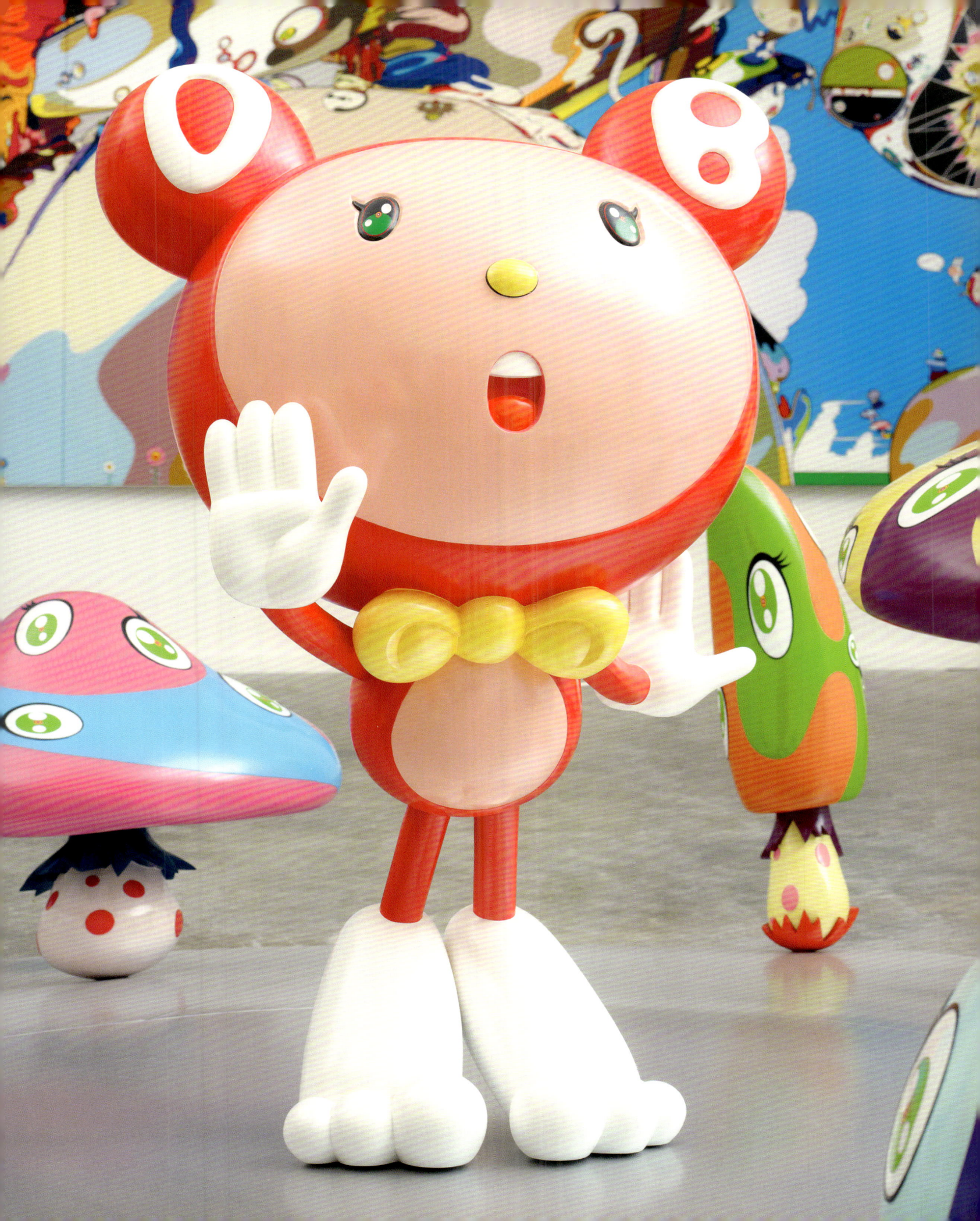

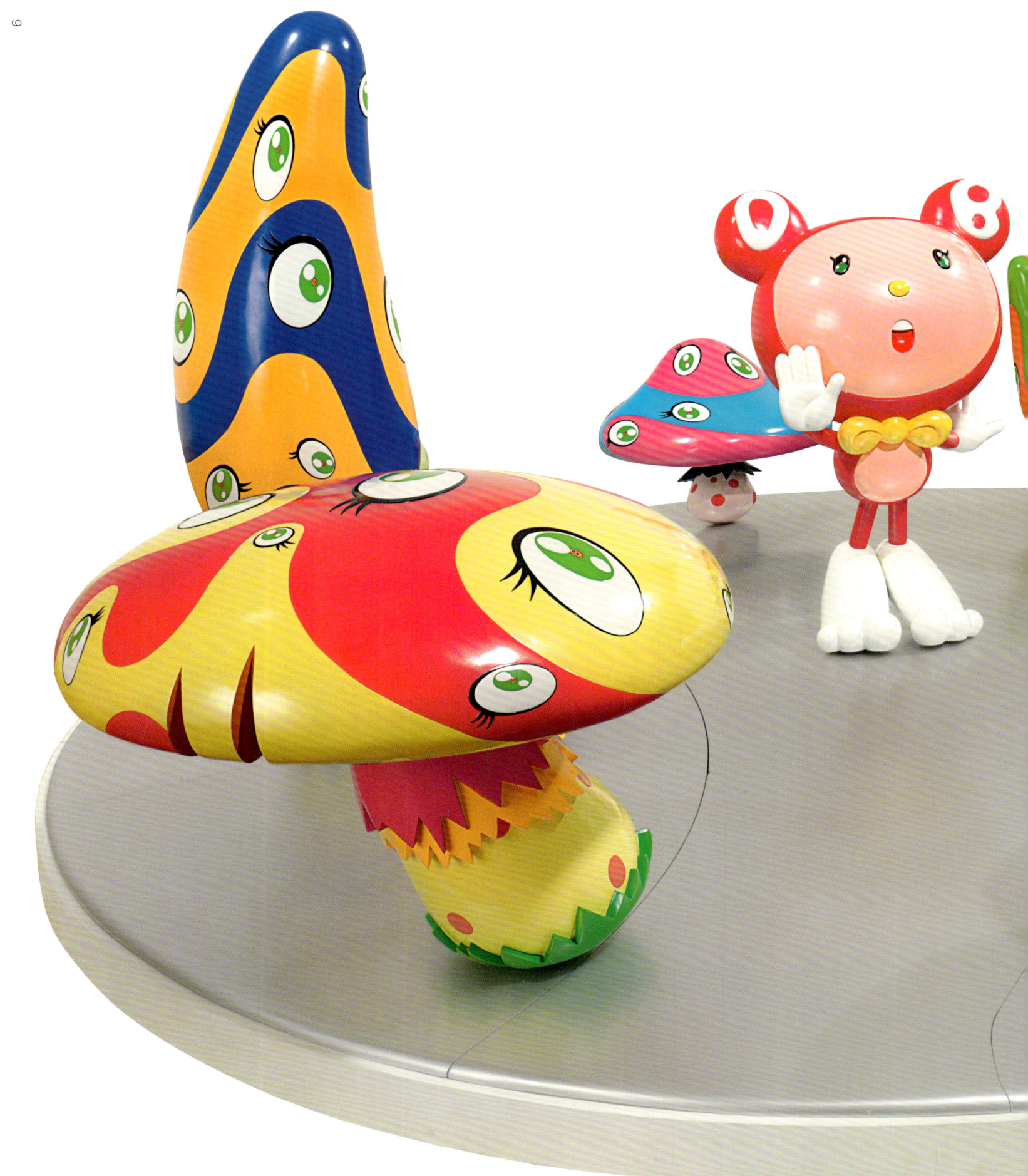

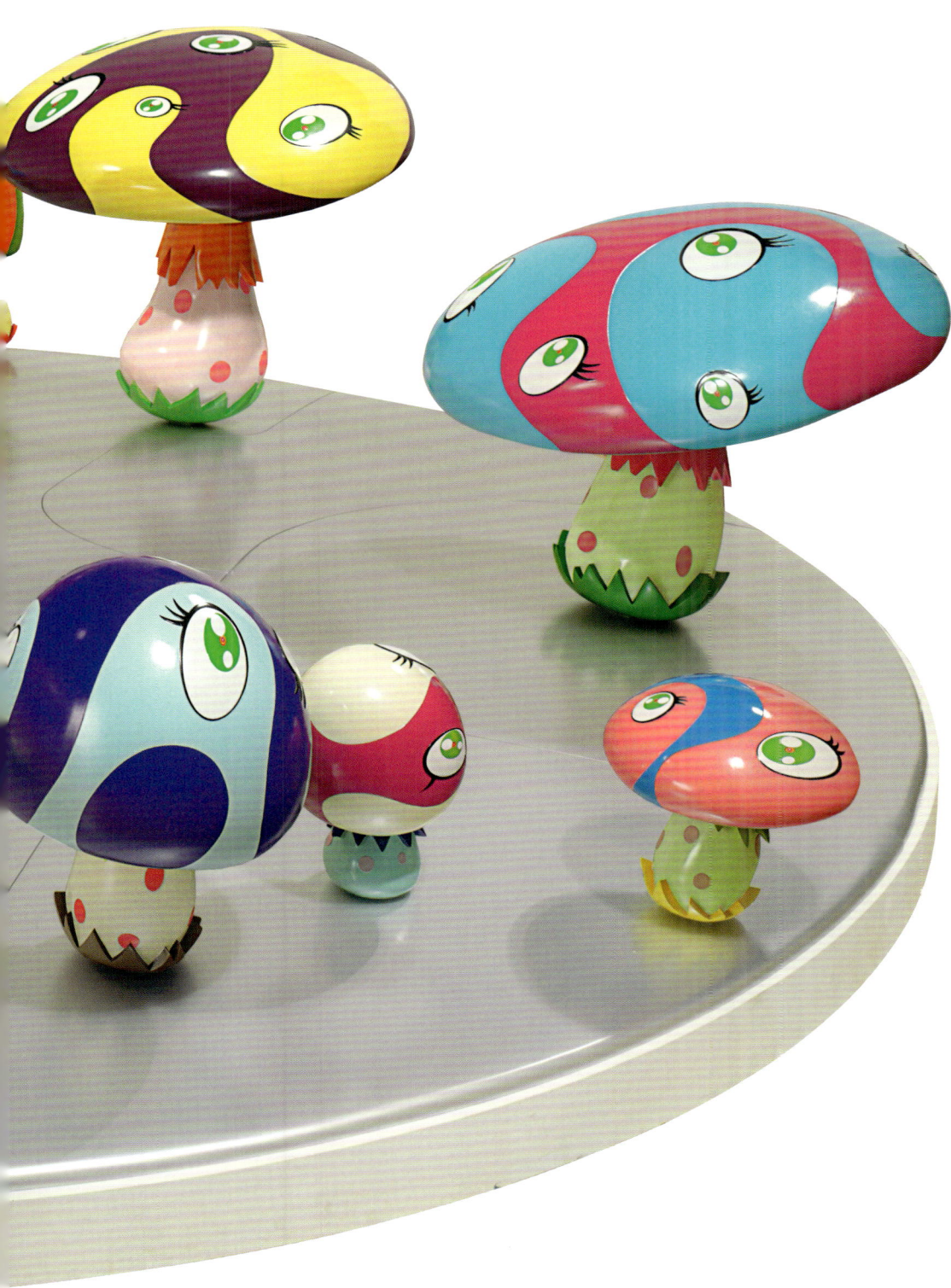

DOB in the Strange Forest (Red DOB) 1999

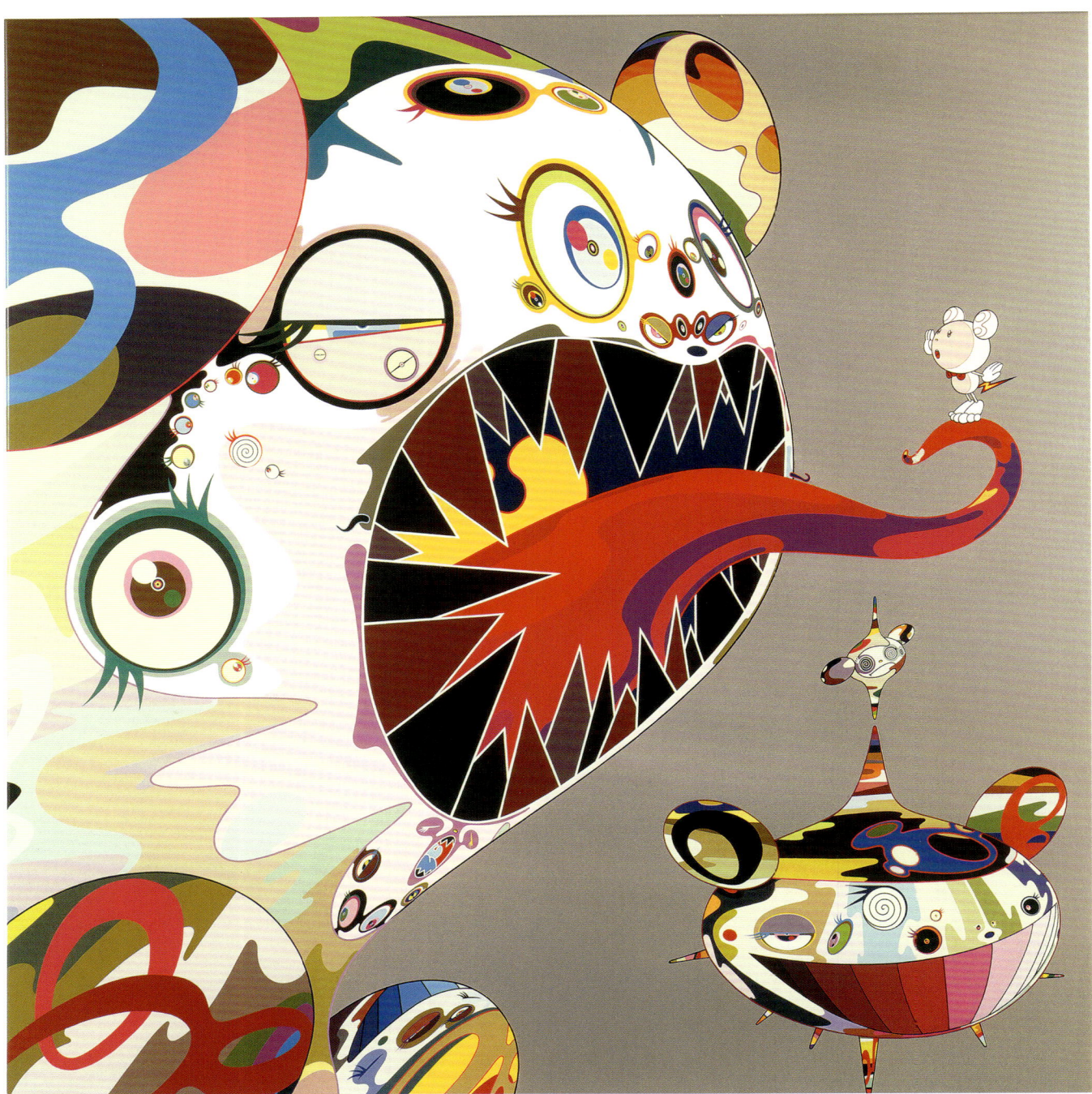

Homage to Francis Bacon (Study of George Dyer) 2002

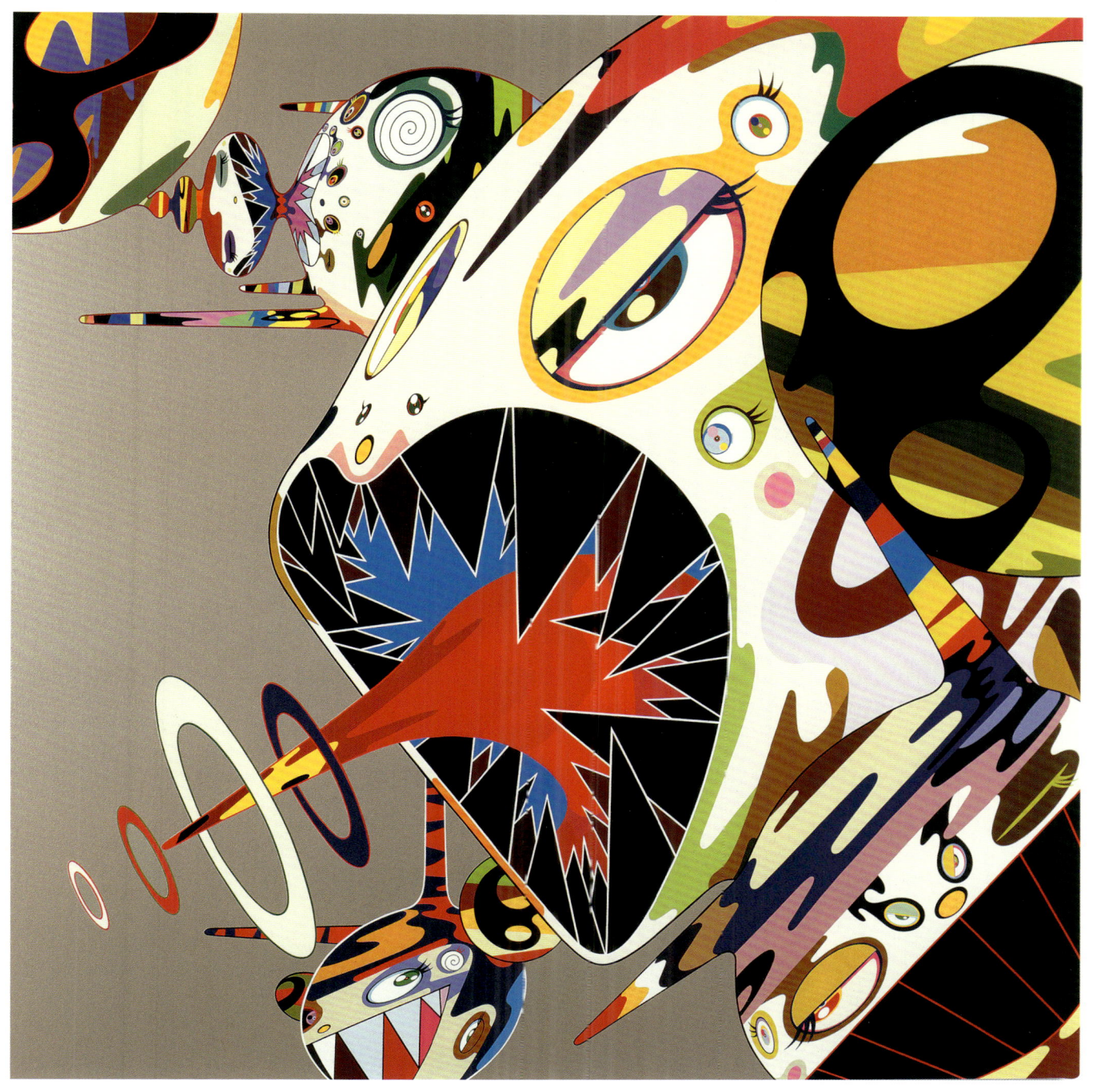

Homage to Francis Bacon (Study of Isabel Rawsthorne) 2002

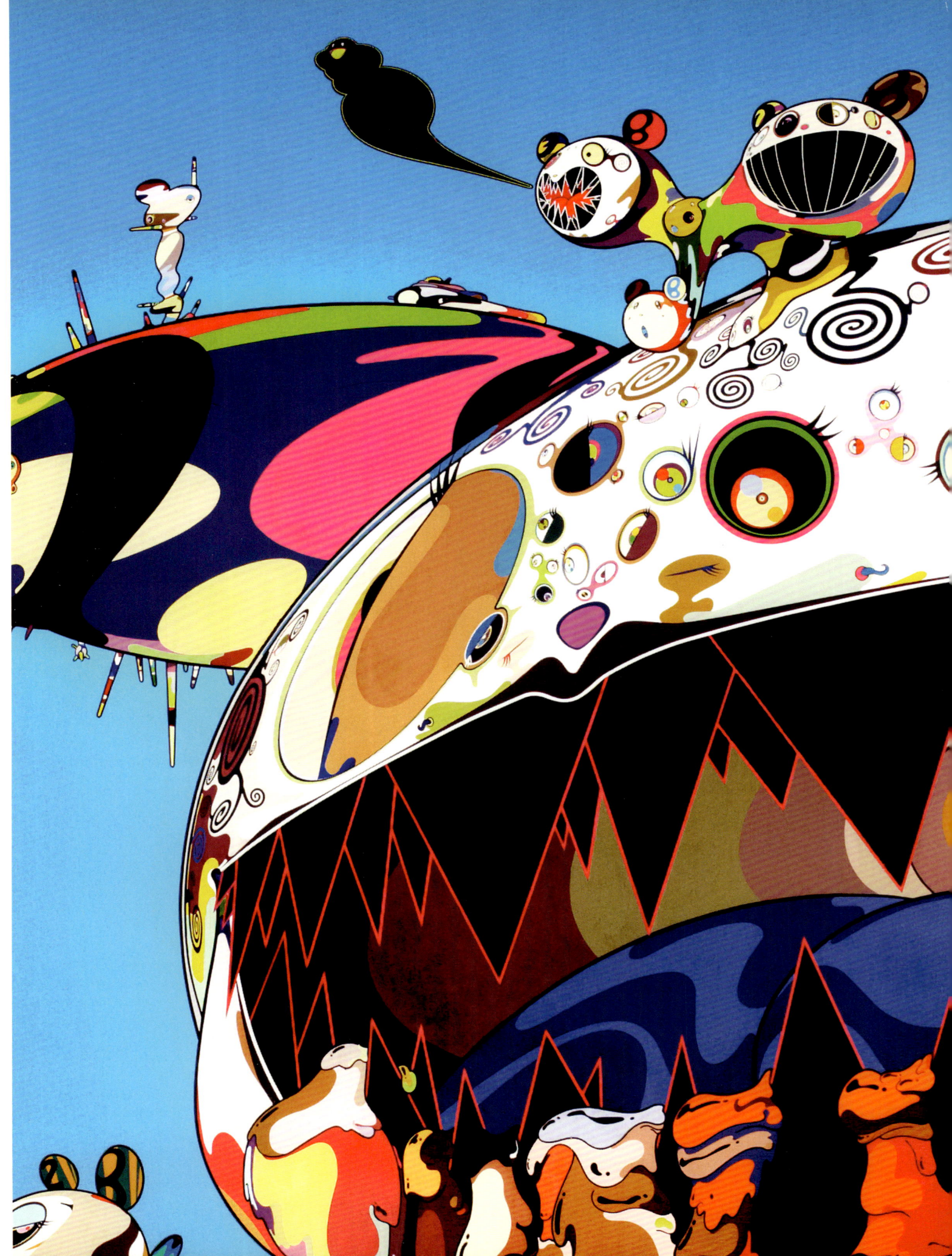

Tan Tan Bo Puking—a.k.a Gero Tan (detail) 2002

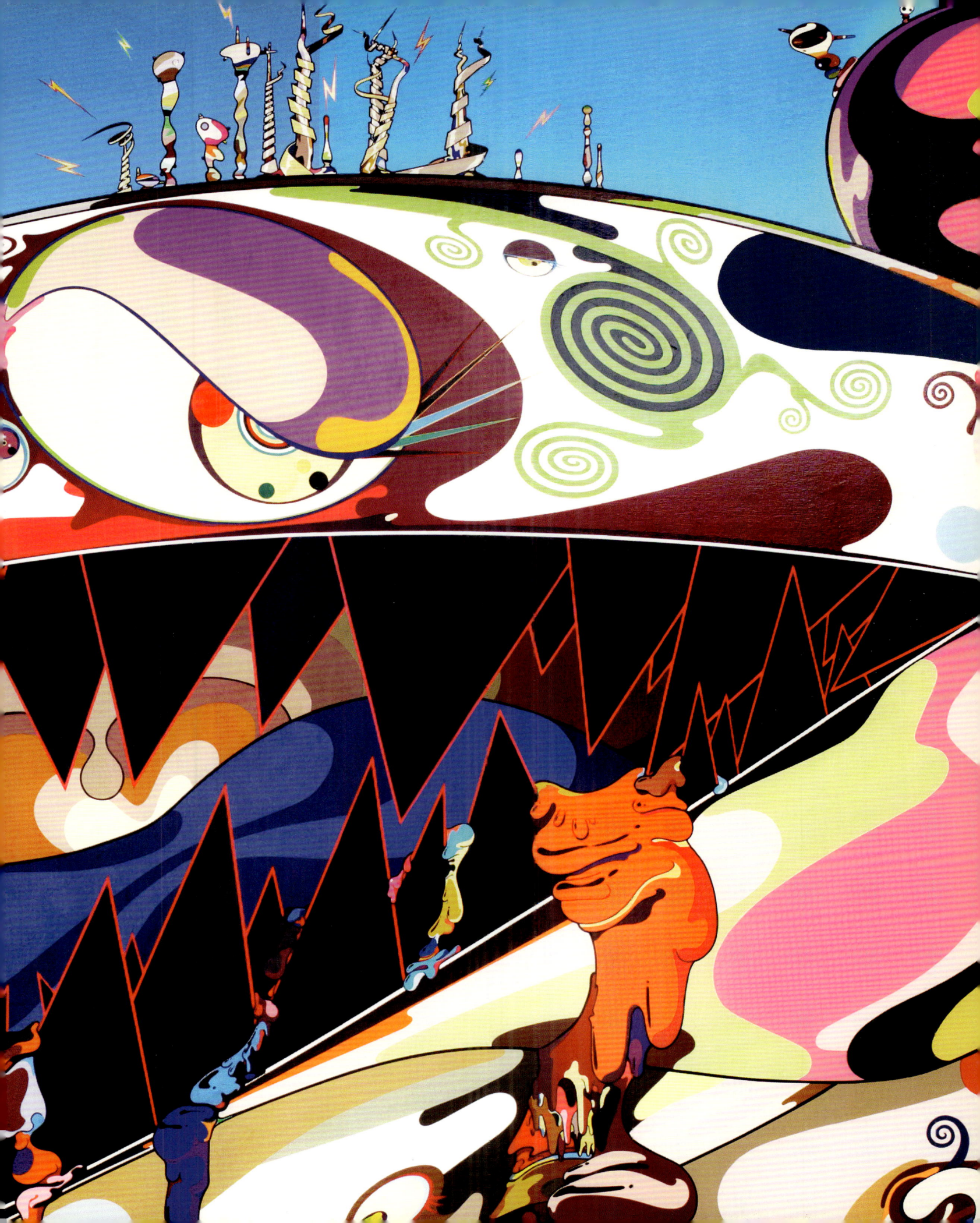

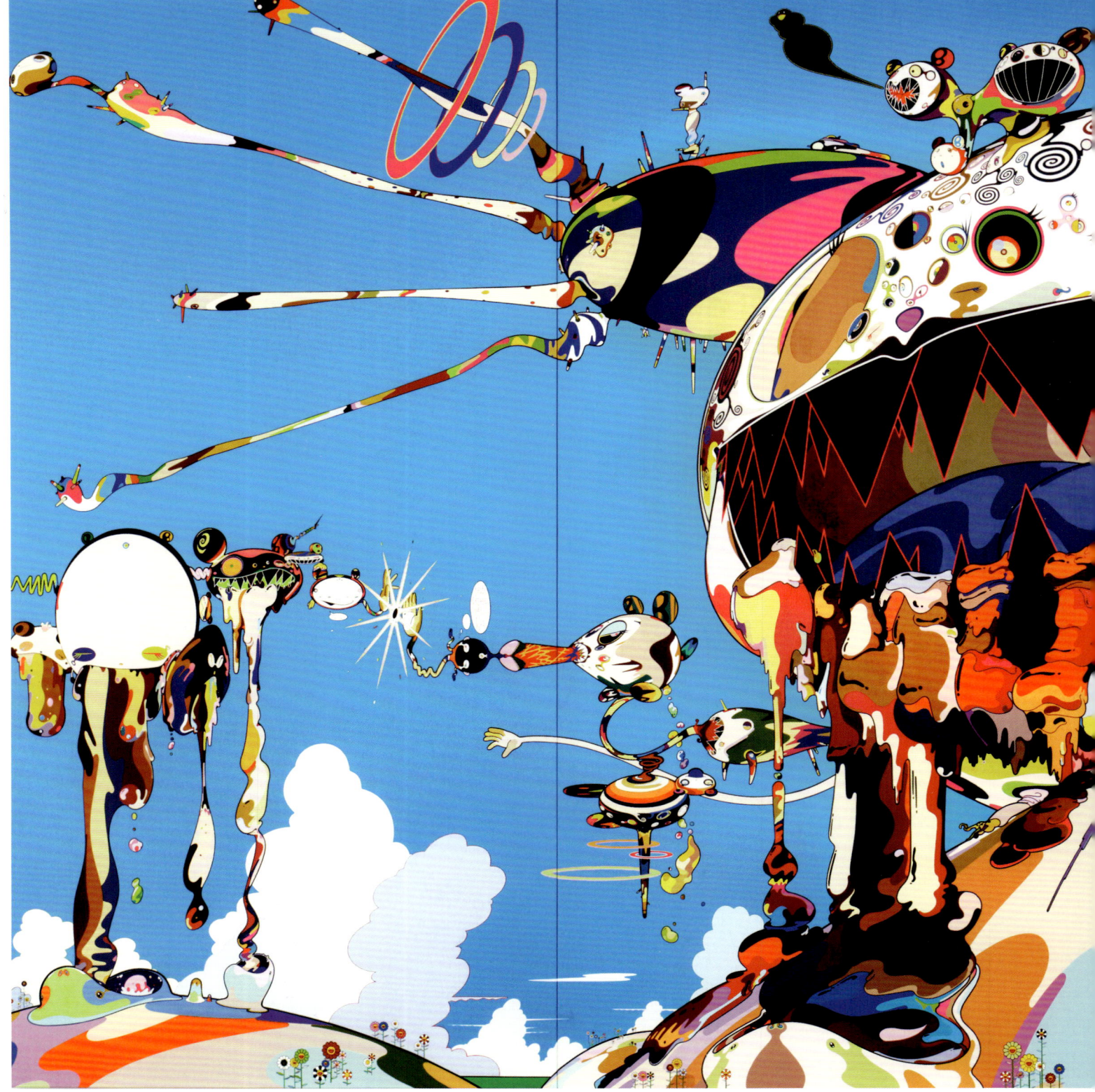

Tan Tan Bo Puking—a.k.a. Gero Tan 2002

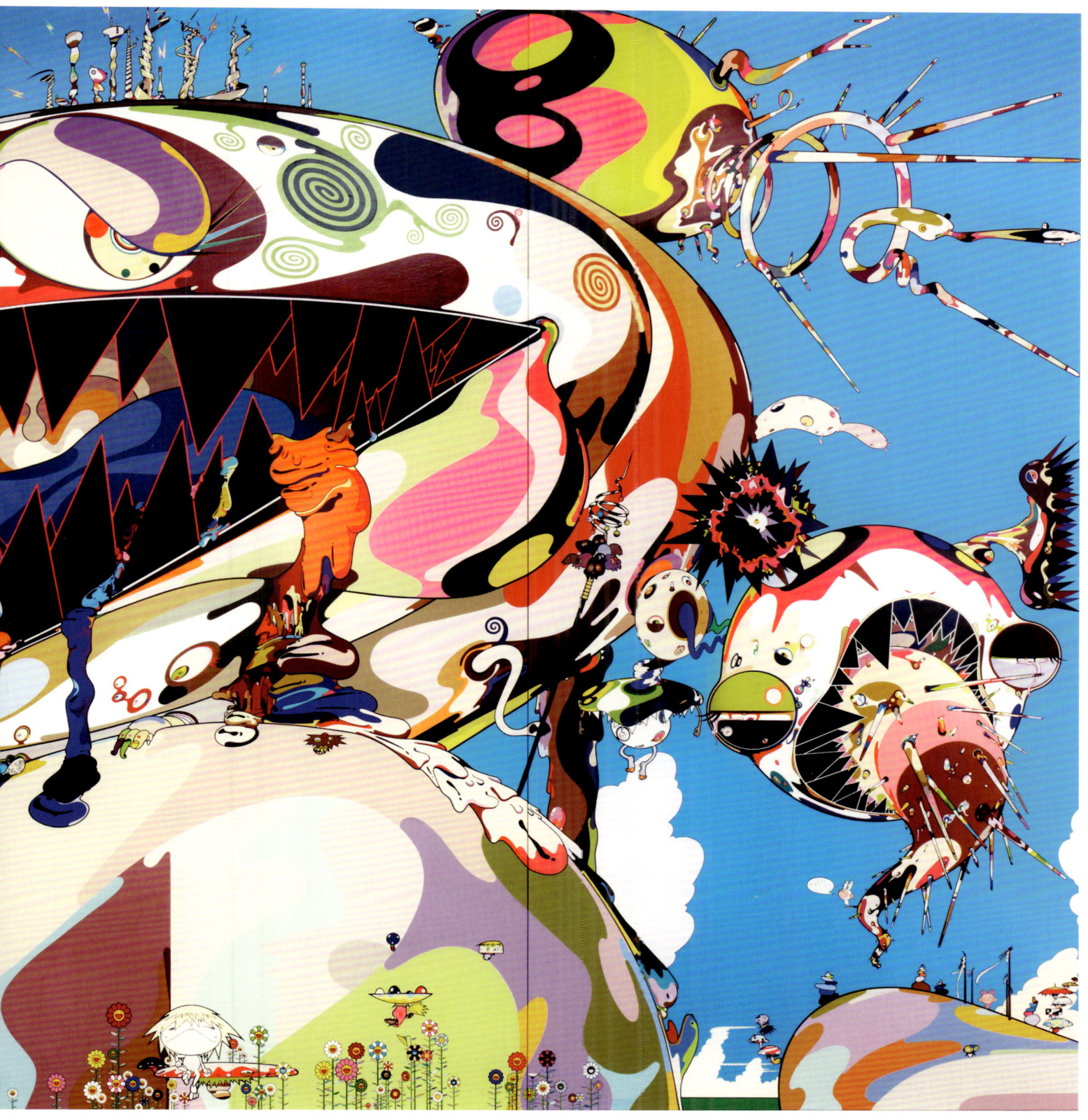

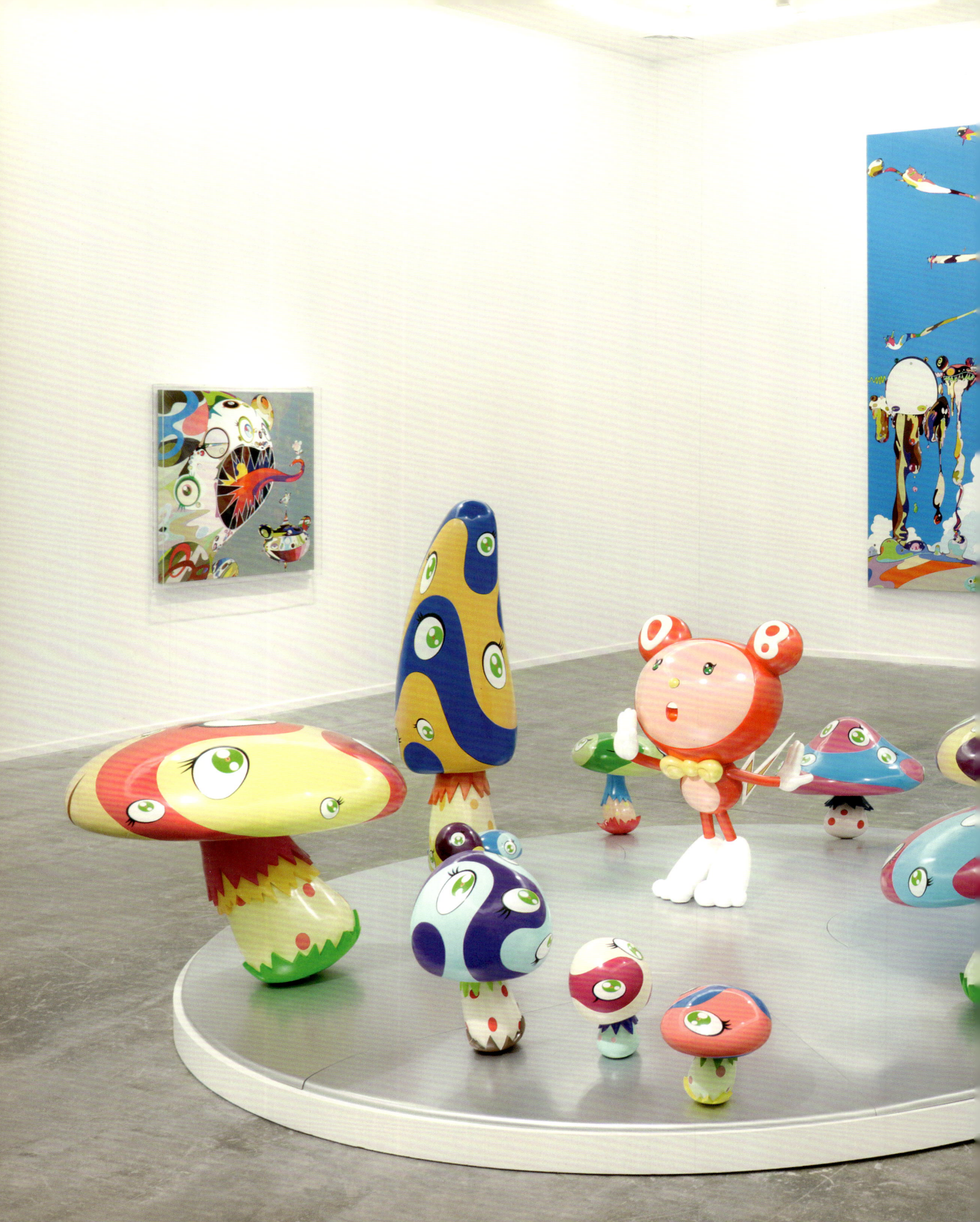

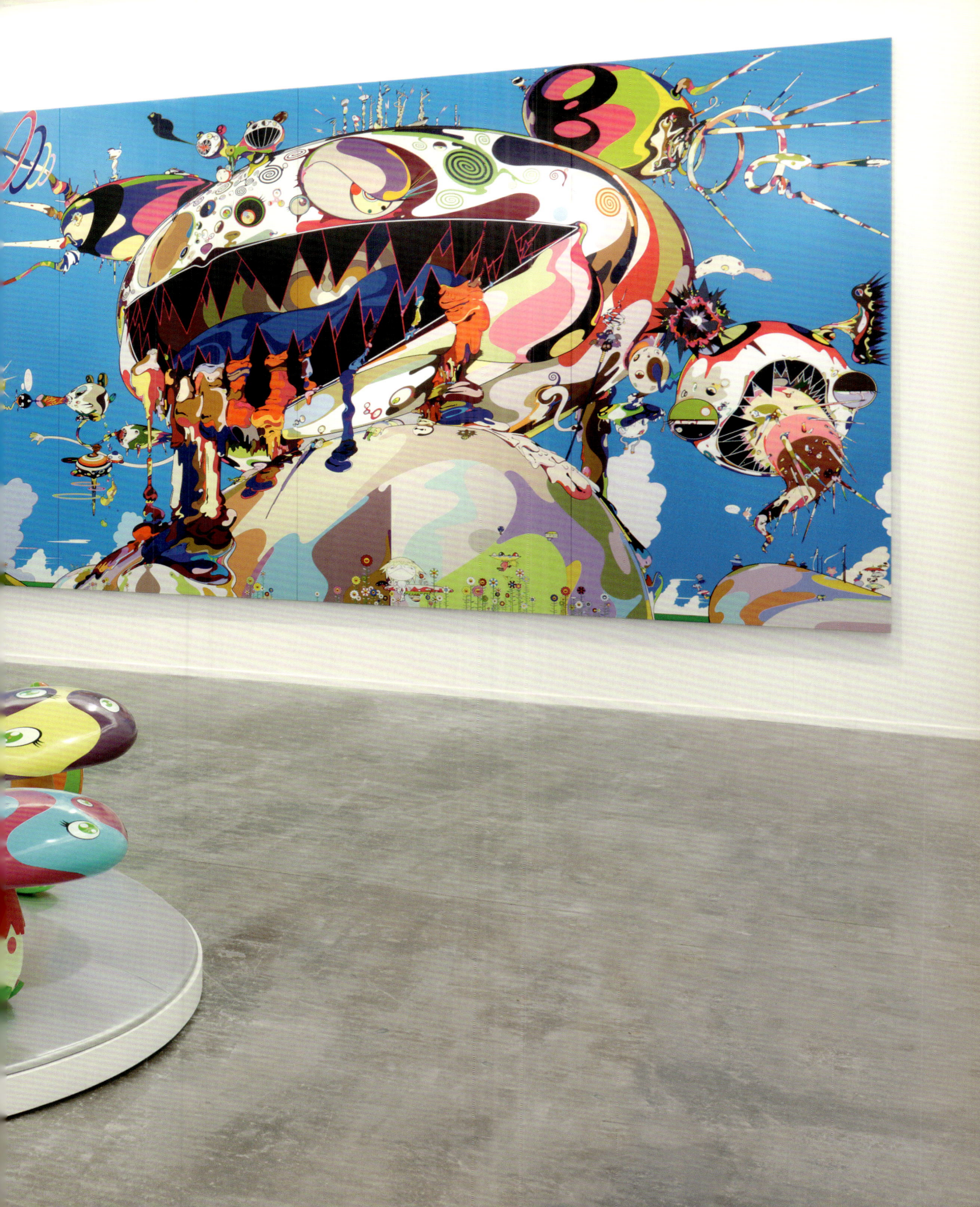

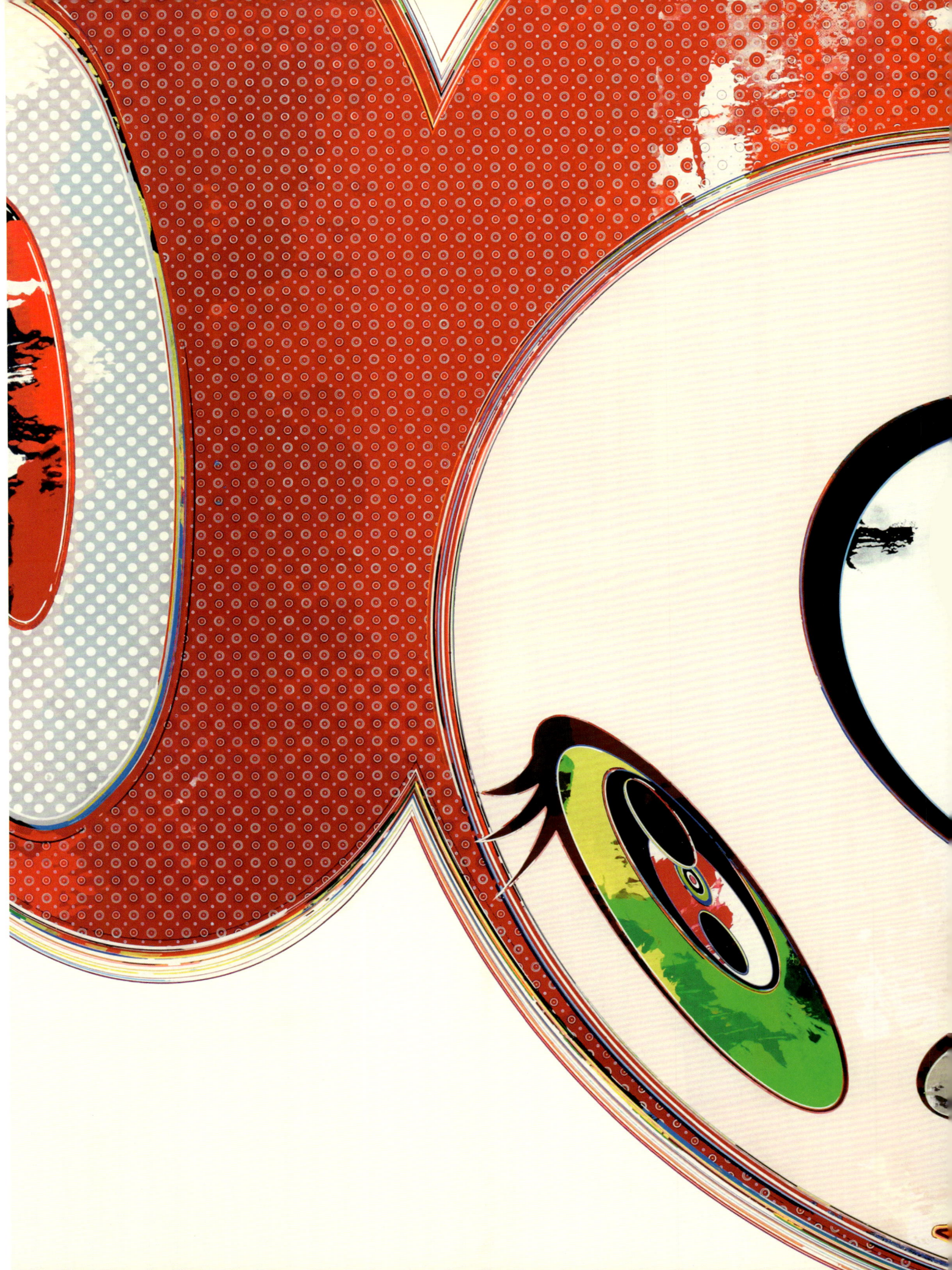

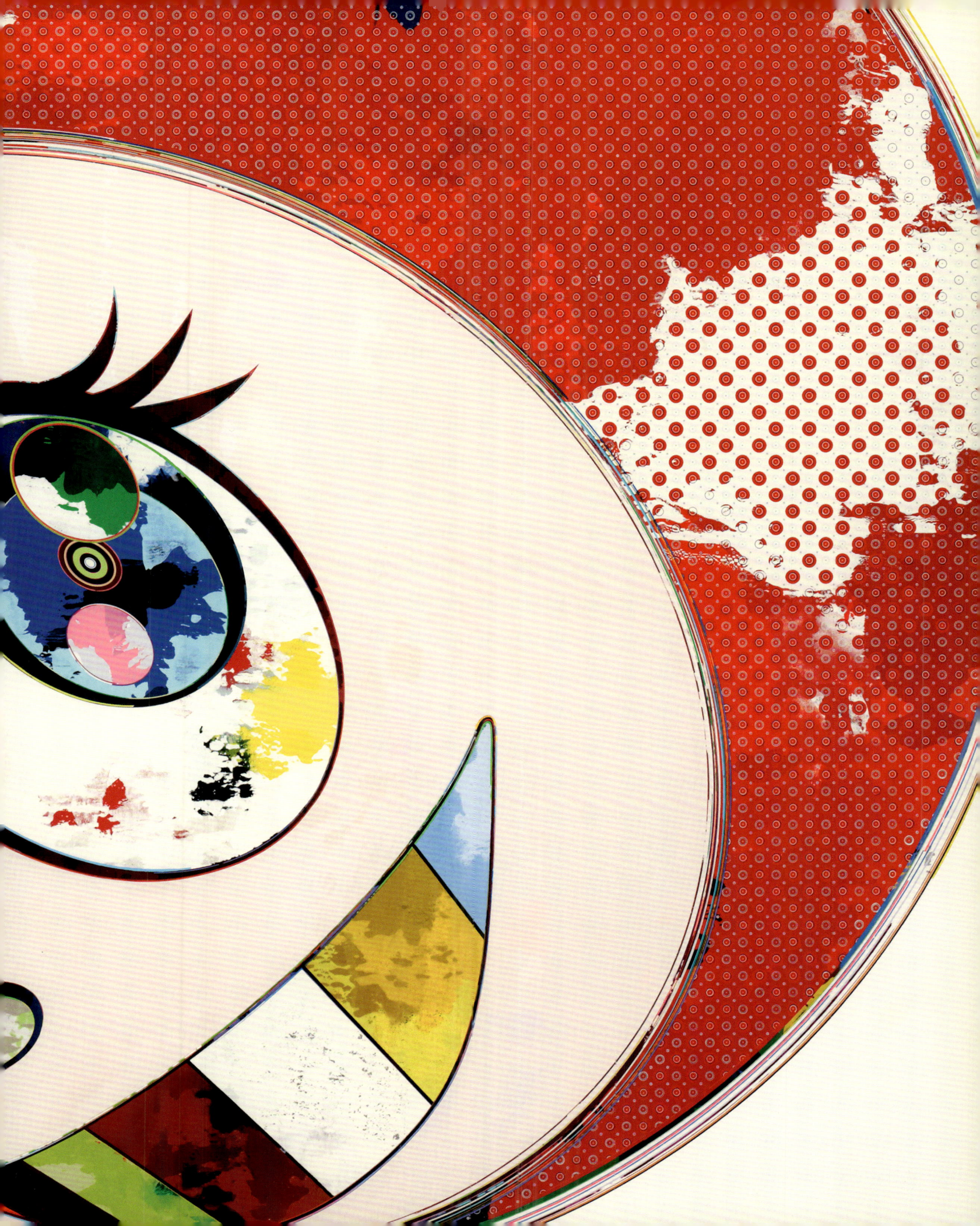

To create Mr. DOB, I took the first three letters from the transliteration of the nonsensical Japanese phrase *"Dobojite, dobojite, oshamanbe."* At the time, Jenny Holzer had an exhibition underway in Japan, and Barbara Kruger imitations were catching on, so pseudo-Roman-letter art was becoming popular. Of course, the Japanese contemporary art scene went right along with the boom, which made me mad. It even spread to the critics responsible for evaluating the art. I think, in part, DOB was my attempt to crush that art scene I despised.

To come up with the design, I talked about characters with my student assistants in Nagoya. In the course of our discussions, we came up with the simple but essential answer that the development of a character is a long process of mixing and matching, and we began the design. Manabu Koga of Pepper Shop, who was in vocational school at the time, took my rough design and touched it up, after which we decided to get graphic designer Gento Matsumoto's help on the project. For the very first blocky "D" and "B" we used a font he had designed.

We gradually smoothed out the letters, making them more rounded. In the end, a lot of people contributed to making DOB the way he is today. In the beginning, the "D," "O," and "B" had three ears on its head. This got pared down to two, and we were finished. In the beginning, the project received loads of criticism from the art community. I guess I can understand why. After all, DOB was partially an attempt to crush the art scene.

TO ME, IT FELT LIKE I HAD SUCCEEDED:

I had created an icon.

Once a character is born and begins to move, I think one has to follow its demands. If you let it be, it will take care of itself. With DOB as my excuse, I sometimes untie the cords of art history, touching on the school of Chuck Close–esque portraiture, African or Polynesian art, Op or psychedelic art, Rinpa school or Momoyama period presentations, and even contemporary Japanese character art. Now I have a face that can transform at will.

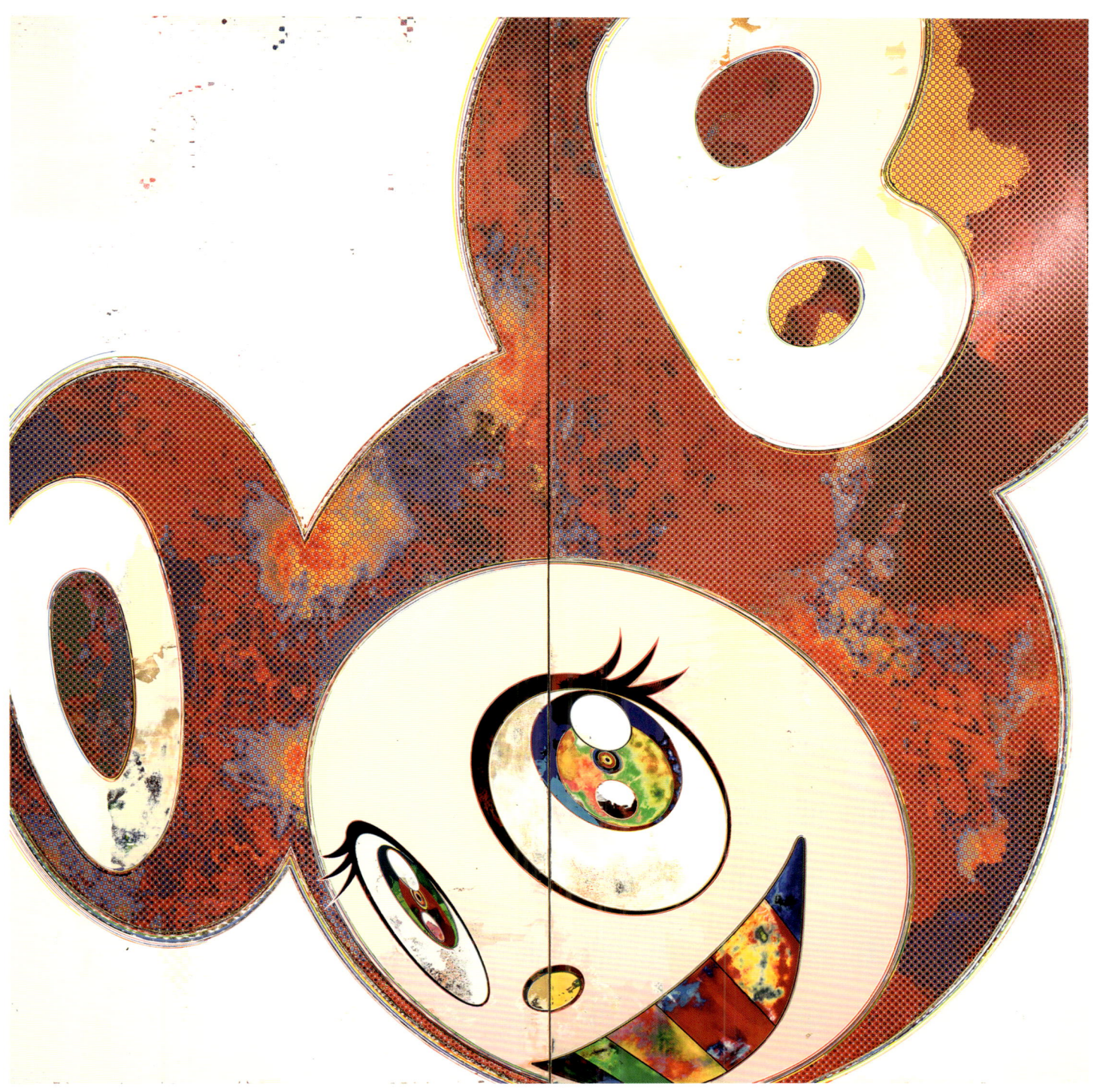

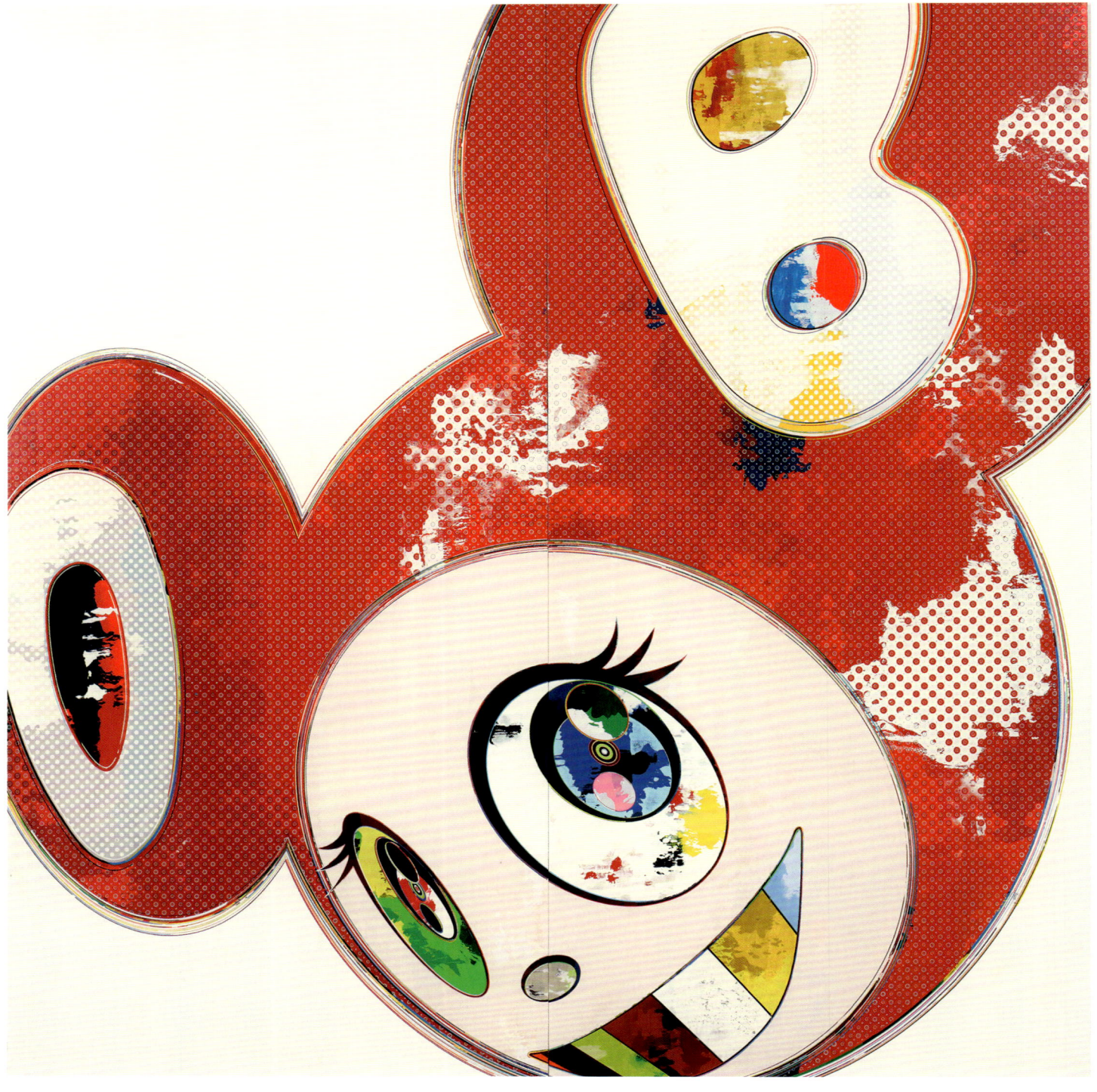

And Then x 6 (Red) 2012

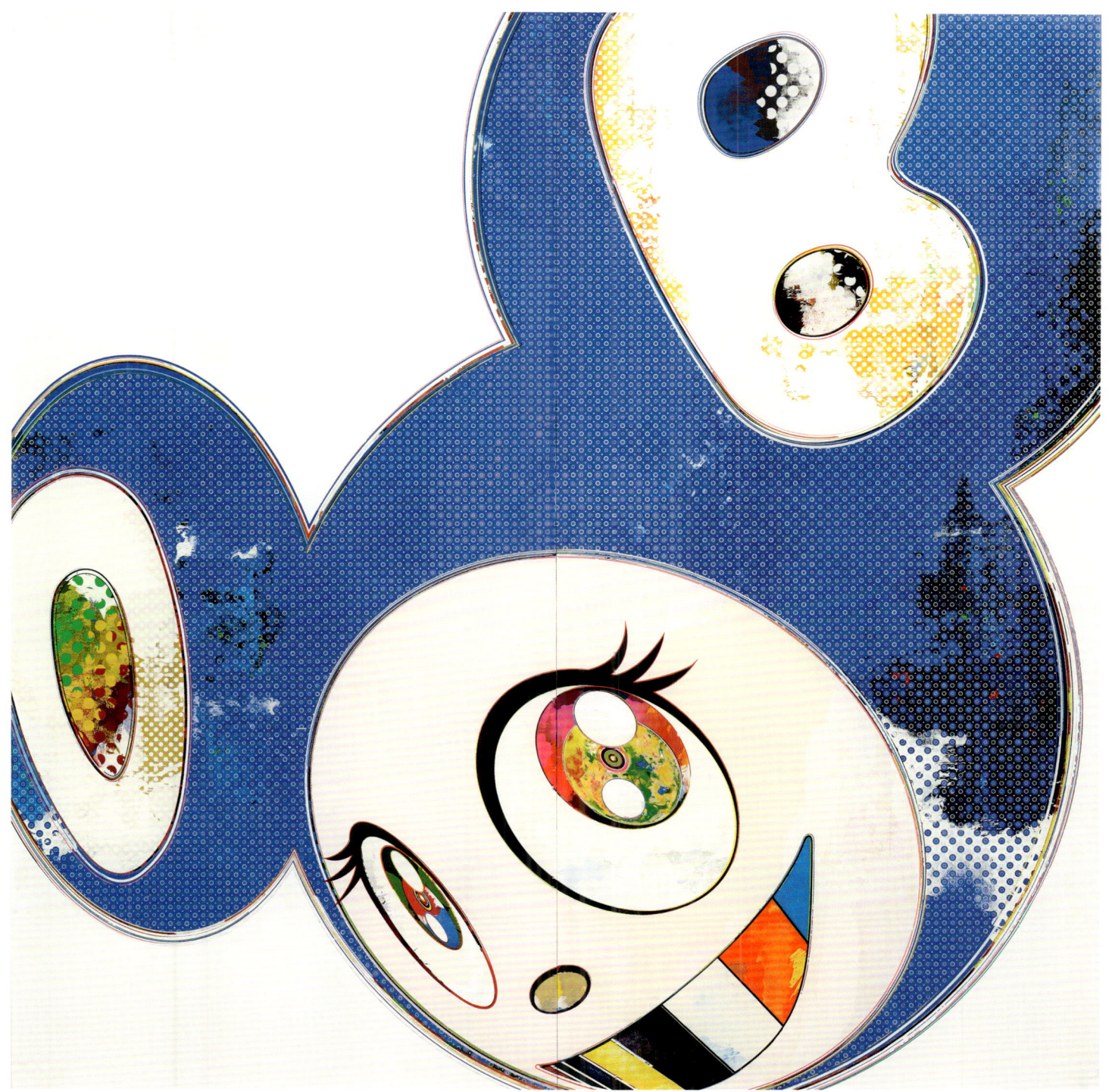

And Then x 6 (Blue) 2012

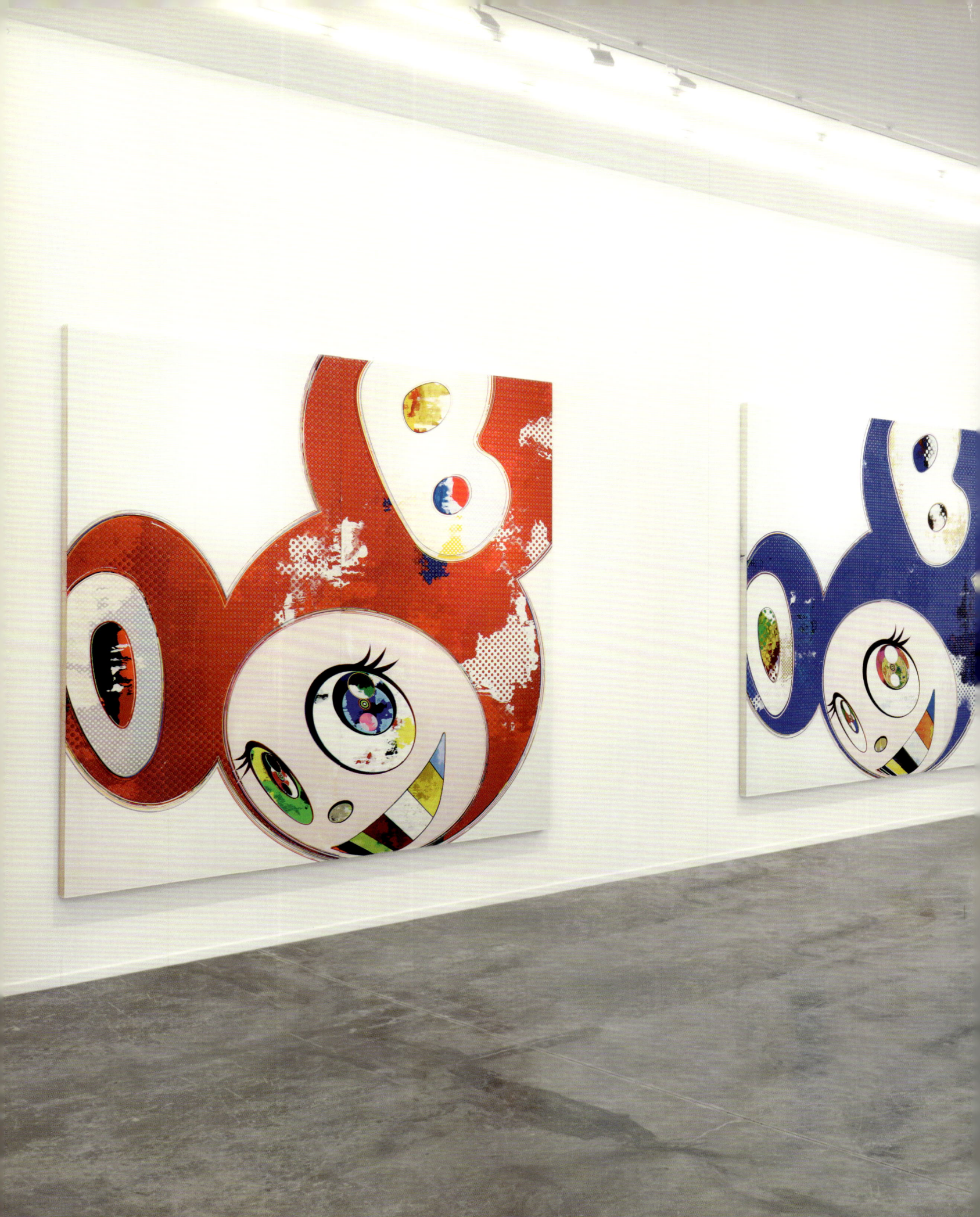

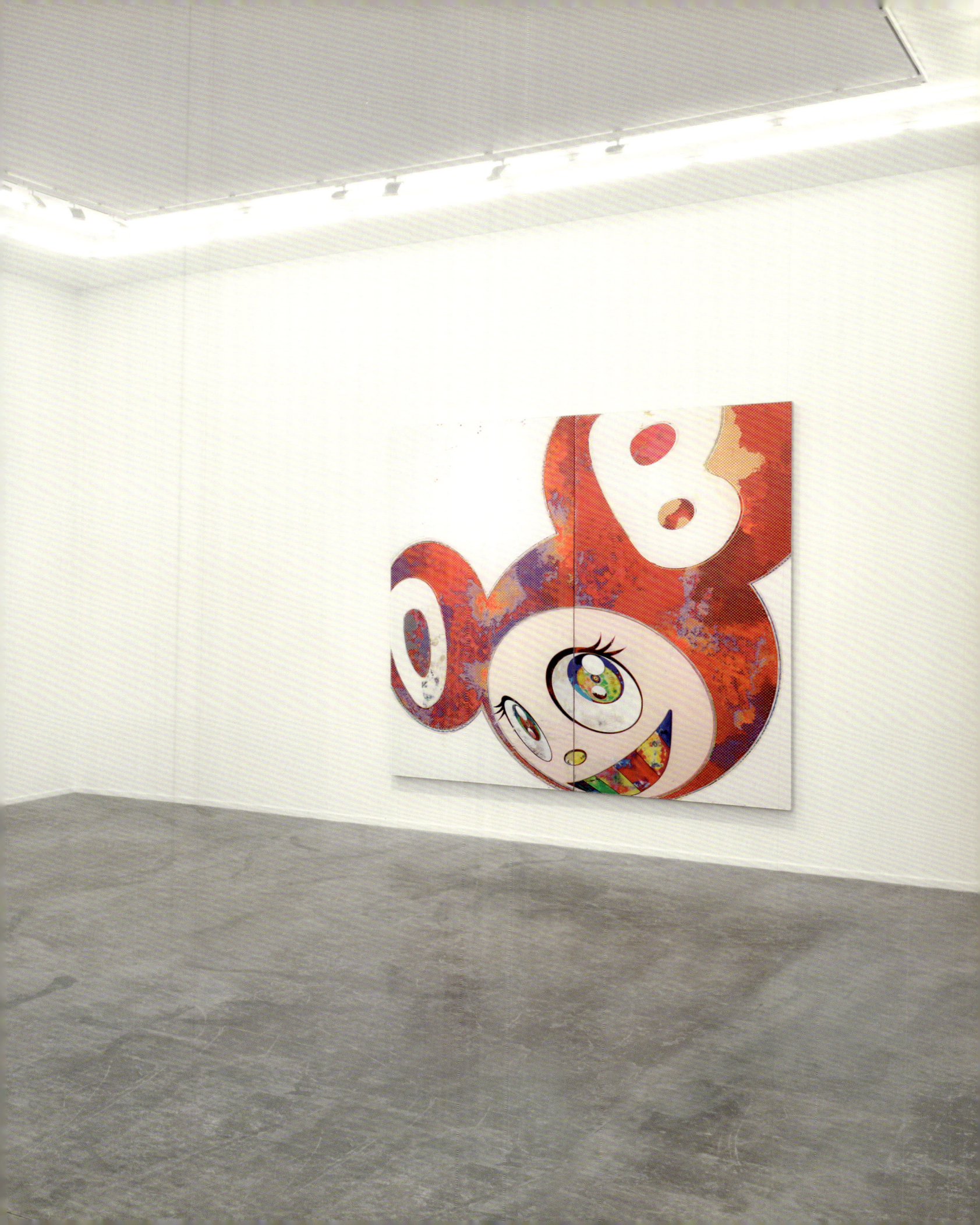

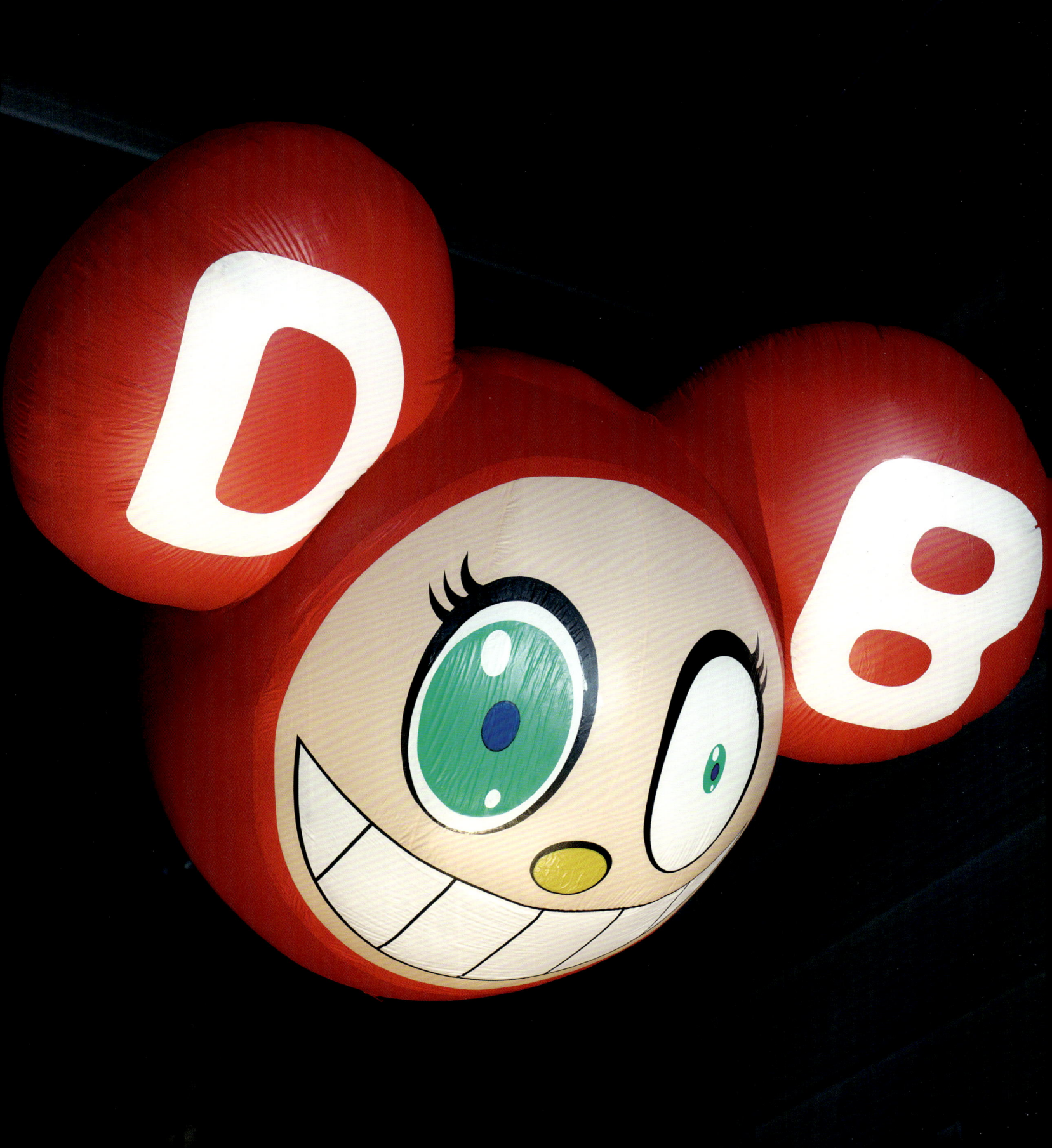

THE FIRST SCULPTURES I MADE WERE BALLOONS FOR AN ART FAIR.

The US and Europe presentations needed something big, but it wasn't easy to take something big out of Japan; plus, my studio was very small. When I went to New York for the first time, I couldn't make big paintings and sculptures.

At that time, I didn't have any kind of sculptural vocabulary. I never thought that I was a professional sculptor, but in the past few years I've come to gradually understand the key to making sculpture. With this understanding, I've been able to create three-dimensional works of all of my characters, experimenting with scale and surface. Over time, I have turned my own image into the inspiration for sculptures that can be monumental and light as air.

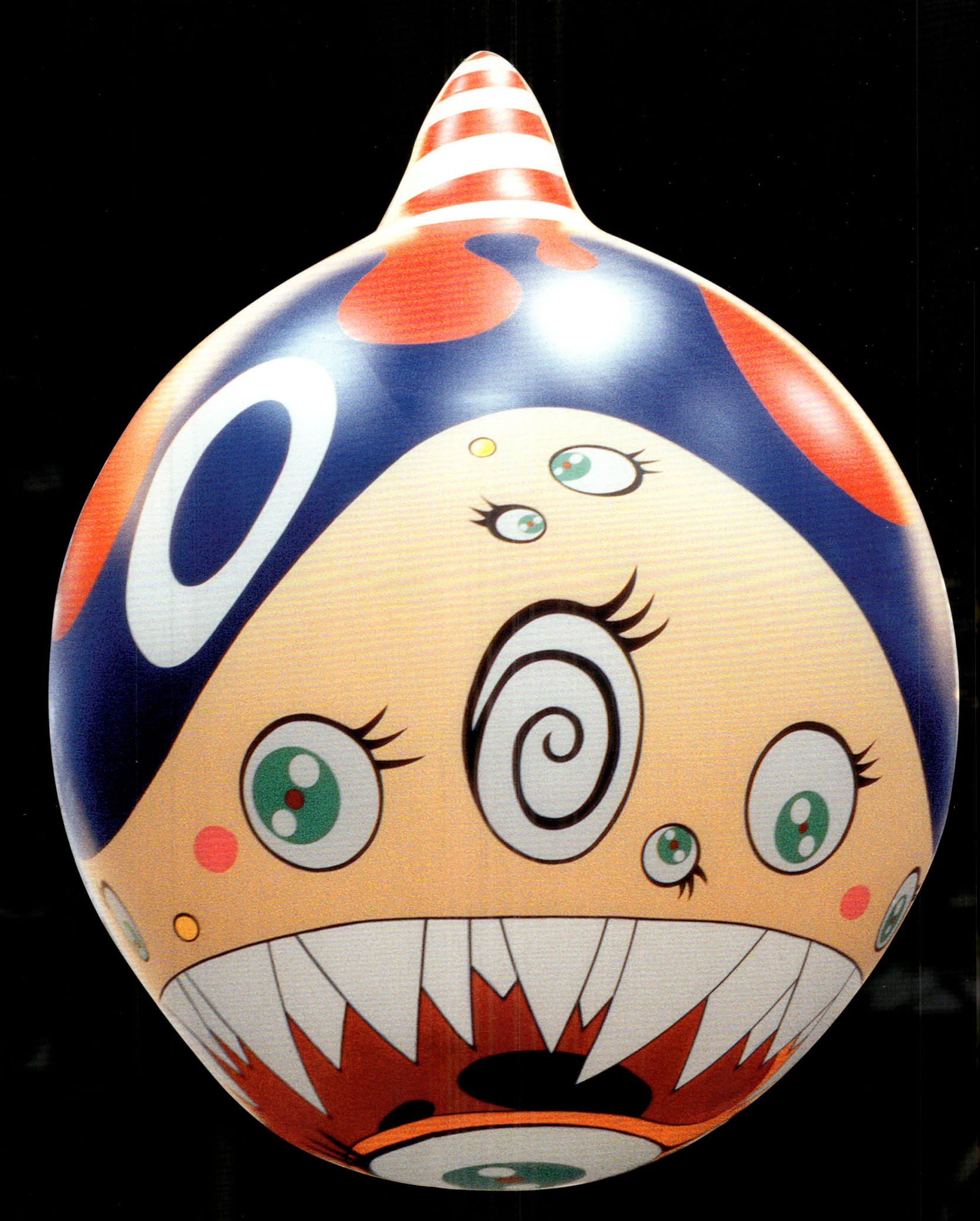

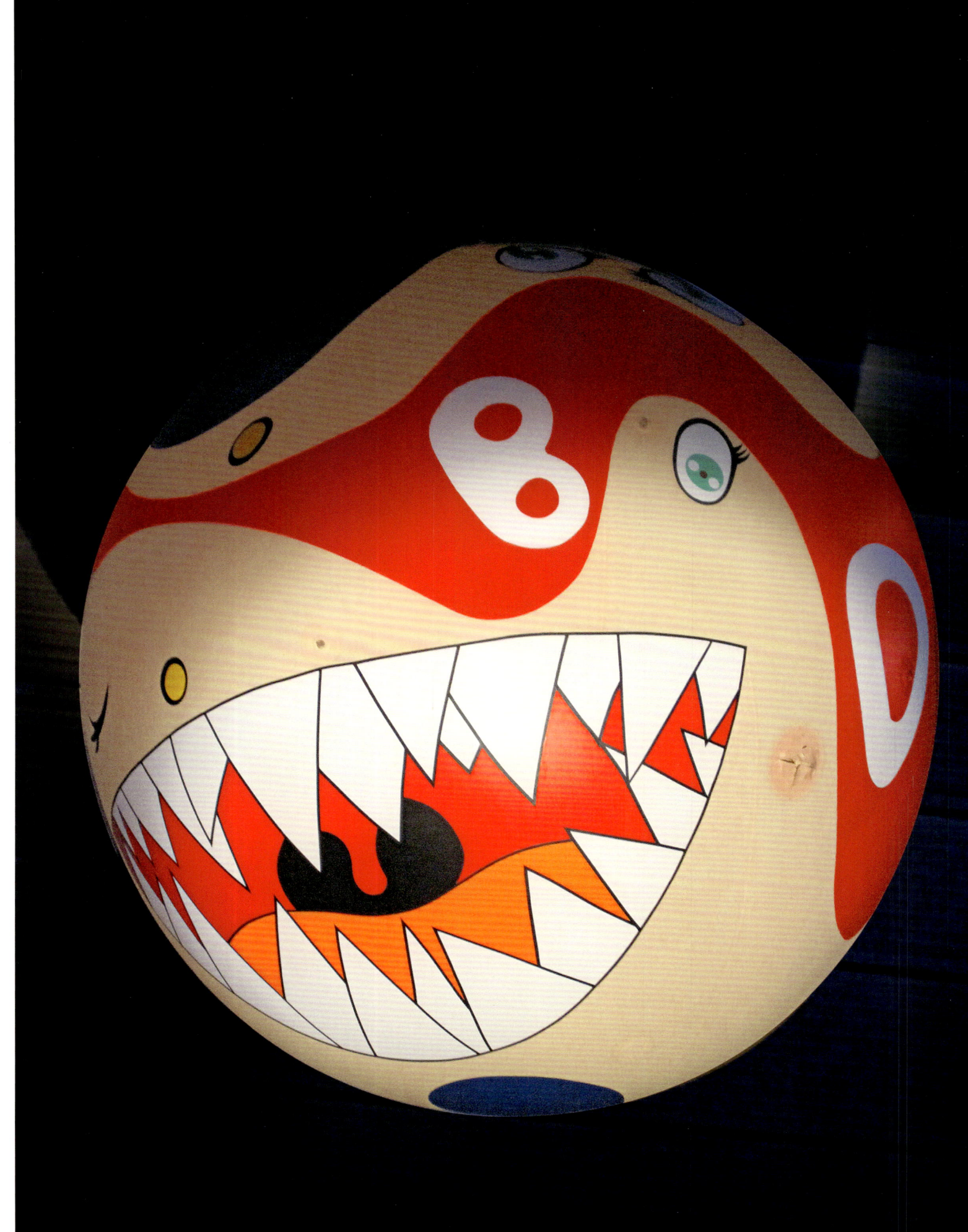

My mother was born in a town called Kokura, in the Kyushu region. Apparently, it was the place the atomic bomb was originally going to be dropped, rather than Nagasaki. So when I was a child, she told me,

"IF THE BOMB HAD BEEN DROPPED IN KOKURA, YOU WOULDN'T BE HERE TODAY."

During my childhood, there were a lot of people around me who were damaged by the war and suffered from sicknesses caused by the atomic bomb.

The question of society's responsibility toward these victims was taken up over and over in countless television programs. What is war? What is the nation? What is society? What is the line between good and evil? I have a feeling that I learned a lot about these things from watching those documentary television shows.

The piece *Time Bokan* describes the fear that good and evil might be two sides of the same coin and that human folly is capable of repainting everything.

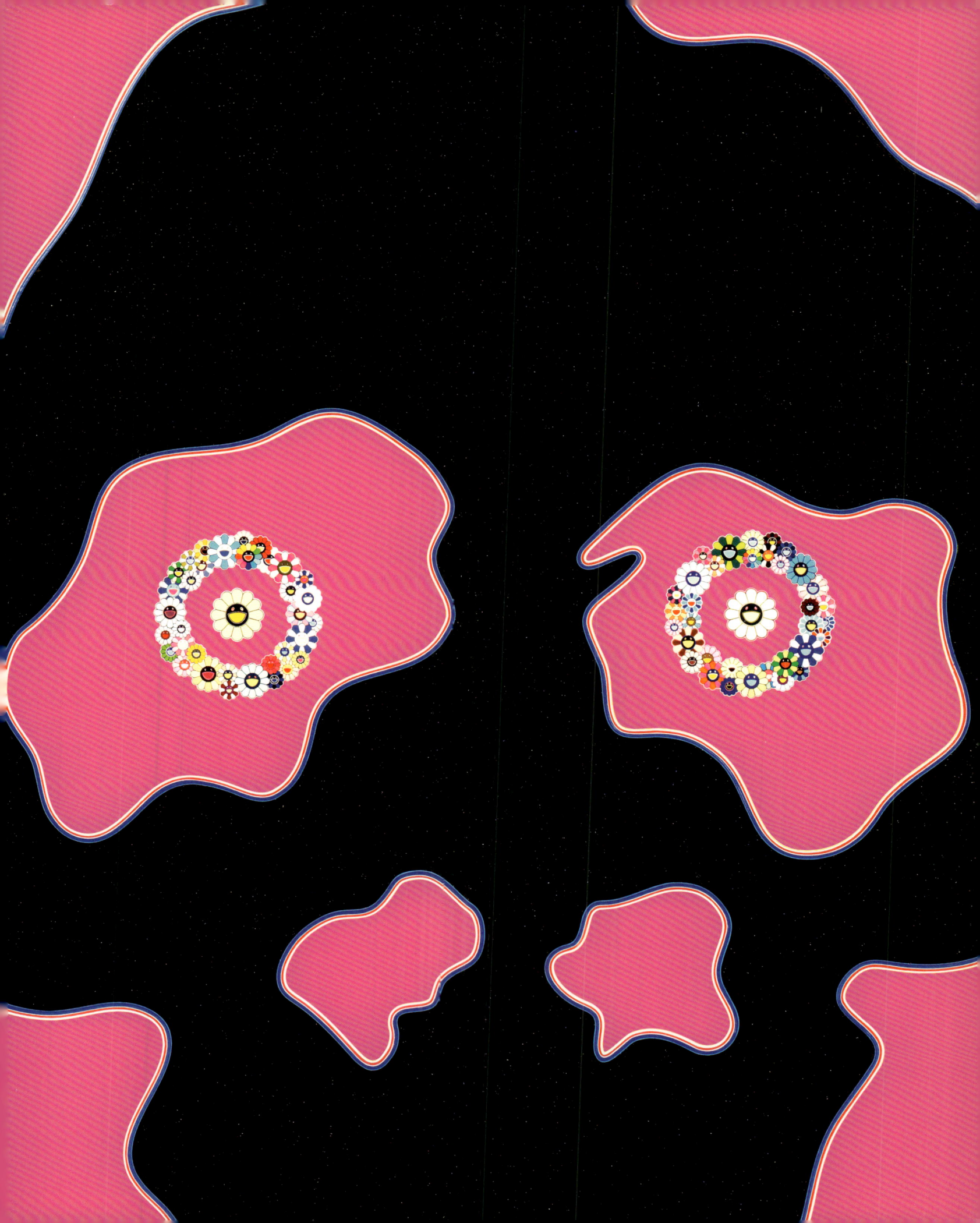

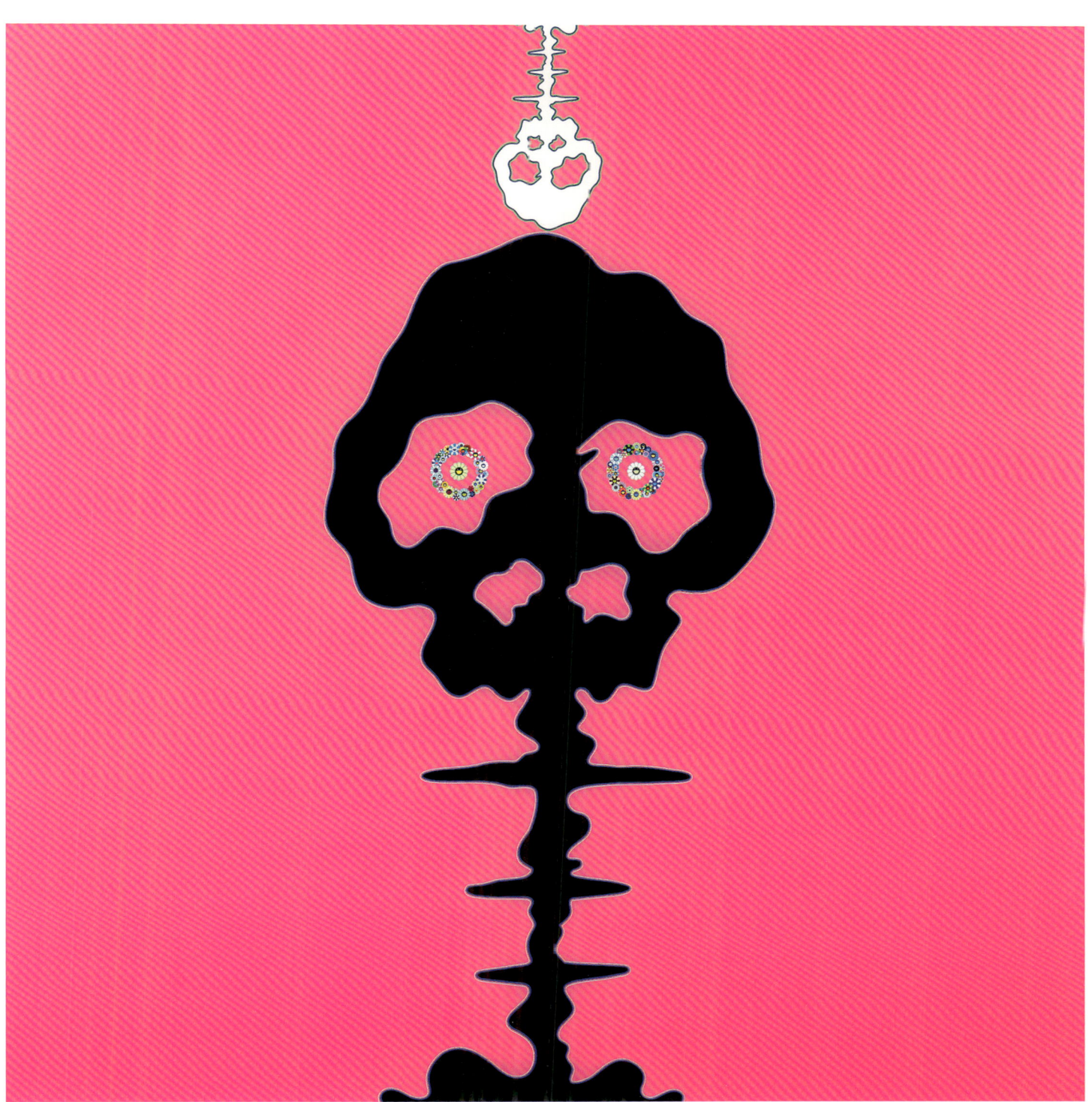

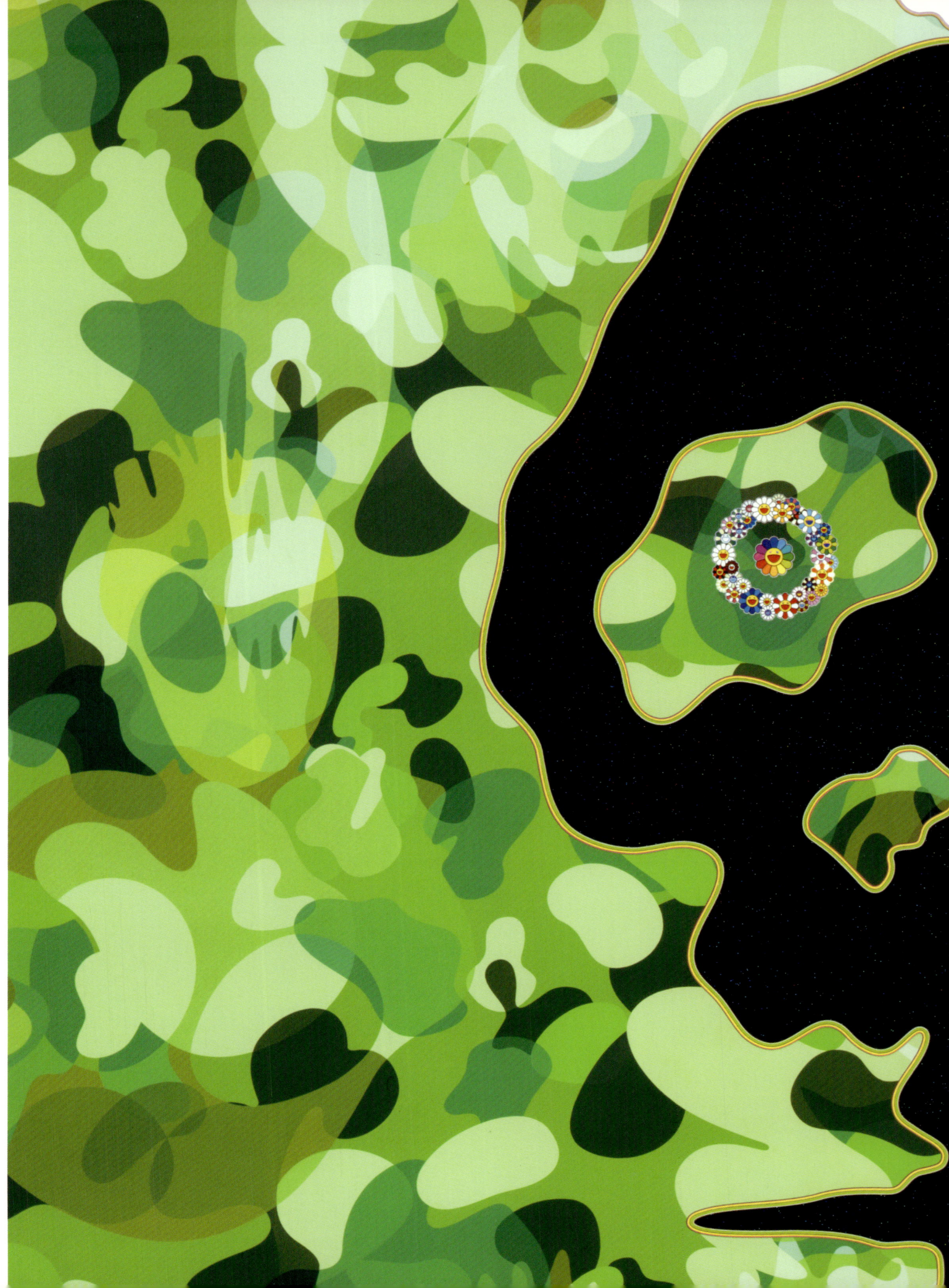

TIME – camouflage moss green (detail) 2009

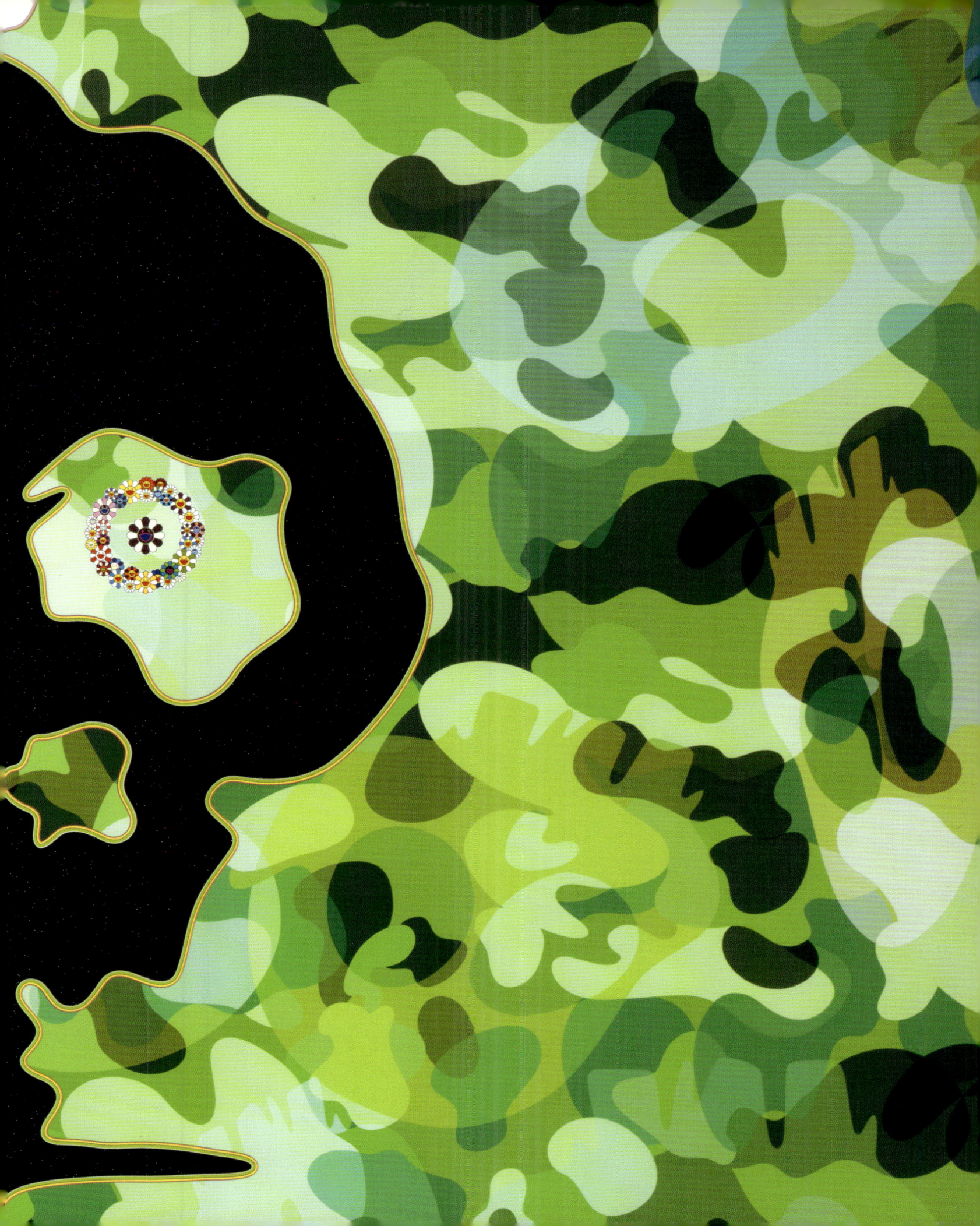

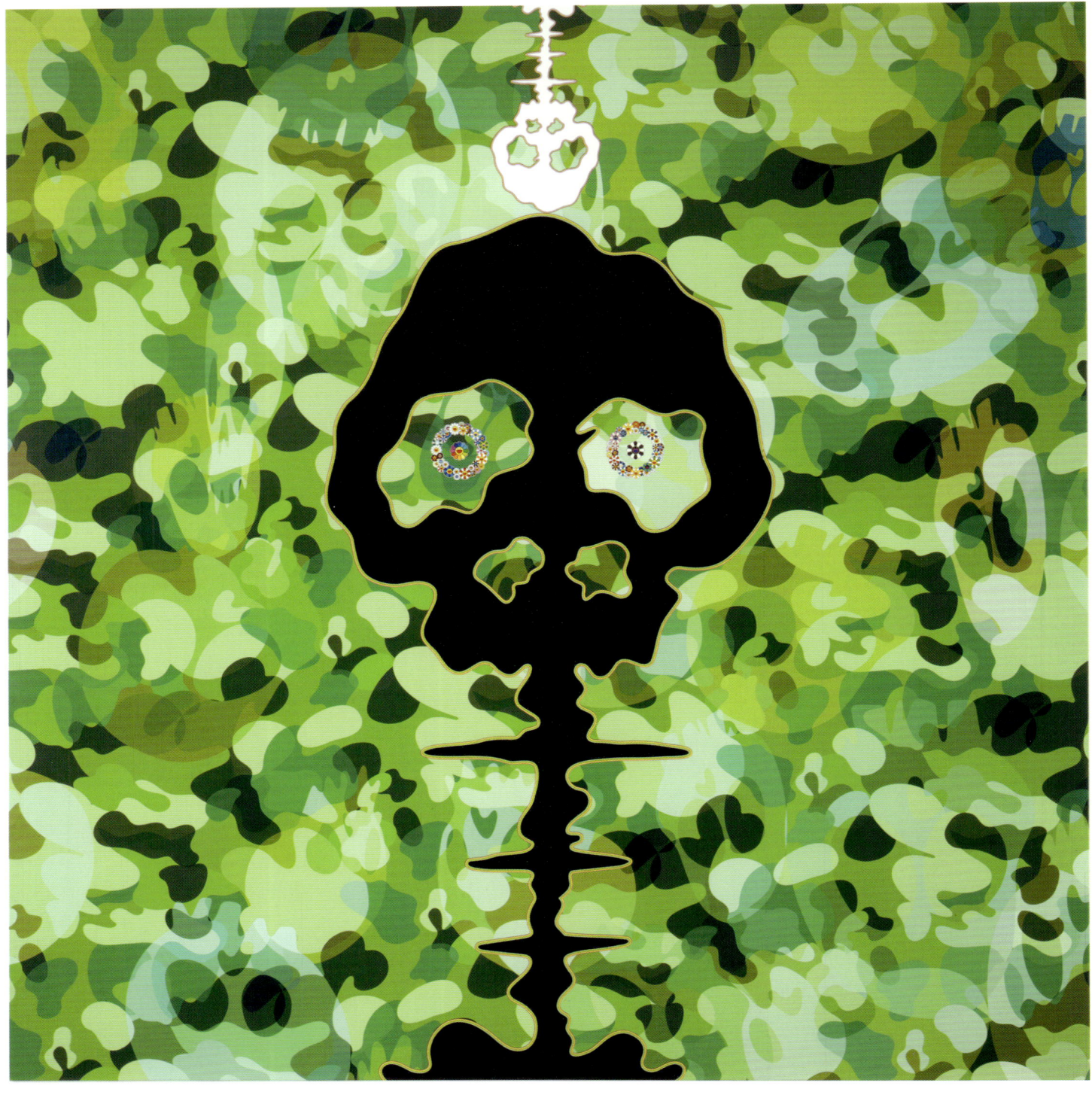

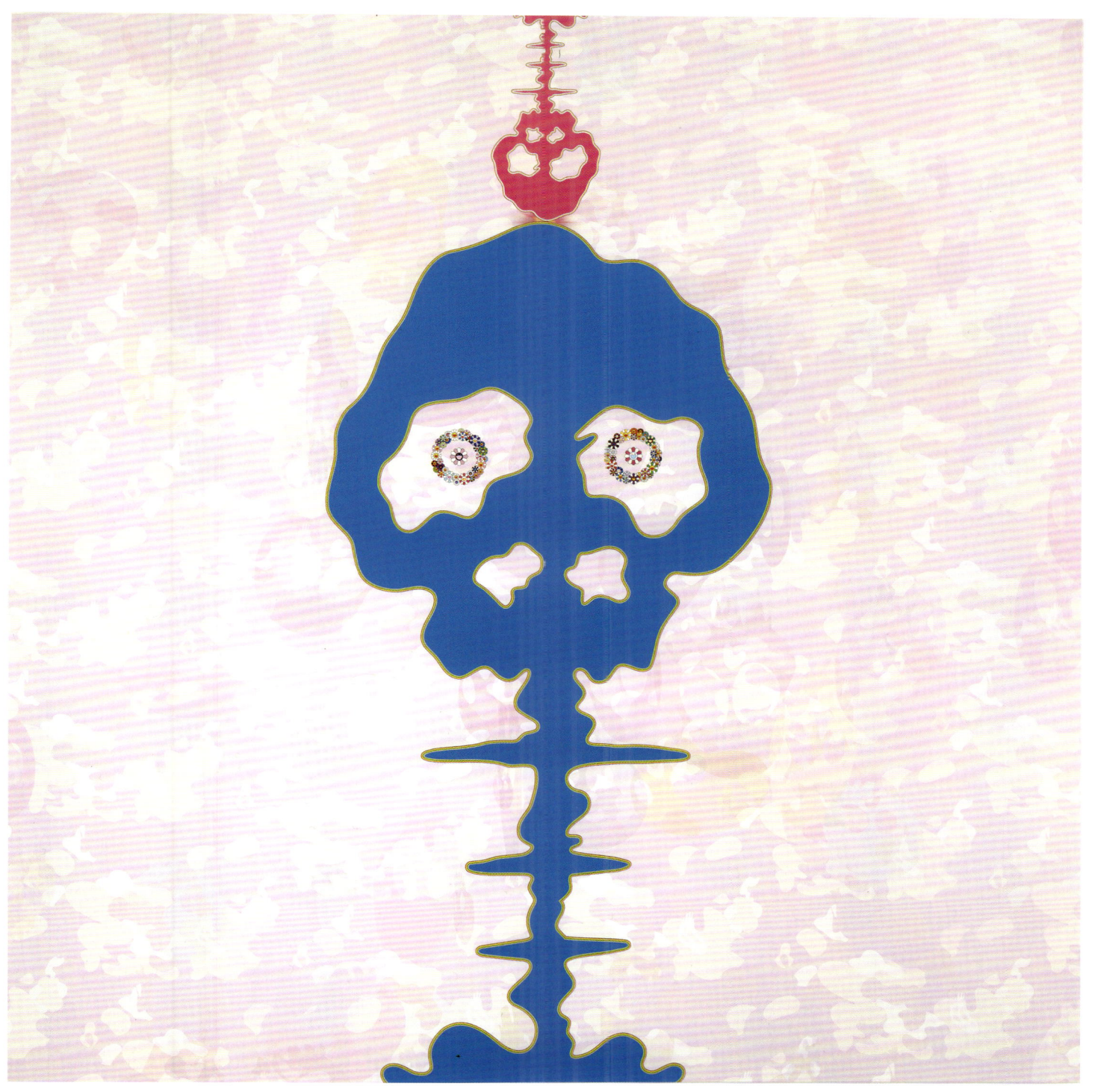

BOKAN — camouflage pink 2009

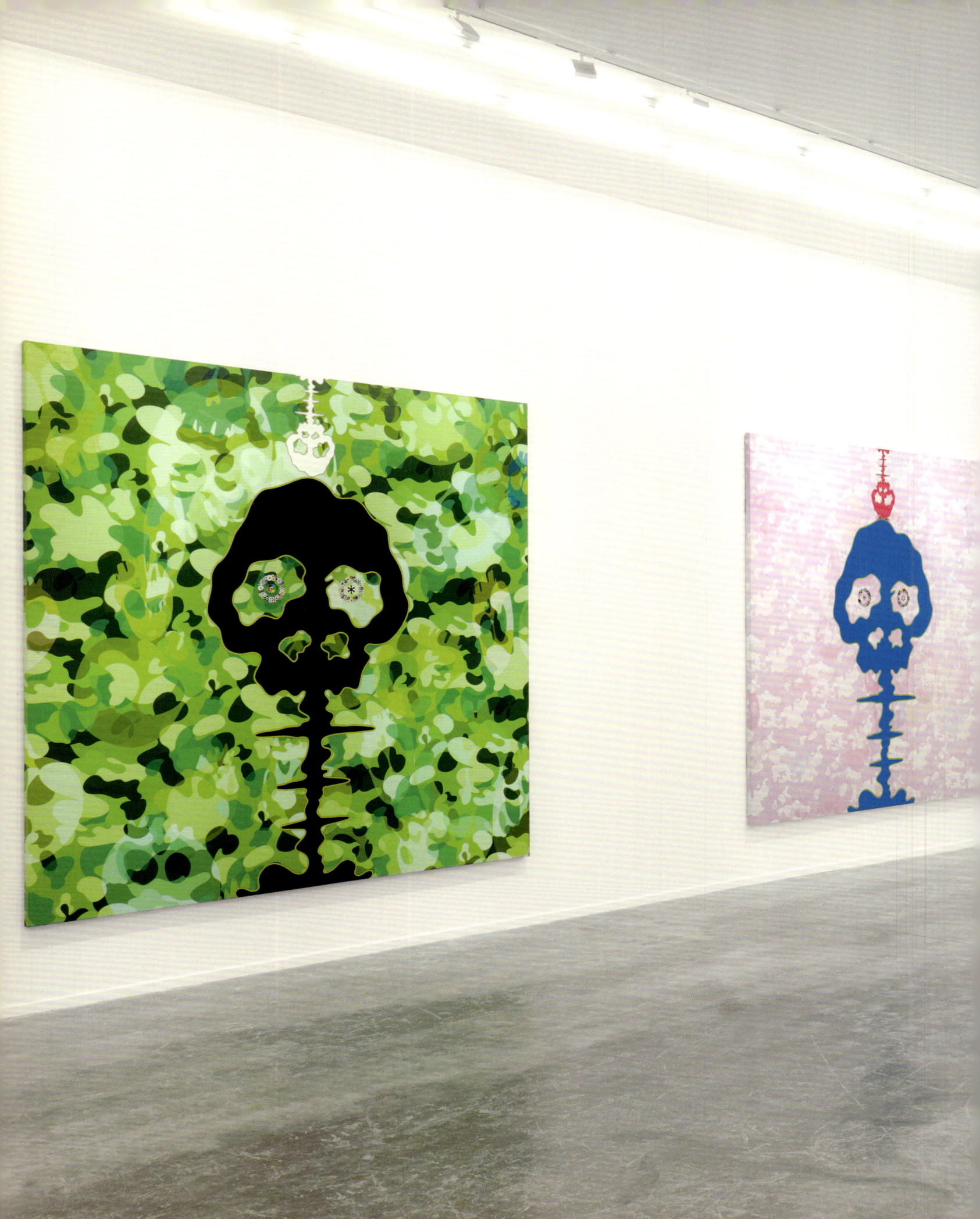

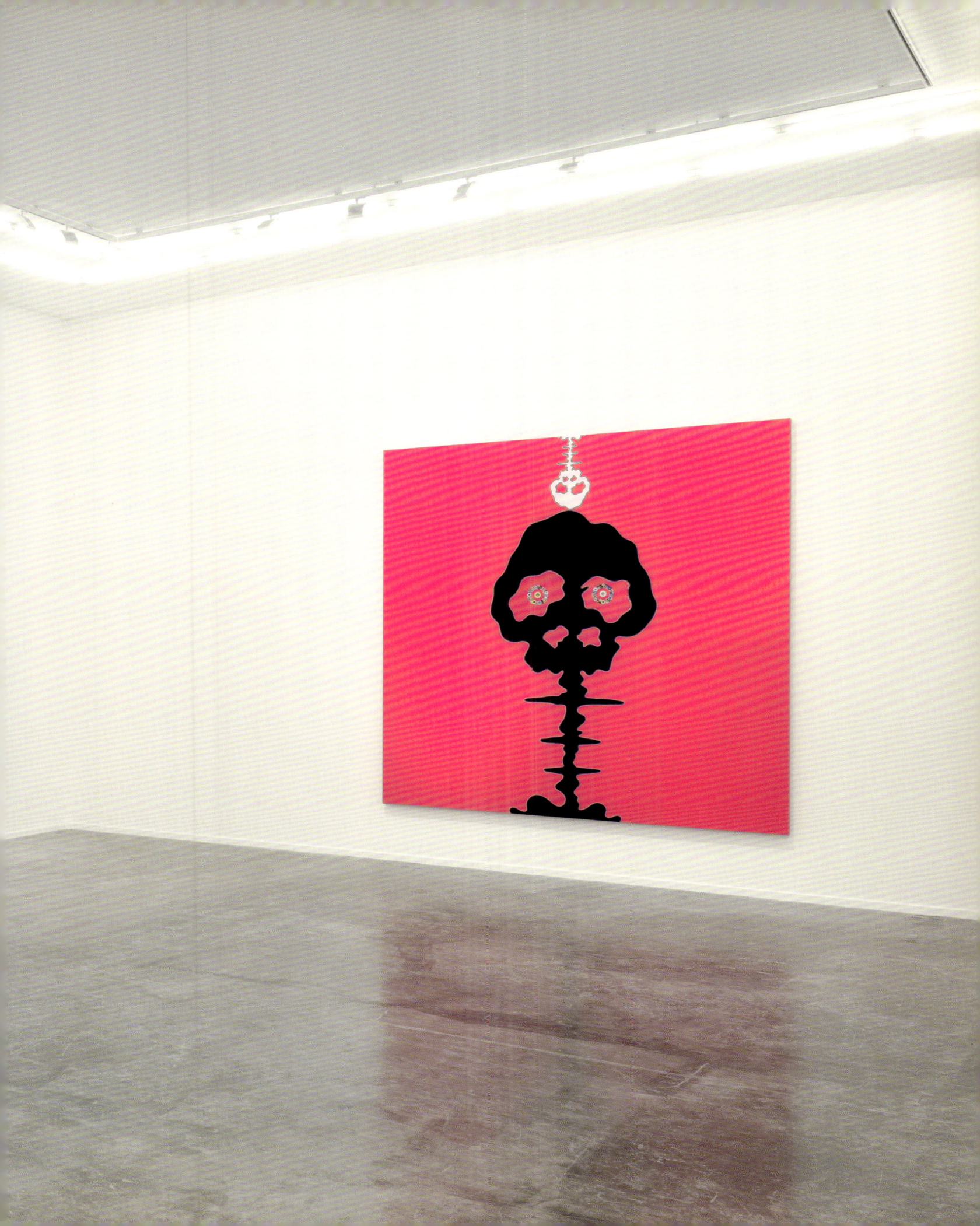

I ONLY UNDERSTAND THE SURFACE. THAT'S WHY I HAVE NO EGO.

I am a kind of B-movie filmmaker. I know very well that I will not be getting an Oscar. I'm constantly making B-movies, but making a B-movie can be just fine. That's where I start from. Sometimes this attitude can mislead the critics. And misreadings can be productive.

A very good example of what I have in mind is Steven Spielberg. Spielberg is the greatest B-movie director: He can get the money and make incredible movies. He has a very strong desire for quality, has a major impact on the industry, and knows how to make use of marketing strategies—just like George Lucas. Serious movie people have no respect for Lucas, but he has reinvented the industry. Lucas and Spielberg are my heroes. I try to work like them: I want to be honest, use my resources to keep the quality of my work at the highest level, and develop new marketing ideas.

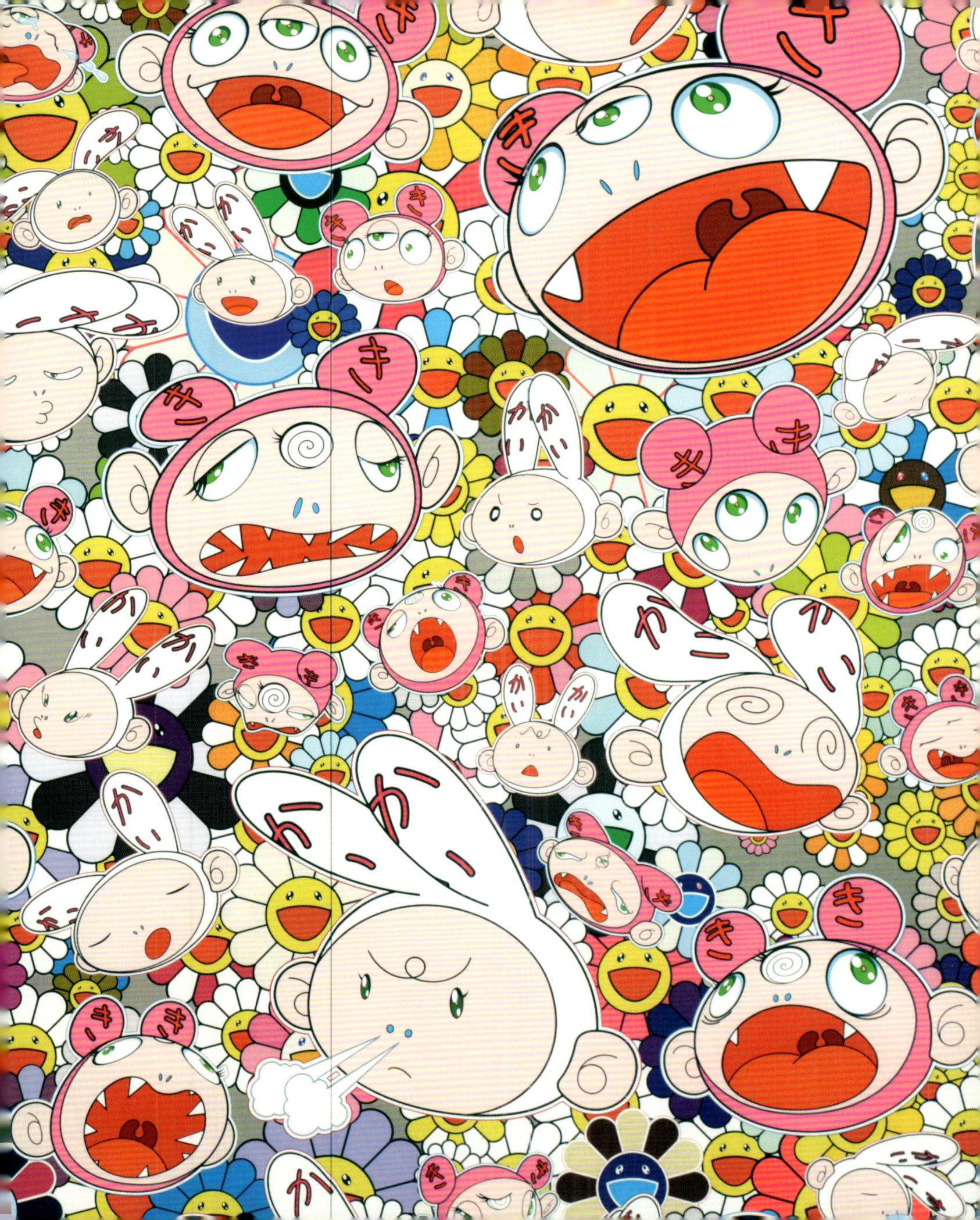

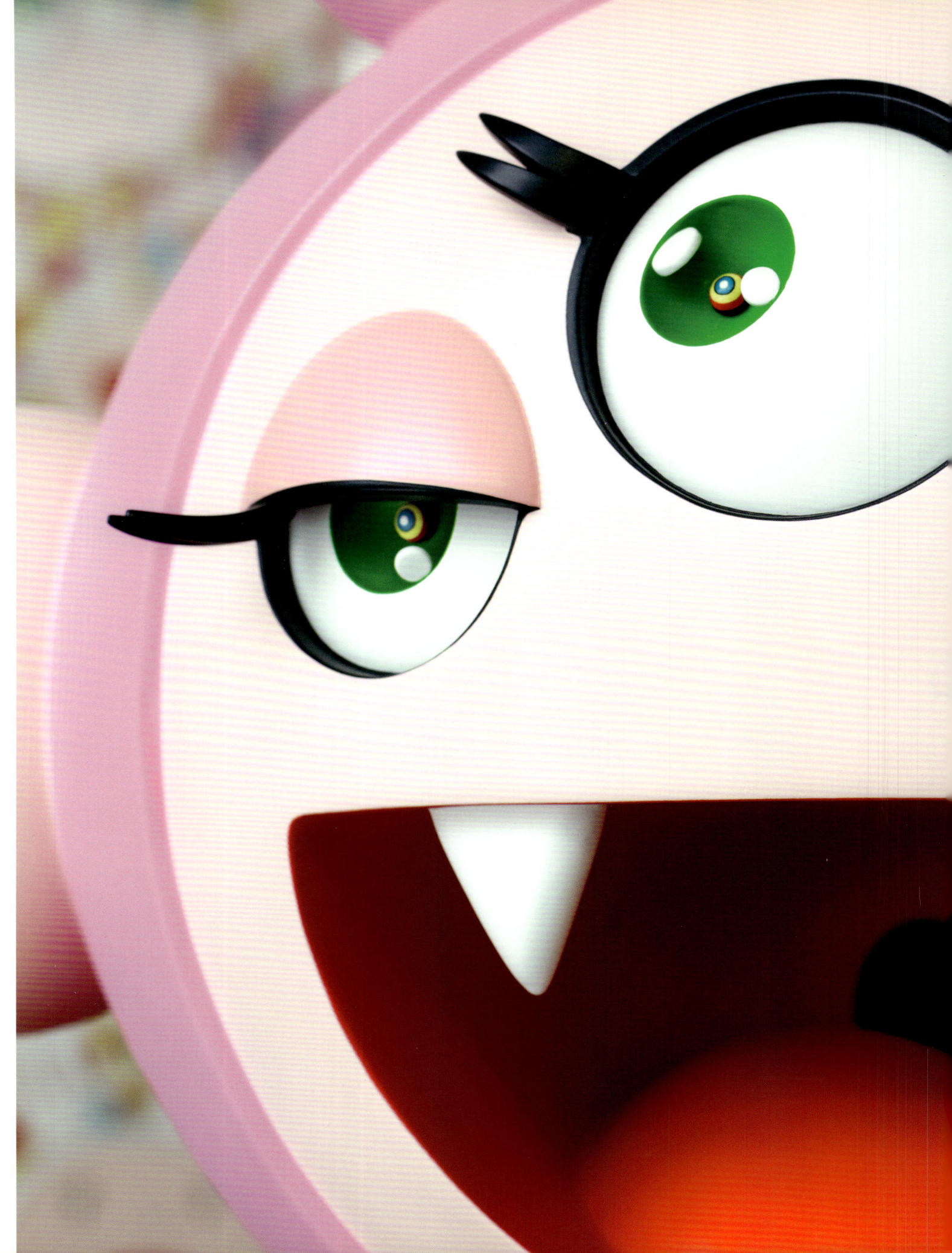

Kiki **(detail)** 2005

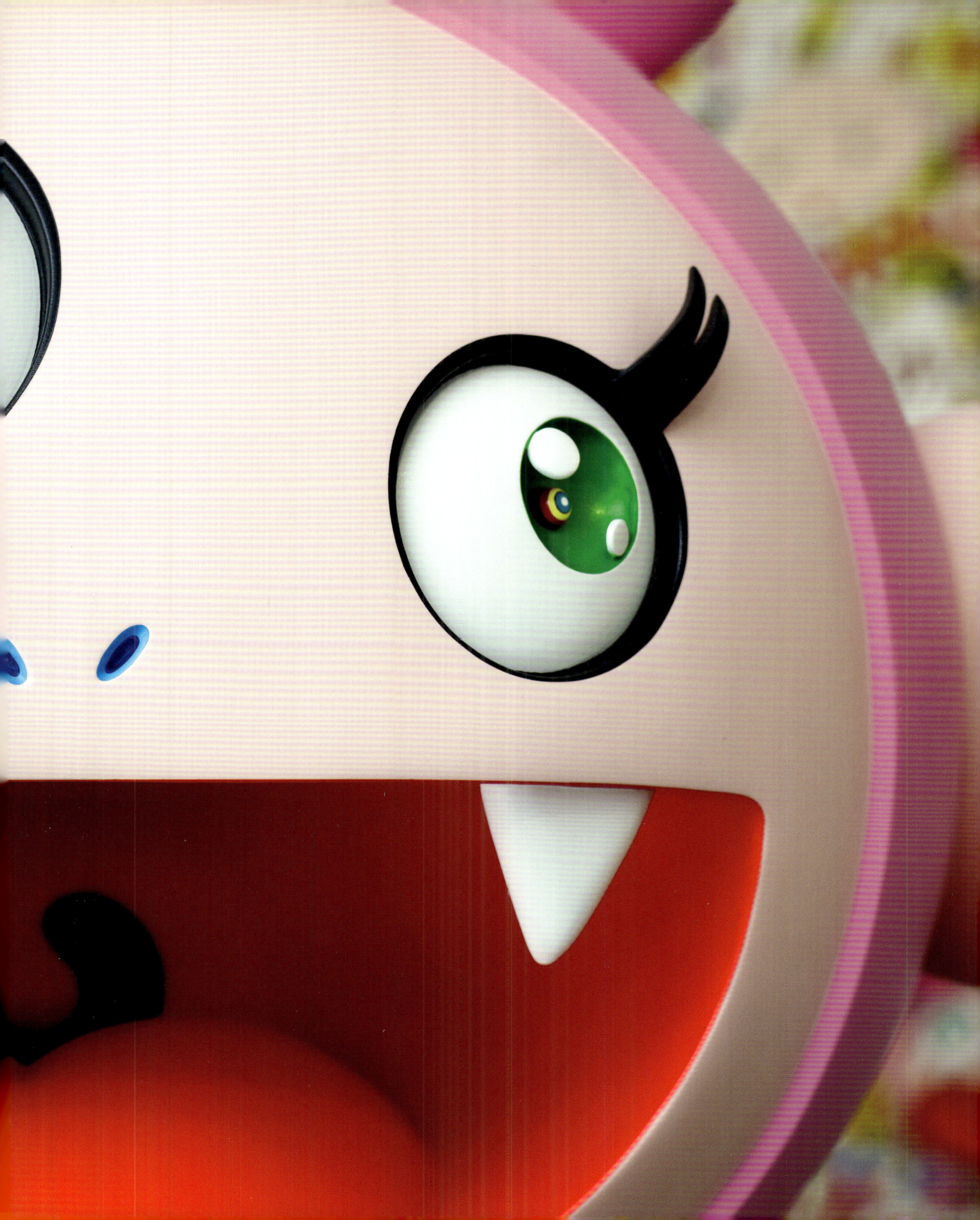

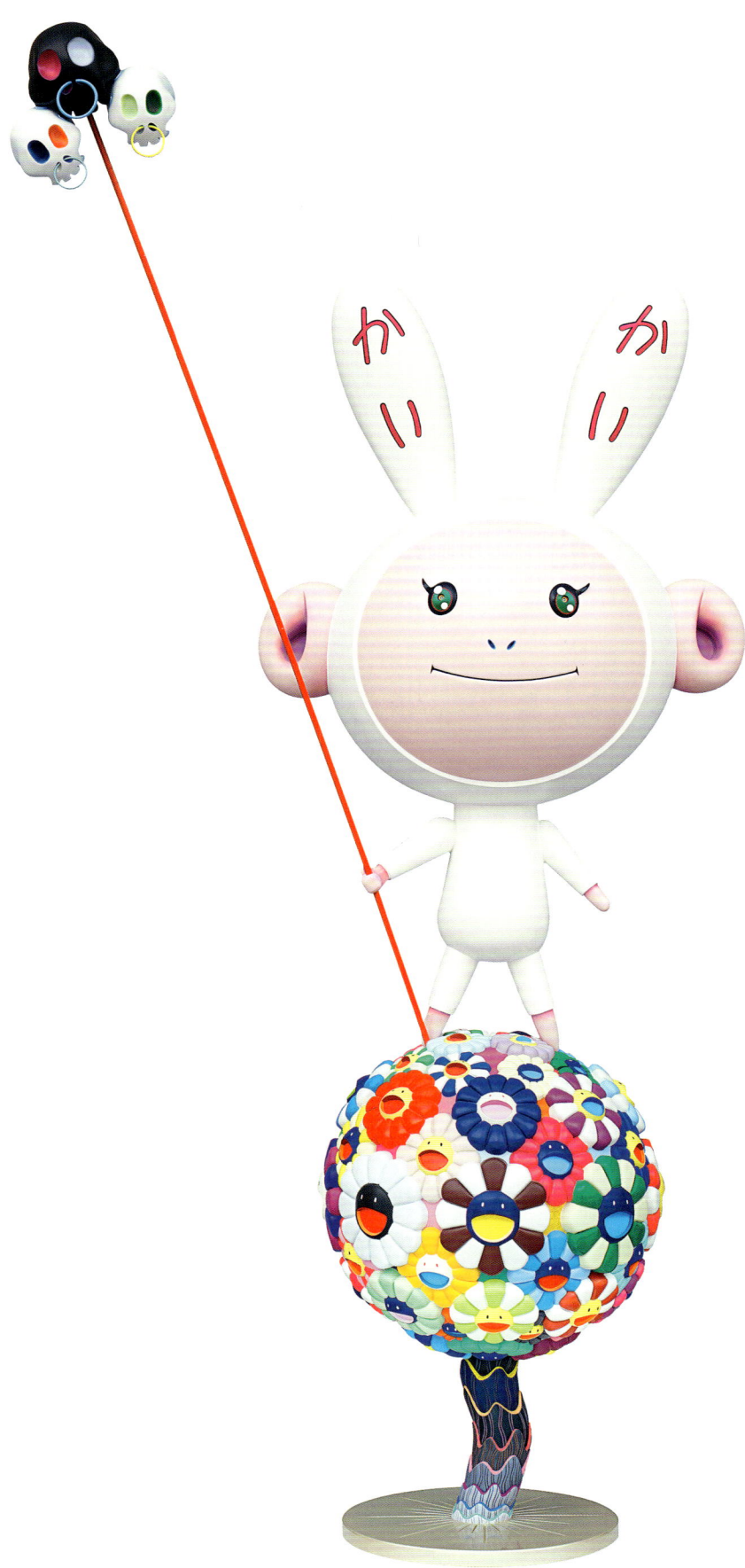

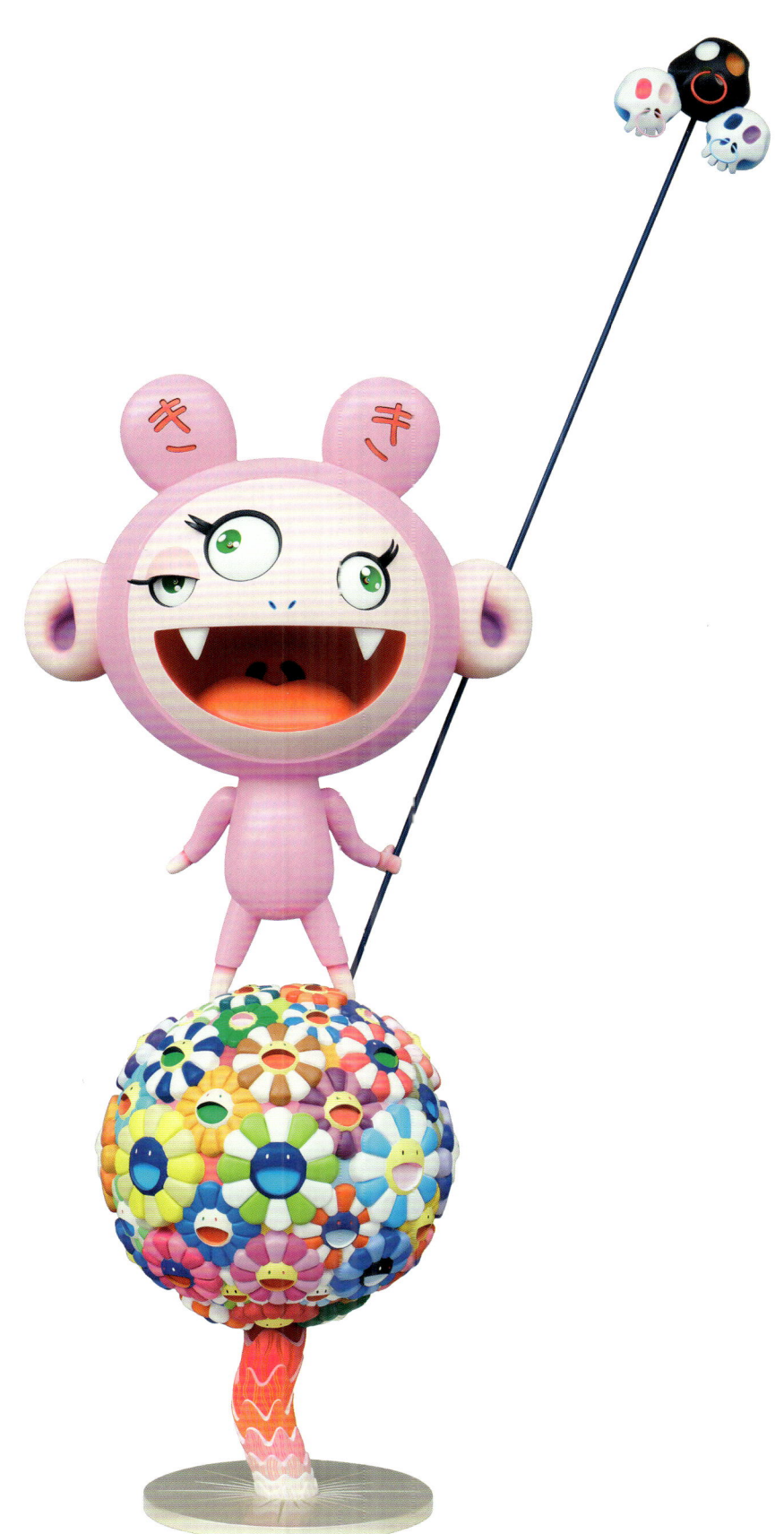

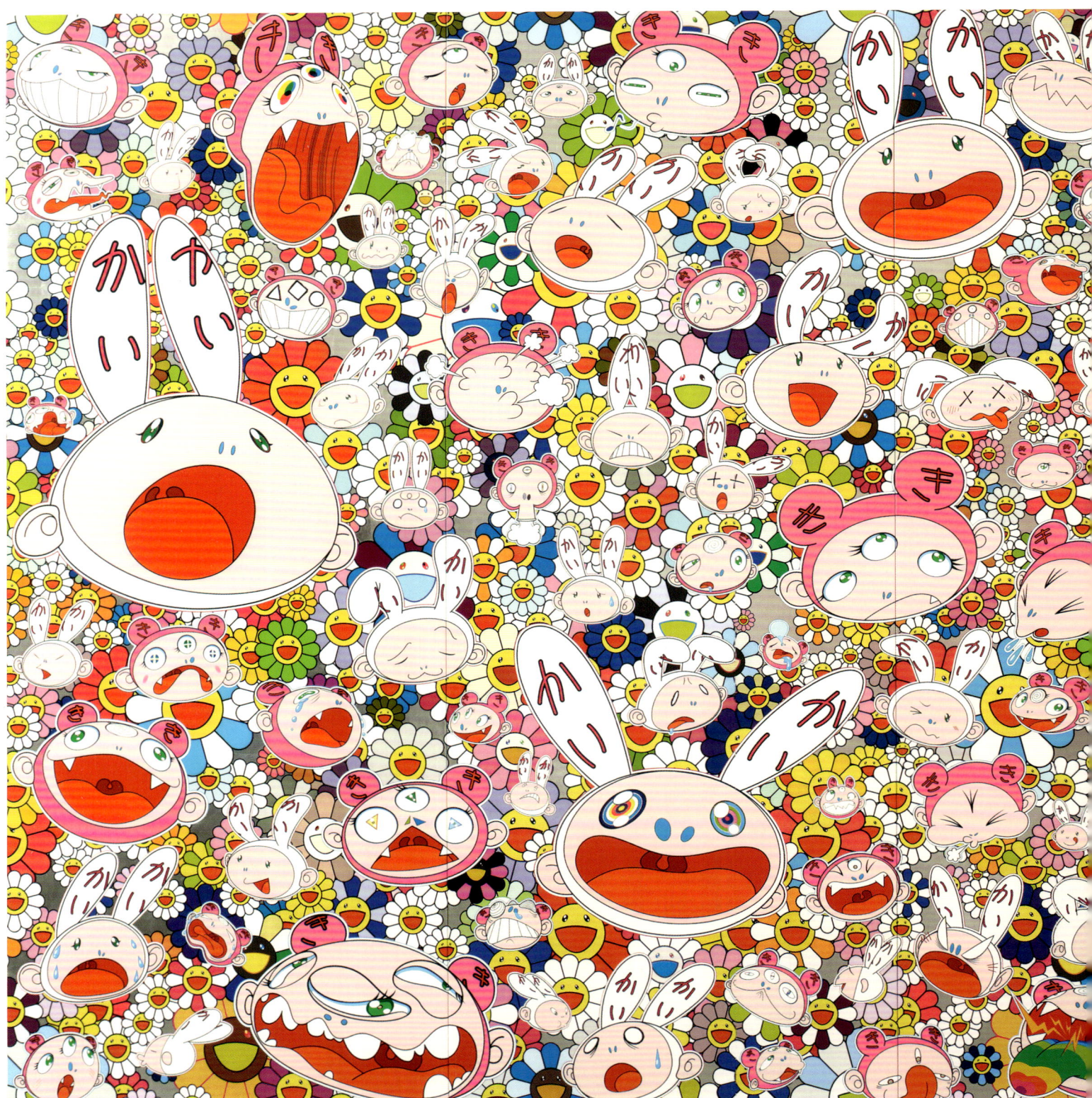

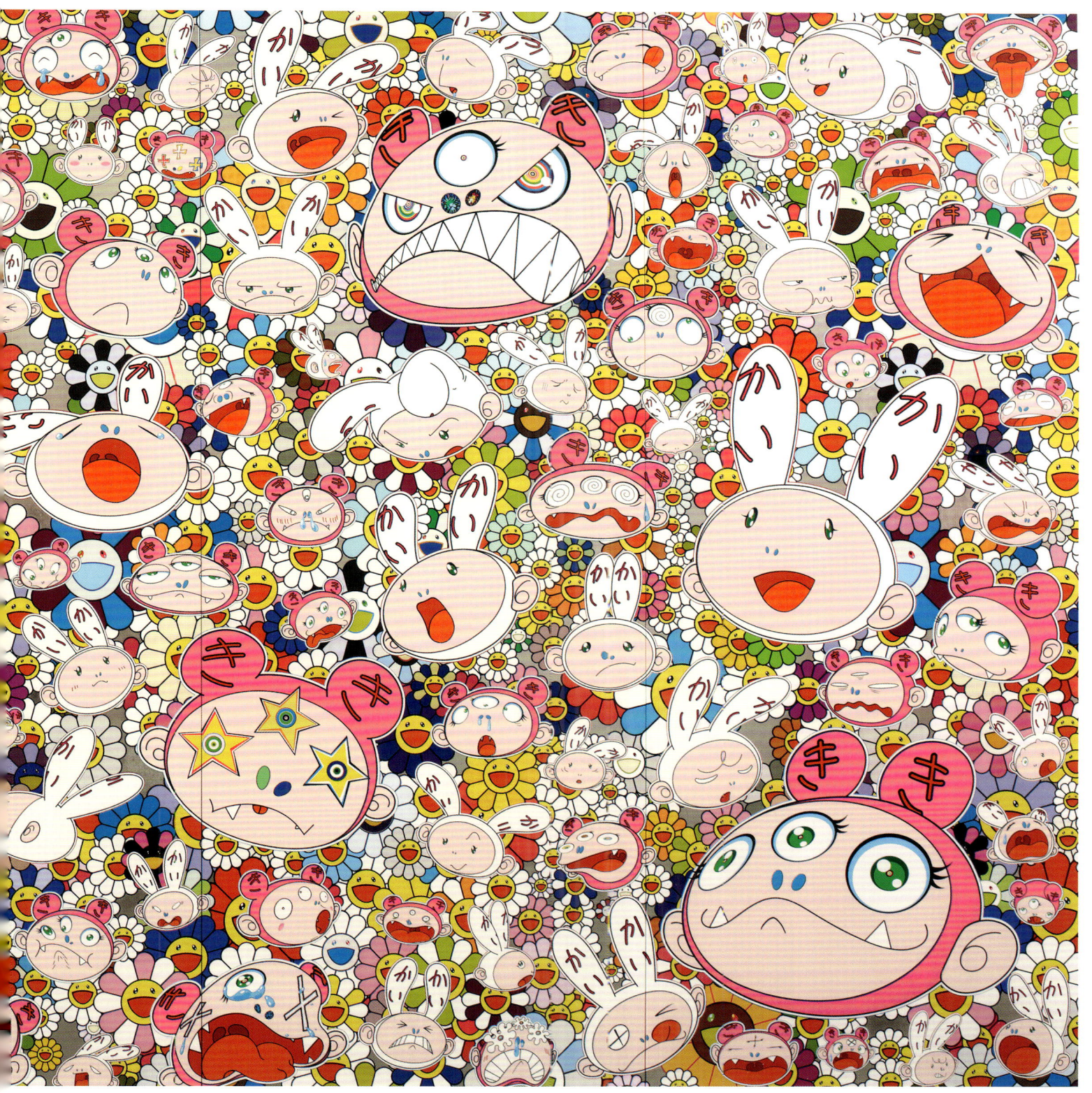

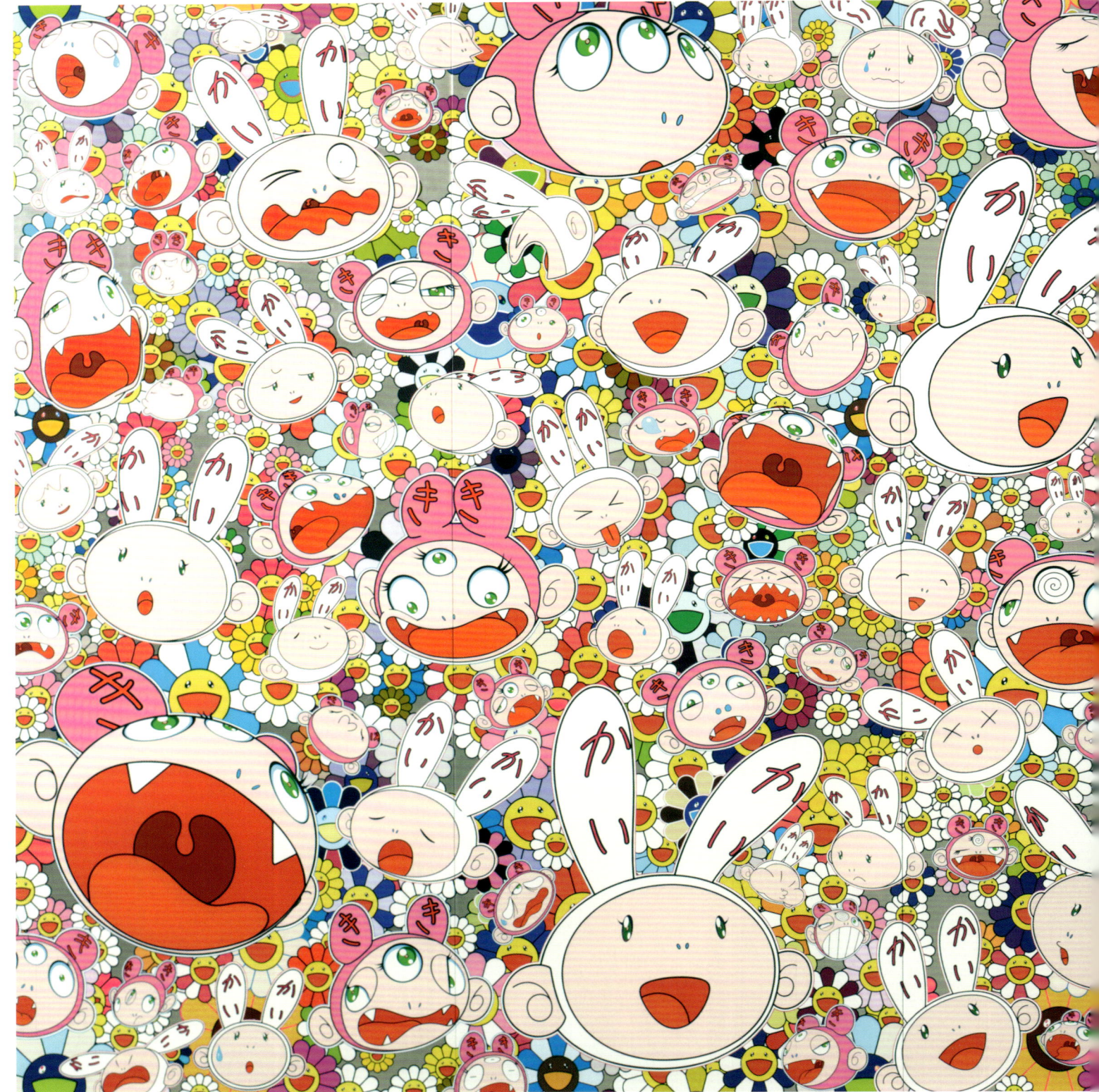

Lots, Lots of Kaikai and Kiki 2009

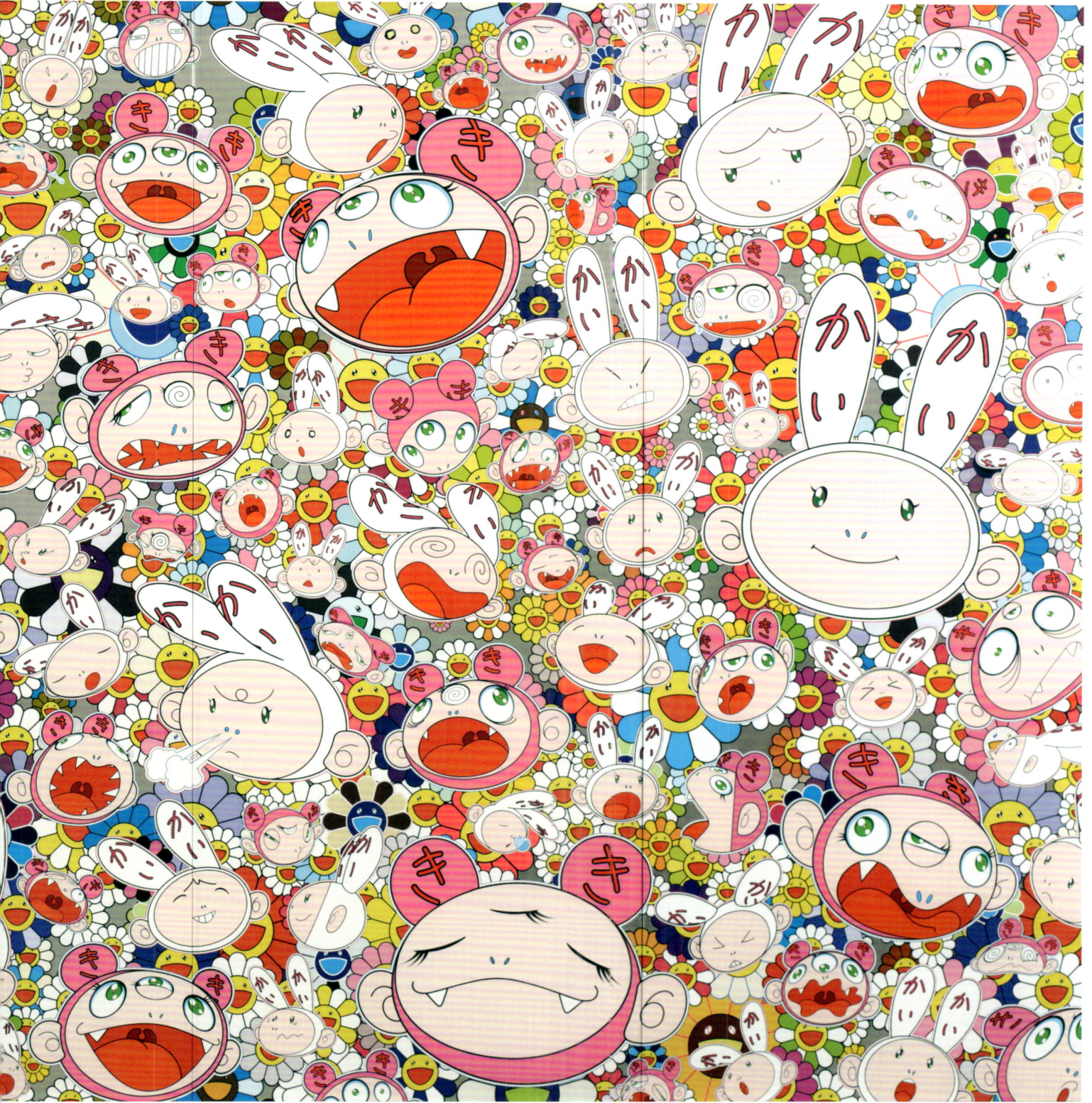

Hustle 'n' Punch by Kaikai and Kiki 2009

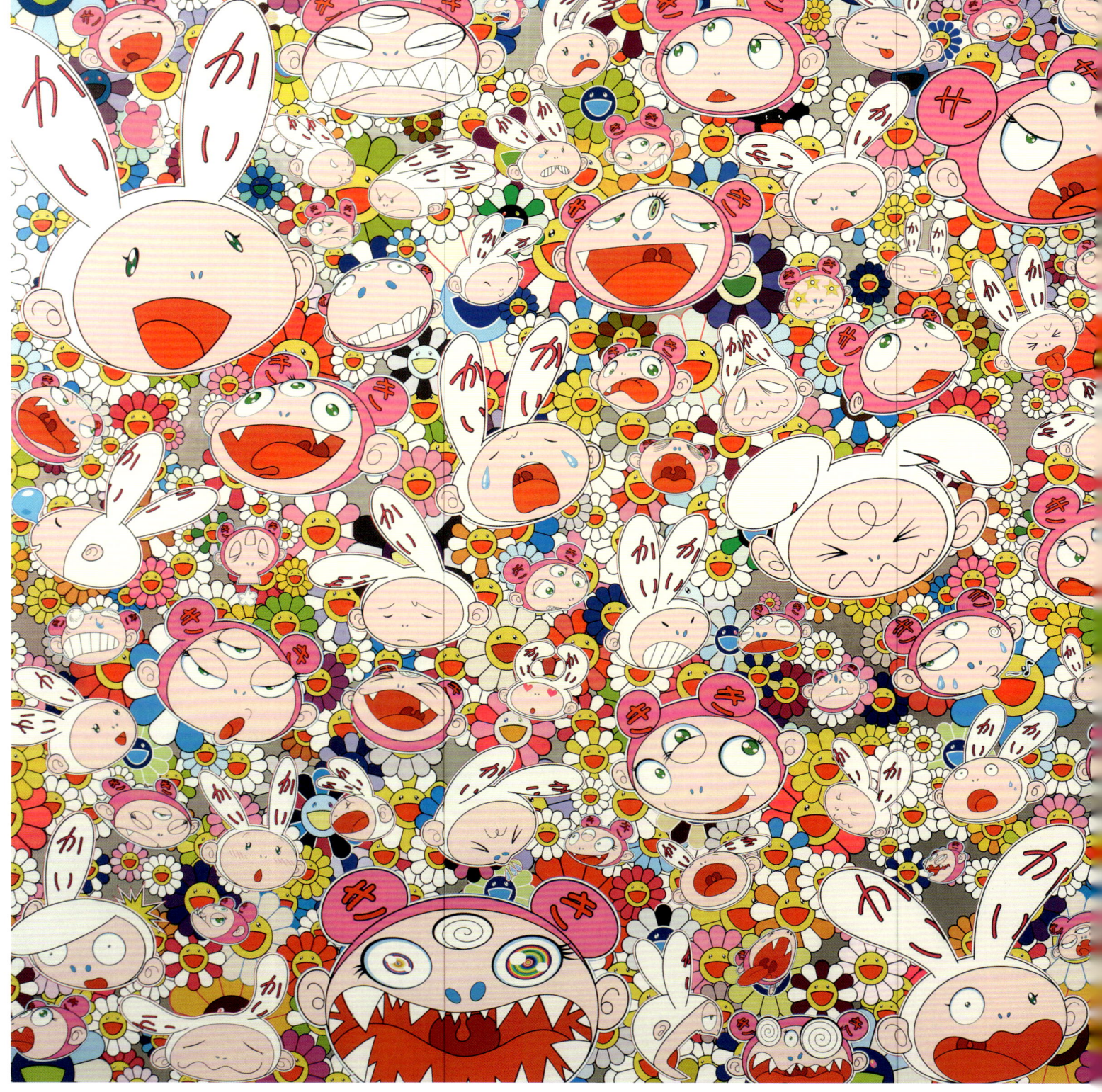

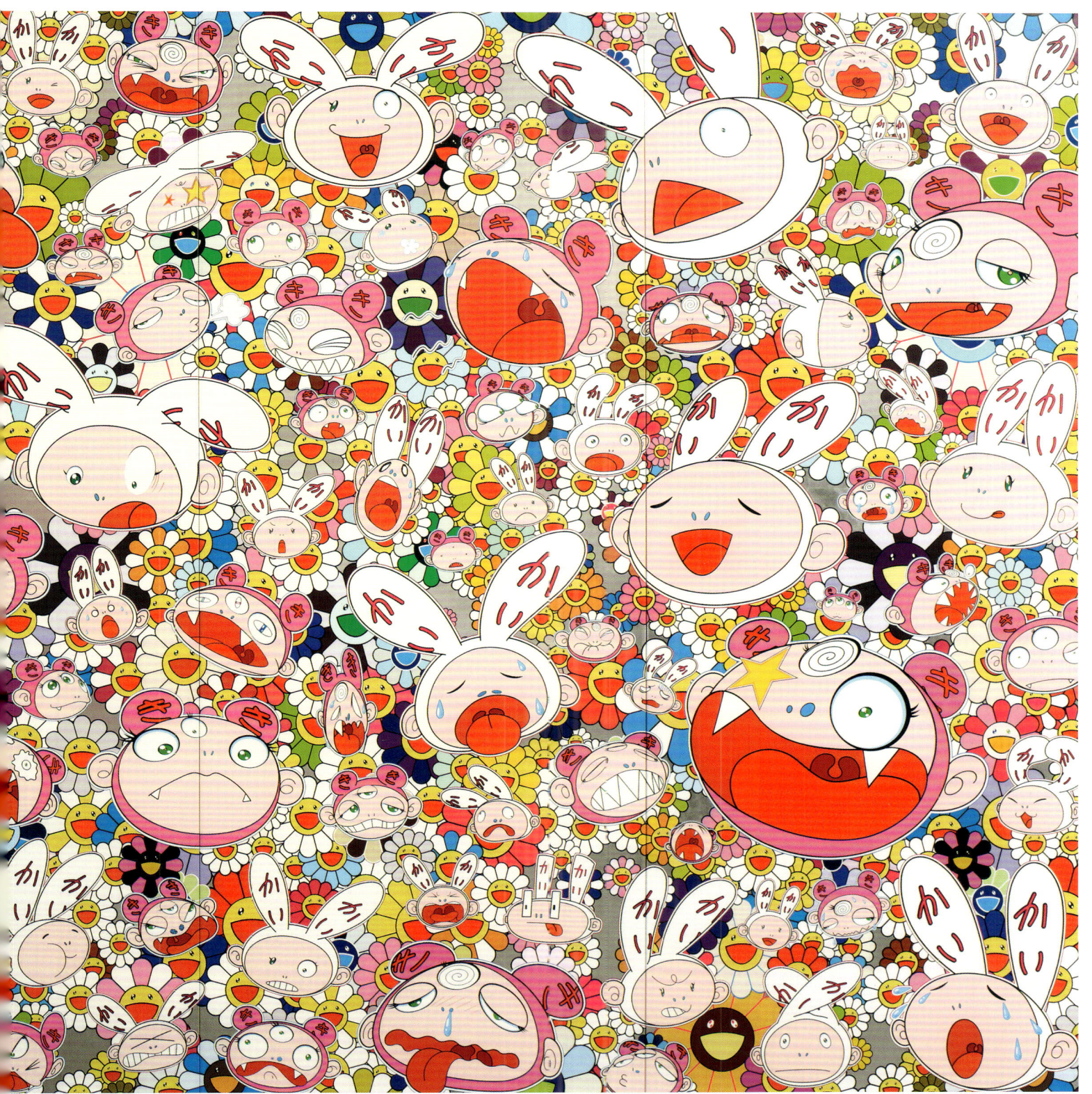

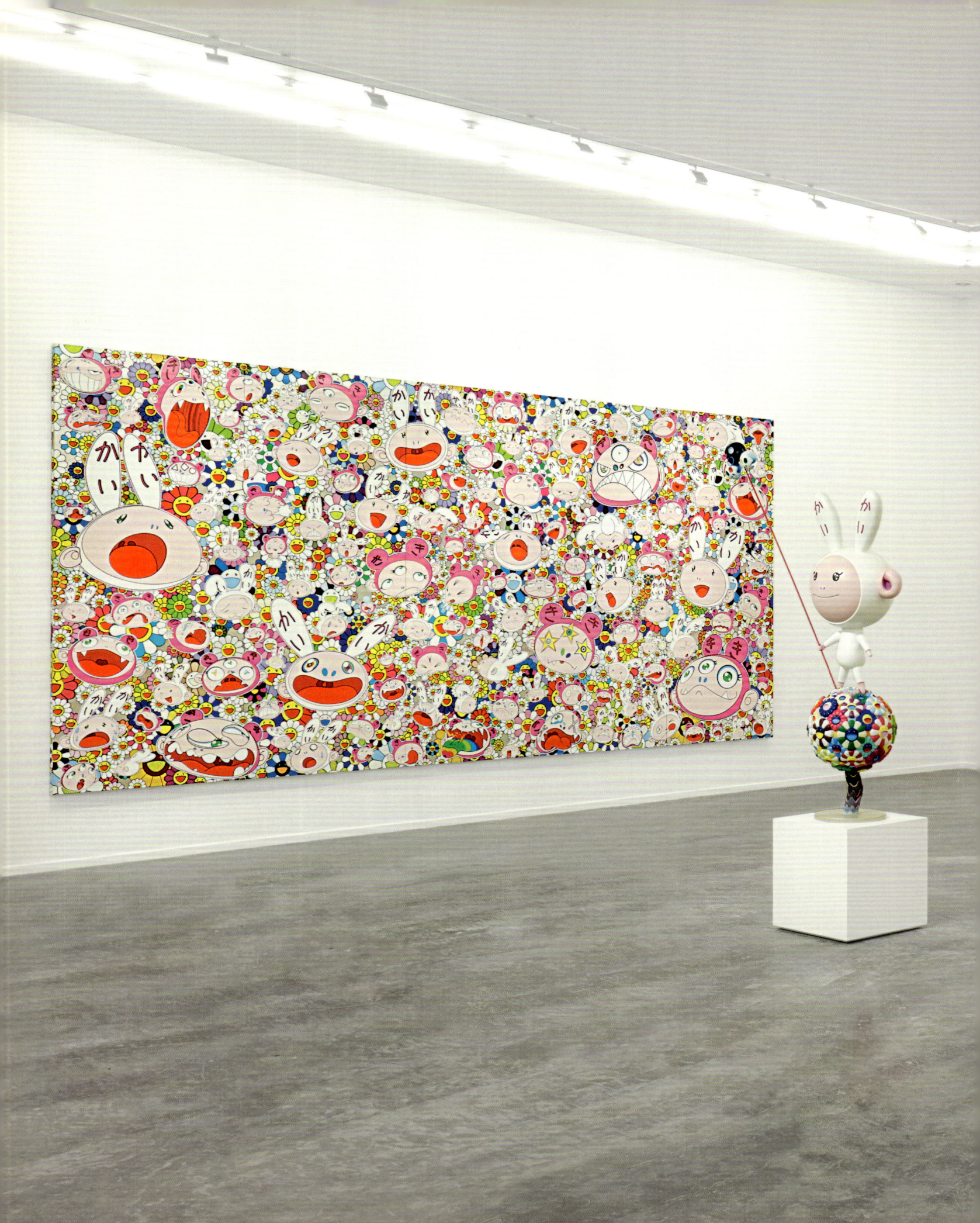

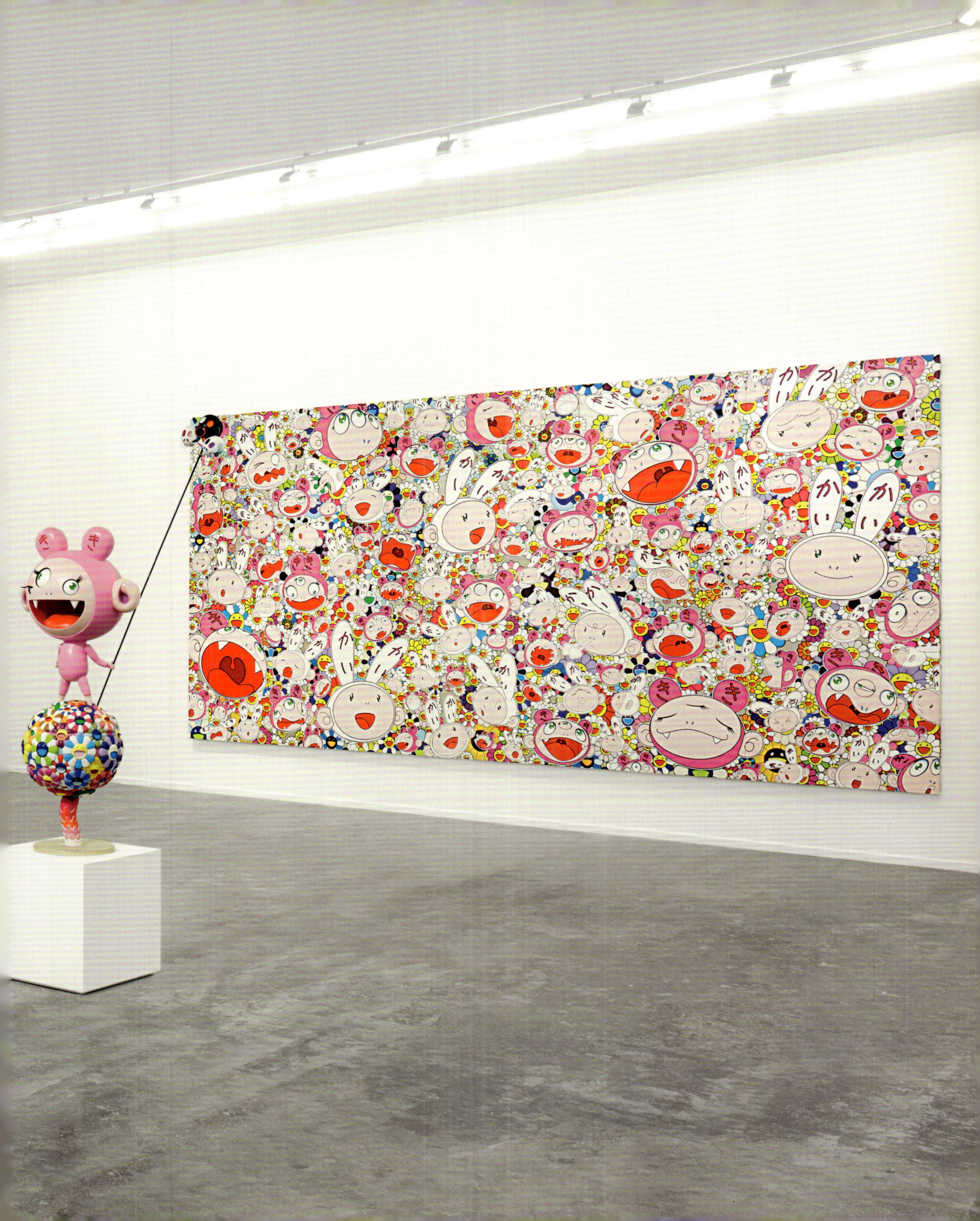

Kaikai Kiki Balloons (Macy's Parade) 2010

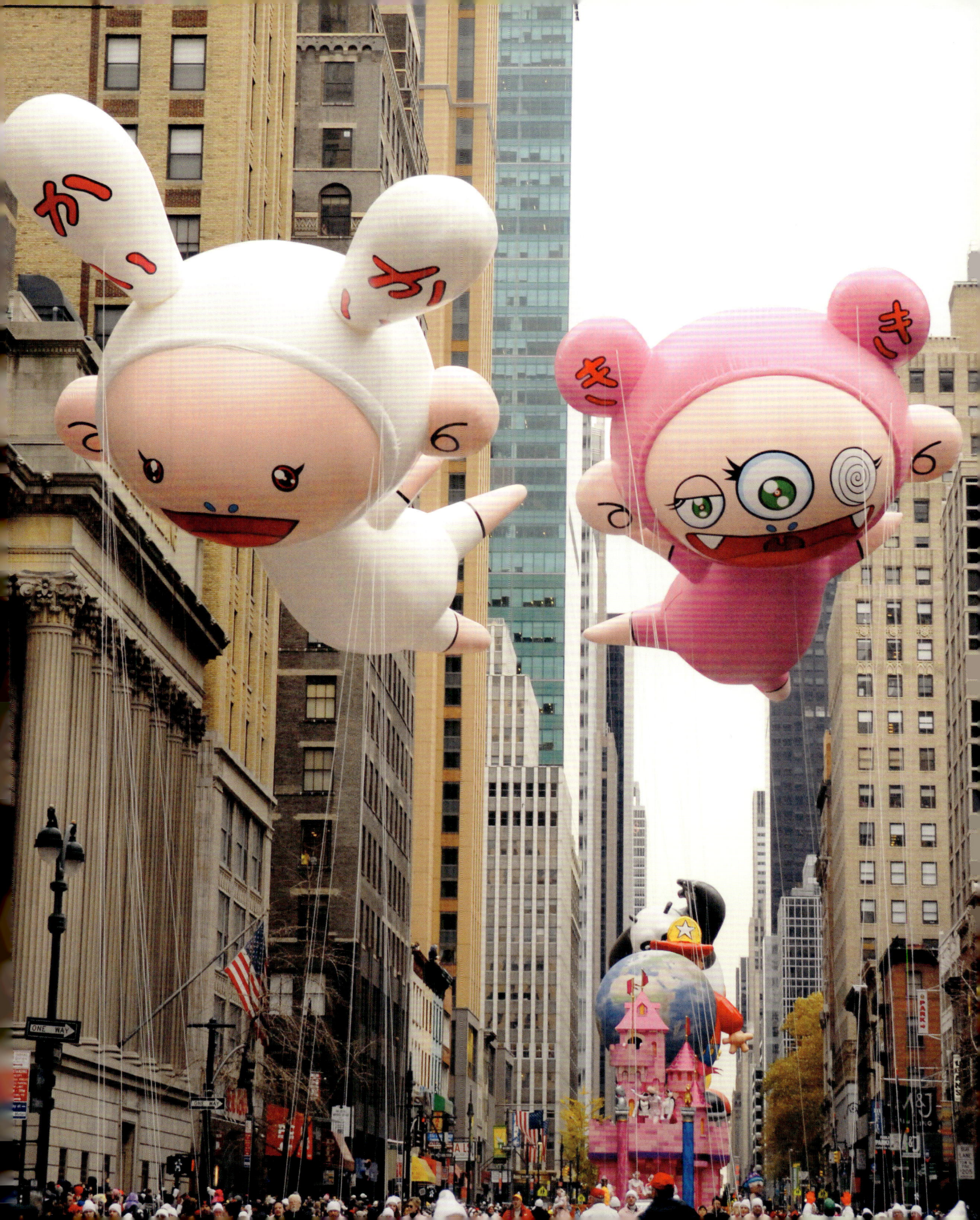

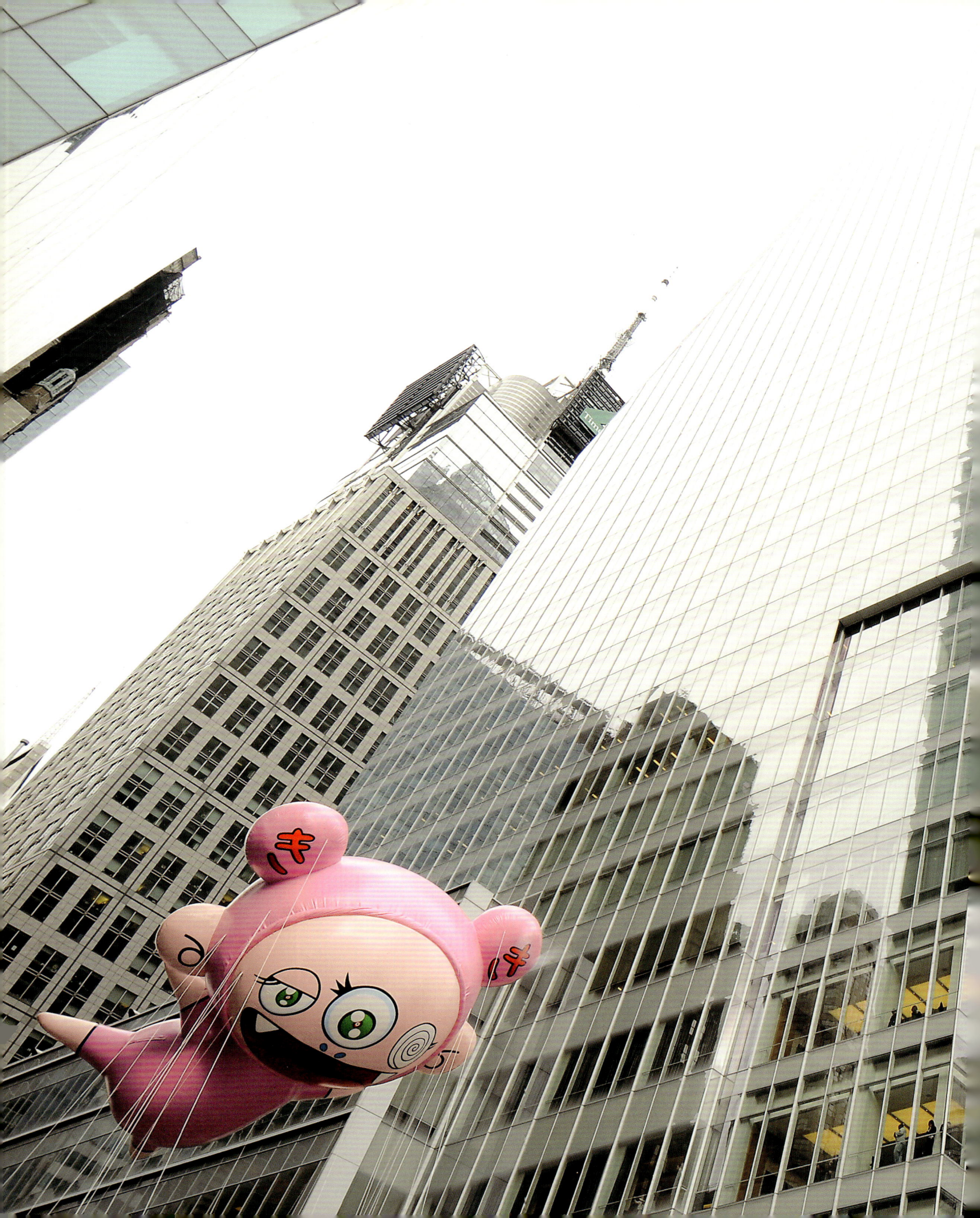

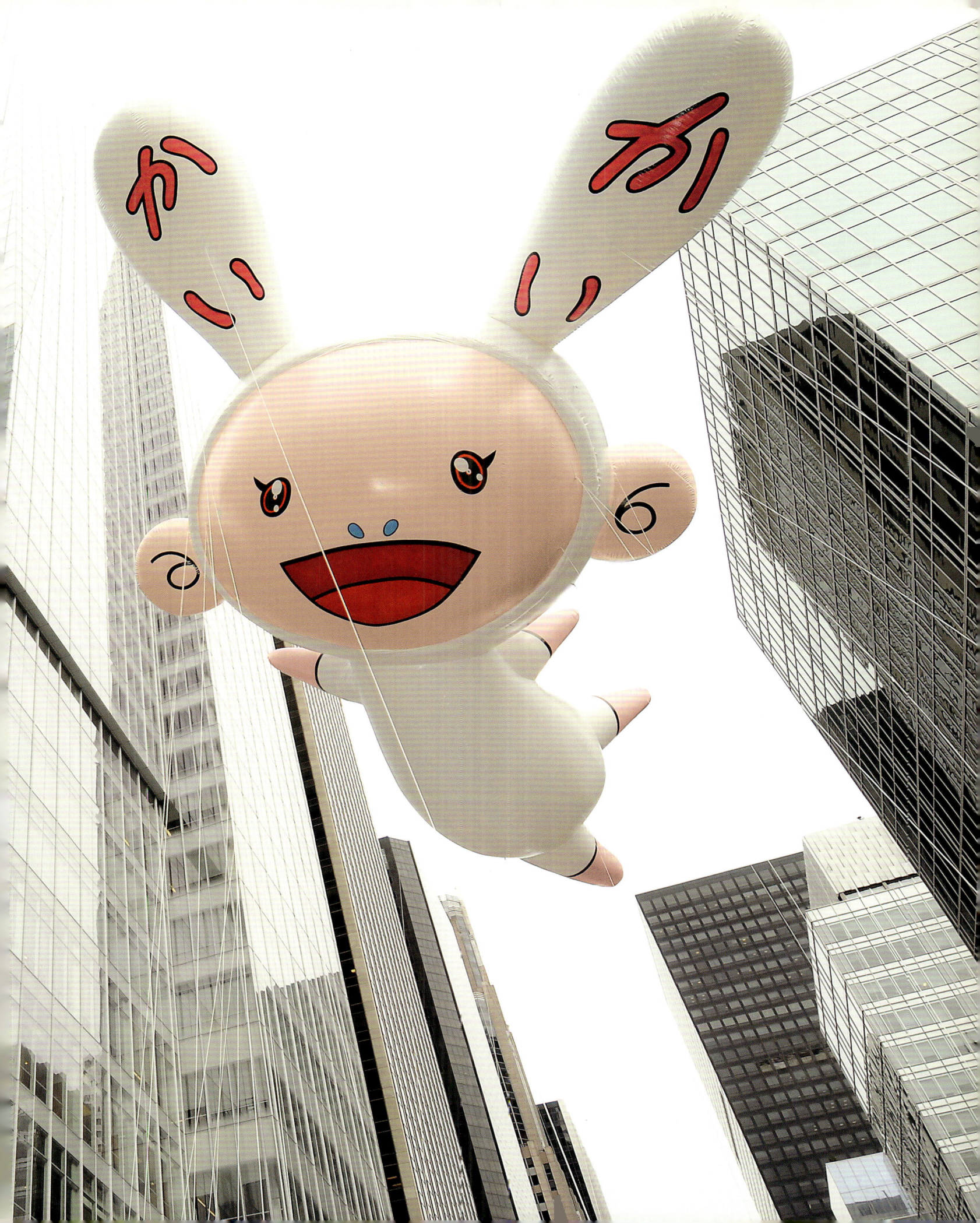

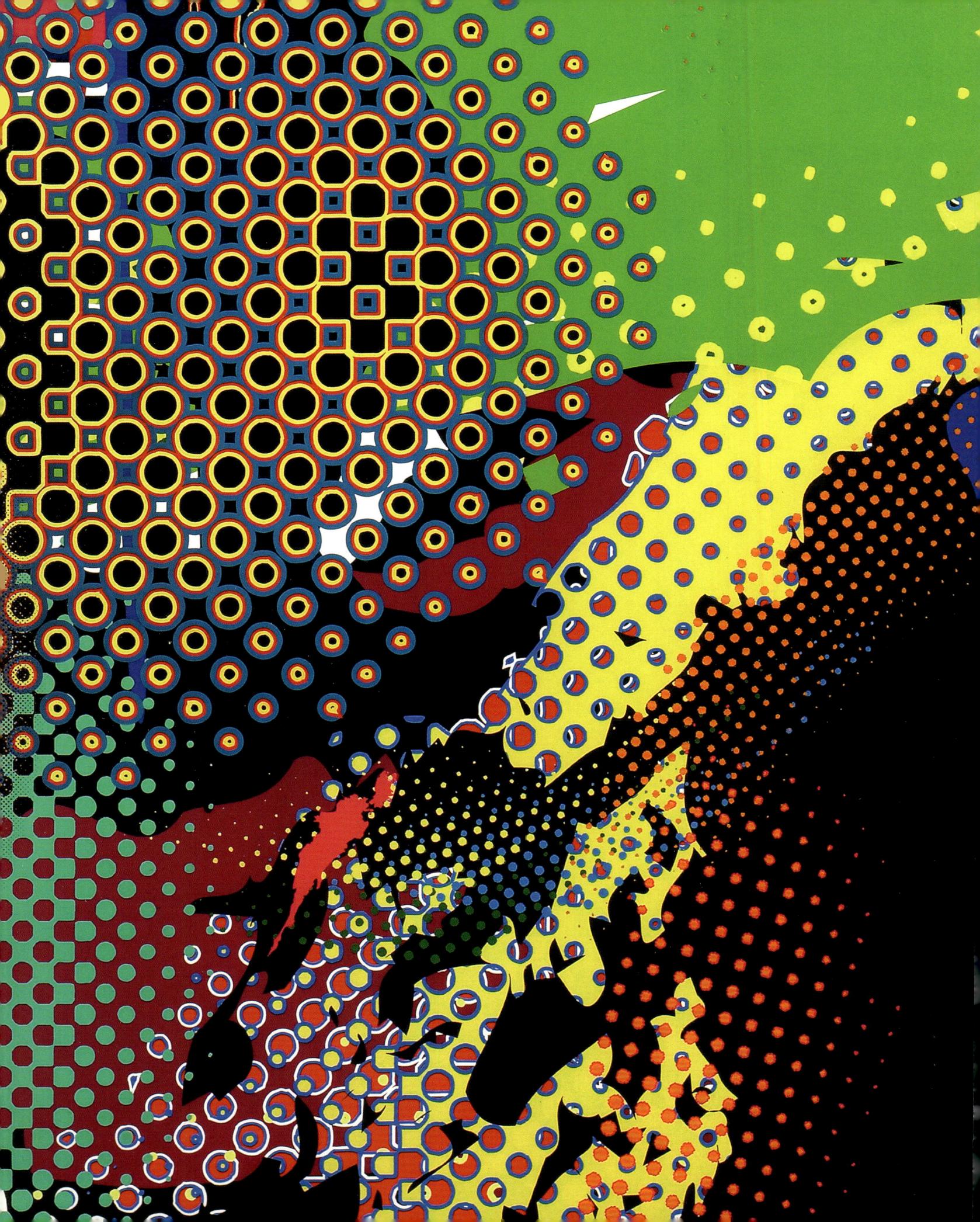

Before we actually start painting, we create a reduced scale model image—about an inch (3 cm) in diameter—and gradually scale it up to a larger image, aiming for maximum smoothness in the contour lines. Then my assistants start their collaborative work, using the Bézier curve tool in Adobe Illustrator to further enhance the smoothness of the outline. It's an extremely difficult, even painful task.

After this back and forth is complete, we begin communicating with the painting studio. The data has to be converted to a format suitable for silk-screen printing, which means again creating a whole new file. When we work on a large-scale piece, we need six full-time staff members present at all times to manage this data-creation process. Even if they are stuck at their desks for more than sixteen hours a day, it can take three whole weeks to complete. What's more, the job requires an incredible amount of technical skill.

Next, we mix the paint and begin printing silk screens, carefully to maintain precision. The process can result in as many as a thousand different screens for one painting.

Even then, we're still not finished. After three months of work by my assistant painters, the "finishing painters" will refine the results. Rather than use data or models as their guide, they have an eye for balance. Their job is to ensure the piece holds together as a complete work of art. This task is extremely sensitive and subjective, requiring an aesthetic sensibility that differs from data management and technical skill and is more similar to what you might have found at Rubens's workshop long ago.

Here, the piece will inevitably take a turn toward something that clashes with my own aesthetics. Which brings us to the most important part: To confront this clash, I myself make an appearance and must decide what to leave alone and what to change. At times, I make drastic changes that affect the work on every level, which of course earns me the ire of my staff. This leads to more back and forth, which ultimately adds to the strength of the work.

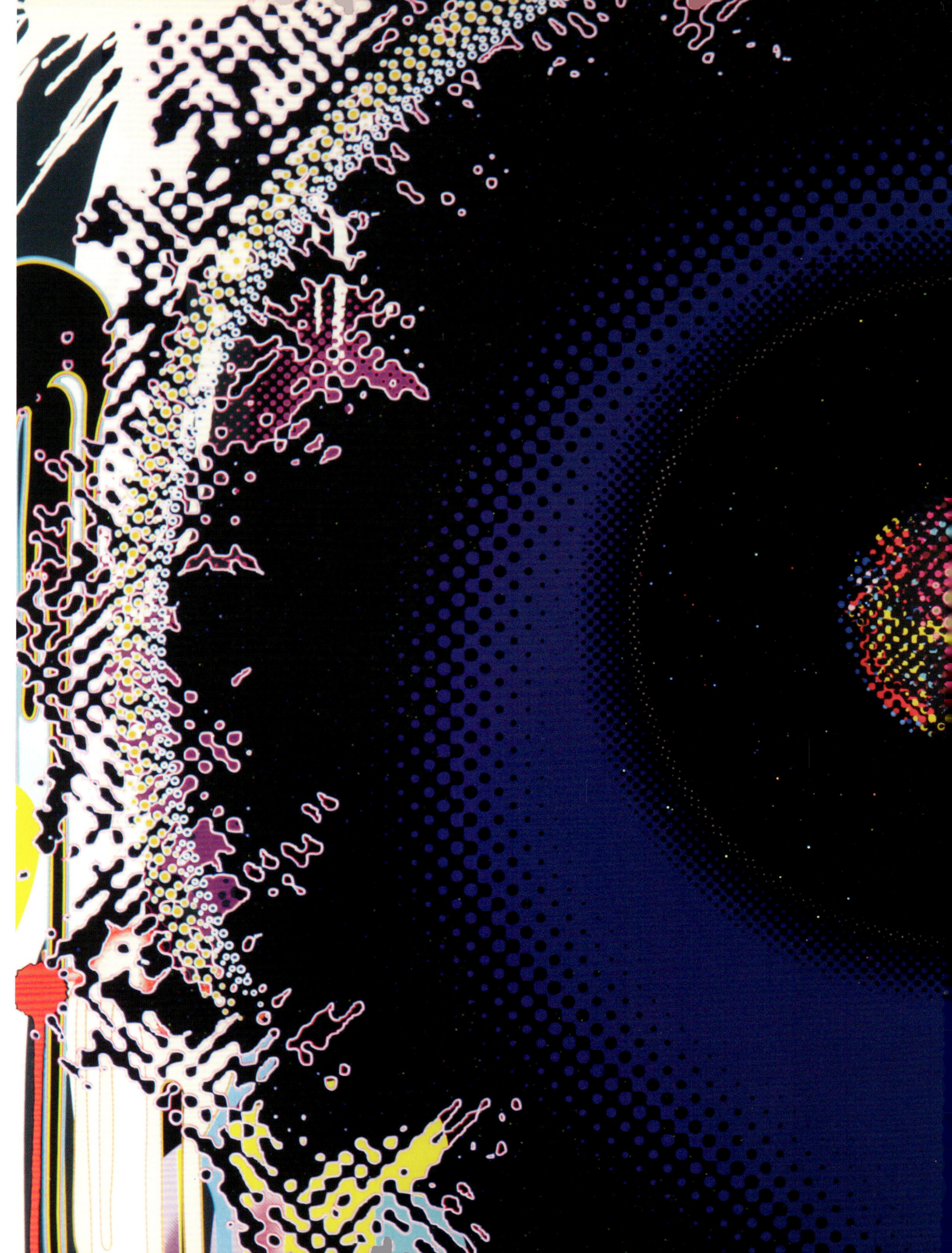

NGC2371-2 (Gemini Nebula) (detail) 2009

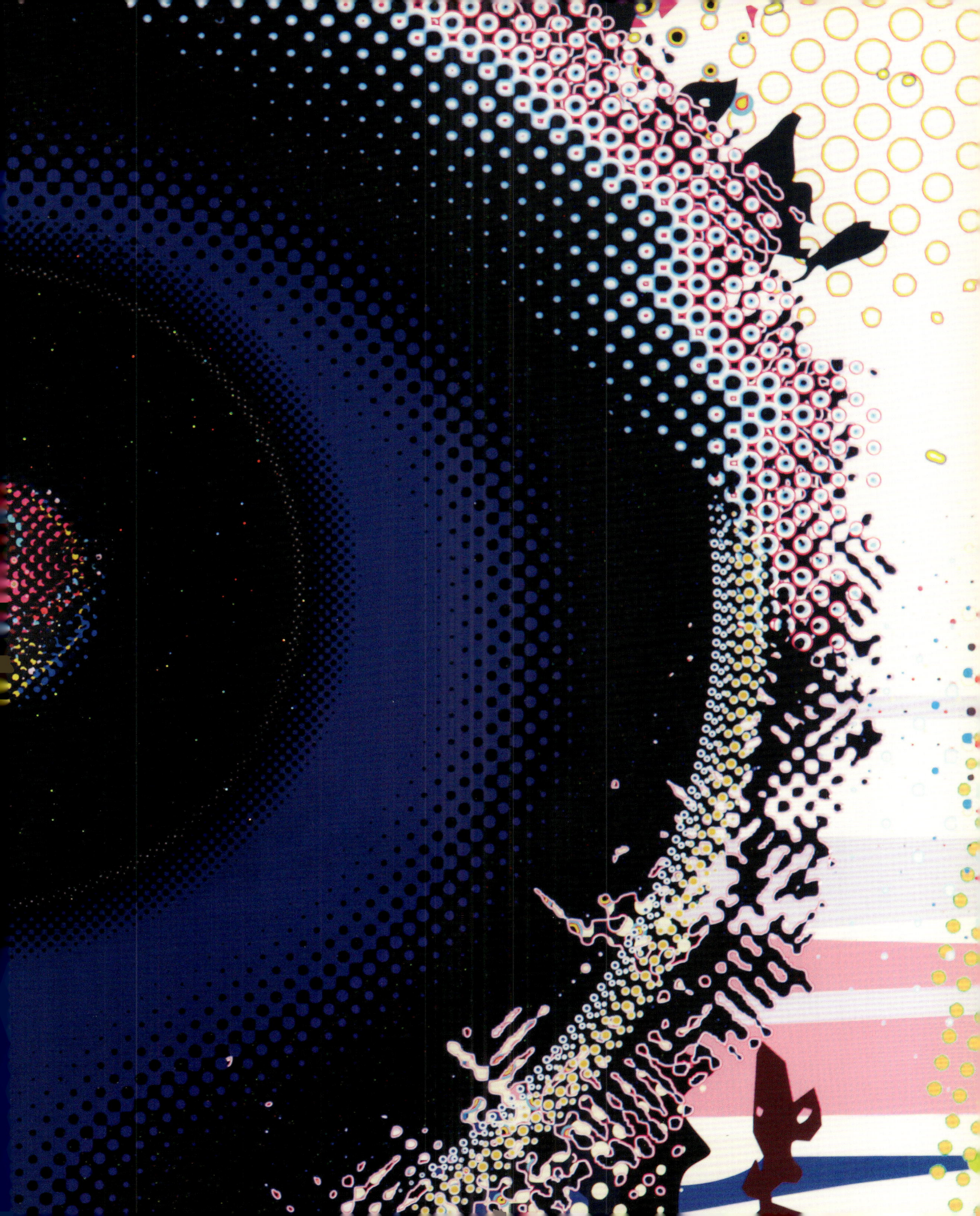

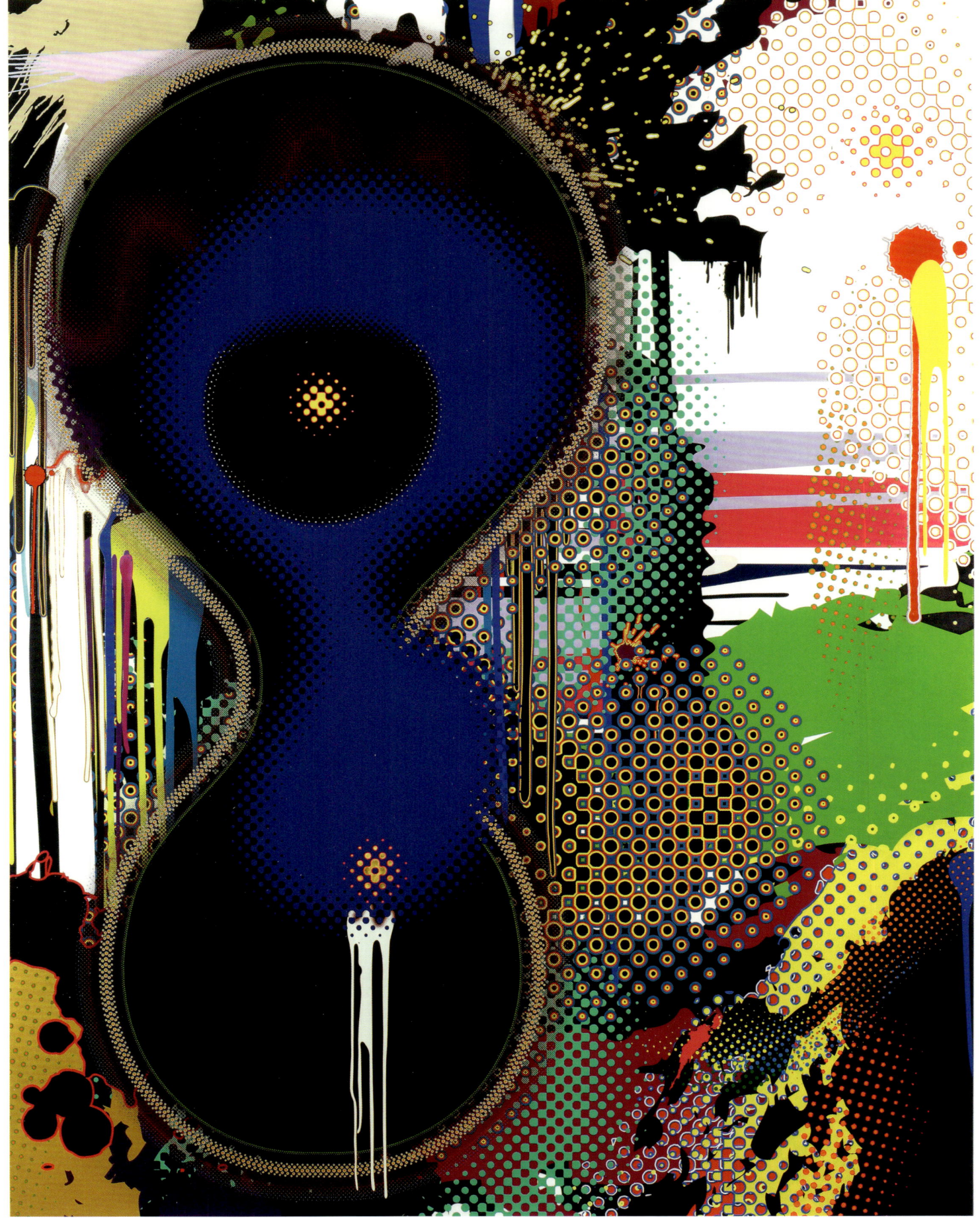

NGC2371-2 (Gemini Nebula) 2009

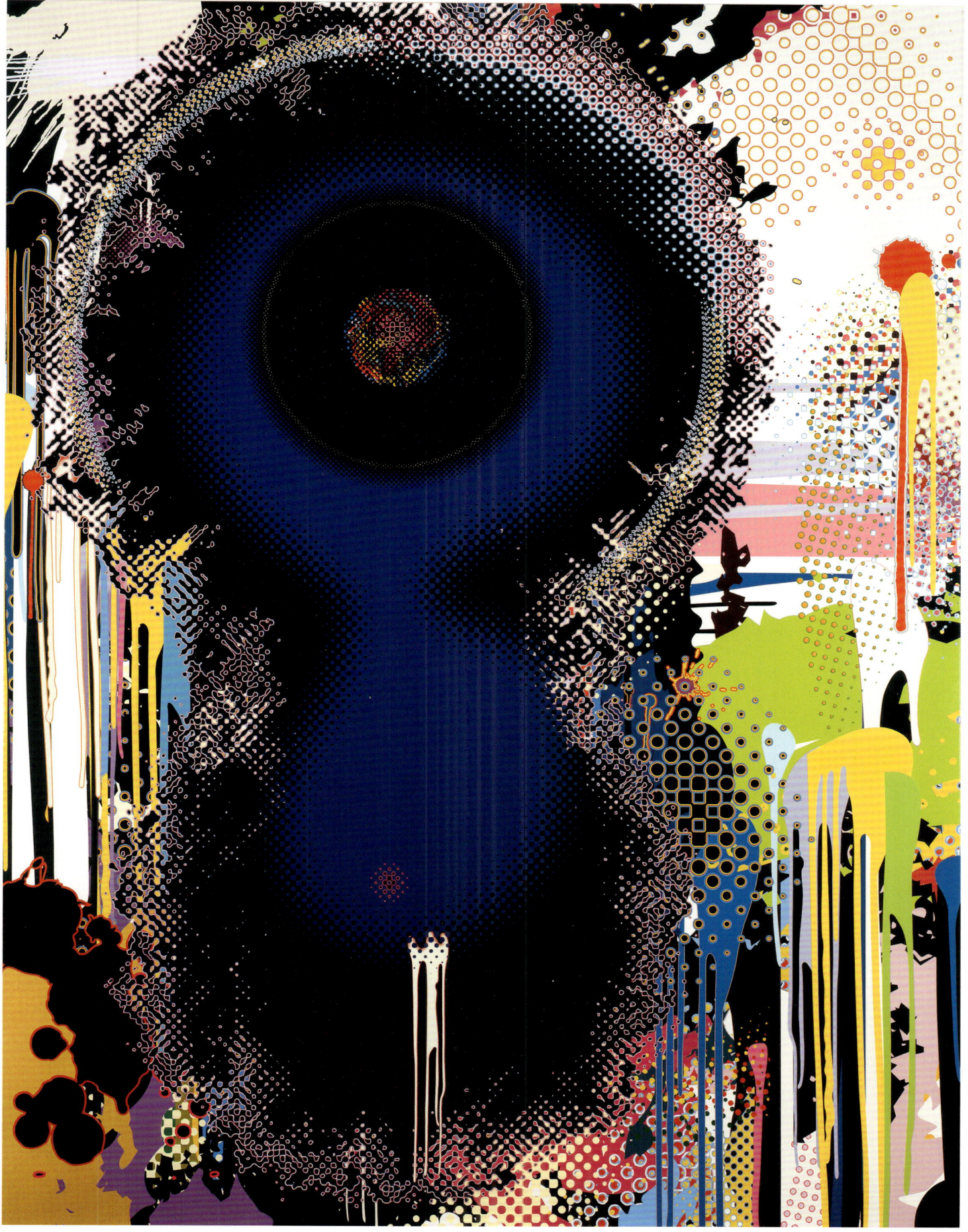

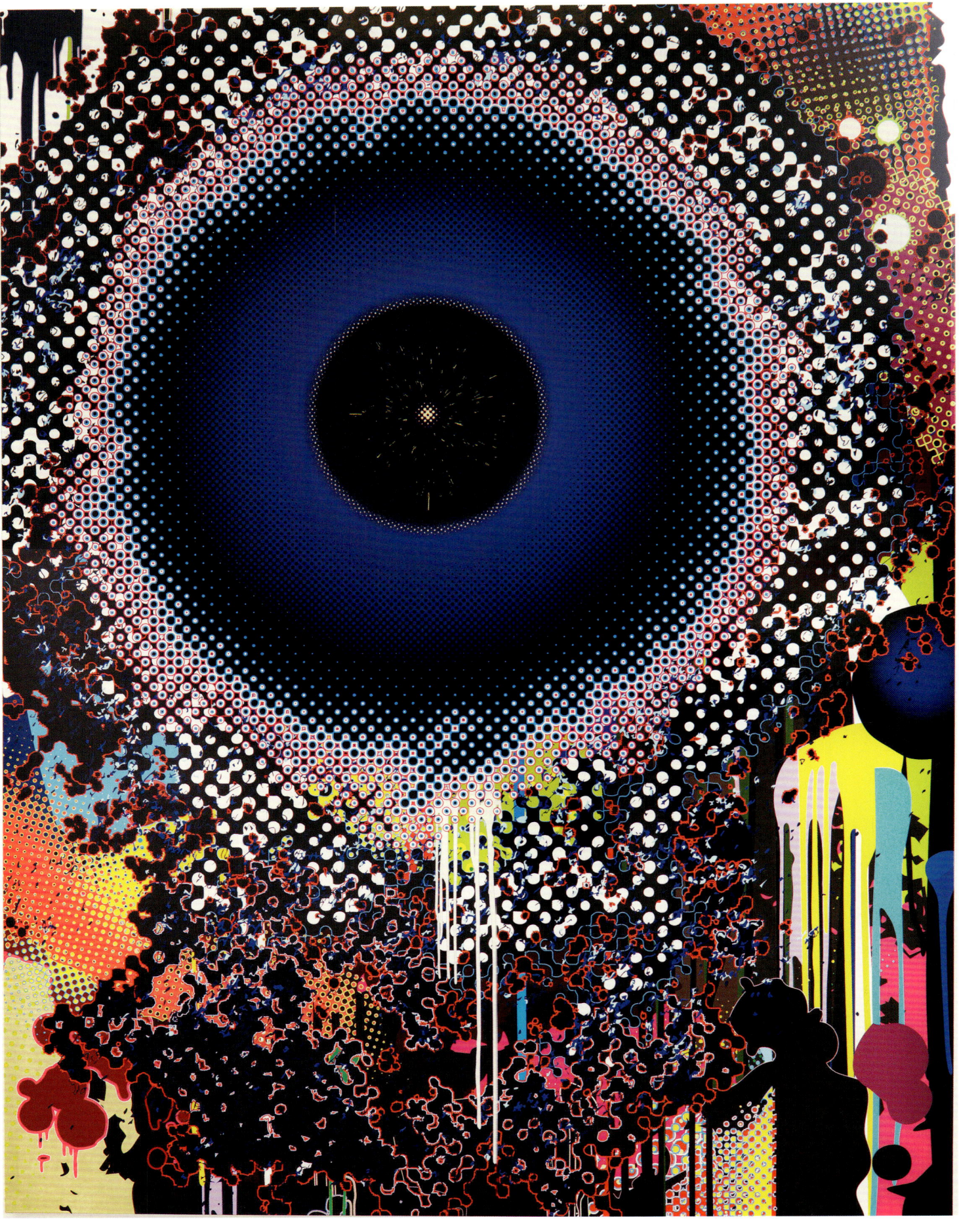

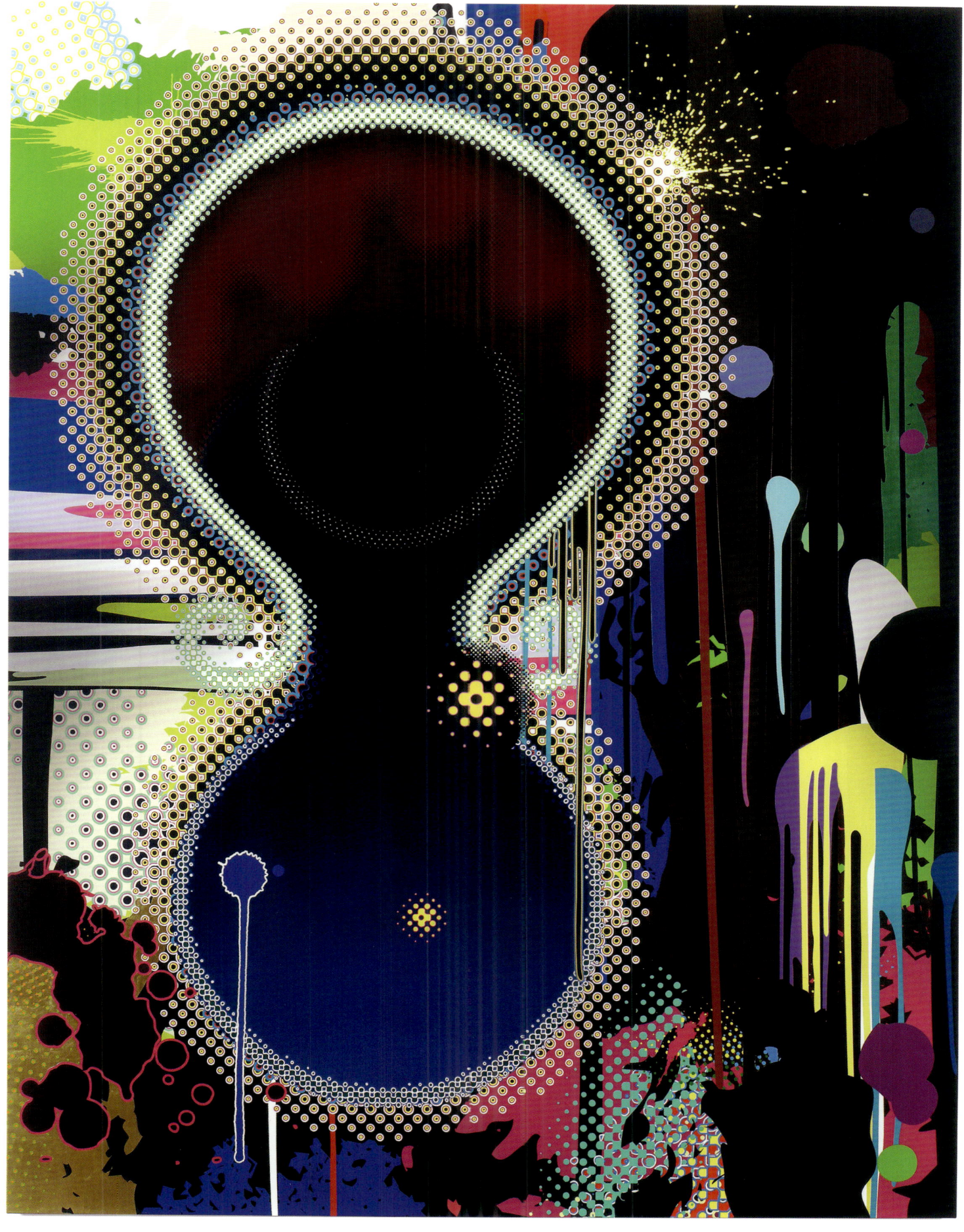

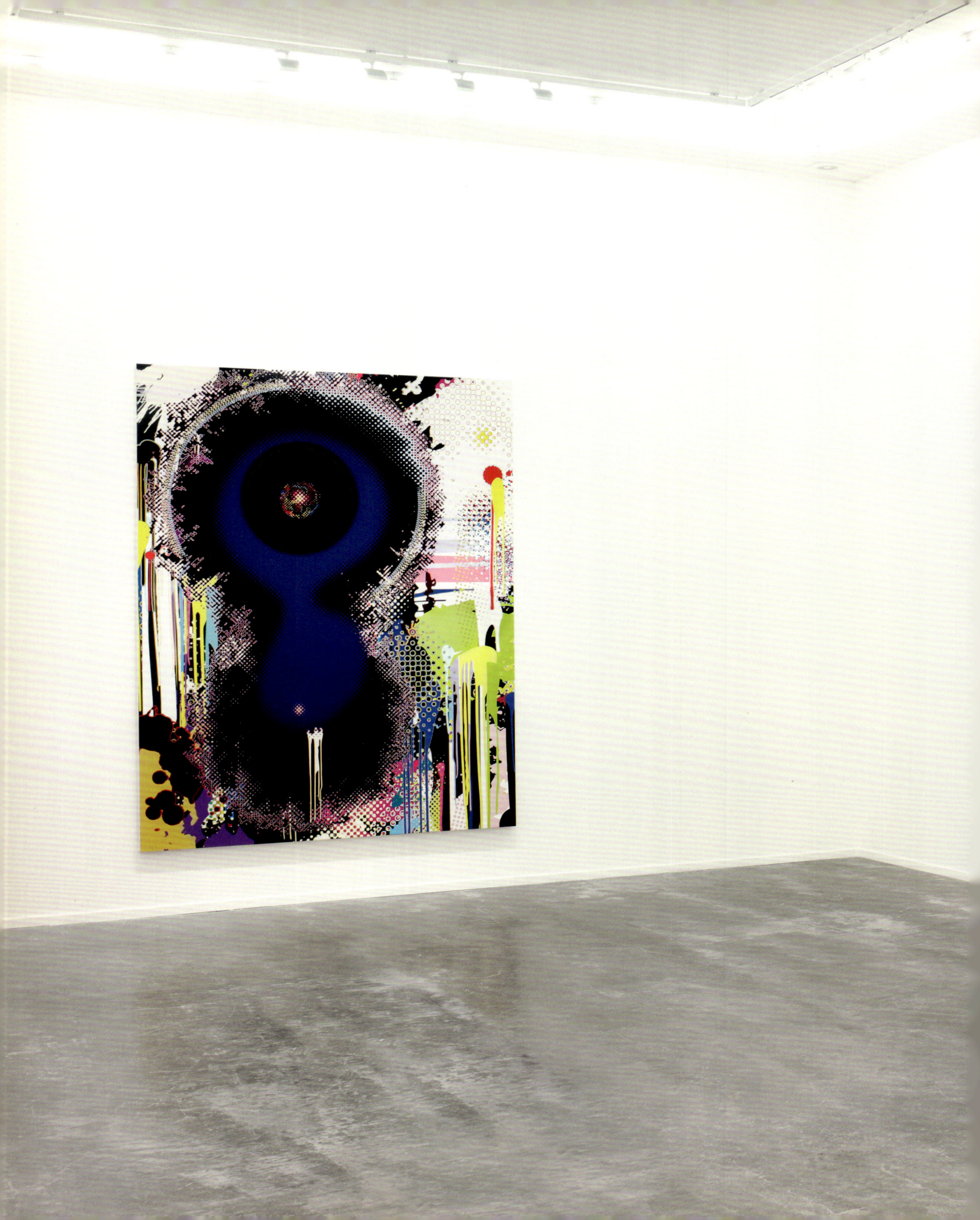

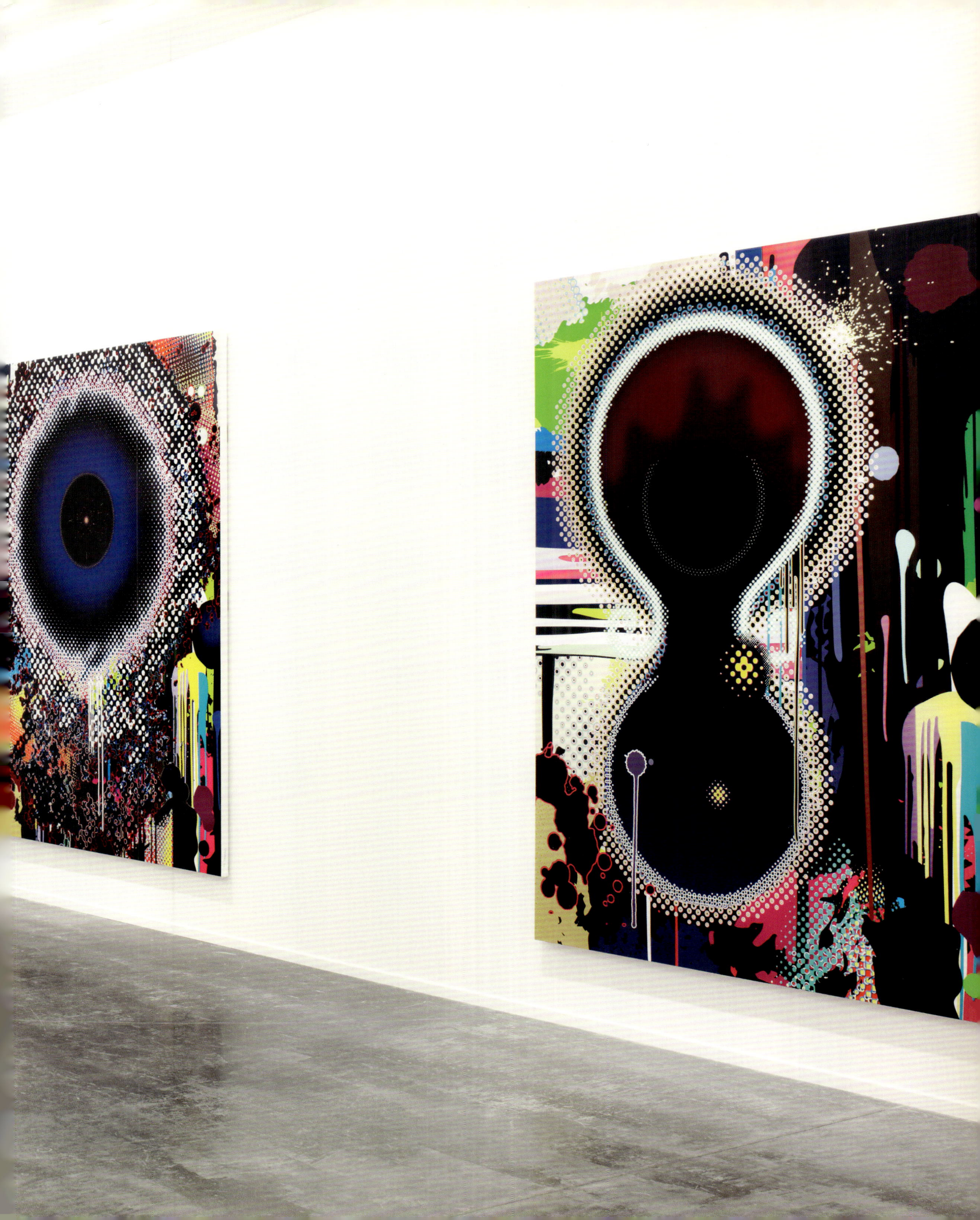

When I was a student of Japanese painting, I was fascinated by new interpretations of the traditional genres in the canon, such as

"SNOW, MOON, FLOWER," AND "FLOWER, BIRD, WIND, MOON." THESE ARE CLASSIC SUBJECTS,

but there are very few iconic treatments that you can point to and say, "This is it!" Most of the modern attempts lack any trace of originality and are content to reproduce dead motifs. I became enchanted with observing plants and flowers, and this became my own personal approach to understanding the canon of Japanese painting. Soon after DOB was born, I had a sudden leap in my progress. Character designs in Japanese popular culture always contain flowers. I discovered that I could combine these flowers with the "snow, moon, flower" theme. This was the birth of the "Cosmos" series of projects. The name was chosen out of respect for my biology teacher at the Tokyo National University of Fine Arts and Music, Professor Miki, who first opened my eyes to the spiral universe.

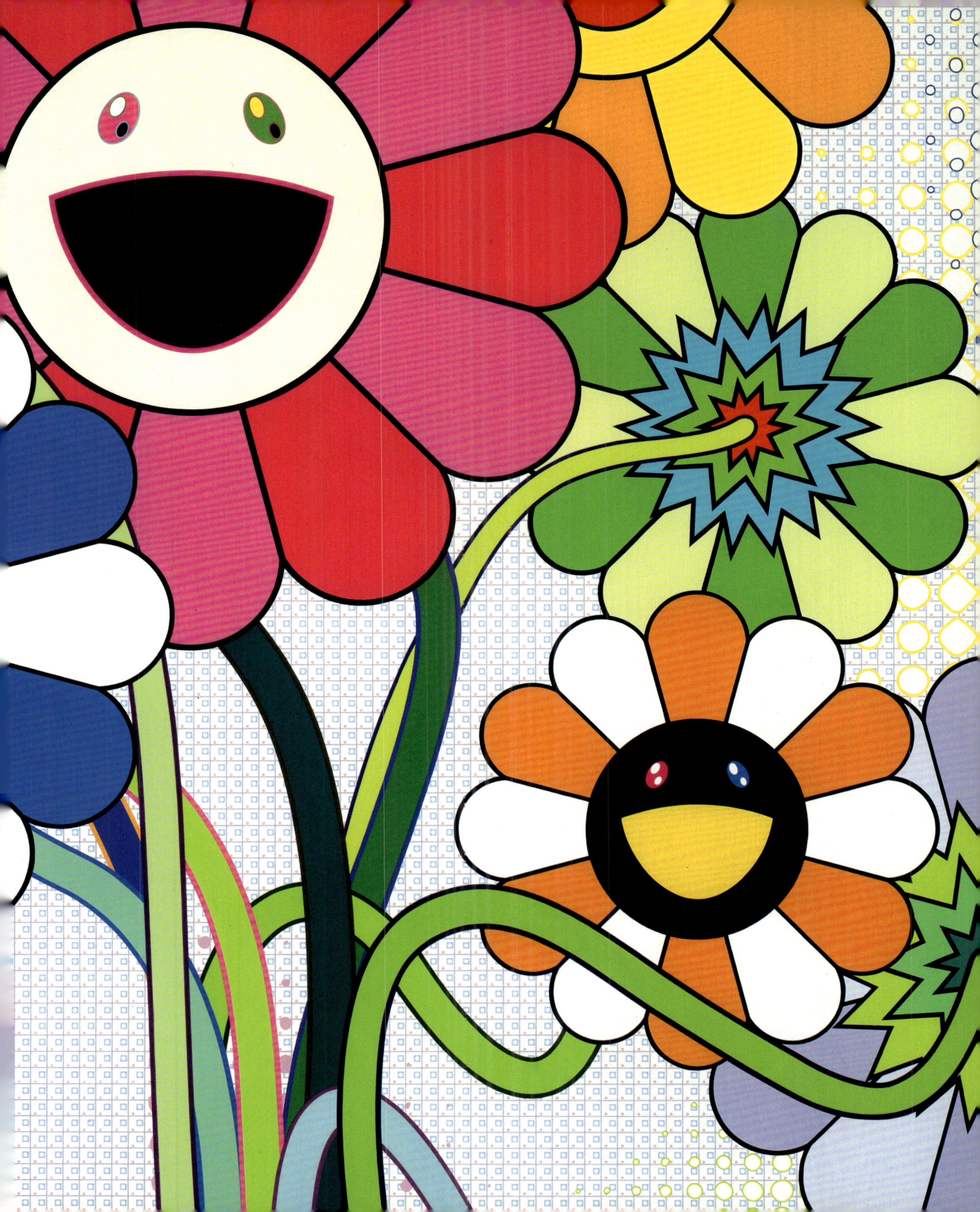

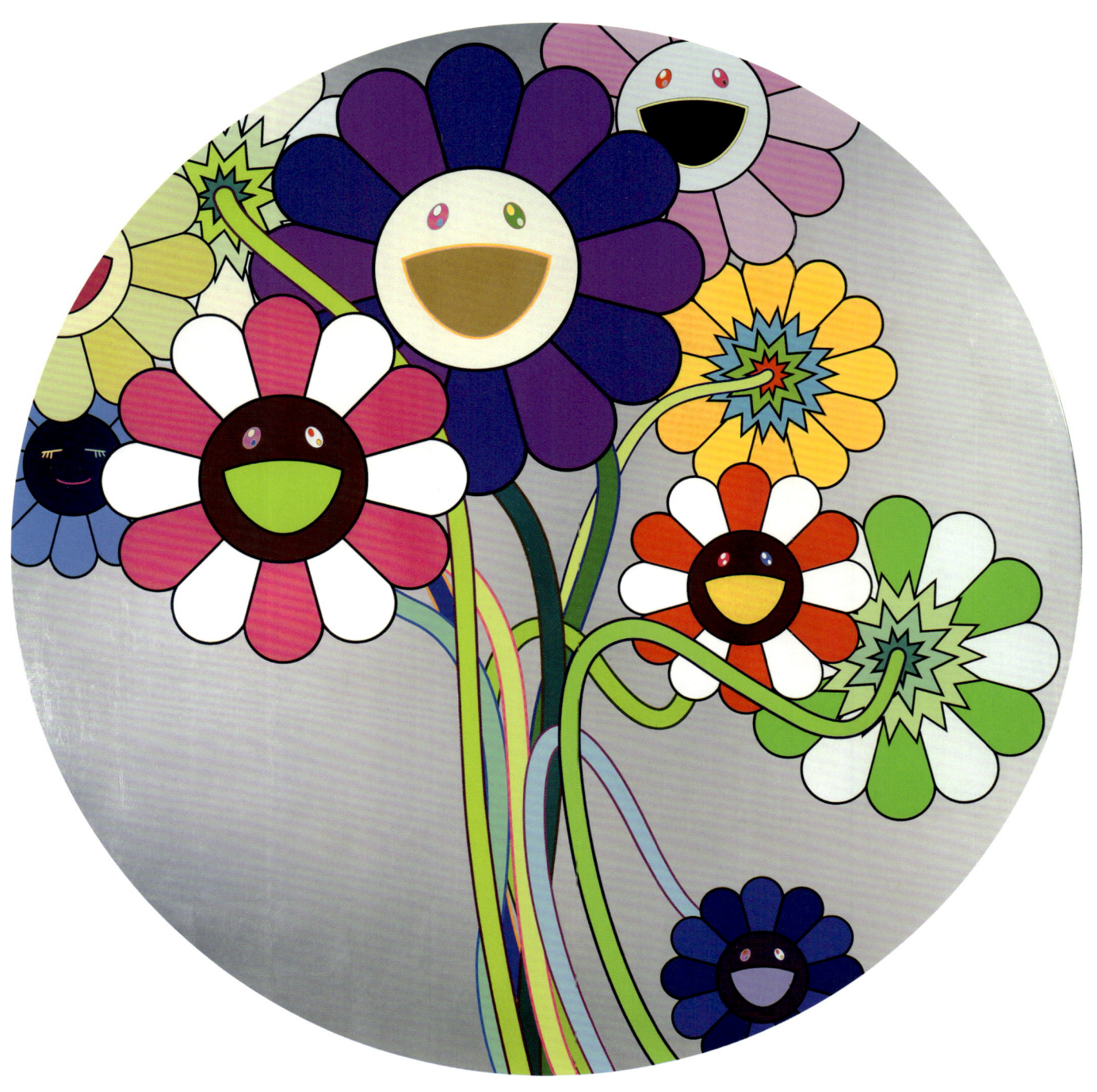

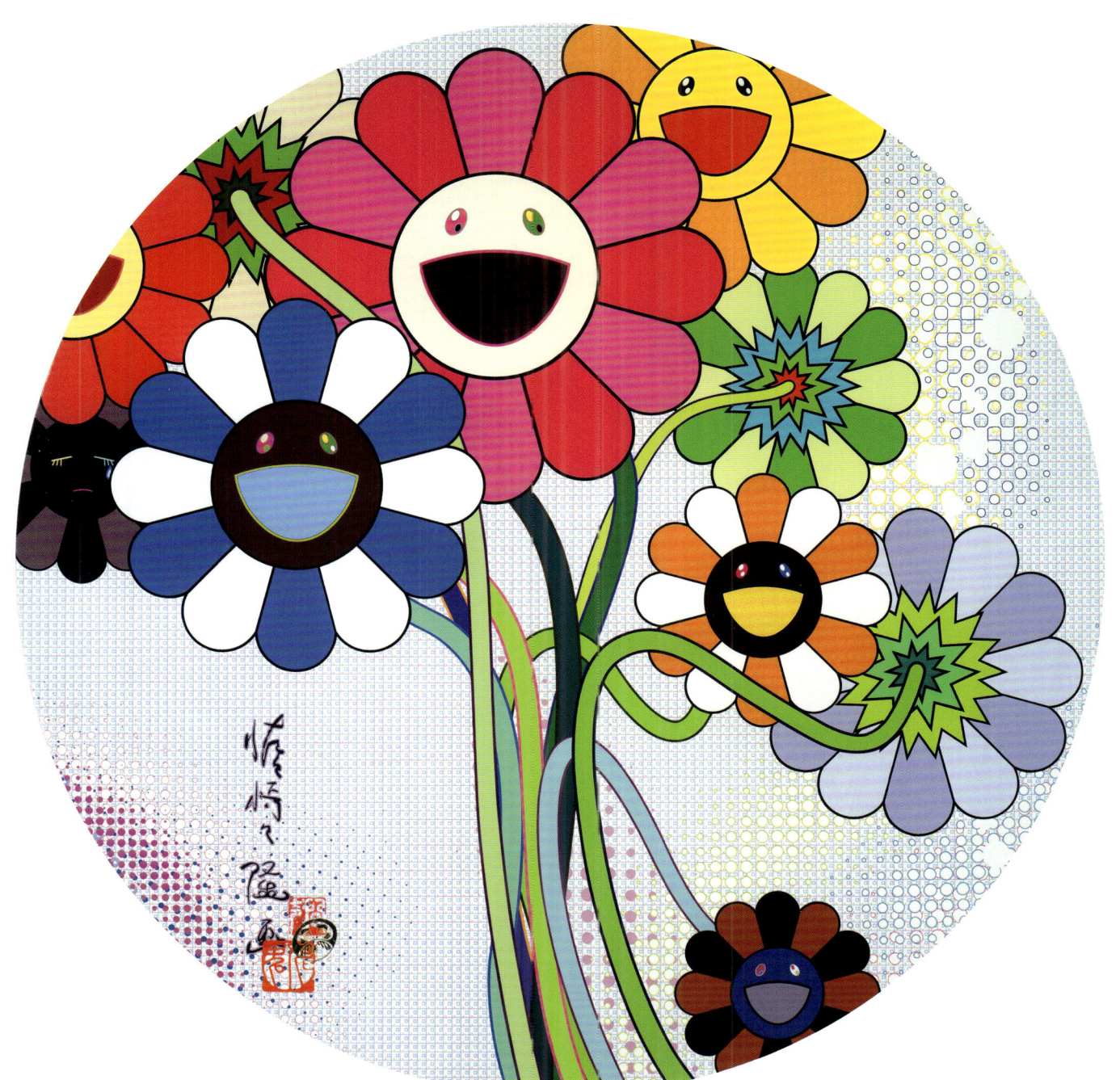

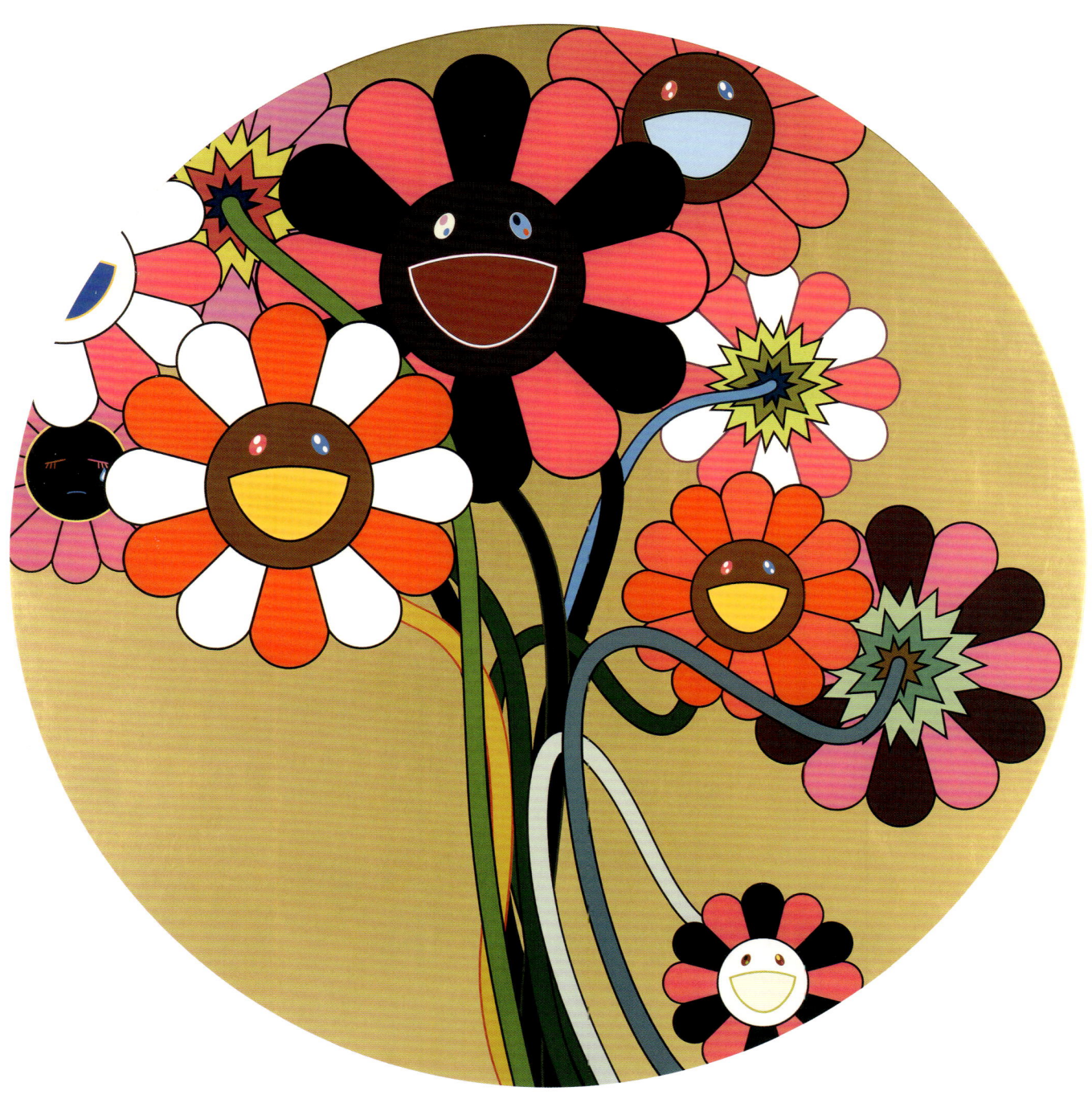

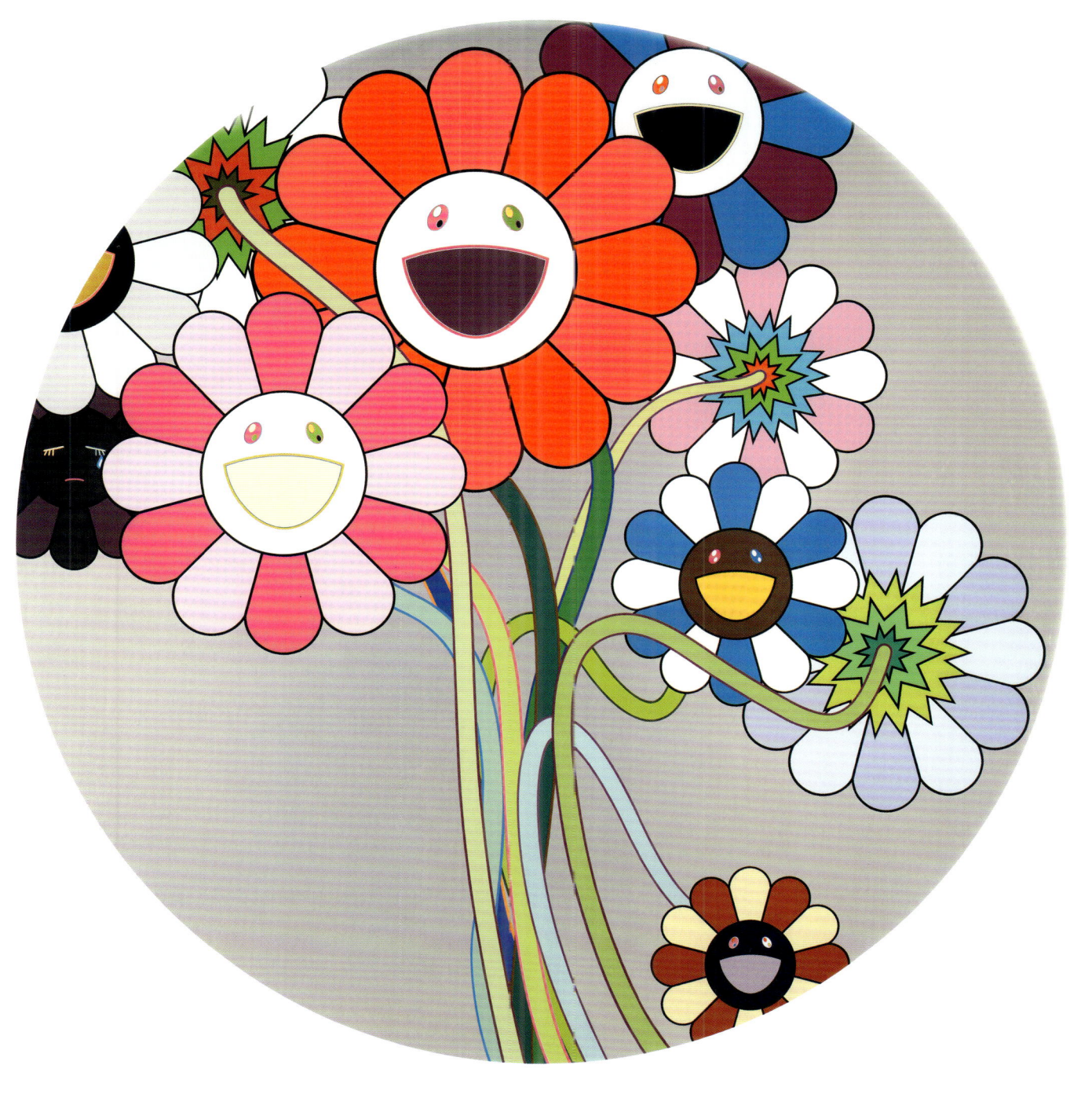

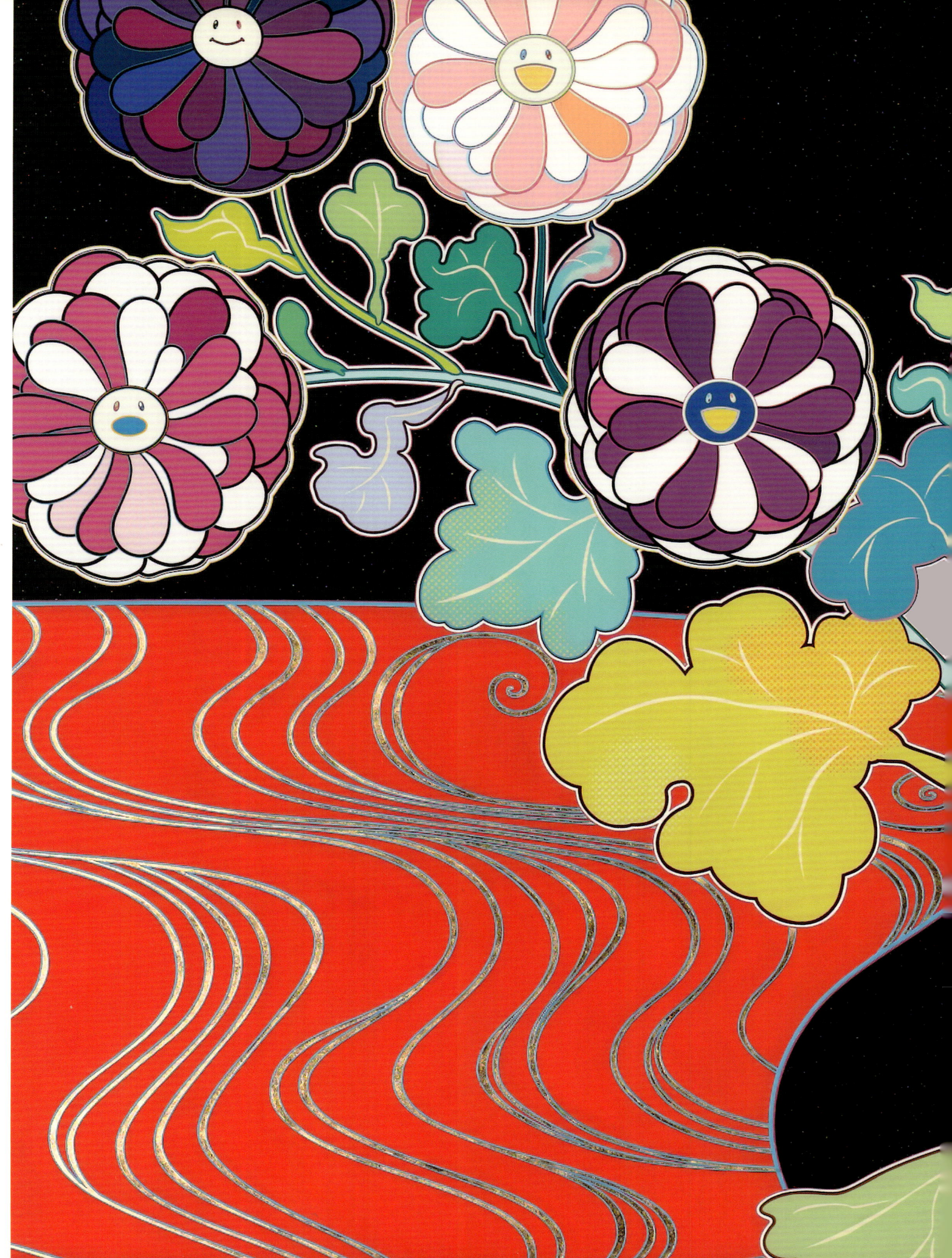

Kansei Kōrin Red Stream (detail) 2009

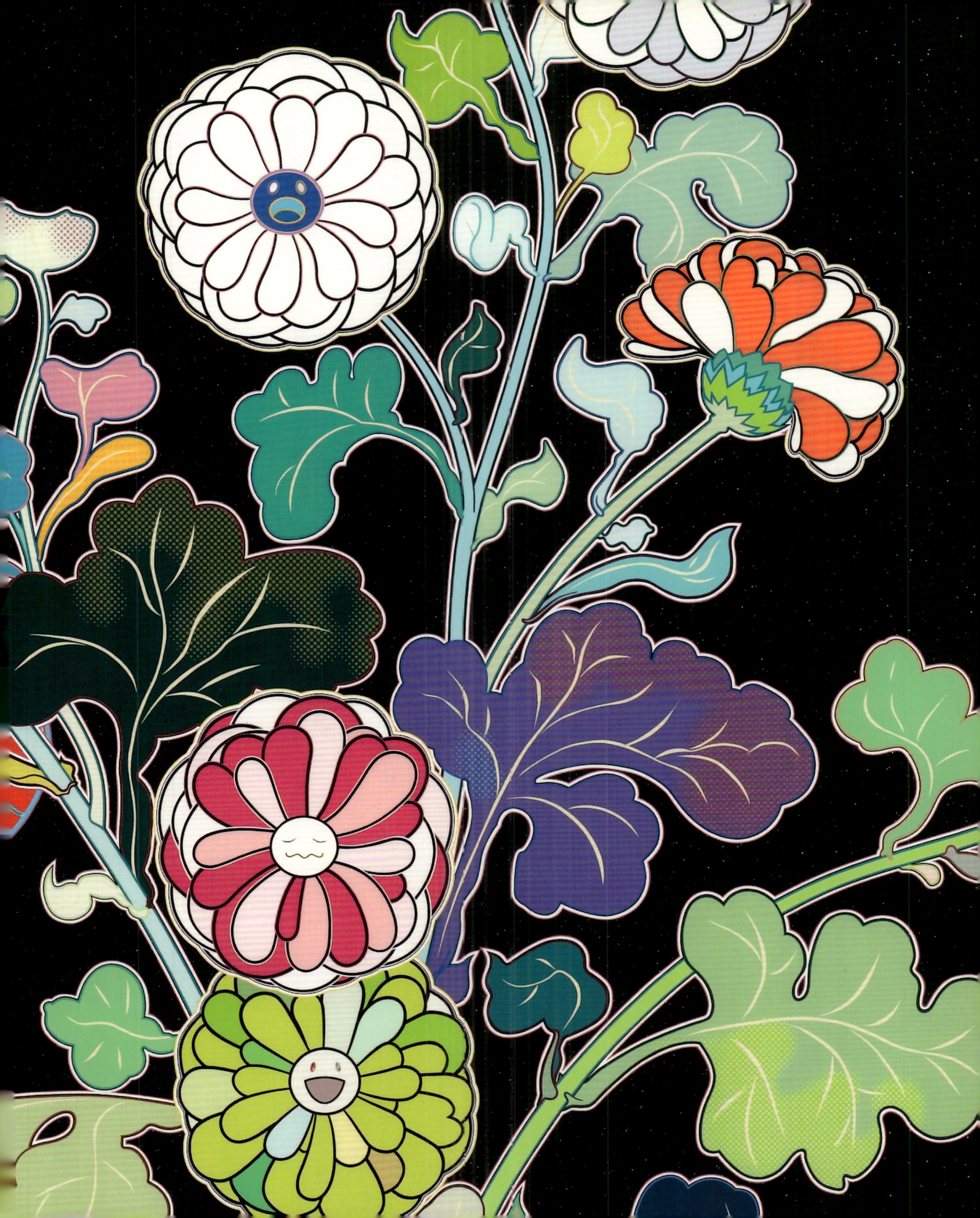

Kansei Kōrin **Red Stream** 2009

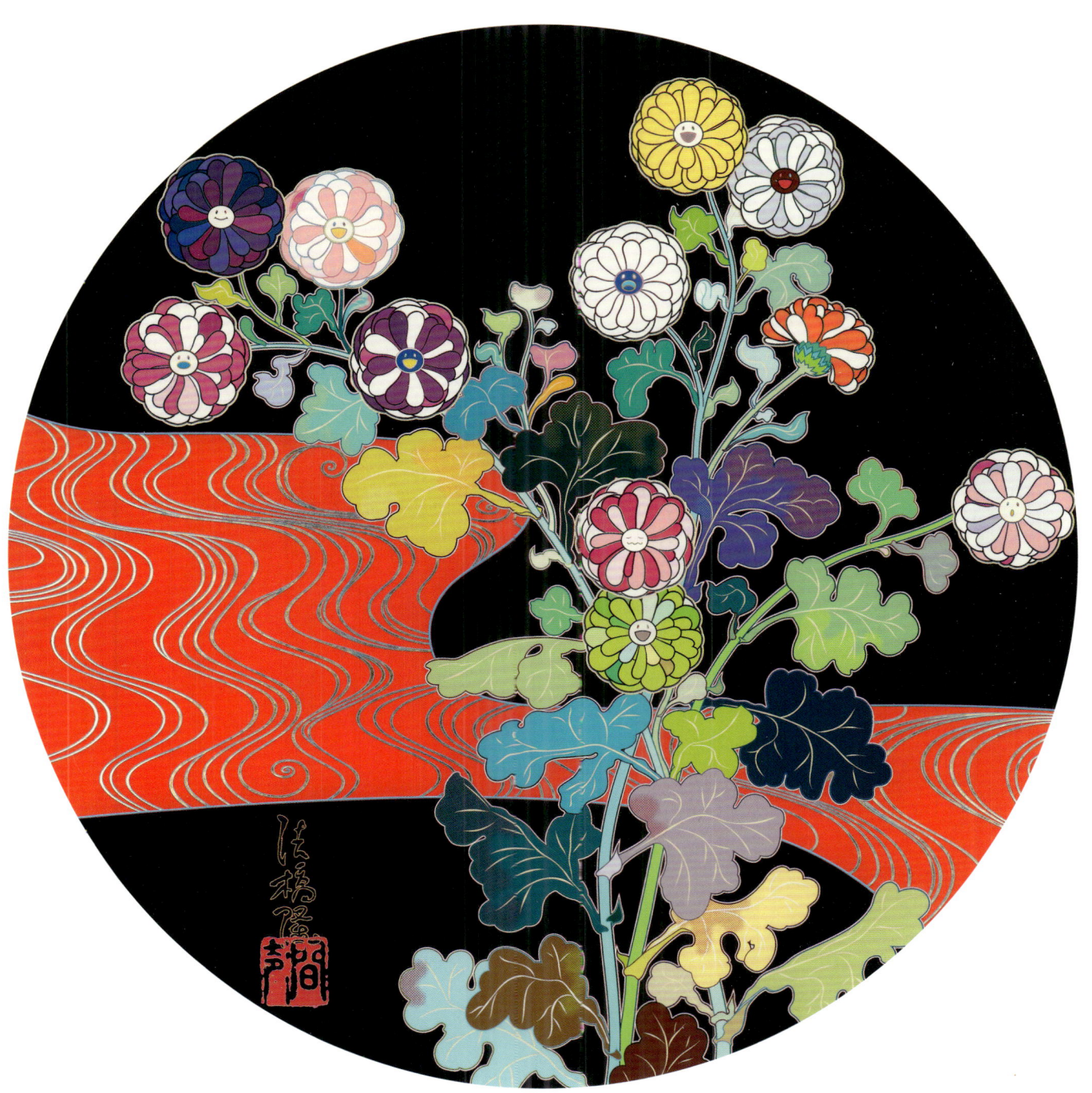

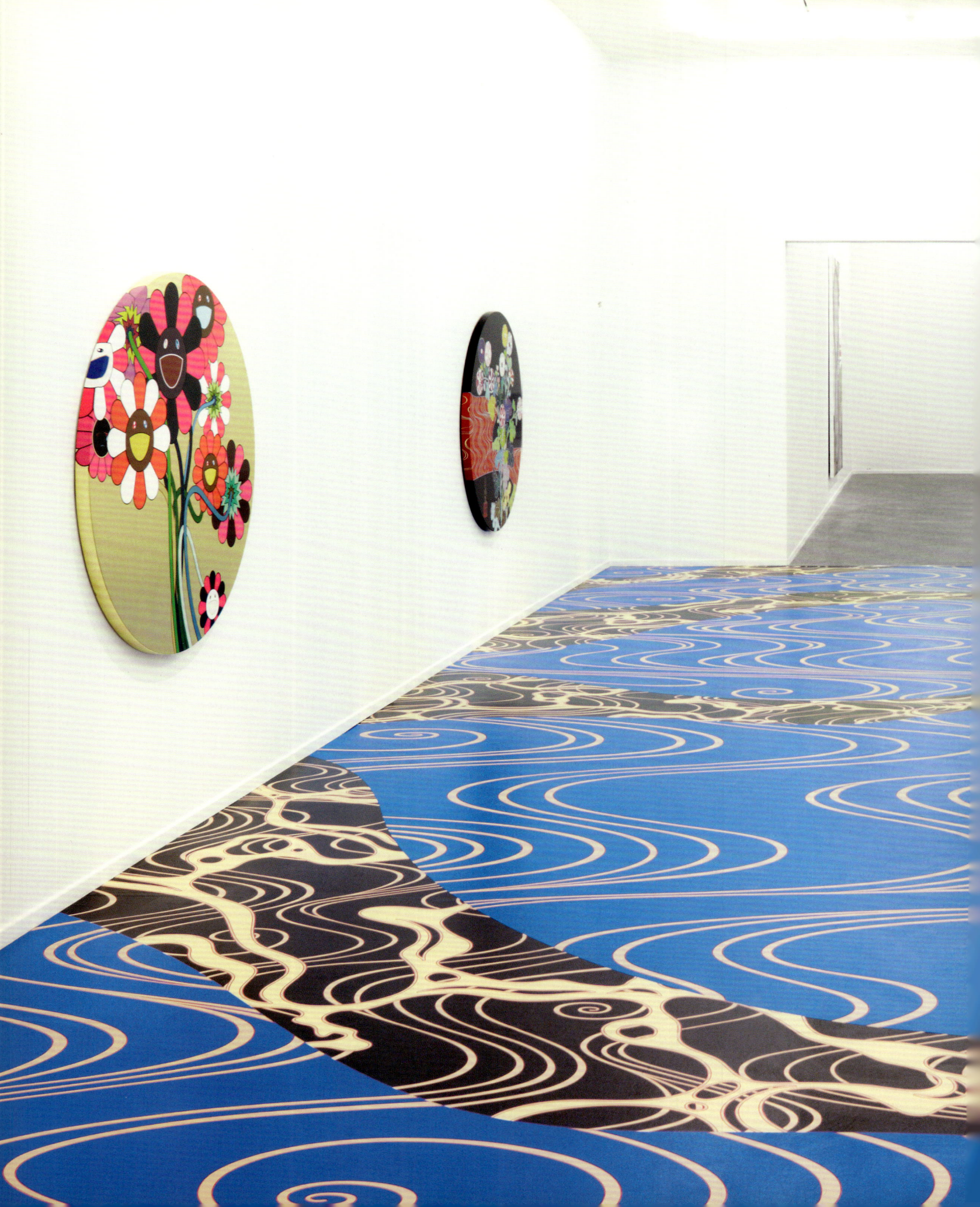

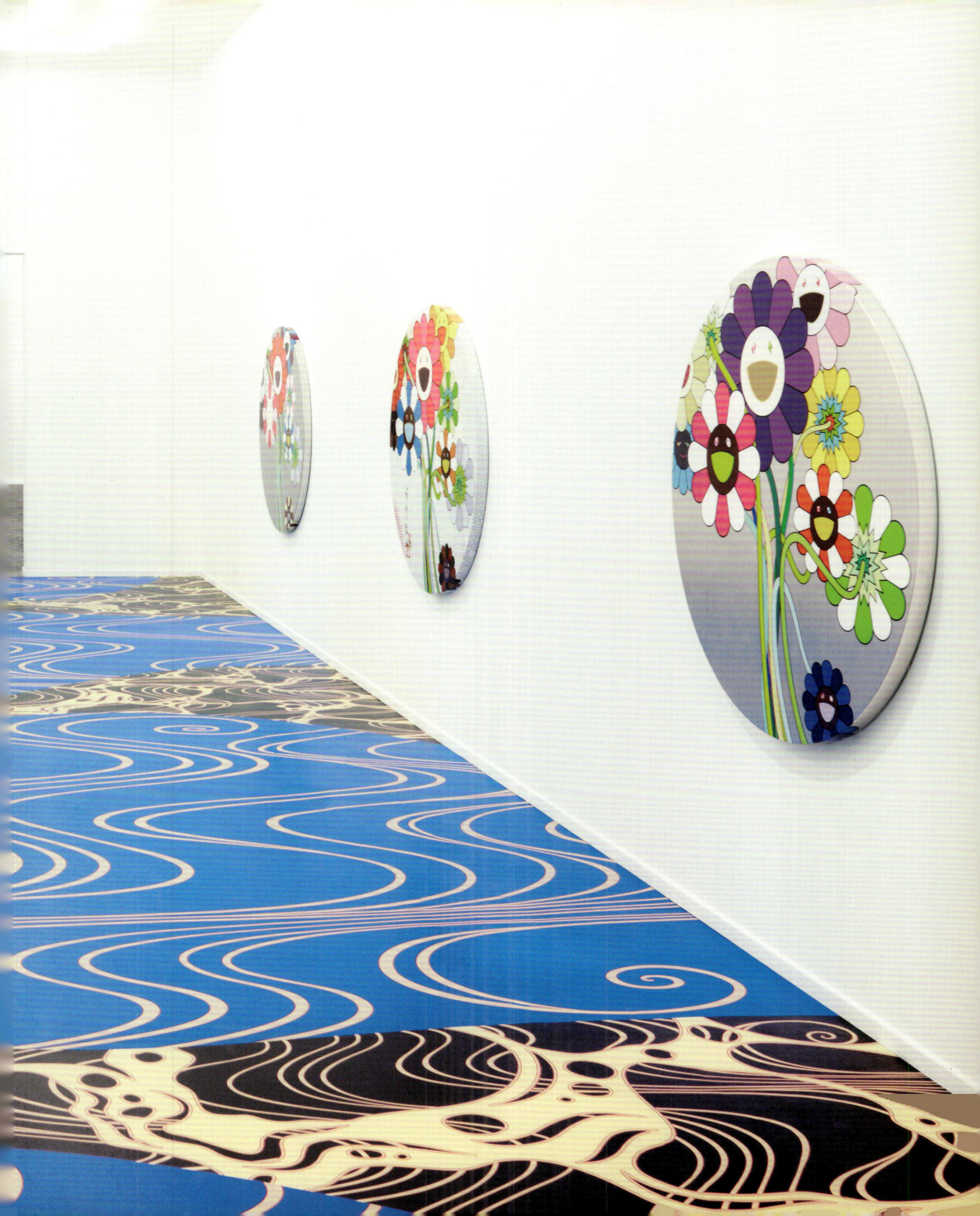

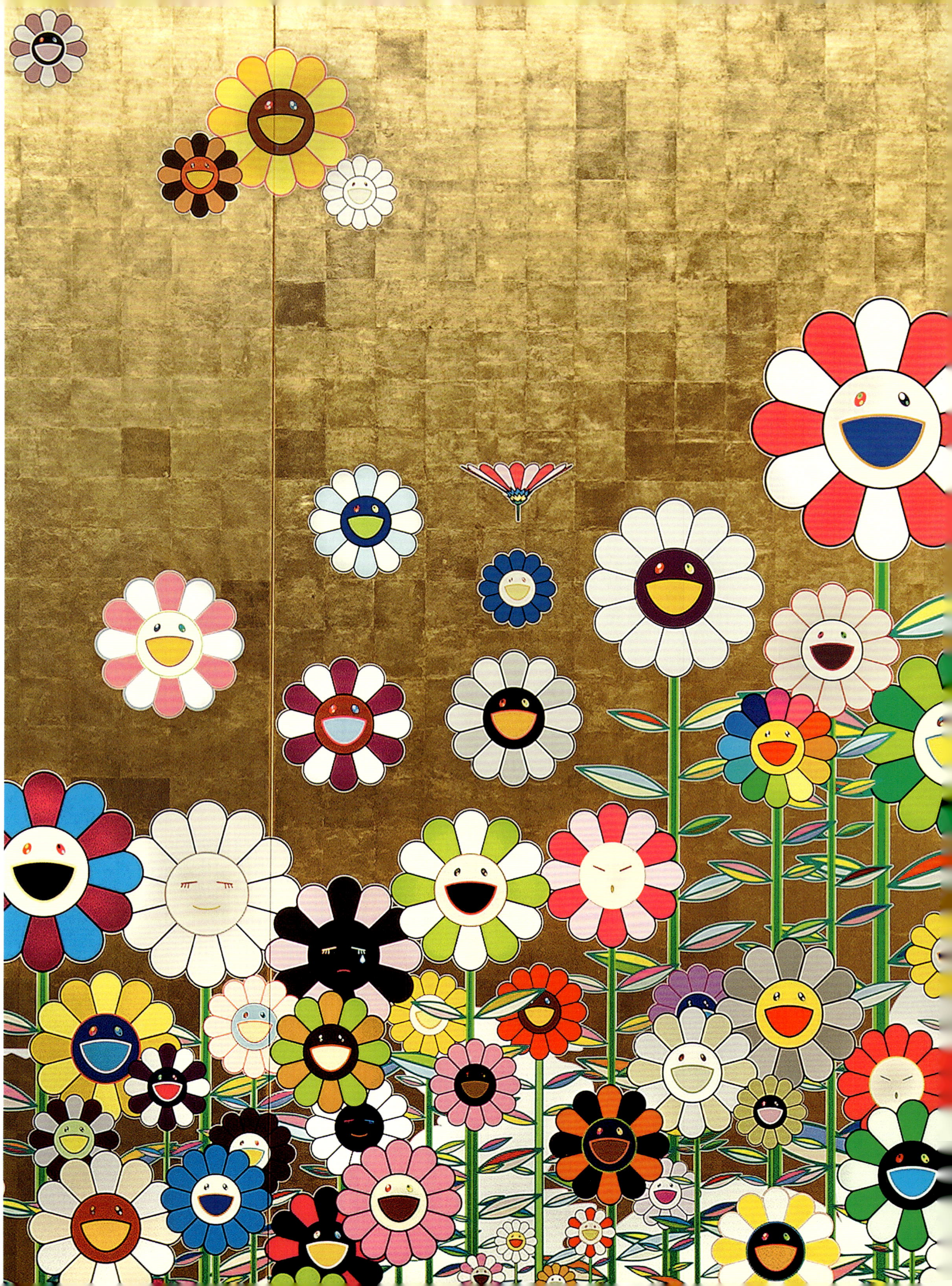

Kawaii — vacances <Summer vacation in the Kingdom of the Golden> (detail) 2008

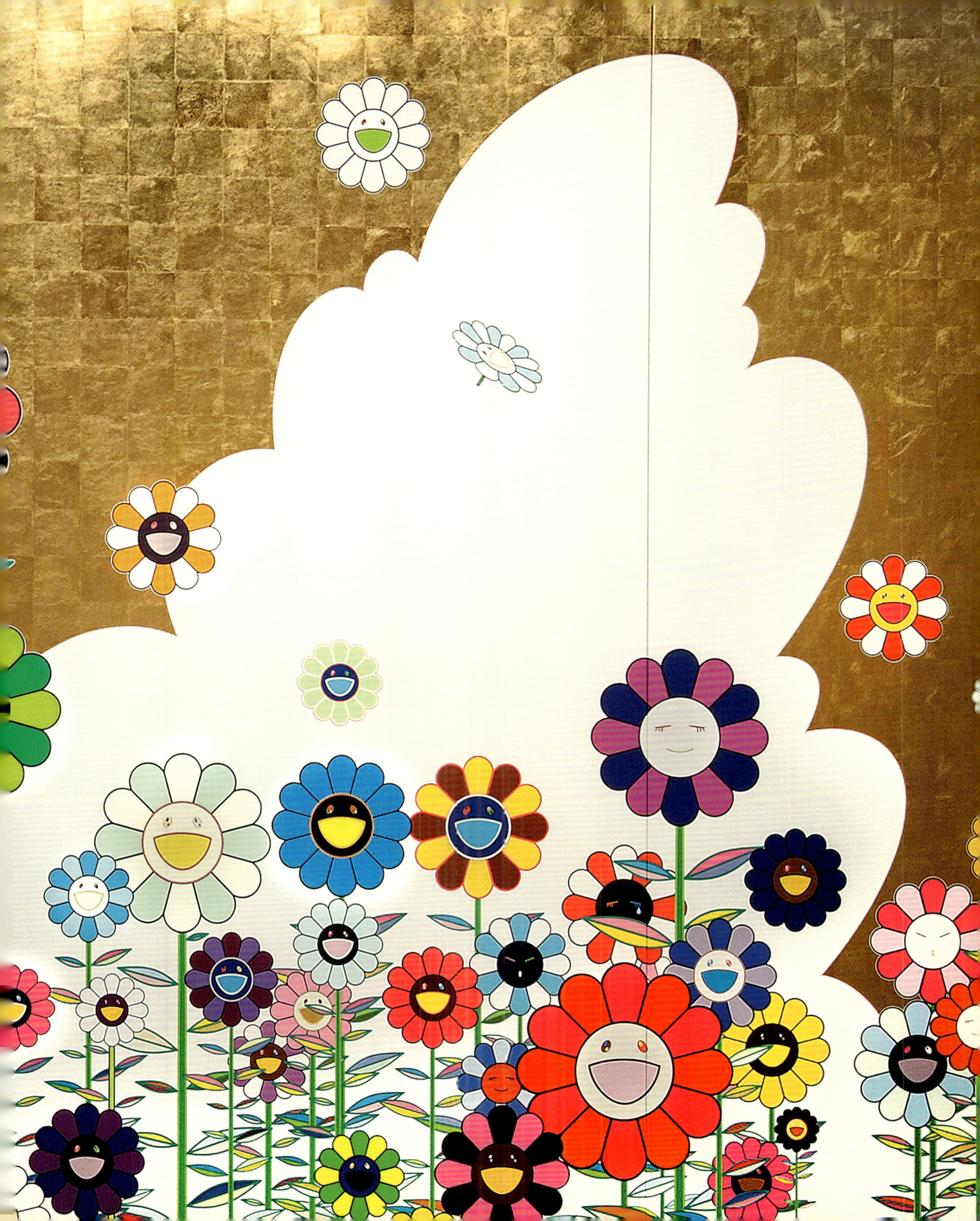

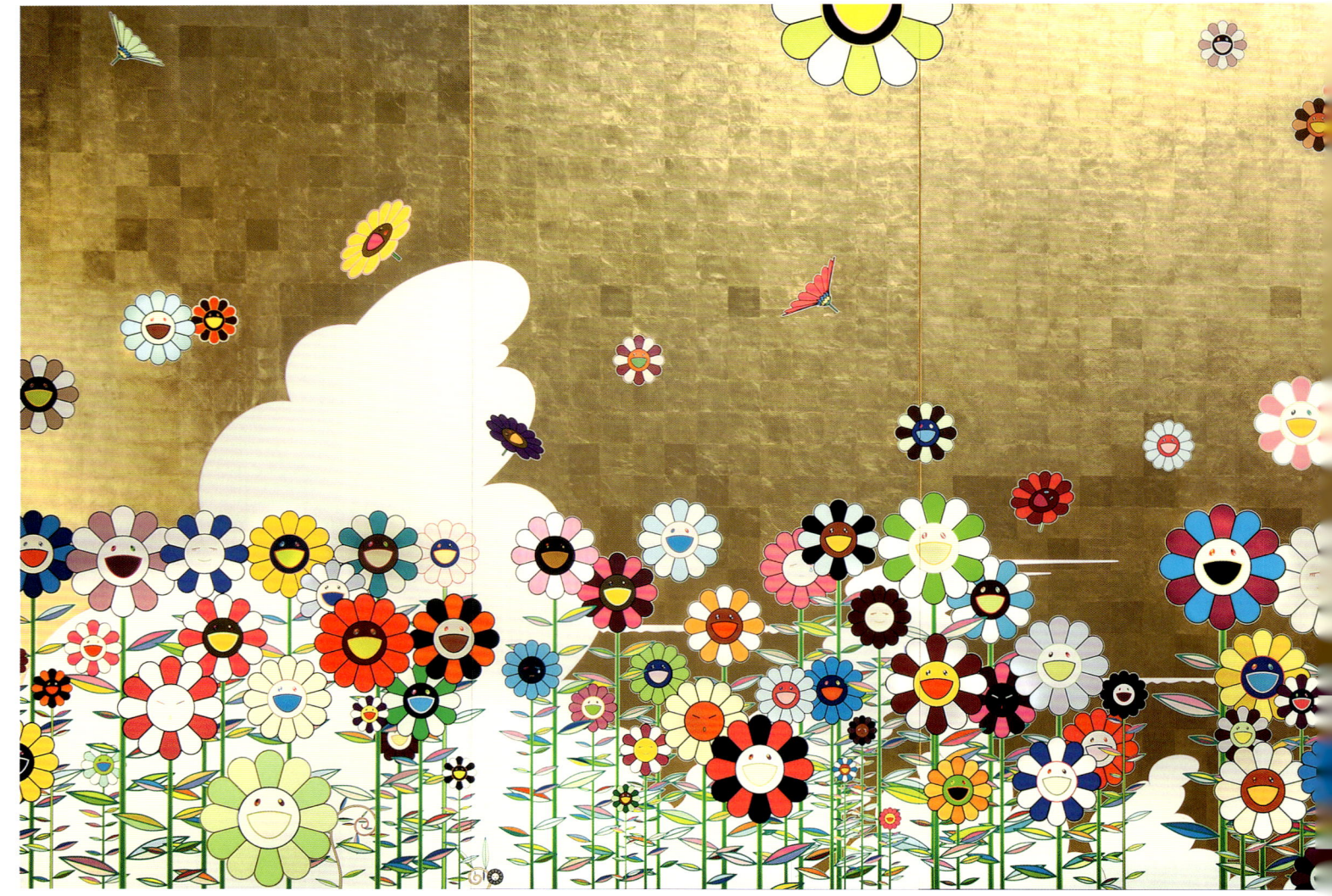

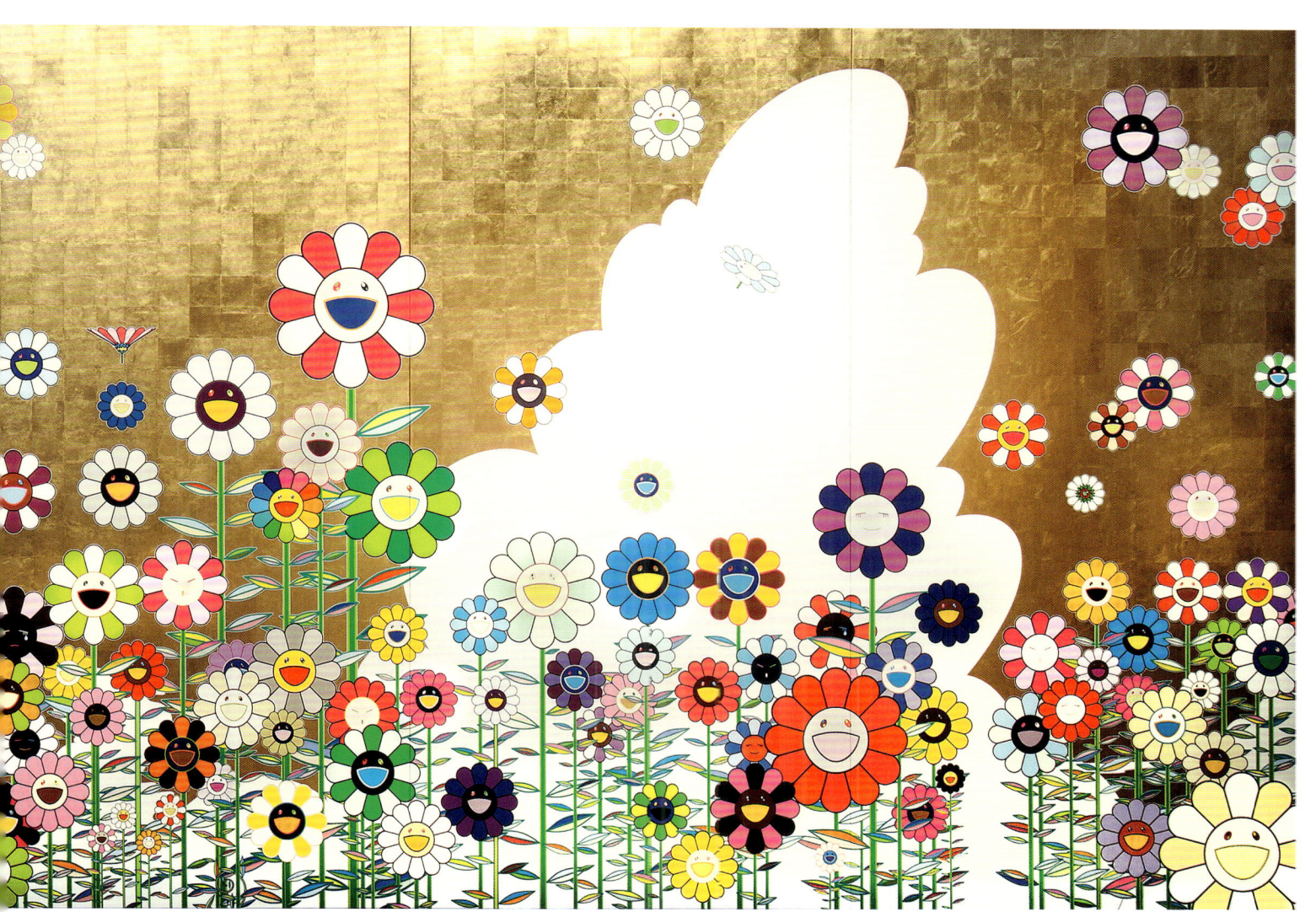

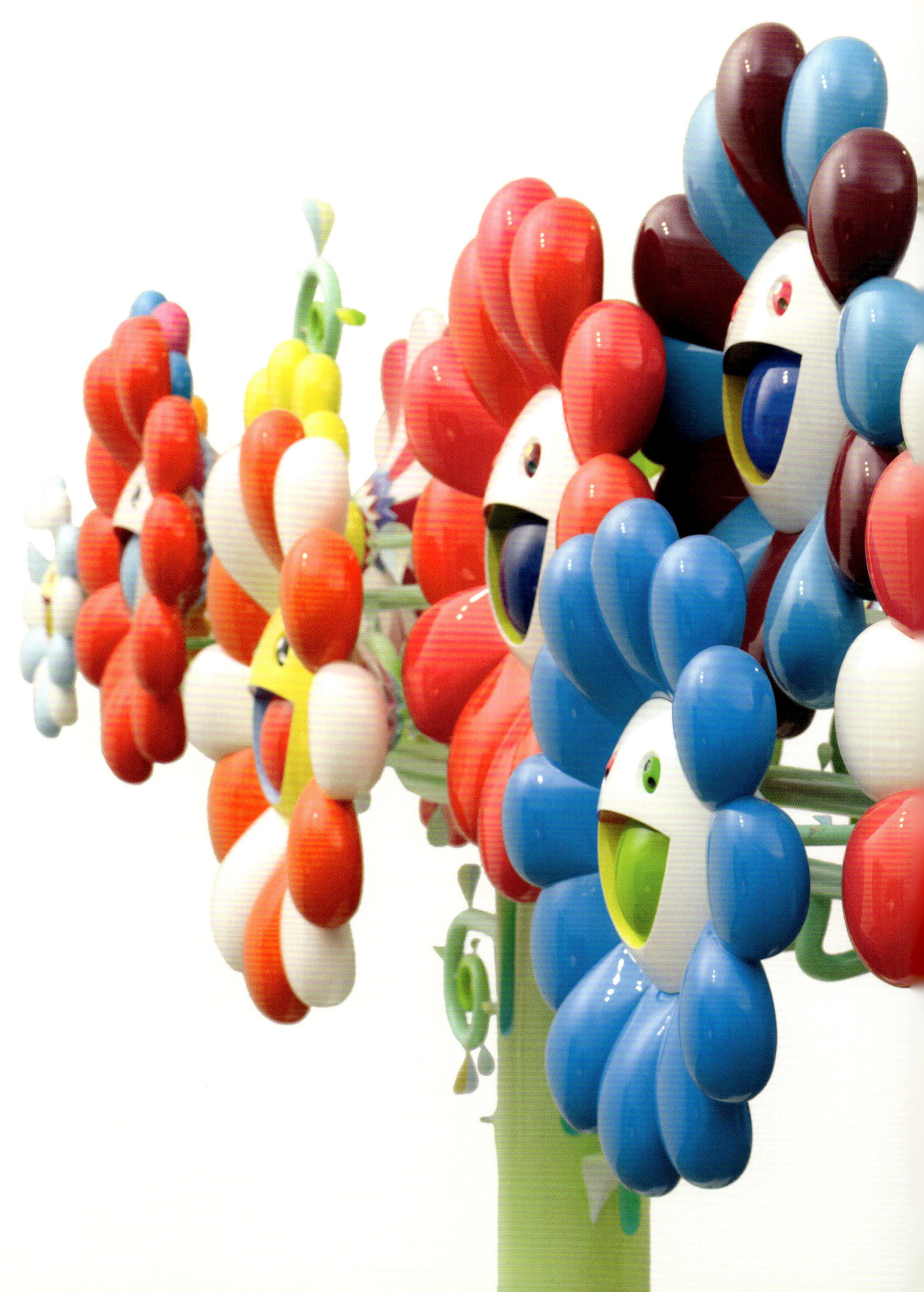

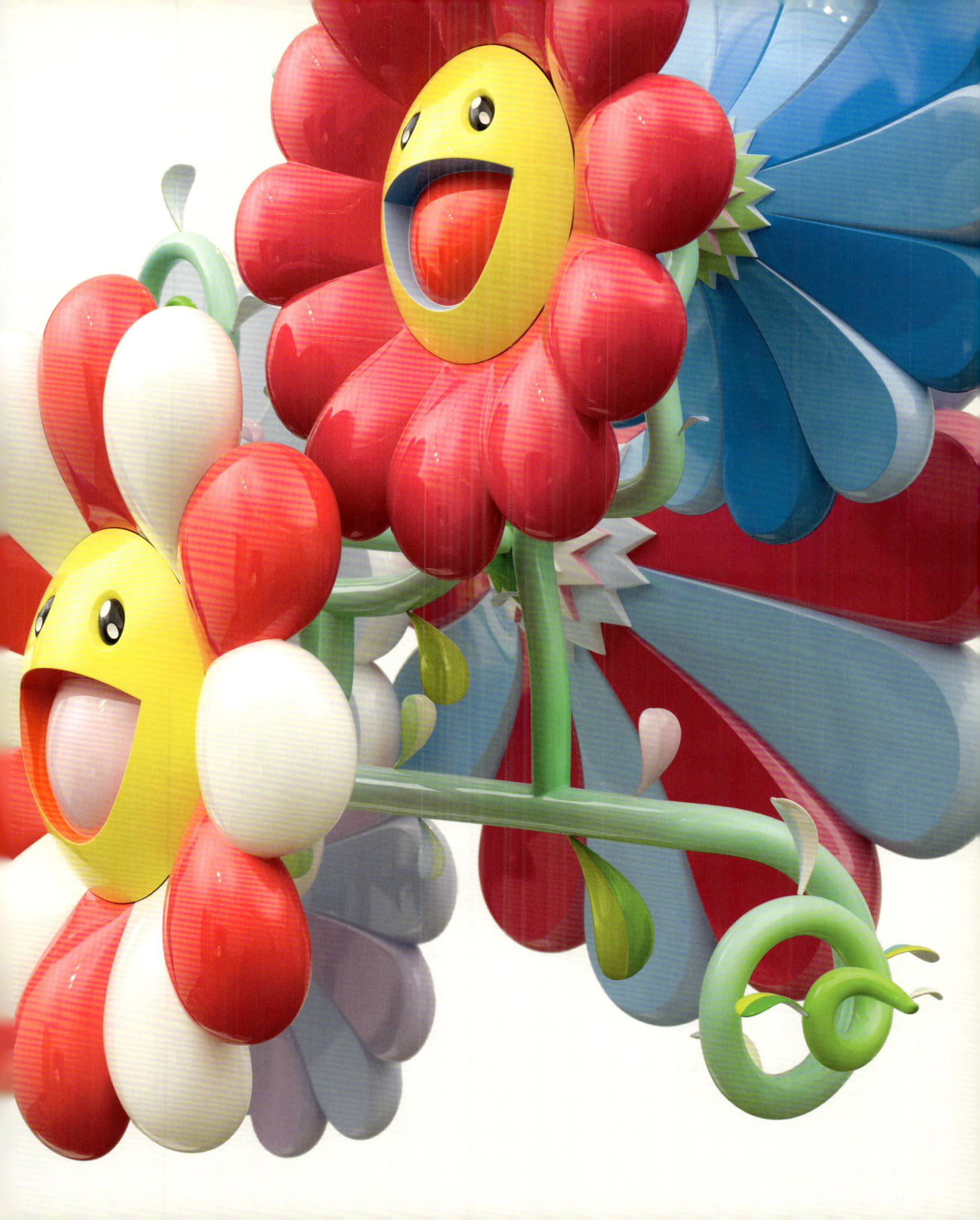

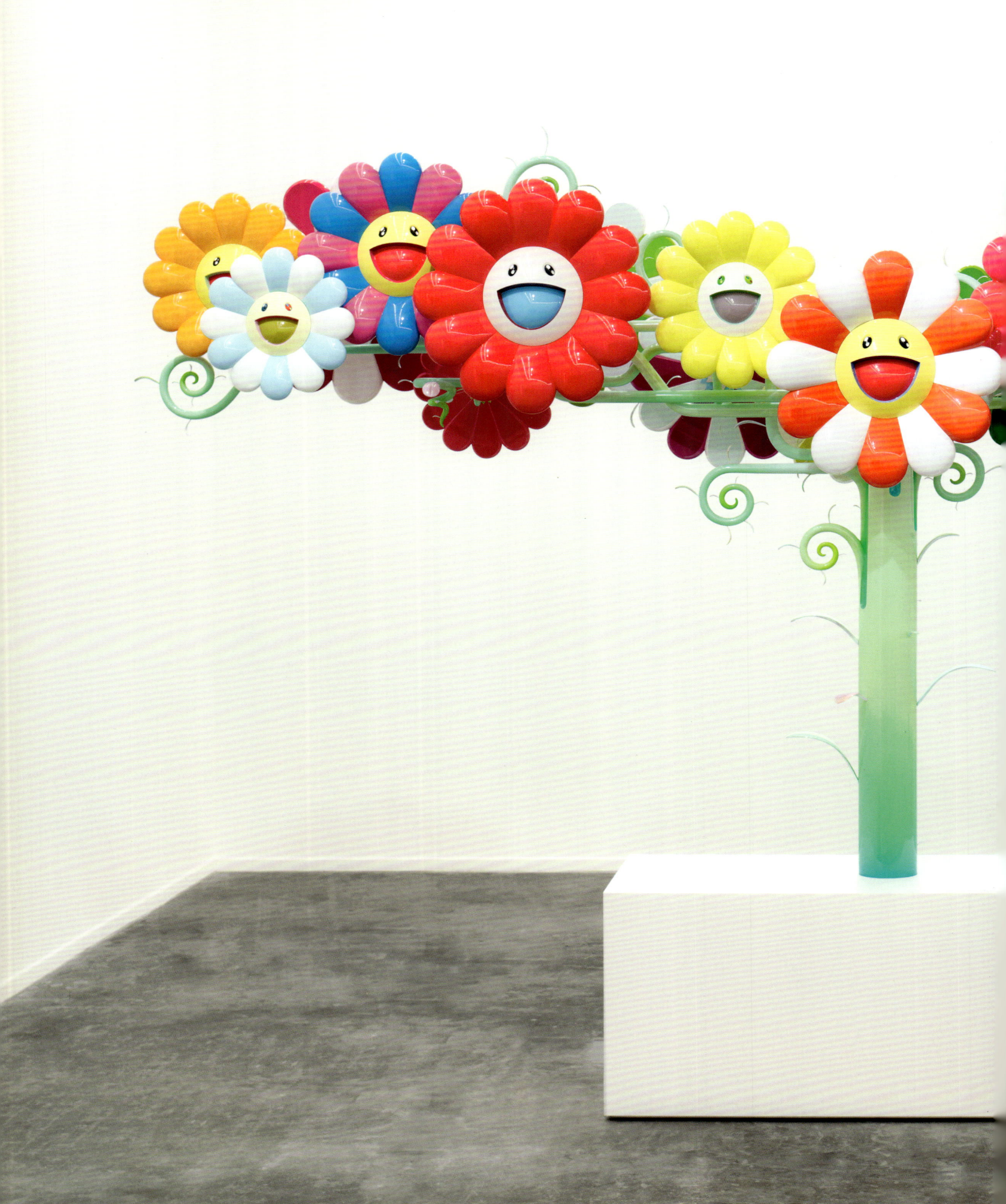

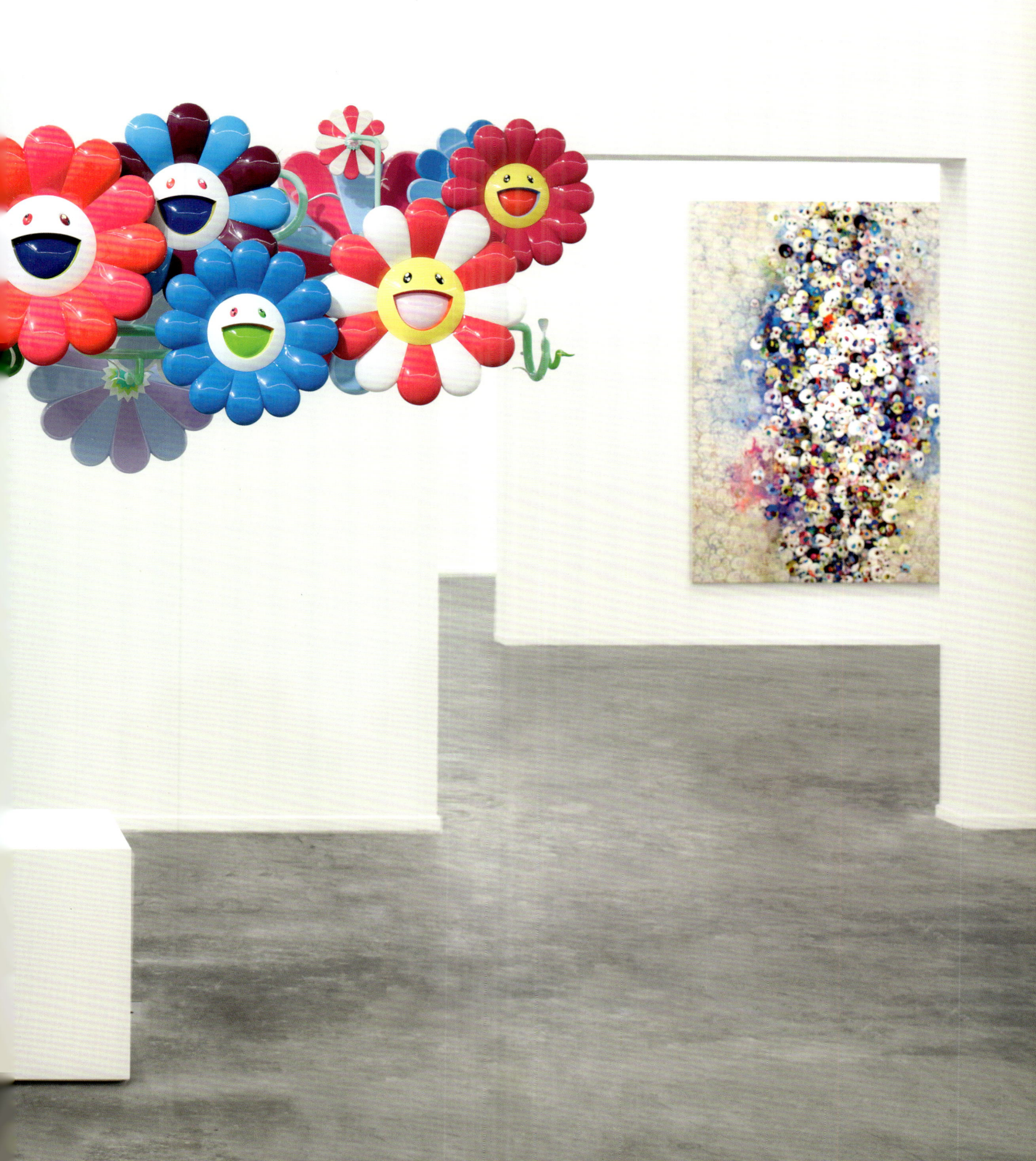

Tongari-kun (detail) 2003–04

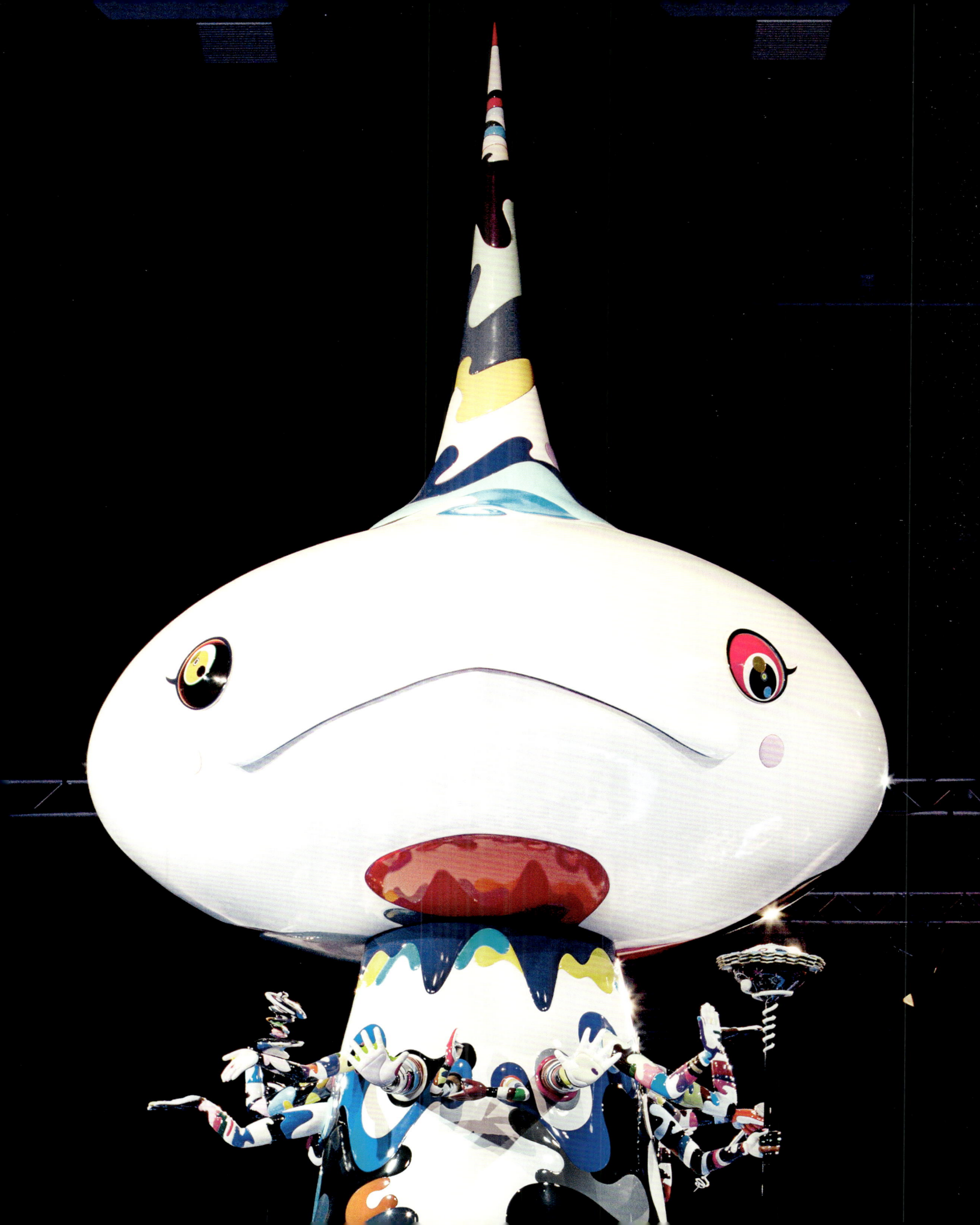

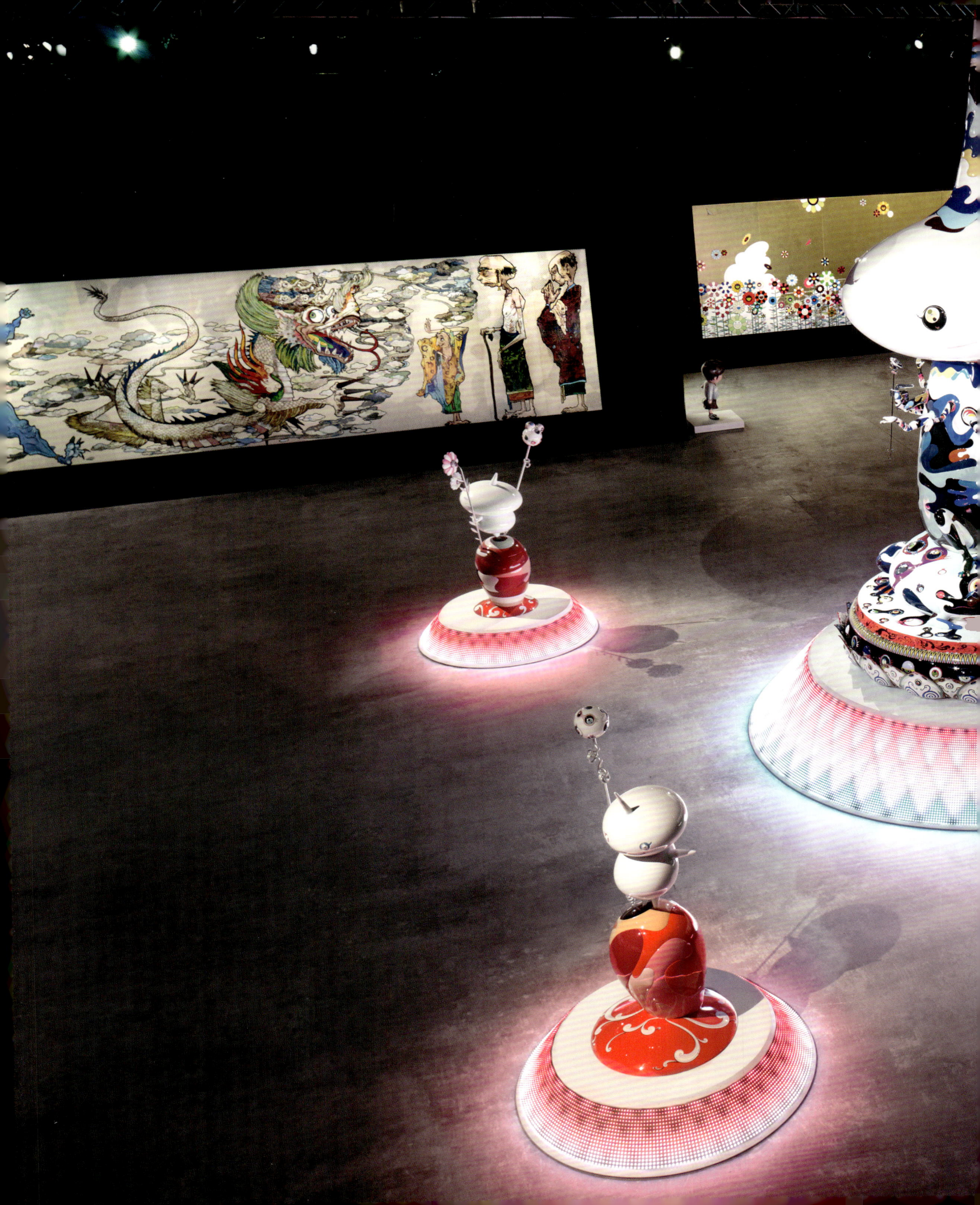

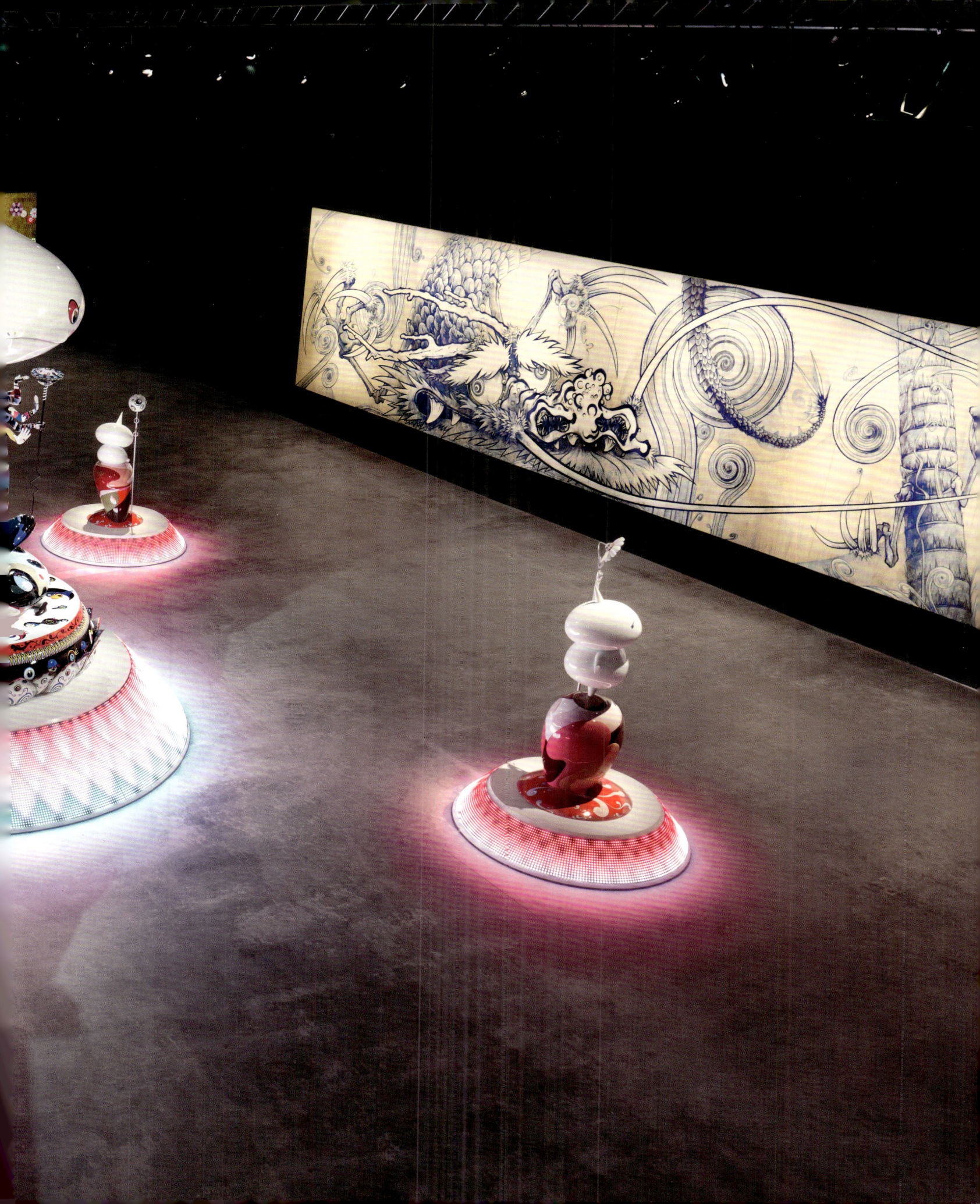

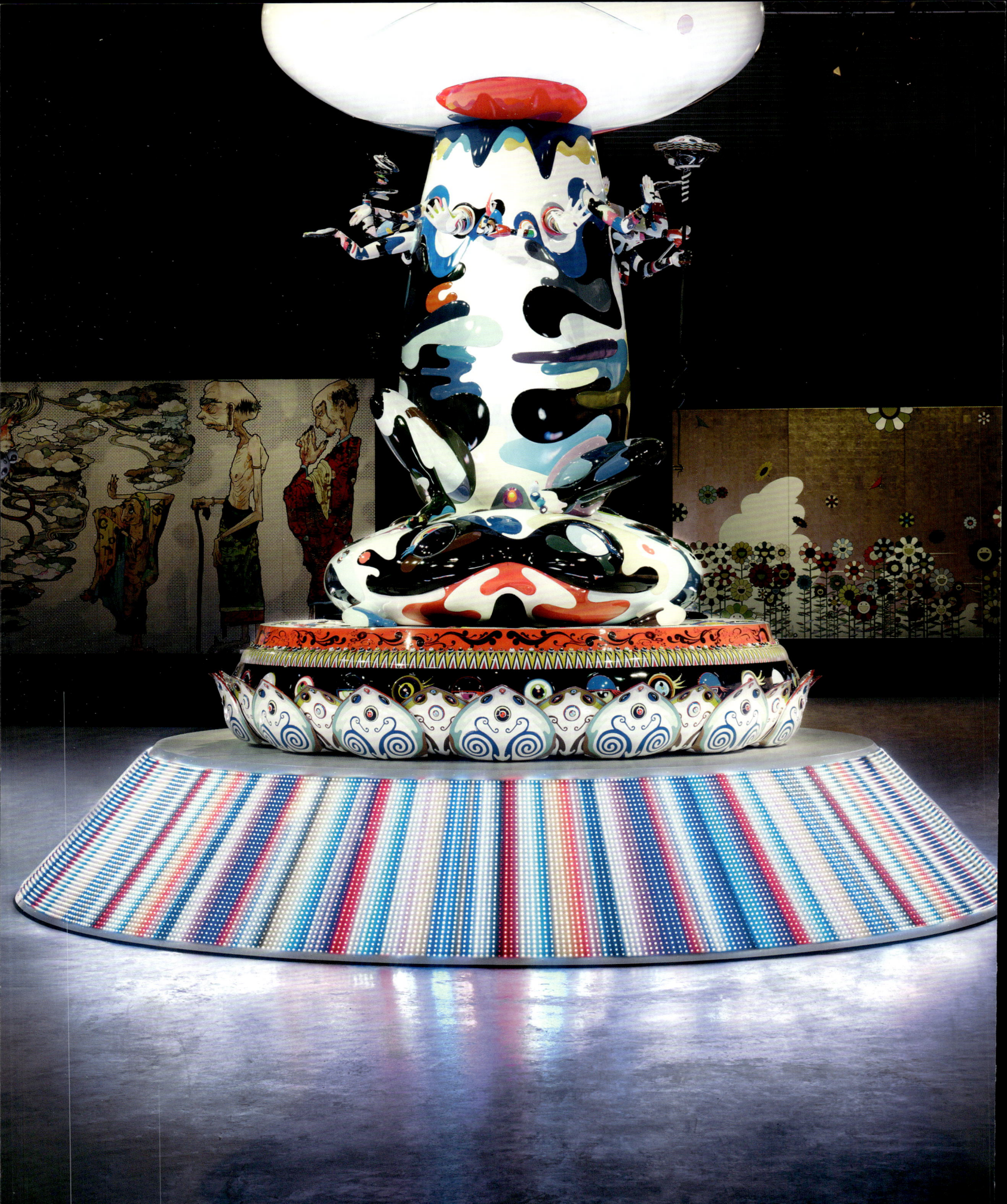

"MURAKAMI—EGO" WAS BORN IN A SCI-FI CITY IN THE DESERT,

in the super-artificial landscape of Doha, Qatar.

I was very impressed by the skyline of Doha when I visited the first time. I was also very interested in understanding the reasons why Qatar feels it is important to exhibit contemporary art. In a way, it's the same reason why, after World War II, the Japanese people really wanted to build museums: They wanted to leave their mark on culture. Of course, here things are very different: After the war, Japan was very poor, and today the situation is difficult again; in Qatar, on the other hand, the cities seem super-rich. That's why "Murakami—Ego" is shot through with an artificial feeling, a sci-fi feeling.

I have imagined a new audience for "Murakami—Ego," an audience that has grown up at the crossroads between Western culture, the Middle East, and Asia. I transformed my work so that it could compete with these new sci-fi cities that are growing in the Middle East. "Murakami—Ego" is a state of mind, like a gigantic amusement park. It's very dramatic. I made these new LED pedestals for my sculptures, so they can glow in the dark. "Murakami—Ego" is a pop-up village, a temporary city, very emotional and very amusing. Now it's time to be more artificial and supernatural.

Heaven's Gate (Bases for Tongari-kun and the Four Guards) 2012

clockwise from top left: **Koumokkun** 2003–05, **Jikokkun** 2003–05, **Tamon-kun** 2003–05, **Zoucho-kun** 2003–05

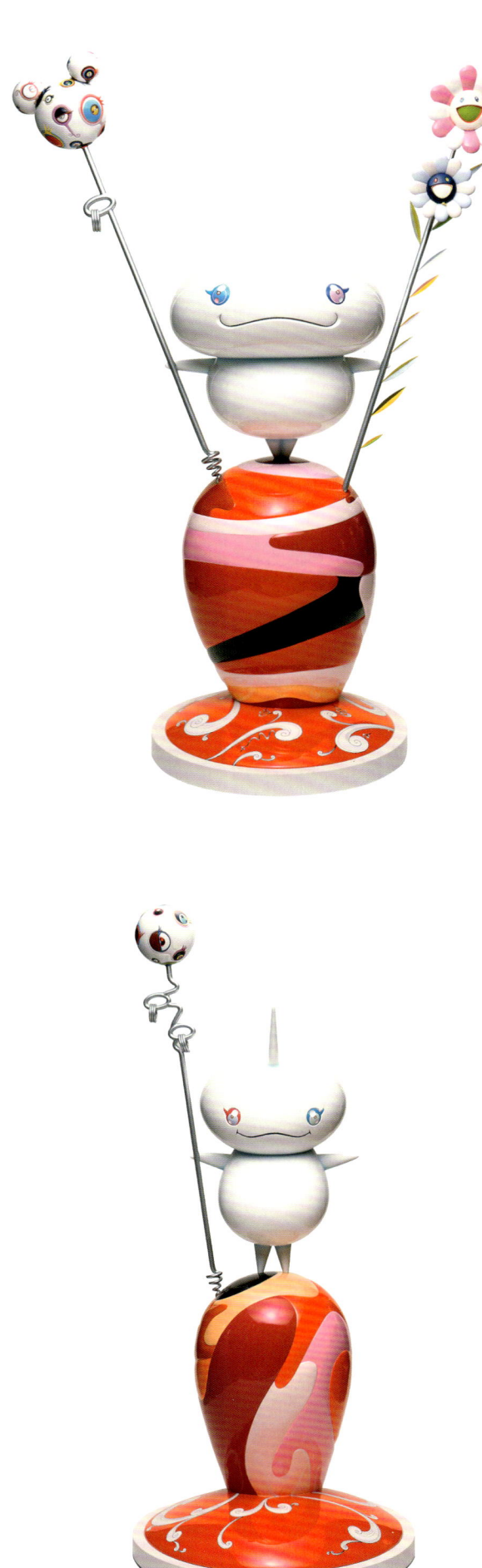

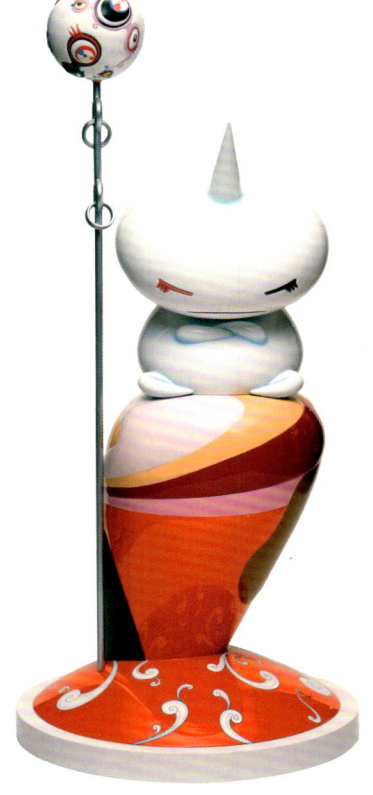

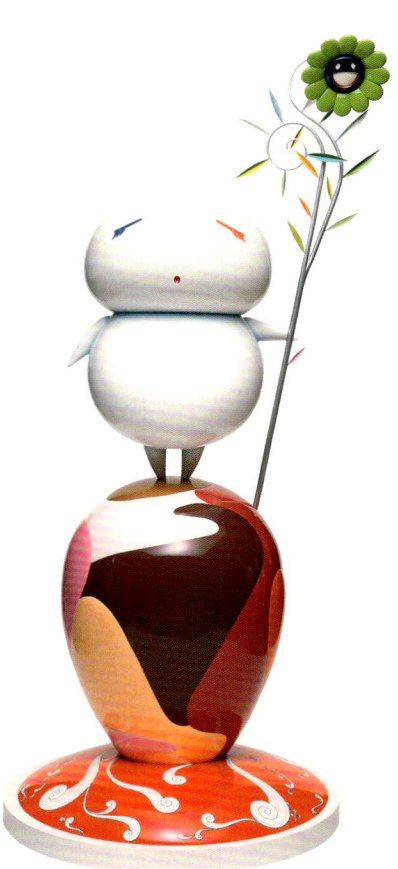

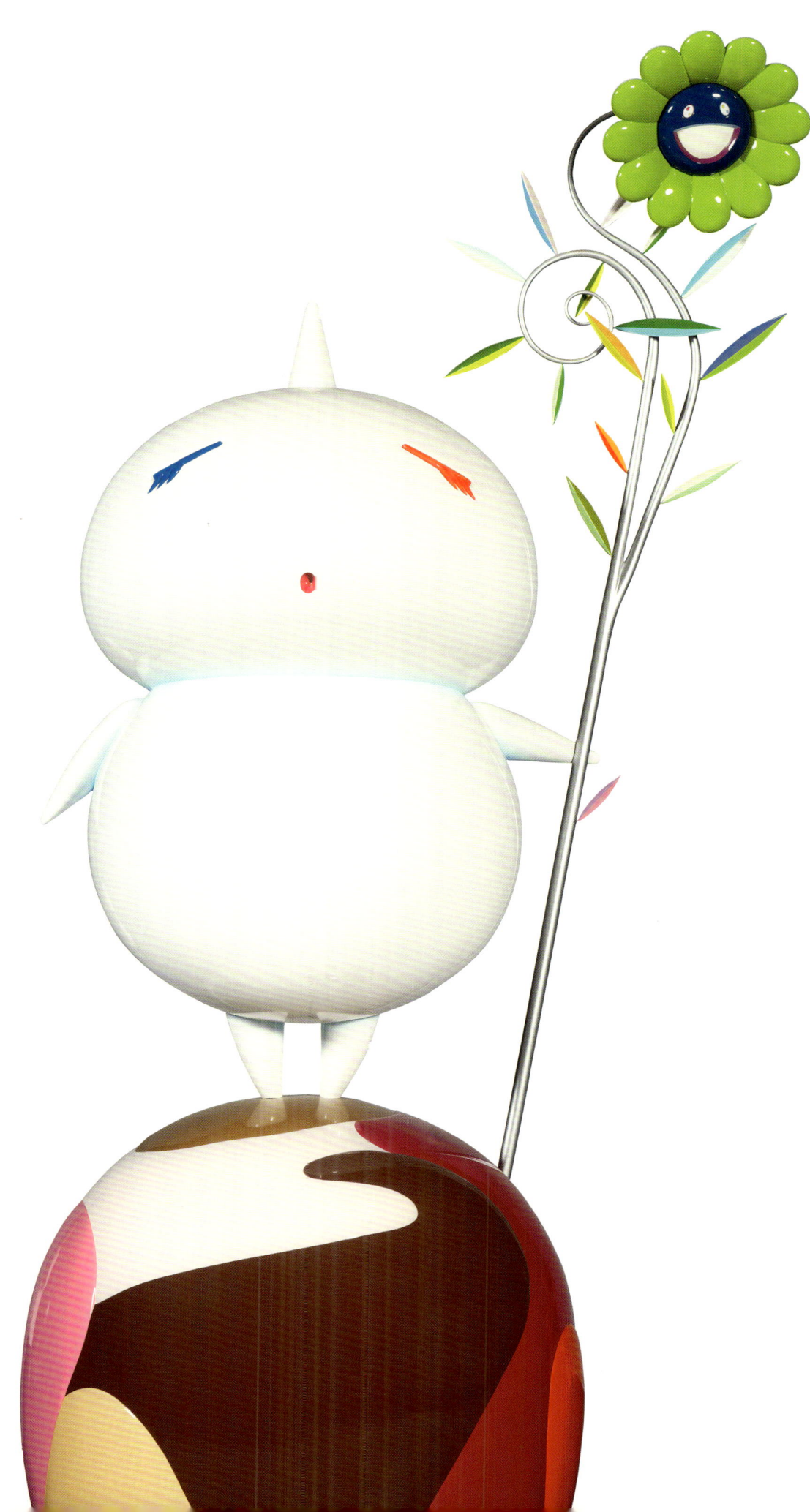

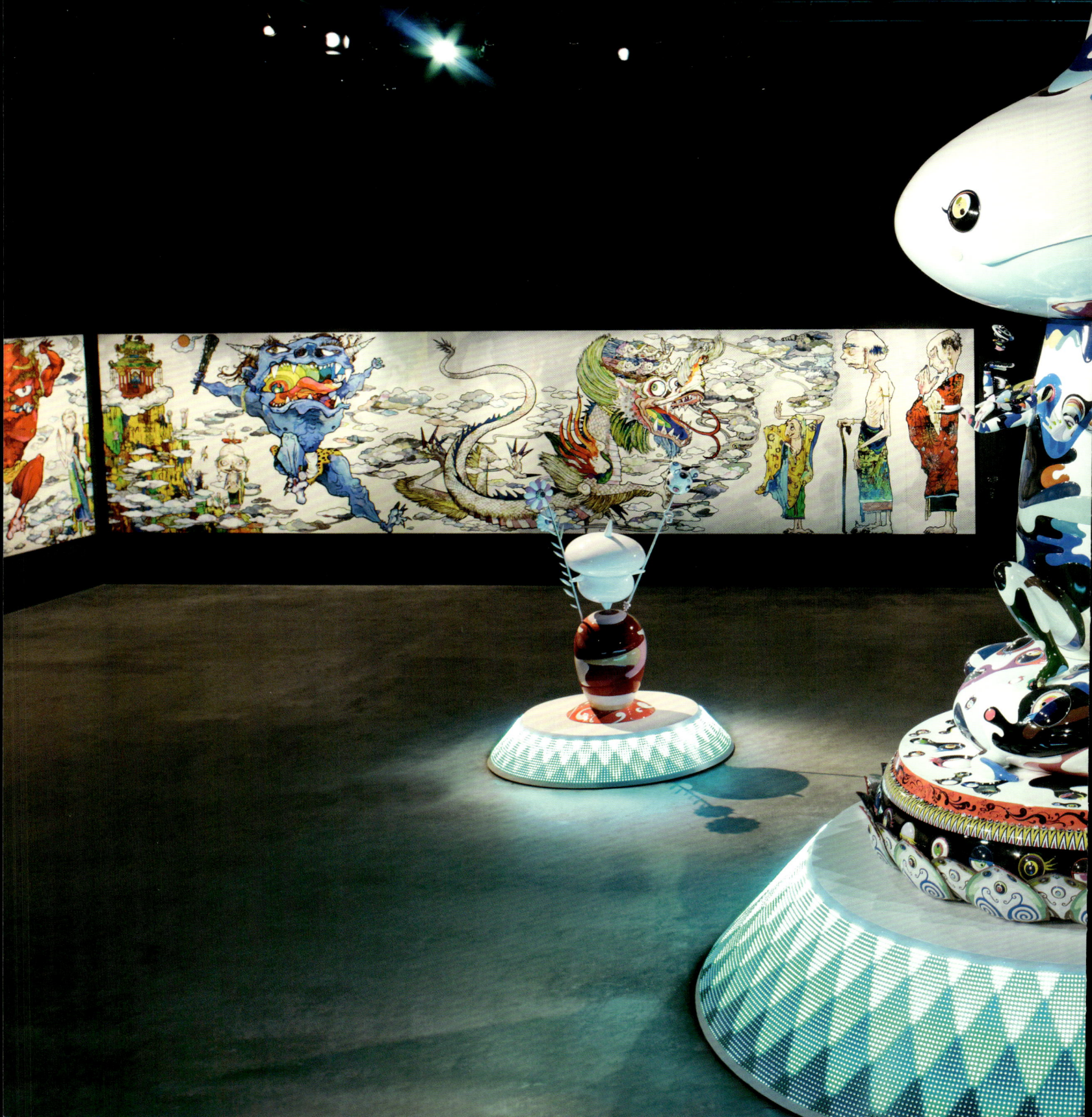

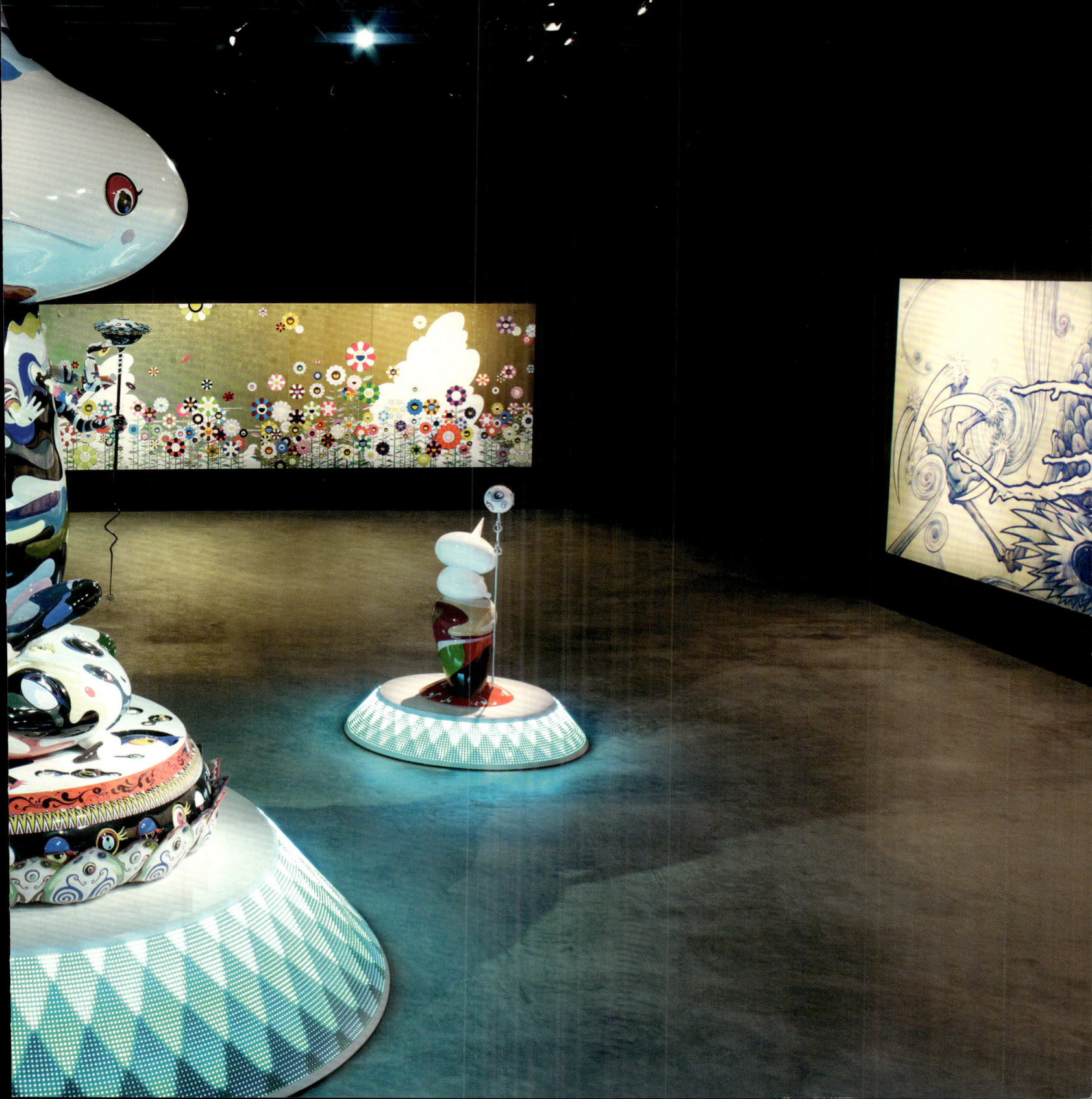

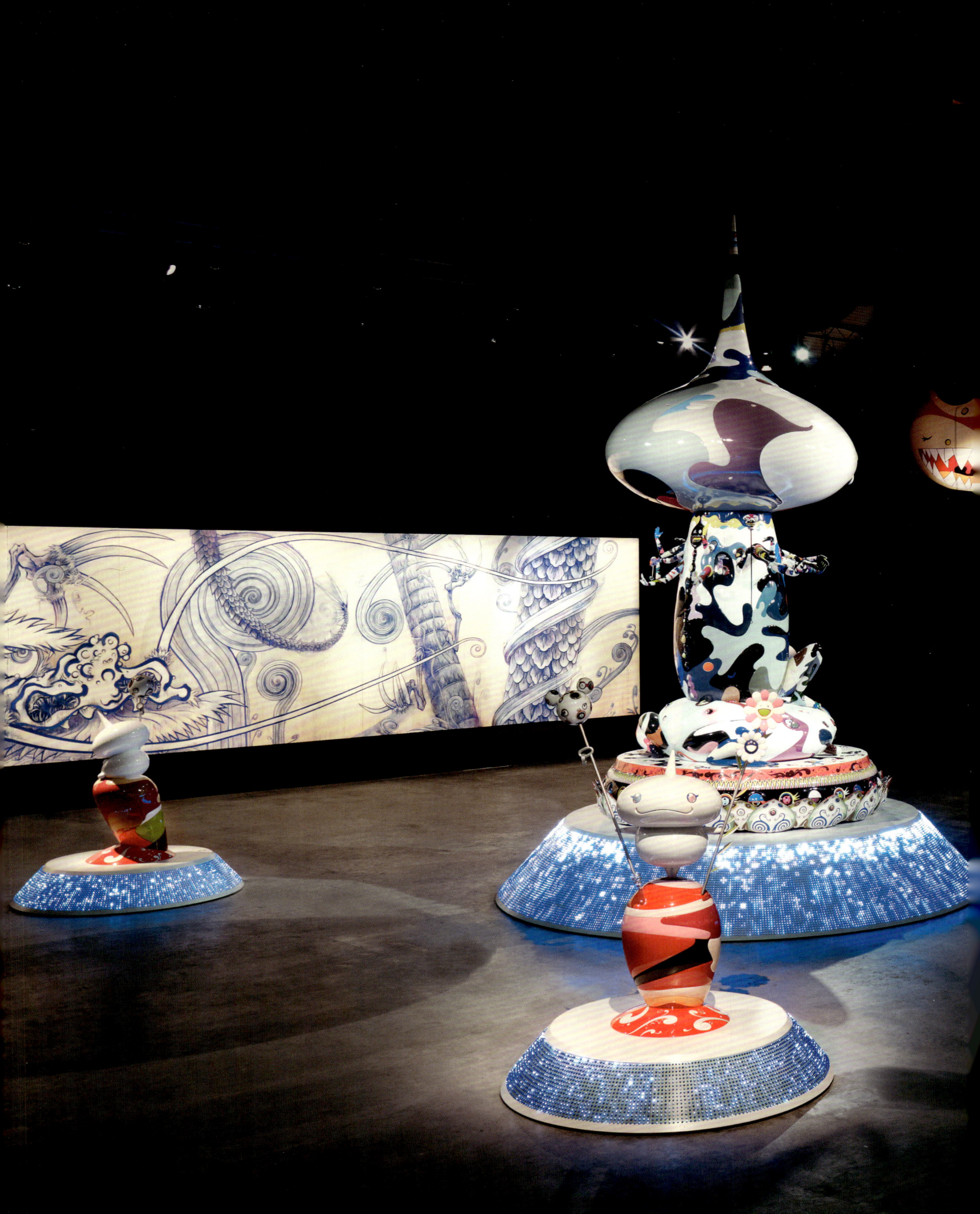

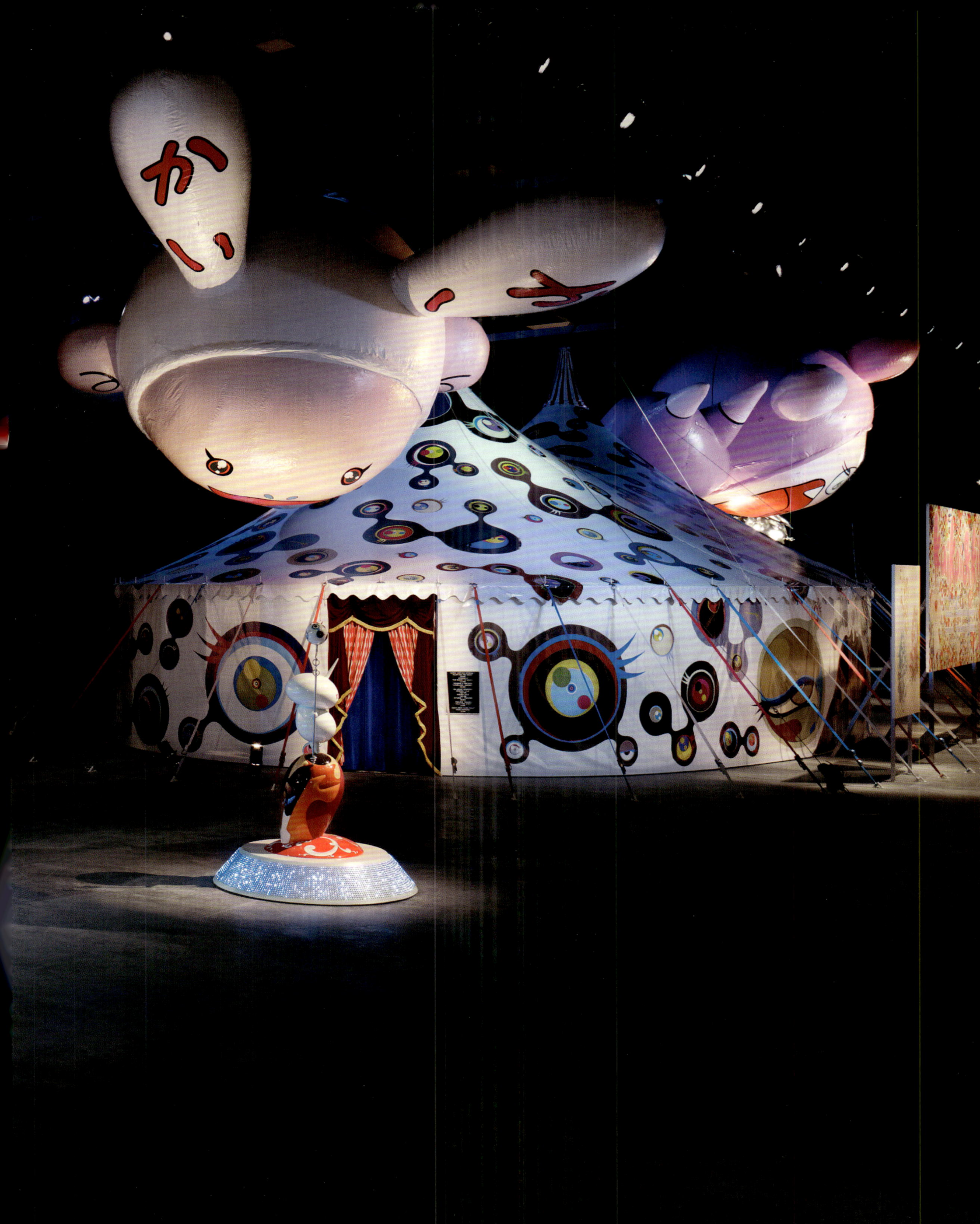

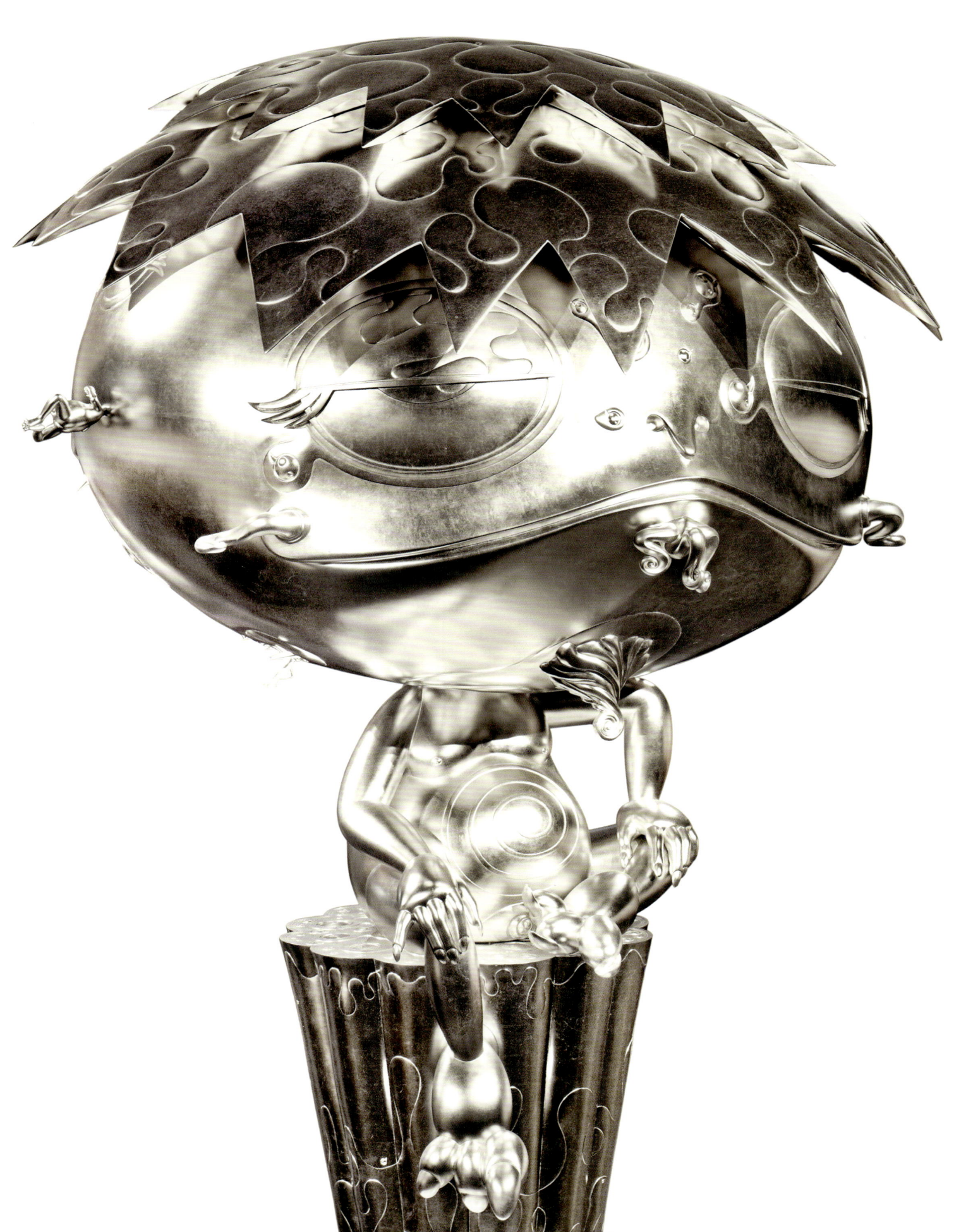

A few years ago, I created a character named Oval. This was in response to a request from fashion designer Issey Miyake, who wanted me to develop a figure based on Humpty Dumpty, which I interpreted in my own way. I was also influenced by Hyakume, or "Hundred Eyes," a ghostlike character beloved from my childhood. Oval is endowed with a large number of eyes. In Western fashion circles, Miyake has managed to achieve a fusion between a Japanese specificity and something more universal. And so, by combining Humpty Dumpty with something Japanese, I too was trying to create a universal character.

I thought of Buddhist sculpture, where statues often appear in threes—Buddha with an acolyte on either side, each holding a staff. When I started, I wanted to make Oval a representation of Buddha. As Buddha is always depicted on a lotus leaf–shaped base, I thought I would make a reference to this by installing Oval on a sphere covered with my flowers. But before creating Oval in that particular posture, I set about making his two acolytes: Kaikai and Kiki. In Japanese, we have this adjective, *kikikaikai*, which we use for strange things or phenomena, things that are frightening, disturbing, or make us uneasy. But when I named Kaikai and Kiki, I was not referring directly to that expression but instead to another one; although based on the same sounds, I write it with different Chinese ideograms, *kaikaikiki*. This term, used by an art critic in the late sixteenth century to describe the works of painter Eitoku Kanô, embraces several different notions: bravery and power, with all the seductiveness those traits may have, and at the same time keen sensitivity. This was the mixture of qualities that was considered elegant at the time, aesthetically speaking. This appreciation of Eitoku Kanō's work made a very favorable impression on me, and I thought that I too would like to create a form of art that was at once vigorous, sensitive, and intelligent. And since I found the expression *kaikaikiki* had a very attractive sound and the names suited them, I baptized these two characters Kaikai and Kiki. With these three characters—Oval, Kaikai, and Kiki—I wanted to create my own gods of art.

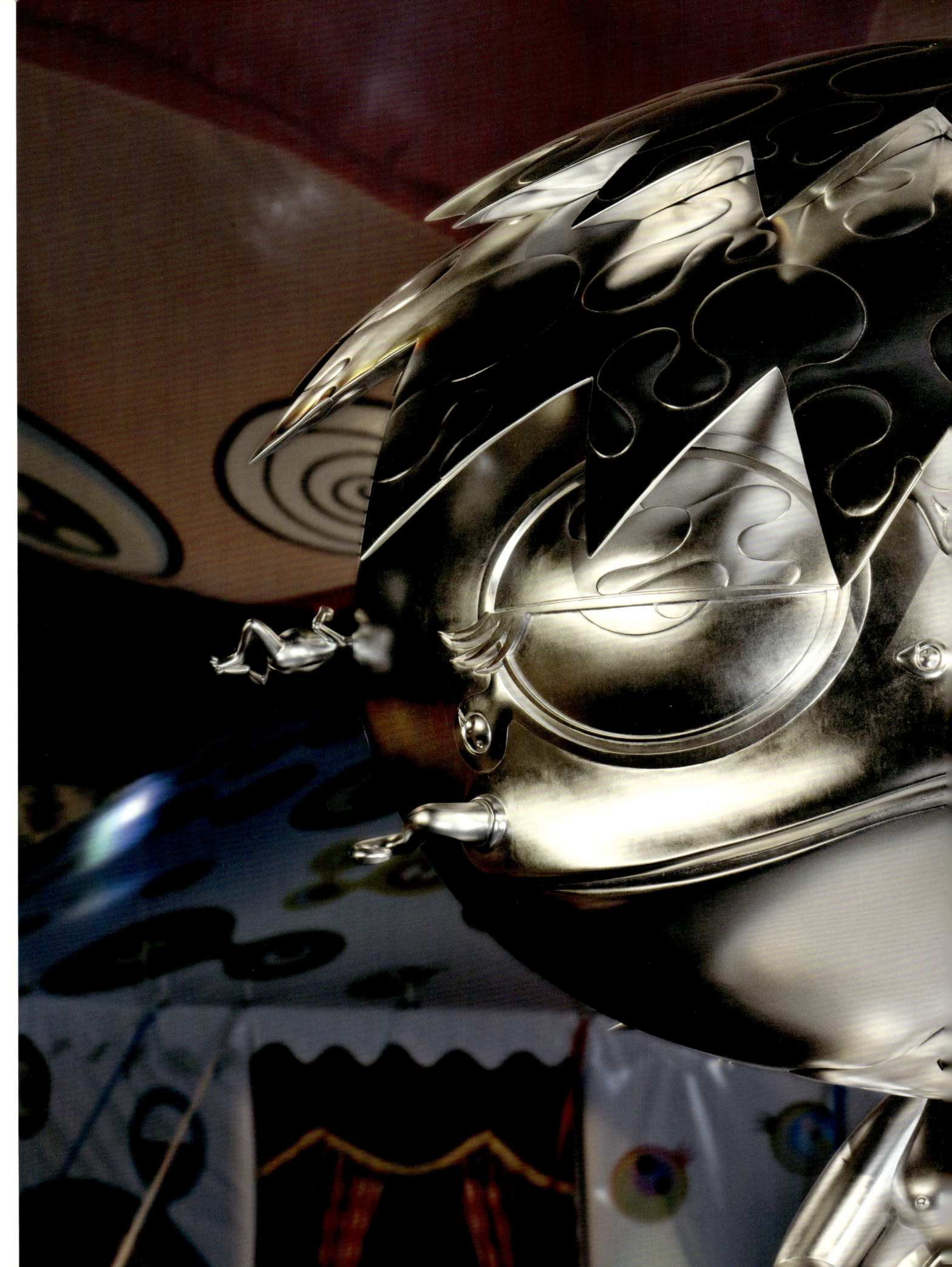

Oval Buddha (detail) 2007–10

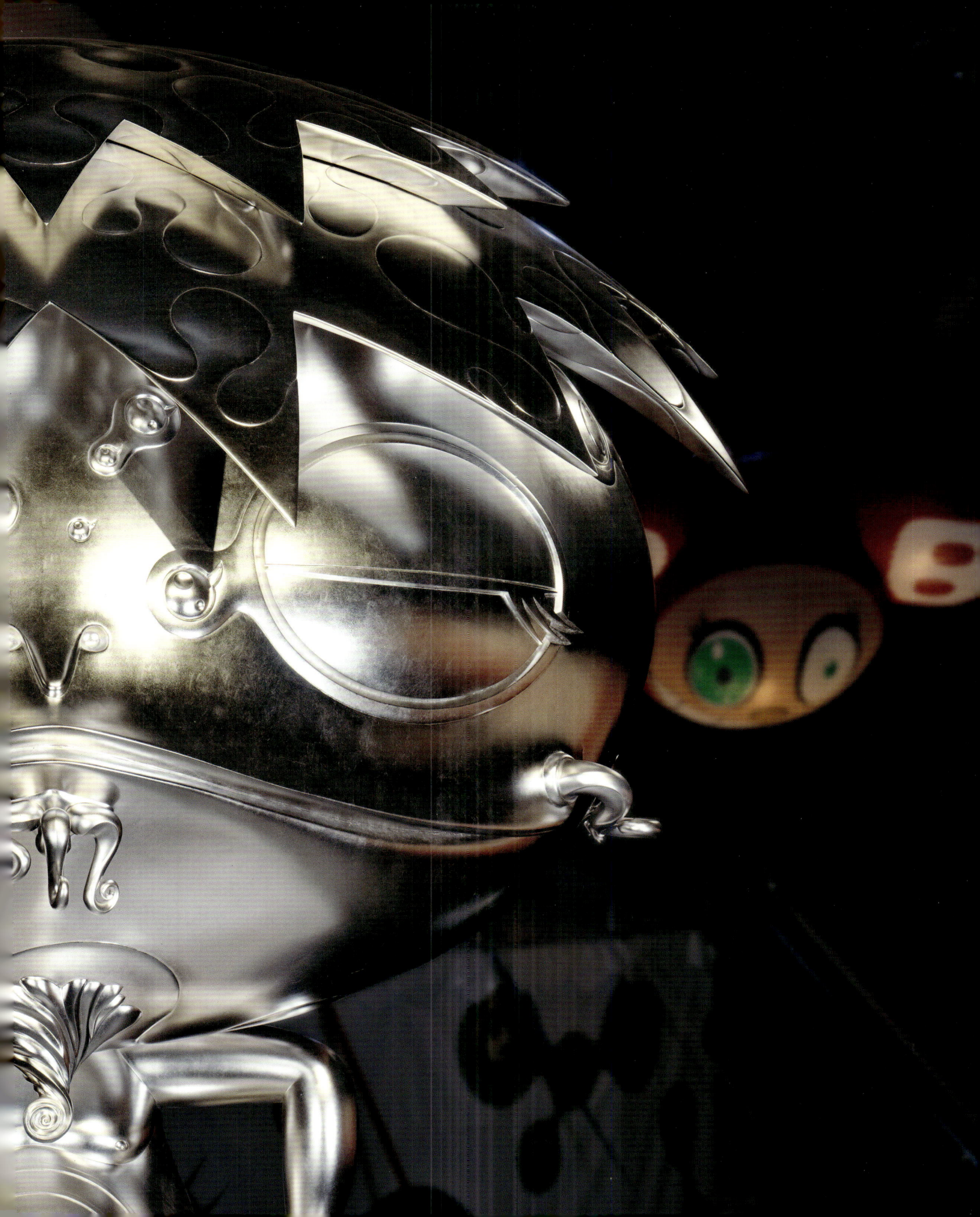

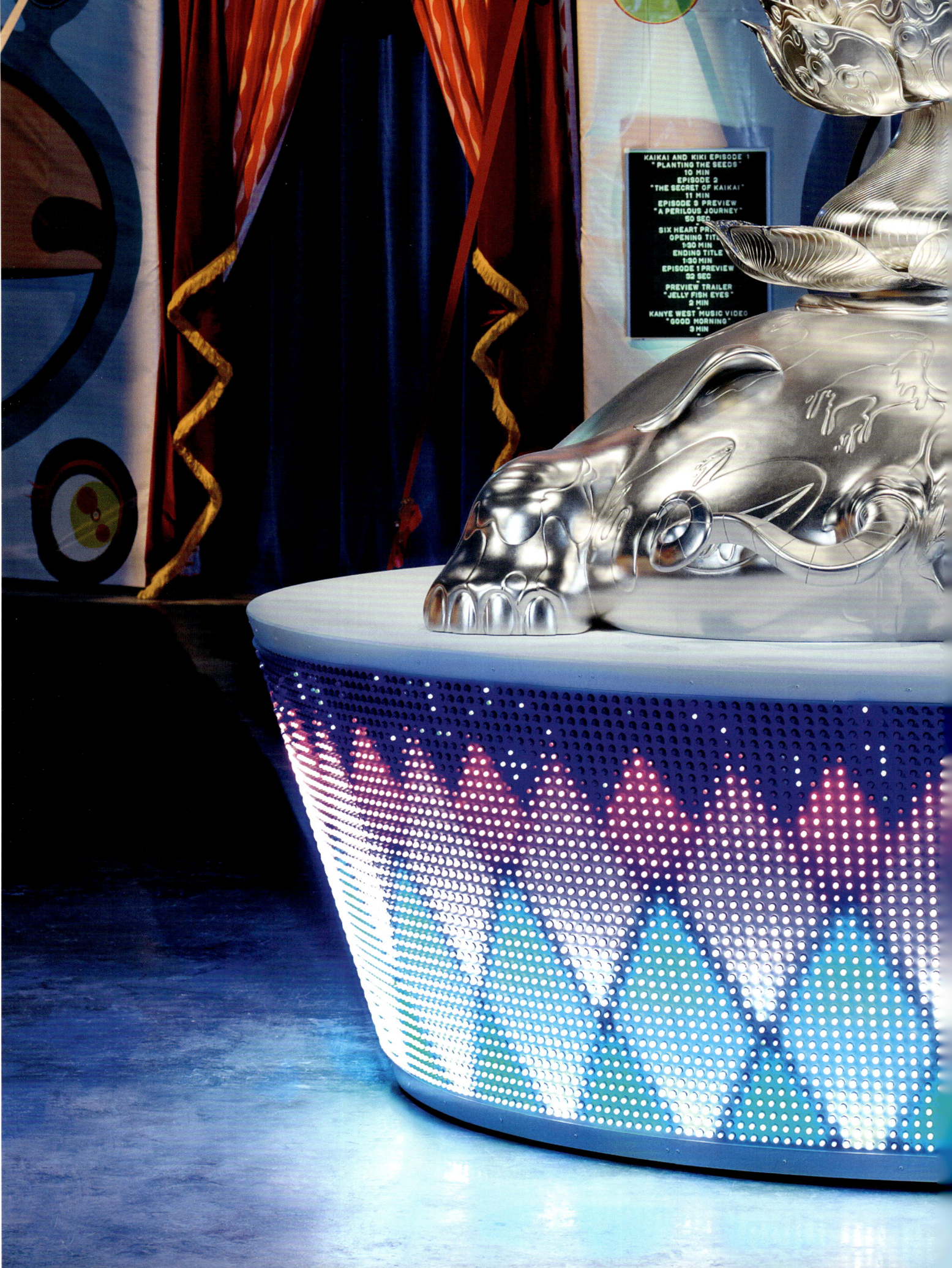

KAIKAI AND KIKI EPISODE 1
" PLANTING THE SEEDS "
10 MIN
EPISODE 2
" THE SECRET OF KAIKAI "
11 MIN
EPISODE 3 PREVIEW
" A PERILOUS JOURNEY "
50 SEC

SIX HEART PR...
OPENING TITL...
1:30 MIN
ENDING TITLE
1:30 MIN
EPISODE 1 PREVIEW
32 SEC

PREVIEW TRAILER
" JELLY FISH EYES "
2 MIN

KANYE WEST MUSIC VIDEO
" GOOD MORNING "
3 MIN

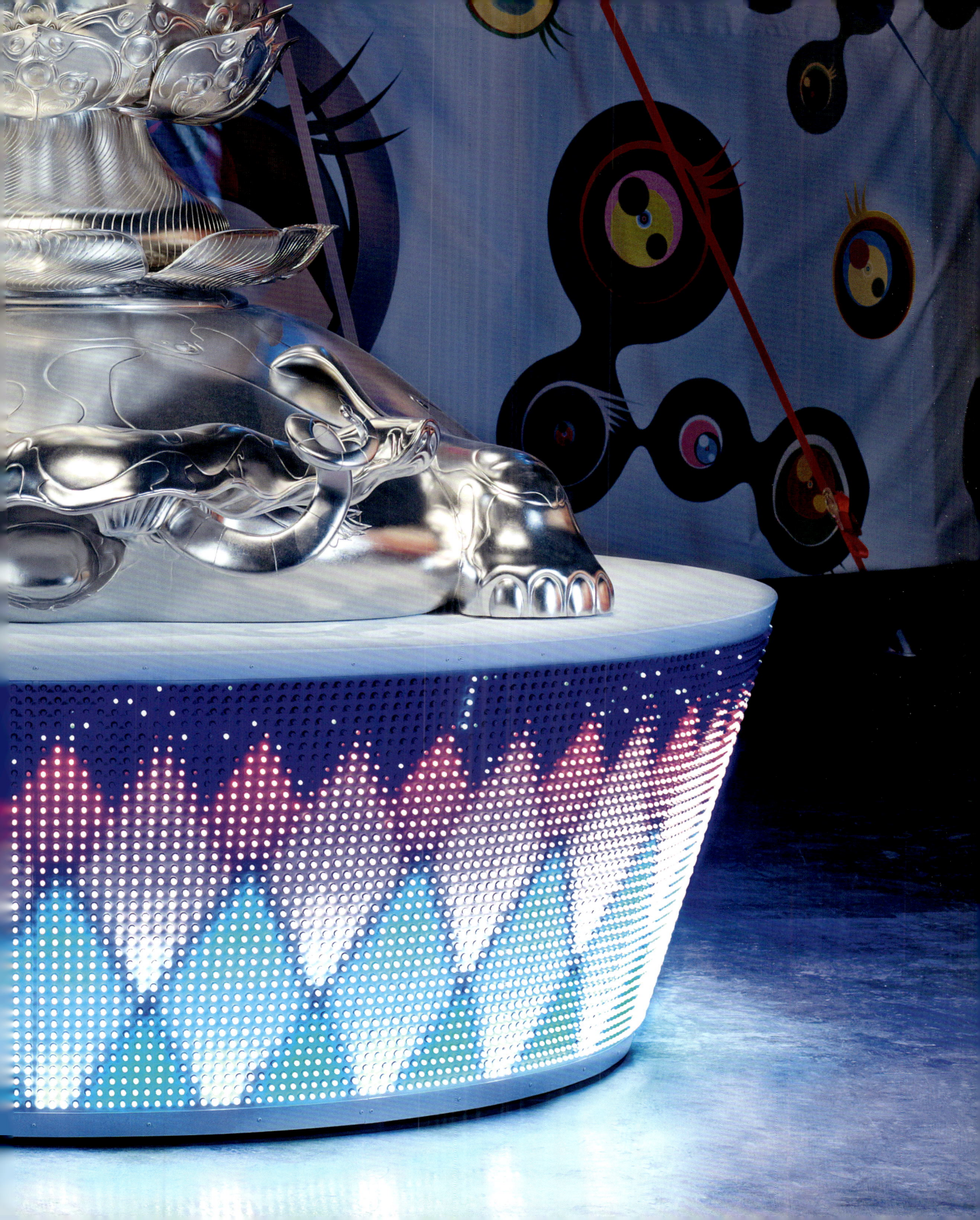

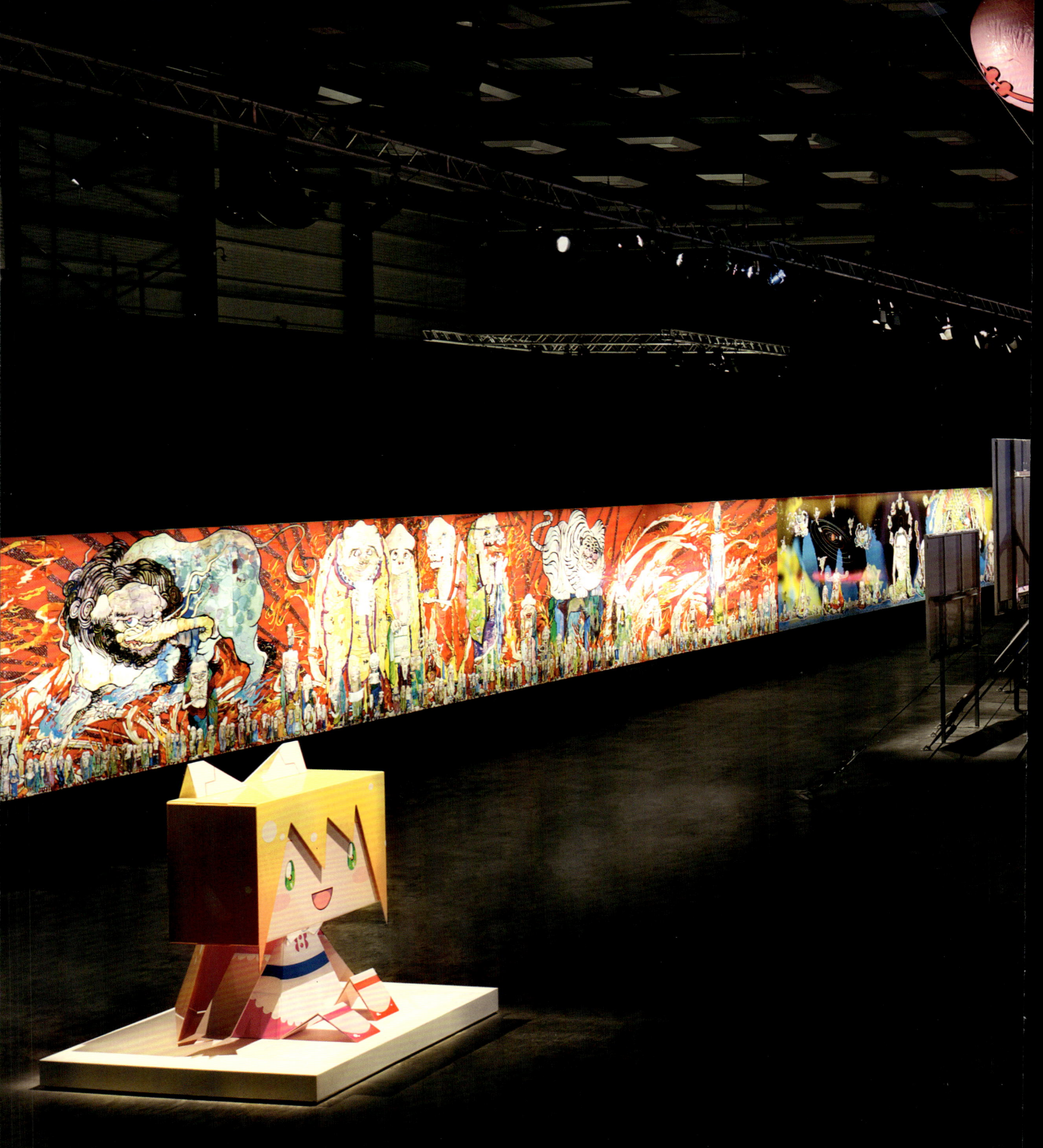

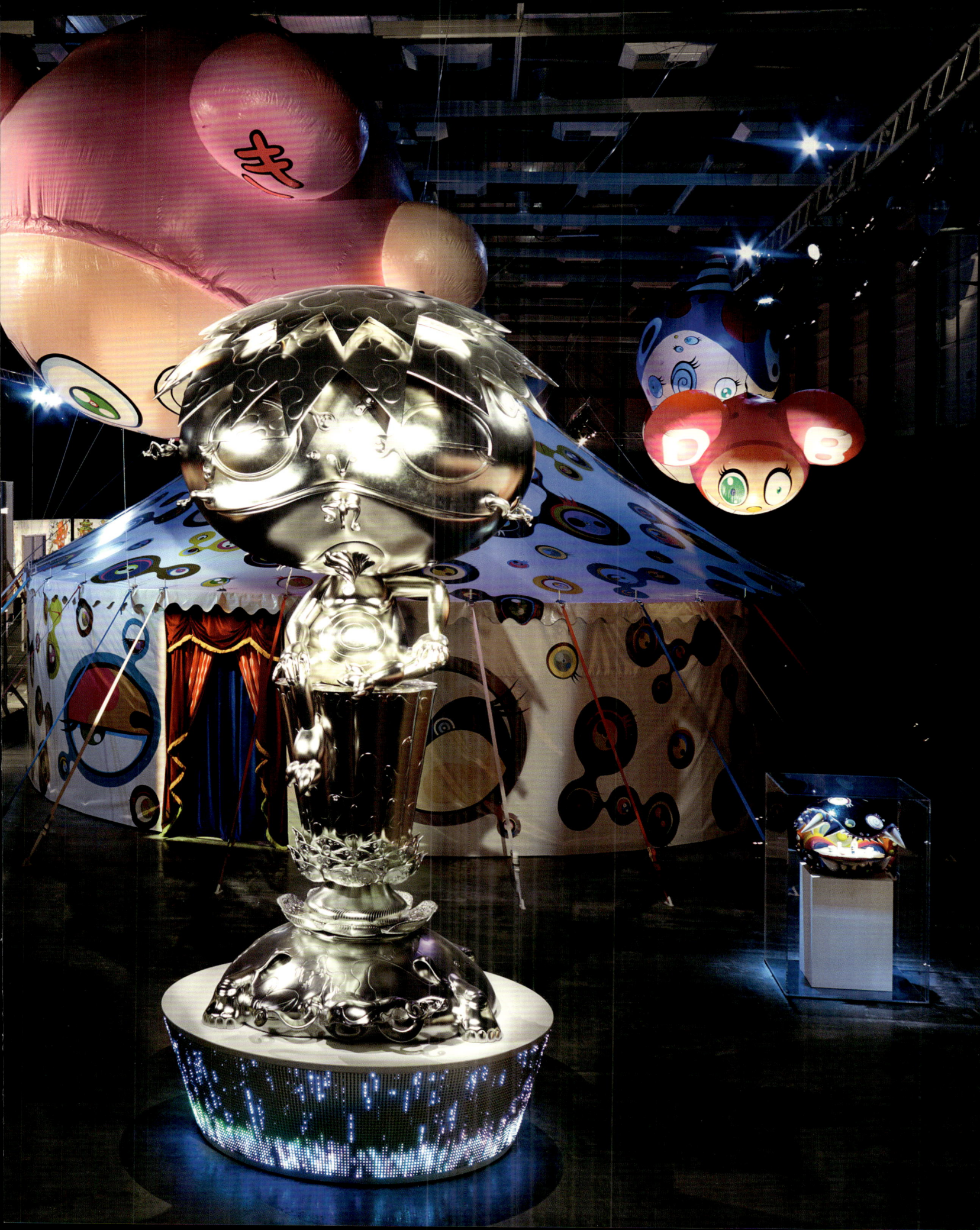

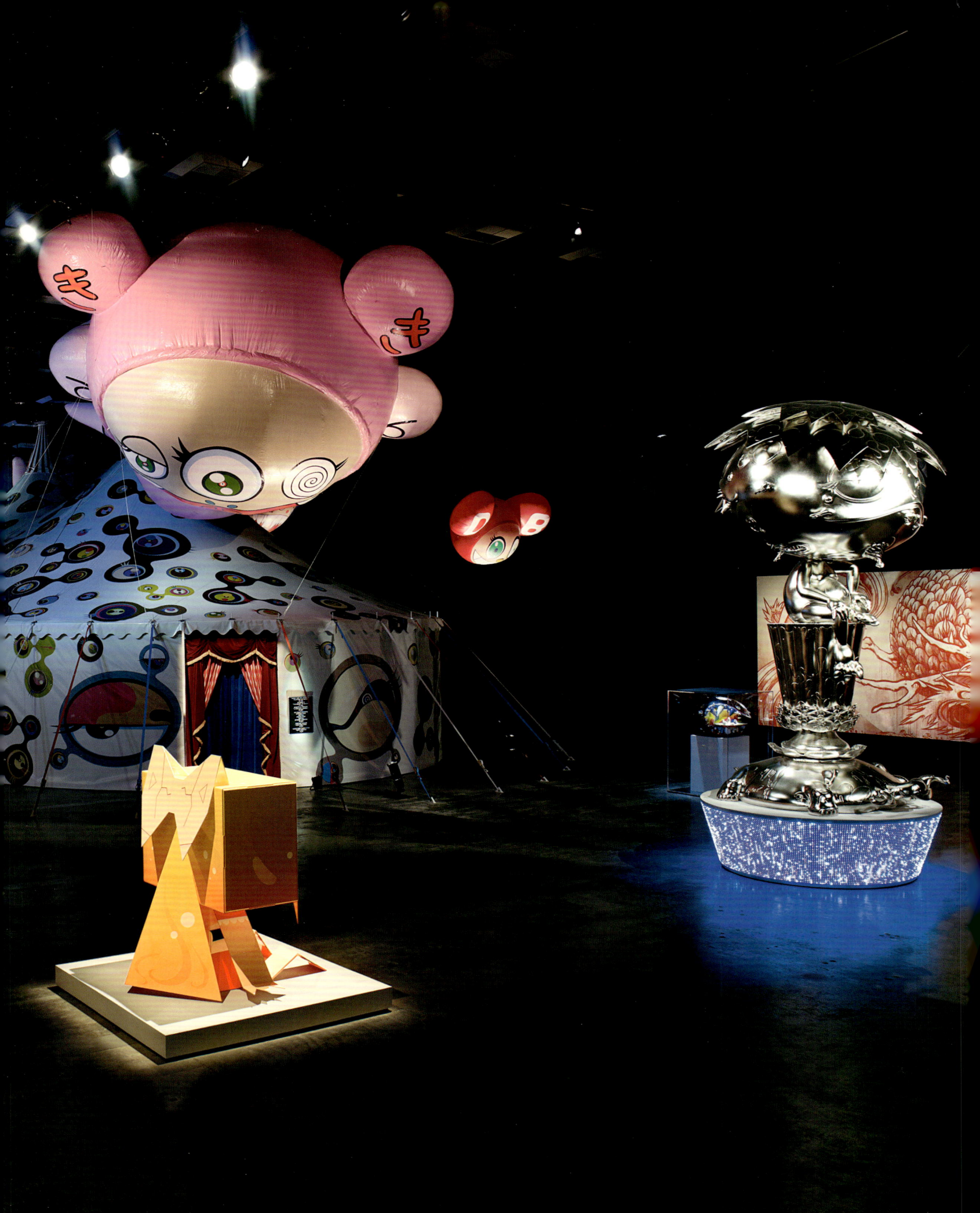

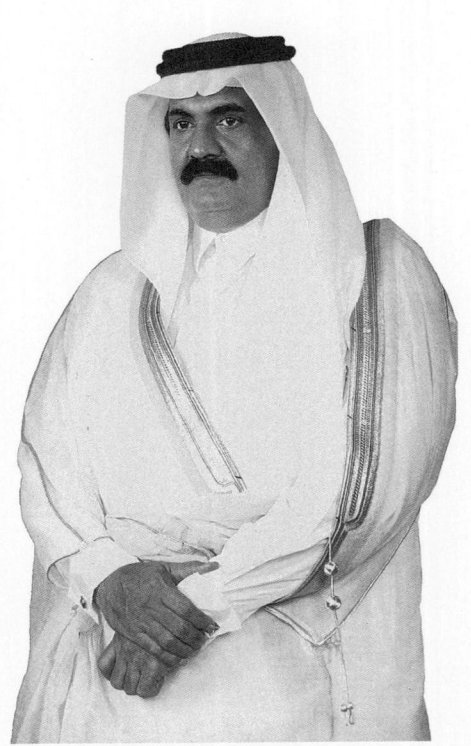

His Highness Sheikh Hamad bin Khalifa Al Thani
Emir of the State of Qatar

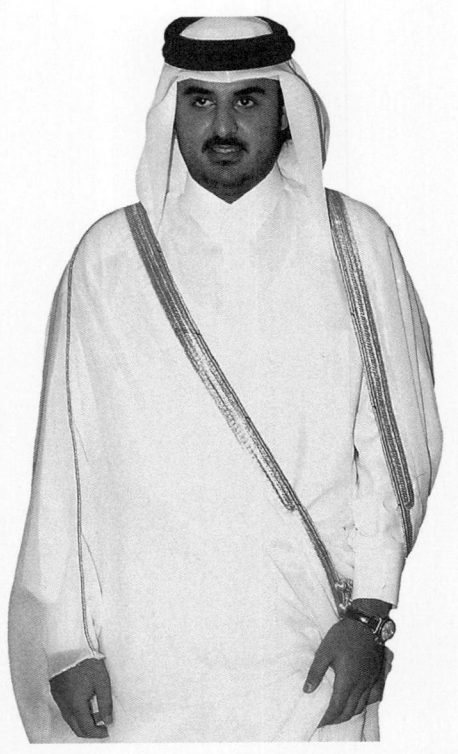

His Highness Sheikh Tamim bin Hamad bin Khalifa Al Thani
Deputy Emir of the State of Qatar, Heir Apparent

FOREWORD

Sheikha Al Mayassa Bint Hamad Bin Khalifa Al Thani

The Qatar Museums Authority is pleased to present "Murakami—Ego," the first solo exhibition of the renowned Japanese artist Takashi Murakami to be held in the Middle East. One of the most innovative artists working today, Murakami creates in his art a private universe that combines the highs and lows of culture, art history and pop, innovation and tradition, East and West, past and present. His interests in the forces of cultural production and his own singular aesthetic led to the idea of "Superflat," a term Murakami coined to describe aspects of post-war Japan as well as his own artistic style, which is instantly recognized the world over. In his multifaceted practice, Murakami has collaborated with esteemed art institutions and fashion powerhouses. He has supported the work of numerous young artists through his company Kaikai Kiki Co., Ltd., and has established new models for artist management, project development, and promotion.

Murakami's expansive vision exemplifies the Qatar Museums Authority's mission to promote cultural dialogue and programs that build bridges between nations. 2012 marks 40 years of positive multilateral relationships between the State of Qatar and Japan, and a yearlong series of activities will be held under the banner of Qatar Japan 2012. This initiative will showcase the unique aspects of each nation, as well as the shared interests of their citizens. As the first event to launch Qatar Japan 2012, Qatar Museums Authority invited Murakami to produce his most ambitious project to date. He has transformed the galleries of the Al Riwaq Exhibition Center into an immersive environment reflective of his personal universe, containing many of his most famous works, groundbreaking technological sculptural displays, an extraordinary 100 meter long painting created explicitly for this exhibition, an enormous circus tent that also functions as an indoor cinema, and a spectacular larger-than-life inflatable self-portrait. The exhibition itself is a work of art.

The Qatar Museums Authority is committed to the invention of new formats and modes for producing and realizing exhibitions of contemporary art by today's most influential artists. "Murakami—Ego" is the largest one person show ever realized in Doha but it is firmly placed in a context of exhibitions and support to contemporary art and culture: in the last few months Qatar Museums Authority has initiated important solo shows by Louise Bourgeois and Cai Guo Qiang, expansive investigations of art in the Middle East, the inauguration of a new major piece by Richard Serra and a series of public art projects.

It is our hope that contemporary art will help Qatar and its visitors understand and put in perspective the present, the past, and the future of our culture, while constantly expanding and enriching international dialogues and local education.

The Qatar Museum Authority would like to thank the many individuals whose dedication to this project has made it possible. The staff at Kaikai Kiki Co., Ltd., and Galerie Perrotin were absolutely essential in the development of the exhibition. In particular I would like to thank Shinichi Kitahara for his unflagging commitment and impressive knowledge of exhibition making. Sayaka Toyama and Brad Plumb at Kaikai Kiki spent many sleepless nights coordinating the exhibition. At Galerie Perrotin Guillaume Ziccarelli supervised the production of the show with great precision and Marguerite Lauras' contribution was crucial in turning the plans for the exhibition into a reality. I am particularly thankful to Emmanuel Perrotin for the enthusiasm, the knowledge, and the energy he brought to this project. Curator Massimiliano Gioni lent his inspiring vision. The team at Qatar Museums Authority has beautifully managed this ambitious exhibition, which is going to forever change the way we experience art in Doha. For this reason, I would like to thank CEO Abdulla al Najjar and, particularly, Director of Public Art Programs Jean-Paul Engelen, who flawlessly brought to completion an incredibly complex project. I am thankful to Katharina Schulz Hertzog, Hala al Khalifa, Tarik Mountassir, and Jeroen Vahrmeijer for their outstanding work: their commitment, expertise, and persistence are fundamental in developing the resources that will continue to make Doha into an important place for contemporary art.

We would like to thank the numerous exhibition lenders from around the world including private collections, art institutions, galleries, and the artist's studio. We would like to thank them for sharing these works with Qatar and the international public. Most of all, Qatar Museums Authority would like to express gratitude to Takashi Murakami whose talent and magnificent art has inspired new avenues of global cultural dialogue and exchange.

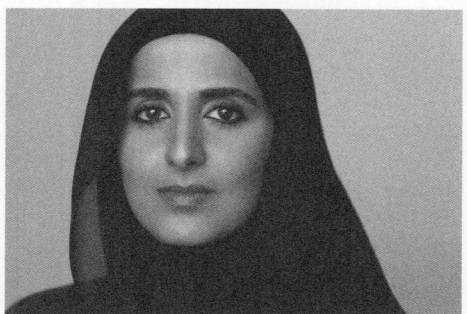

Sheikha Al Mayassa Bint Hamad Bin Khalifa Al Thani
President of the Qatar Museums Authority

TAKASHI MURAKAMI—EGO MIX:
Some facts and fictions about the life and work of Takashi Murakami

Massimiliano Gioni

Takashi Murakami has no home; he just sleeps wherever he happens to be. Whenever he gets drowsy, he stretches out on a piece of cardboard, wraps himself in a sleeping bag and snoozes for twenty minutes or so.

Murakami runs three studios, one in New York and two in Tokyo, as well as a sculpture atelier and, for a few months now, a gallery in Taiwan—all are part of the Kaikai Kiki enterprise. In periods of peak production, his studios operate seven days a week, twenty-four hours a day. His assistants and associates often do not go home for days on end, sleeping at work.

To stay in constant contact with his studios, Murakami has abolished the night; he abides by no time zone. Work is what dictates the rhythm of his days.

A single painting may be worked on by up to two hundred people, organized in different shifts.

Takashi Murakami's studio and Kaikai Kiki, his production company, are a cross between charismatic dictatorship and direct democracy. From the outside, Kaikai Kiki can seem like an impregnable fortress, a Kafkaesque castle governed by inscrutable laws and untranslatable codes. And yet every time I visit the studio, or look through photos documenting the creation of Murakami's pieces, I see only smiling faces; the atmosphere seems filled with the sense of a collective, shared project.

Abnegation is the word I would automatically associate with Takashi Murakami and his assistants.

Or perhaps *ataraxia*.

There is something obsessive—others might say ascetic, even mystical—about the way Murakami and everyone who works with him are focused on carrying out the artist's projects.

Murakami is always dressed the same way: in cargo pants, tennis shoes or slippers, T-shirts, and various layers of sweatshirts, jackets, and coats.

Murakami is very sensitive to cold, and his studios are overheated, often to the point of being rather uncomfortable for visitors. Legend has it that in the mid-1990s, when Murakami was living in New York and just beginning his career, his landlord tried to evict him by cutting off the radiators, forcing the artist to spend the winter in an unheated apartment. Ever since, Murakami has been terrified of chills and always travels with an extra supply of sweaters and heat patches.

During particularly intense periods, it is not uncommon for Murakami to go for days, sometimes even weeks, without a shower.

One of Murakami's most famous series depicts the sixth-century monk Bodhidharma. According to legend, after meditating for seven consecutive years, always facing the same wall, Bodhidharma dozed off for a few seconds. To keep that from happening again, he cut off his eyelids, then went back to staring at the wall for two more years without ever blinking. After spending a few days with Murakami and his team, a story like that sounds perfectly credible. I wouldn't be at all surprised if someone told me that Murakami had cut his eyelids off or demanded one of his collaborators to do so.

Murakami says he loves the moment of waking up, opening his eyes, and seeing his paintings in front of him.

Eyes are a strong presence in many of Murakami's works: His universe seems built on the multiplication of vision, on the desire to see more and more. His paintings—but I'd also say his studios, his whole world—are swarming with gazes, with hundreds upon hundreds of eyeballs.

The society dreamed up by Murakami is organized like a microscopic, molecular structure: His paintings and imaginary universes are anthills.

In Murakami's world, everything is surface. He is the first to point out the importance of the thin film or epidermis that envelops all of his works. It is like a mutant tissue of cells that seem capable of multiplying themselves ad infinitum. If you could cut off a little patch of the skin that covers each of his paintings, it would probably start to reproduce itself, instantly growing to wrap around the entire universe.

Murakami's work has always had sweeping ambitions; he aspires to restructure the world. His merchandising, T-shirts, toys, and fashion and design projects are more than just marketing experiments or products for a new mass economy of art. They are attempts to rebuild the universe.

The exhibition "Murakami – Ego" is his first urban-scale exercise in imagining the outlines of a new world: Welcome to Murakami City.

It is not a coincidence that this imaginary metropolis has sprung up cheek by jowl with the skyscrapers of Doha. Murakami's world is a *fata morgana*, a desert mirage.

Rather than architecture, Murakami takes the movie industry, as his model. He identifies with Steven Spielberg and George Lucas, and he isn't ashamed to describe himself as a B-movie director. One can think of him as comparable to Roger Corman, if only because of the impact Murakami has had on dozens of other artists and colleagues, whom he has often supported and exhibited in his galleries and contemporary art festivals.

Although Murakami is an avid collector of comics, books, ceramics, and art, the concept of ownership is utterly alien to his life.

Every drawing, sketch, or note that Murakami jots on any scrap of paper during a meeting, luncheon, or a briefing is quickly swept up by his assistants and filed away.

A few years ago, Murakami was followed around everywhere by a film crew that documented every minute of his existence.

Murakami and Kaikai Kiki are obsessed with copyright issues, often to the brink of dysfunction. For authorization to reproduce even a single image, one must submit a formal application, and then several members of his team must present a series of additional documents and requests. The same procedure is followed every time, even after one has been working for months on a show with the artist and has the illusion of having entered his circle of collaborators.

Lawyers are mentioned dozens of times a day when working on an exhibition with Murakami: every request presented to the studio must be "run by the lawyers" or "is with the lawyers." I've come to imagine these lawyers as men in bowler hats à la Magritte or secret agents out of *The Matrix*.

Data is another key concept in Murakami's universe. Dozens of employees work on the production of Data, obviously covered by stringent copyright rules and jealously guarded by a phalanx of lawyers. One's potential access to Data creates a sort of internal hierarchy at the studio: Being given clearance to receive Data amounts to a form of investiture.

If Warhol's Factory was a perverse, hypertrophic emulation of assembly-line systems, Kaikai Kiki is a demented replica of a multinational corporation.

Kaikai Kiki is a bachelor machine; and like any bachelor machine, it is both perfectly functional and utterly useless.

The fact that Kaikai Kiki generates monsters—sculptures of mutant creatures, paintings of sometimes cute, sometimes grotesque figures—should come as no surprise. It is a megacorporation gone mad, and its products are genetically modified.

Murakami's world has evolved from the Superflat aesthetics of his early work towards a fascination with the supernatural. His most recent paintings are not simply shiny, metallic, and new: they resonate instead with references to ancient legends and myths. Murakami has become a history painter.

His new 300-foot (100-meter-long) painting is composed of vast panoramas in which the Japanese tradition of nineteenth-century scroll painting has been updated to offer a new image of the sublime. Conceived in response to the recent disasters in Japan, this new cycle of paintings is Murakami's most realistic, yet most hallucinatory work to date: It suggests a shift away from the stylized reductions of his previous work towards a much more intricate imagery.

The 500 Arhats is populated by hundreds and hundreds of characters, gigantic figures, symbolic beasts, and immense fragments of landscape. The devotion to detail is stunning, the inventiveness unending. This painting is the Noah's ark of Murakami's personal universe: an attempt to preserve all the infinite variations of his imagination. While he still works the surface of his paintings with the precision of a goldsmith, Murakami also reaches new emotional and psychological depths. Simultaneously desperate and hopeful, this painting radiates a cathartic power that had never before permeated Murakami's work. It is as though the wind of fate has wiped away the perennial present of his previous paintings and his creatures have suddenly discovered their fragility and their complexity. This is perhaps what Murakami means when he says that this is his first religious, consolatory painting: one that takes both its characters and its viewers from the algid realm of artificial perfection to the warm, tragic kingdom of humanity.

TAKASHI MURAKAMI
The 500 Arhats

Gary Carrion-Murayari

The title of Takashi Murakami's largest exhibition to date, "Murakami—Ego," is both extremely apt and somewhat deceptive. This exhibition is remarkable in the way it completely immerses the viewer in the artist's visual and psychological universe. Murakami has described the exhibition as a giant self-portrait. The assembled artworks cover the entire range of his iconography and the signature cast of characters who animate his fears and fantasies. He has also turned himself into one of his cartoon creations, inhabiting the same fantasy landscapes he creates for Mr. DOB, Kaikai, and Kiki. Yet, this exhibition is also, less obviously, a self-portrait of Japan. As personal as the work may be, "Murakami—Ego" also reflects his complicated relationship with his home country. Murakami's work cannot be discussed without referencing the wide array of sources from which he borrows. Murakami's art is an attempt to assemble a collaged image of Japan from the bits and pieces of visual information he has ingested over the years: His work consumes and digests manga and otaku culture, as well as historical Japanese painting and sculpture, recreating these images as products for the international art market. The result is an image of a country as a body that is grotesque, banal, irreverent, and apocalyptic all at once.

Gradually, Murakami has erased the distinction between himself and the cultural position he inhabits. The complex iconography he has built may have been extracted from Japanese entertainment, but these images have become Murakami's own icons—or better yet, avatars—which he uses to negotiate the relationship between East and West. If Murakami's ego is one that is synchronous with Japan, then his work becomes an expression of latent trauma and continual adaptation. The destructive force of the two atomic bombs dropped on Japan in 1945 can be seen as the engine that has driven the Murakami art machine. The artist continues to trace the echoes of their devastation as they are manifested in every corner of Japanese culture. His work is a reminder of the ways in which Japan has failed to come to terms with its own past and the way its trauma shapes the country's particular modes of visual expression. Murakami's practice is a kind of sustained investigation into or analysis of the Japanese visual unconscious. The tragedy of the Japanese people always looms somewhere below the surface, sometimes imperceptible to Western audiences. In the past, however, his work has rarely touched upon the monumental events of the present. It is only recently that

Murakami work has attempted to bear witness to the destruction, pain, and suffering of his own time.

On March 11, 2011, a magnitude 8.9 earthquake struck off the eastern coast of Japan. Following the earthquake, the eastern coast of Japan was ravaged by a massive tsunami that reached heights of 133 feet. The devastation caused by this deadly wave was nearly indescribable. Among the effects of the disaster, the Fukushima nuclear power plant suffered extensive damage to its reactors causing radiation leaks and contamination of food and water supplies that affected millions. The total death toll from the event eventually surpassed 18,000, with an economic impact that will take years to recover from. The Tohoku Earthquake (or Great East Japan Earthquake) was the largest natural disaster ever to hit the country. The psychological trauma of the event may not be fully comprehended for generations.

Over 150 years earlier, another massive earthquake struck Japan causing similarly overwhelming devastation. The Great Asei Edo Earthquake of 1855 measured 6.9 on the Richter scale and devastated the city of Edo (eventually renamed Tokyo). Nearly five thousand people died and thousands of houses, temples, and businesses were destroyed. The earthquake was one of a number of tremors and other natural disasters which struck Edo around this time. Residents of the city inhabited a world where the potential for death and destruction on a seemingly apocalyptic scale was almost always present. It was in this fraught environment that the painter, Kanō Kazunobu, created his monumental series of paintings depicting the five hundred arhats (or *rakan* in Japanese).

The five hundred rakan were a popular subject within Buddhist art in Japan at the time. These men were purported to be followers of the historical Buddha who met at the First Buddhist Council and protected his teachings for generations to come. They were revered figures whose cult of devotion only increased in the years after Buddhism moved from India to China and then Japan. Kazunobu's work, in the form of one hundred painted scrolls, was created as a commission for the wealthy Zōjōji temple in Edo. The scrolls took Kazunobu over ten years to complete (the last scrolls were completed by assistants after his death) and remain a remarkable achievement for their narrative complexity, formal inventiveness, and emotional intensity.

As the popularity of the rakan increased, they became a favorite subject of Japanese painters and sculptures. Kazunobu's rendition of the subject is one of the most spectacular and idiosyncratic ever created. As the historian Pamela Graham has noted about one of the scrolls:

> [The work] shows the artist at the height of his talent, masterfully synthesizing various painting styles. His inclusion of raking light, shading, and precise anatomical definition stemmed from

recently introduced Western influences; his brush techniques and color application originated in Kanō teaching methods; and he derived basic composition and figural forms from old Chinese and Japanese prototypes.

In essence, Kazunobu brought together all of the tools at his disposal to realize his multifaceted vision of the rakan. Over the course of the one hundred painted scrolls, the highly individualized figures float dramatically above vivid landscapes, sometimes behaving like ordinary, unremarkable beings, and other times, dishing out punishment or salvation to the helpless humans below. Tiny human figures boil in fiery pits of hell, languish in earthquake-inspired destruction, or flounder amidst tsunami like waves. Kazunobu's "Five Hundred Rakan" responds to Japan's natural disasters with an overwhelming visual spectacle meant to inspire piety in the hopes of redemption.

Coincidentally, Kanō Kazunobu's "Five Hundred Rakan" paintings were on view in Tokyo in spring 2011. It was the first time the original series of one hundred scrolls was exhibited in its entirety since its original temple home was destroyed in 1945. For an artist like Murakami who regularly draws on the so-called "eccentric painters" of the late Edo period, the Kazunobu scrolls served as the perfect model to craft an appropriate response to the horrors that were happening in Japan. Murakami's painting *The 500 Arhats*, created specifically for "Murakami—Ego," echoes the monumental scale of Kazunobu's work, while creating a uniquely contemporary vision. The painting is the largest and perhaps most dramatic painting Murakami has ever created and a uniquely personal response to the events of March 2011.

The 500 Arhats is divided into four distinct sections, each measuring eighty-two feet (twenty-five meters) in length. Each section is its own pictorial universe, dedicated to a natural element—Wind, Fire, Mountain, and Wood—as found in the canon of traditional Japanese painting. These visionary land-scapes are populated by a countless army of arhats, big and small, as well as a host of other creatures, including dragons, lions, birds, and demons. Informed by Chinese mythology, each of the four sections is dominated by a particular creature and corresponds to a particular cardinal direction moving from the Azure Dragon (East/Spring) to the Vermillion Bird (South/Summer) to the White Tiger (West/Autumn) and ending with a Black Tortoise (North/Winter). Murakami renders the natural world with a spectacular array of colors, patterns, and forms. Each wave, cloud, gust of wind, or nebulous galaxy is painted with rich color and surface. The arhats themselves are grotesque creatures. In spite of their sheer number, each figure has a different set of facial features, style of dress, and emotional expression. They are painted in Murakami's typically flat style: intricately detailed, but seemingly at a remove from the world around them. They clearly exist on a supernatural plane immune to the ferocity of nature. Individual figures seem to tame the billowing gusts of wind with beams of light, puffs of smoke, or focused gestures of prayer.

Certain parts of Murakami's work resonate with Kazunobu's scrolls—in particular, Murakami's "Fire" landscape recalls Kazunobu's earlier depictions of the torments of Hell. More often than not, however, Murakami's work is a unique production of his own contemporary imagination. Aside from the stylistic differences between the works, Murakami chooses to render the arhats alone, without humans to rescue from tragedy or condemn to damnation. Murakami also eschews Kazunobu's approach of individual narrative panels in favor of a composition that borders on an immersive architectural environment. In doing so, he implicates the viewer in the nightmarish world of his painting. *The 500 Arhats* becomes less didactic and more experiential, and in spite of its stylized nature, the resulting environment is both disorienting and slightly terrifying. The canvas collapses cultural history and iconography into a singular, psychedelic space. Of course, Murakami's arhats inhabit neither the painful reality of the physical world, nor the kind of spiritual realm that was meaningful in Kazunobu's time: They are monks of the digital realm, materializing to an audience whose connection to Japan's suffering is through an undifferentiated stream of images.

Coming as it does after one of the most powerful demonstrations of nature's destructive power, *The 500 Arhats* seems to express the struggle to comprehend these forces in a world that is increasingly virtual rather than physical. The arhats are no longer discernible presences in the human world; they appear as relics of a past spiritual age, or ghosts who have returned to haunt us with our own powerlessness in the face of nature. Like the earth-quake itself, they are a reminder of the transience of life. When speaking about this new body of work, Murakami has invoked the Japanese expression, *shogyō mujō*, a Buddhist phrase that means "everything must pass." In a post-spiritual age, this line is repeated often but seldom felt on the level of everyday experience. For Kazunobu, his arthats served as both an explanation of the suffering caused by natural disasters and a prescription for how to behave in response. Murakami, on the other hand, can promise no solace through the possibility of spiritual redemption. His arhats convey no message other than the ferocity of nature and the reminder that it will eventually come to reclaim all of us. They no longer intervene in the lives of men; instead they surround us as we suffer and remind us that this has come before and will come again. It is without a doubt a bleak message, but one that is deeply rooted in the history of Japan and therefore in the art of Takashi Murakami.

THE METAMORPHOSIS OF LIGHT

A poem by Fahad Al-Mursel
inspired by Takashi Murakami's world

In the beginning there was a flower.

"Alas, oh, flower of spectrum and despair, my desert cherishes your incense. Your dew is due or I shall perish!" said the Arabian knight while falling asleep in the shadow of the mighty ink dragon.

In the beginning there was a flower.
Kaikai and Kiki were chasing young circles of light sneaking on the canvases.

The light grew until it became an atomic smoke.

In the beginning, there was smoke in the form of Takashi's skull when his body was stolen by the God of the Flower.

In the beginning was the God of the Flower
knitting Takashi from the threads of an ancient ego until Takashi was created in the form of a pet Tiger yawning at a Superflat nebula.

On the Shores of the Arabian Gulf, the Dragon is awakened, gazing upon the falling sun like an Arabian lover who lost his beloved.
In the Mosques' yards, the incense of the mad Monk within fills up our lungs until every word of the unknown matches the unknown itself.

"The numbers shall prevail!" shouted the demon in the mountain/God of the heights.
A digital storm—armed with five hundred monks—hit the ground. The storm cleared, but the monks were left behind roaming the "I," between the desert I yearn for, and my delicate photogenic city of glass; between "Beauty" and its opposite; between "Love" and the unreachable.

The "Corniche" water ripples under a Qatari sunset, until "Orange & Red" burst out as a character for Doha's tranquil evenings, and the hopes for a better tomorrow in a world that already consumed itself:
Orange: just like another flower that Takashi wrote about himself.
Red: just like another story of the blood and wine of ancient Arabian poets, and my virtuous estranged camel.

Oh Superflat spectra, you have released me into the alphabets to realize that we are nothing but vessels. We contain only what is poured into us by the world's ideologies—pain—revolutions.

The vessel/"us" is made of mute brass; filled with water, hence we shall forever produce that familiar water in a "brassy" yellow color. Yet Takashi/ the vessel was made of the "Anti-Absolute," and so it shall forever pour keys to a new realm.

Takashi the elephant with twisted tusks and huge bored heart, guide me— I beg of you—to the "Suhail" star in the desert's sky so I find my beloved. Inspire me with the poems of my forefathers until I master the virtue of "Understanding" and satisfy my slim burgundy horse.

In the beginning there was an elephant.
The tusks weren't twisted then, and the Bedouin knight was dismounting his ego.

But now, that Bedouin is sleeping next to Takashi–the Hyaena in a digital tent, as he listens to the distant chanting of Daruma while we all try to embrace the future.

"Our new founded heritage is horrifying and shrewd!"
said the water monk while crossing a lake of dreams—which long inhabited my nights—as I falter behind the many open mouths of Takashi's unfinished plaster monster. A monster just like the cities it came from: never satisfied.

The questions multiply:

Where does happiness reside?
In Murakami's footed realism? Or his winged imagination?
Where does beauty emerge?
In the physical nature of his creations or the metaphysical? The soul or its surroundings?
Where are the wishes granted?
In the color or in the thought of the color? In the "I" or the other claw-full "I"?

Pour me a cup of illusion, oh sane traveler. The Bedouin has no desire in God's food, but will certainly beg for a dream that once blessed the meditation of a dedicated slave.

In the presence of Takashi's light and its metamorphosis, destiny preys on me like a falcon.

Like my pearl-diving father whom I don't remember well, Takashi's monks traveled the sea searching for salvation. The monks' salvation was a mere sign or a godly whisper in the horizon; my father's salvation was a pearl sleeping on the sea-bed of time.

Alas oh "Danah" of Salvation! I lost you…

I never searched…
…
…

The God of the Flower seems angry now.

Still stitching Takashi together using threads of light.
Still perfecting the talent between the sharp edges of Art and Love.
Still living in the realm of the super ego.

still…

and will ever be…

Oh Takashi
In the beginning, there was the ultimate ego.

WORKS IN THE EXHIBITION

Mr. DOB, 1997
Inflatable vinyl chloride
236 x 304 x 180 cm
Courtesy Galerie Perrotin, Paris
Page 24

Untitled, 1997
Inflatable vinyl chloride
300 cm diameter
Courtesy Galerie Perrotin, Paris
Page 28

Guru Guru, 1998
Inflatable vinyl chloride
395 x 288 cm
Courtesy Galerie Perrotin, Paris
Page 27

DOB in the Strange Forest (Red DOB), 1999
FRP, resin, fiberglass, acrylic, and iron
152.4 x 304.8 x 304.8 cm
Private collection
Courtesy Galerie Perrotin, Paris
Pages 5, 6–7

Kaikai, 2000–05
Oil paint, acrylic, synthetic resins,
fiberglass, and iron
222 x 96 x 46 cm
Courtesy Galerie Perrotin, Paris
Page 44

Kiki, 2000–05
Oil paint, acrylic, synthetic resins,
fiberglass, and iron
222 x 96 x 46 cm
Courtesy Galerie Perrotin, Paris
Pages 42–43, 45

Homage to Francis Bacon (Study of George Dyer), 2002
Acrylic on canvas mounted on board
120 x 120 cm
Private collection
Courtesy Galerie Perrotin, Paris
Page 8

Homage to Francis Bacon (Study of Isabel Rawsthorne), 2002
Acrylic on canvas mounted on board
120 x 120 cm
Collection Galerie Perrotin, Paris
Page 9

Tan Tan Bo Puking—a.k.a. Gero Tan, 2002
Acrylic on canvas mounted on board
360 x 720 cm
Private collection
Courtesy Galerie Perrotin, Paris
Pages 10–13

Kitagawa-Kun, 2002–04
Oil paint, acrylic, synthetic resins,
fiberglass, steel, and Corian base
125 cm high
Page 237

Tongari-kun, 2003–04
Oil paint, acrylic, synthetic resins,
fiberglass, and iron
702 x 350 x 350 cm
Page 91

Jikokkun, 2003–05
Oil paint, acrylic, synthetic resins,
fiberglass, and iron
206.1 x 90 cm
Page 96

Koumokkun, 2003–05
Oil paint, acrylic, synthetic resins,
fiberglass, and iron
240 x 84 cm
Page 96

Panda, 2003–09
Acrylic on fiberglass with antique
Louis Vuitton trunk
255.3 x 165.1 x 109.2 cm
With cooperation from Louis Vuitton
Page 231

Tamon-kun, 2003–05
Oil paint, acrylic, synthetic resins,
fiberglass, and iron
275 x 110 cm
Pages 96, 97

Zoucho-kun, 2003–05
Oil paint, acrylic, synthetic resins,
fiberglass, and iron
263 x 112.5 cm
Page 96

In the heart's eye, a universe, 2007
Acrylic on canvas mounted on board,
signage in gold leaf
180 x 213.2 cm
Private collection
Courtesy Gagosian Gallery
Page 260

*My arms and legs rot off and though my
blood rushes forth, the tranquility of my
heart shall be prized above all. (Red blood,
black blood, blood that is not blood)*, 2007
Acrylic and platinum leaf on canvas
mounted on board, signage in platinum
and gold leaf
180 x 213.2 cm
The Broad Art Foundation, Santa Monica
Courtesy Blum & Poe, Los Angeles
Page 261

Oval Buddha, 2007–10
Aluminum and platinum leaf
568 x 318.9 x 311.5 cm
Private collection
Courtesy Blum & Poe, Los Angeles
Pages 102, 104–05

Dumb Compass, 2008
Acrylic, gold leaf and platinum leaf on
canvas mounted on aluminum frame
300 x 234.4 cm
The Pinchuk Art Centre, Kyiv
Courtesy Blum & Poe, Los Angeles
Page 67

Infinity, 2008
Acrylic, gold leaf and platinum leaf on
canvas mounted on aluminum frame
300 x 234.4 cm
Private collection
Courtesy Blum & Poe, Los Angeles
Page 58, 62

*Kawaii — vacances <Summer vacation in the
Kingdom of the Golden>*, 2008
Acrylic and gold leaf on canvas mounted on
aluminum frame
300 x 900 cm
Private collection
Courtesy Galerie Perrotin, Paris
Pages 82–85

PINK-TIME, 2008
Acrylic on canvas mounted on aluminum
frame
300 x 300 cm
Private collection
Courtesy Galerie Perrotin, Paris
Pages 31, 33

Release Chakra's Gate at This Instant, 2008
Acrylic and platinum leaf on canvas
mounted on board
160 x 351 cm
Private collection
Courtesy Blum & Poe, Los Angeles
Pages 262–65

*And Then, When That's Done......I Change.
What I Was Yesterday Is Cast Aside, Like an
Insect Shedding Its Skin*, 2009
Acrylic on canvas mounted on board
300 x 300 cm
Private collection
Courtesy Galerie Perrotin, Paris
Page 19

BOKAN — camouflage pink, 2009
Acrylic on canvas mounted on
aluminum frame
300 x 300 cm
Private collection
Courtesy Gagosian Gallery
Page 37

Hustle 'n' Punch by Kaikai and Kiki, 2009
Acrylic and platinum leaf on canvas
mounted on aluminum frame
300 x 608 cm
The Broad Art Foundation, Santa Monica
Courtesy Galerie Perrotin, Paris
Pages 50–51

Kansei Kōrin Red Stream, 2009
Acrylic and gold leaf on canvas mounted
on board
150 cm diameter
Private collection
Courtesy Galerie Perrotin, Paris
Pages 76–77, 79

Kanye Bear, 2009
Aluminum, carbon fiber, urethane paint,
steel, and Corian base
121.5 x 64 x 64 cm
"Kanye Bear" is based on a character
appearing on the cover of Kanye West's
"Graduation" album.
Page 229

Lots, Lots of Kaikai and Kiki, 2009
Acrylic and platinum leaf on canvas
mounted on aluminum frame
300 x 608 cm
Private collection
Courtesy Gagosian Gallery
Pages 41, 48–49

Me and Double-DOB, 2009
Acrylic and platinum leaf on canvas
mounted on board
150 x 150 cm
Private collection, Taiwan
Courtesy Galerie Perrotin, Paris
Pages 189–91

Me and Kaikai and Kiki, 2009
Acrylic and platinum leaf on canvas
mounted on aluminum frame
160 x 160 cm
Private collection, Taiwan
Courtesy Galerie Perrotin, Paris
Page 192

NGC2371-2 (Gemini Nebula), 2009
Acrylic, platinum leaf and gold leaf on
canvas mounted on aluminum frame
300 x 234.4 cm
Private collection
Courtesy Galerie Perrotin, Paris
Pages 60–61, 65

Self-Portrait of the Distressed Artist, 2009
Acrylic and platinum leaf on canvas
mounted on aluminum frame
160 x 160 cm
Collection of Lisa and Steven Tananbaum
Courtesy Galerie Perrotin, Paris
Page 193

TIME — camouflage moss green, 2009
Acrylic on canvas mounted on
aluminum frame
300 x 300 cm
Private collection, Asia
Courtesy Gagosian Gallery, New York
Pages 34–36

Warhol/Gold, 2009
Acrylic and gold leaf on canvas mounted
on board
150 cm diameter
Collection of Adriana Abascal
Courtesy Galerie Perrotin, Paris
Page 74

Warhol/Silver, 2009
Acrylic and platinum leaf on canvas
mounted on board
150 cm diameter
Collection of Scott Hoffman
Courtesy Galerie Perrotin, Paris
Page 75

Warp, 2009
Acrylic, platinum leaf and gold leaf on
canvas mounted on aluminum frame
300 x 234.4 cm
The Broad Art Foundation, Santa Monica
Courtesy Galerie Perrotin, Paris
Page 66

Pom & Me, 2009–10
Aluminum, gold leaf, steel, and Corian base
133 x 107 x 90 cm
The Frank Cohen Collection, England
Courtesy Galerie Perrotin, Paris
Pages 179, 183

Pom & Me, 2009–10
Bronze, steel, and Corian base
133 x 107 x 90 cm
Collection Galerie Perrotin, Paris
Page 181

Pom & Me, 2009–10
Aluminum, platinum leaf, steel, and Corian base
133 x 107 x 90 cm
François Pinault Collection
Courtesy Galerie Perrotin, Paris
Page 183

Pom & Me, 2009–10
Carbon fiber, acrylic, and Corian base
133 x 107 x 90 cm
Page 185

Pom & Me, 2009–10
Carbon fiber, acrylic, and Corian base
133 x 107 x 90 cm
Private collection
Courtesy Galerie Perrotin, Paris
Page 184

Yume Lion (The Dream Lion), 2009–10
Carbon fiber, acrylic, steel, and Corian base
191 x 127 x 110 cm
Collection of Lisa and Steven Tananbaum
Courtesy Galerie Perrotin, Paris with cooperation from Tokyo MX
Page 241

Daruma Scale Models, 2009–11
Foamed styrol and resin
Various sizes from 6 x 23 x 23 cm to 379 x 240 x 240 cm
Pages 254–55, 257

Dragon in Clouds — Indigo Blue, 2010
Acrylic on canvas mounted on board
363 x 1800 cm
Collection of Larry Gagosian
Courtesy Gagosian Gallery
Pages 168–69

Dragon in Clouds — Red Mutation, 2010
Acrylic on canvas mounted on board
363 x 1800 cm
Private collection
Courtesy Gagosian Gallery
Pages 164–67

Even the Digital Realm Has Flowers to Offer!, 2010
Acrylic and platinum leaf on canvas mounted on board
150 diameter
Private collection
Courtesy Galerie Perrotin, Paris
Pages 71, 73

Kaikai Kiki and Me–For Better or Worse, in Good Times and Bad. The Weather Is Fine, 2010
Acrylic and platinum leaf on canvas mounted on aluminum frame
150 x 150 cm
Dr. Hong Family Collection
Courtesy Gagosian Gallery
Page 188

Kaikai Kiki Balloons, 2010
Polyurethane coated with nylon
1097.28 x 853.44 cm and 914.1 x 853.44 cm
Courtesy Macy's
Pages 55–57

Purple Flowers in a Bouquet, 2010
Acrylic and platinum leaf on canvas mounted on board
150 cm diameter
Private collection
Courtesy Galerie Perrotin, Paris
Page 72

Superflat Flowers, 2010
FRP, carbon fiber, steel, acrylic, and Corian base
287 x 450 x 91 cm
Collection Galerie Perrotin, Paris
Pages 86–87

Who's Afraid of Red, Yellow, Blue and Death, 2010
Acrylic on canvas mounted on aluminum frame
300 x 234.4 cm
Private collection
Courtesy Gagosian Gallery
Page 250

Wow, Kaikai Kiki, 2010–11
Acrylic and platinum leaf on canvas mounted on aluminum frame
300 x 608 cm
Private collection
Courtesy Galerie Perrotin, Paris
Pages 46–47

Big Box PKo², 2011
Carbon fiber, acrylic, and Corian base
236.5 x 232 x 233 cm
Sculpture based on papercraft illustration
by Sanpati, design by NC Empire, full scale
sculpture by Lucky-Wide Co., Ltd.
The Lalaland Collection
Courtesy Gagosian Gallery
Pages 238–39

END OF LINE, 2011
Acrylic on canvas mounted on board
300 x 234.4 cm
The Broad Art Foundation, Santa Monica
Courtesy Gagosian Gallery
Pages 248–49, 251

Of Chinese Lions, Peonies, Skulls, and Fountains, 2011
Acrylic on canvas mounted on board
300 x 600 cm
The Broad Art Foundation, Santa Monica
Courtesy Gagosian Gallery
Pages 244, 246–47

Oval Buddha Gold, 2011
Sterling silver, gold leaf and Corian base
161.5 x 84 x 84 cm
Courtesy Galerie Perrotin, Paris
Pages 172, 174–75

And Then x 6 (Blue), 2012
Acrylic on canvas mounted on board
300 x 300 cm
Page 21

And Then x 6 (Red), 2012
Acrylic on canvas mounted on board
300 x 300 cm
Courtesy Gagosian Gallery
Pages 16–17, 20

The 500 Arhats, 2012
Acrylic on canvas mounted on board
302 x 10000 cm
Courtesy Galerie Perrotin, Paris
Gatefolds, 148–49, 151–61

Heaven's Gate (Bases for *Tongari-kun* and the Four Guards), 2012
LED, plywood, steel, aluminum composite
Various sizes from 40 x 165 to 84 x 561 cm diameter
Page 94

Kaikai Kiki Board, 2012
Inkjet mounted on board
326 x 689 cm
Pages 206–07

Murakami—Ego Monster, 2012
Steel structure and fabric
100 x 240 x 150 cm
Courtesy Galerie Perrotin, Paris
Pages 204–05

Six ♡ Princess: Battle Formation, 2012
Acrylic on canvas mounted on
aluminum frame
214 x 270 cm
Courtesy Gagosian Gallery.
Production sketches by Mizutamago
Pages 212–15

Six ♡ Princess: Friends Forever, 2012
Acrylic on canvas mounted on
aluminum frame
275 x 214.8 cm
Courtesy Gagosian Gallery.
Production sketches by Mebae
Page 216

Welcome to Murakami Ego, 2012
Inflatable structure
600 x 545.6 x 623 cm
Courtesy Galerie Perrotin, Paris
Pages 197–99

World of Lotus (Base for *Oval Buddha*), 2012
LED, plywood, steel, aluminum composite
95 x 310 cm
Pages 106–07

Takashi Murakami & Pharrell Williams
The Simple Things, 2008–09
Glass fiber, steel, acrylic, wood, LED and
7 objects made of gold (white, yellow, and
pink) set with rubies, sapphires, emeralds,
and diamonds
188 x 110 x 101 cm
Collection of Adriana Abascal and
Cathy Vedovi
Courtesy Galerie Perrotin, Paris
Pages 234–35

FILMS

Kaikai and Kiki Animation Episode 1:
Planting the Seeds, 10'30", 2008

Kaikai and Kiki Animation Episode 2:
The Secret of Kaikai, 11'20", 2008
Animation production by OLM&OLM Digital

Kaikai and Kiki Animation Episode 3:
Preview *A Perilous Journey*, 50", 2012
Pages 208–09

Six ♡ Princess, **Opening Title, 1'30", 2010**

Six ♡ Princess, **Ending Title, 1'30", 2010**
Pages 218–21

Six ♡ Princess, **Episode 1 Preview, 32", 2012**

Preview Trailer, *Jellyfish Eyes*, 2', 2012
Pages 201–03

Kanye West Music Video, *Good Morning*,
3'30", 2007
©2007 Takashi Murakami/Kaikai Kiki Co.,Ltd./
Kanye West/International West Holdings, LLC.
All Rights Reserved.
Animation Production by OLM Digital
Pages 222–25

ACKNOWLEDGMENTS

This catalog was published in conjunction with "Murakami — Ego," an exhibition organized by the Qatar Museums Authority at Al Riwaq in Doha, February 9 to June 24, 2012.

Exhibition initiated by His Excellency Sheikh Jassim bin Abdulaziz bin Jassim Al Thani

QATAR MUSEUMS AUTHORITY
Her Excellency Sheikha Al Mayassa Bint Hamad Bin Khalifa Al Thani, Chairperson
His Excellency Sheikh Hassan bin Mohammed bin Ali Al Thani, Vice Chairman
Abdulla Al Najjar, CEO
Edward Dolman, Executive Vice Chairperson

Exhibition Curator
Massimiliano Gioni

Public Art Department QMA
Jean-Paul Engelen, Director
Katharina Schulz-Hertzog, Curator Al Riwaq
Jeroen Vahrmeijer, Head of Installation & Design
Hala Al Khalifa, Education Manager
Khalid Ali, Multimedia Specialist
Sheikha Maryam bint Abdulaziz Al Thani, Marketing & Public Relations

We would like to thank all the lenders for their generosity. A special thanks to Blum & Poe; Gagosian Gallery; Galerie Perrotin; Nicolai Frahm and Frahm, Ltd.; Giraud.Pissarro.Segalot, New York-Paris; The Heller Group.

Photography Credits
Pages 1, 5, 14–15, 22–24, 27, 38–39, 42–45, 52–53, 68–69, 80–81, 86–89, 91–94, 98–102, 104–110, 136–149, 151–163, 170–172, 174–177, 179, 186–187, 194–195, 197–199, 204–207, 210–211, 226–227, 232–233, 237, 242–244, 252–255, 257–259, 268: photos Ambroise Tezenas
Pages 6–7: courtesy Christie's Images, Ltd.
Pages 8–13, 19, 21, 31, 33, 46–47, 50–51, 60–61, 65, 66, 71–77, 79, 82–85, 181–185, 189–193, 234–235, 241: courtesy Galerie Perrotin
Pages 16–17, 20, 34–37, 41, 48–49, 164–169, 188, 238–239, 246–251, 260–261: courtesy Gagosian Gallery
Pages 24, 244, 248–49: photos by Christto Saz and Khalid Ali
Page 28: photo Lesley Chi
Pages 55–57: photos GION
Pages 58, 62, 67, 262–265: courtesy Blum & Poe
Pages 84–85: photos courtesy Sylvie Van Roey and Khalid Ali
Pages 112, 114: photos QMA

Catalogue and "Murakami — Ego" logo design
Takaya Goto and Lesley Chi with Jillian Coulton and Sho Momma, Goto Design, New York

The Qatar Museums Authority and Takashi Murakami wish to thank:
QATAR MUSEUMS AUTHORITY
Ibrahim Abbas Abdulrahim, Mohammed Osman Ahmed, Hessa Al Ali, Abdulrahman Ali Al Amadi, Reham Hamdy Al Anany, Dana Al Ansari, Wafaa Salem Al Atawi, Ali Hassan Al Bilal, Nasser Falah Al Dosari, Nahed Al Emadi, Fadalah Yousif Al Fadalah, Ahmed Al Hail, Hamad Al Hajri, Hamad Saeed Al Hassan, Abdulla Abdulla Al Hemadi, Muez Ali, Aisha Al Khater, Mai Ali Al-Kubaisi, Mohammed Jumah Al Kuwari, Sara Al Maadheed, Nisreen Mohammed Al Malek, Fahad Al Mansoori, Mohammed Al Mansoori, Abdulla Al-Athba Al-Marri, Mubarak Al Mohannadi, Aisha Abdulh Al Nameh, Aisha Al Obidly, Sinan Al Qaysi, Sheikha Jawaher bint Abdulaziz Al Thani, Sheikh Fahad Al Thani, Kholoud Yousuf Al Saai, Fatma Al Said, Saad Al Sharim, Yasmin Al Sharshani, Laila Gholam Azad, Steve Barclay, Daniel Brown, Salam Chagary, Omar Chaikhouni, Louise Cutajar, Deanne Dewar, Madian Fatayerji, Andrew Foster, Fani Gouziou, Jasper Hwang, Ibtissam Ibtihaj, Younes Janahi, Taghreed Abas Kamal, Nibras Kardaman, Boushra Kassab, Travers Lee, Roger Earl Mandle, Tarik Mountassir, Melina Gama de Moura, Angelina Mountford, Walid Nashwan, Johanna Olafsdotter, Orlando Vincent Pereira, Rana Refaat, Susan Rees, Olivia Reynolds, Diana Rizk, Christo Sanz, John Shields, Richard Bagnall Smith, Saleh Tayani, Joy Marie Ticod, Merridy Wilson, Federica Zuccarini

KAIKAI KIKI CO., LTD.—**Project Management**—Chiaki Kasahara, Mai Miyazaki, Natsuyo Kawaoka, Tomoko Kuroda, Kensuke Ito, Syuhei Iwamoto—**Legal**—Daisuke Murakoshi—**Reception**—Mizuho Takezawa, Yuka Takahashi—**Translation**—Reiko Anzaki—**Accounting**—Miki Hara, Yuko Ito, Naomi Uema—**HR**—Yuki Kajiwara—**Hidari Zingaro**—Atsushi Taima, Ryo Suzuki, Mai Fukuda, Mami Niijima, Maasa Arai, Sanshirou Ogawa, Eriko Ueda, Ryuji Hikosaka, Kouichi Ohno, Shinpei Miura—**GEISAI**—Takumi "Kasenyan" Kaseno, Haruka Kashiwazaki, Bruna Christina Terayama, Shota Yamada—**Systems**—Norikazu Nemoto, Yusuke Nakaya—**Maintenance**—Koichiro Endo, Masashi Ito, Koji Ito—**Merchandise**—Toshiki Ishii, Teppei Yamazaki, Noriko Takahashi, Misako Sugimoto, Kazumi Muto, Tomoko Kajiyama, Natsumi Kobayashi, Yoshimi Yamagishi, Shizuko Kajiyama, Ryoko Kojima, Kurumi Hisanaga, Yasuhiro Koma, Rikako Kawasaki—**Painting Director**—SHISHO—**The 500 Arhats Painting Production Team (Drafting)**—Yuki Sinoo, Maeri Makuno, Seira Fukuta, Takuya Fukukawa, Aya Saimoto, Yuka Oyama, Yoshihiro Takeuchi, Yuto Sakagami, Mizuki Abe, Satomi Soga, Kiyoshi Muto, Yasuko Eto, Kaori Soutome—**Data Operation**—Yuki Oshima, Nana Miyagi, Ayako Irie, Saki Kobayashi, Ayaki Yamane, Masato Watanabe, Yota Yamashita, Shuro Okayasu, Maaya Shimoda, Yuki Morimoto, Ryo Saito, Takashi Shiraishi, Issei Murakami—**Chief Painters**—Ai Ebato, Taizo Sugimoto, Yutaka Sugiyama, Satomi Kawasaki, Kotomi Shiraishi—**Painters**—Kazuko Suzuki, Haruka Nakajo, Katsuya Kiyota, Ikki Ando, Masaaki Kuno, Moe Matsuhashi, Nozomi Hirata, Gaku Shimogaito, Tomoyuki Mitani, Yoshikazu Hirata, Ryu Saito, Megumi Yamamoto, Naosuke Wada, Ayako Funakoshi, Yoshie Nogami, Maiko Kimura, Masaki Okuten, Yoshihiro Ishiduka, Yoichi Ishikawa, Yoshitaka Fukano, Eriko Mine, Yuki Kawai, Toshiki Kikuchi, Marina Akiyoshi, Sachiko Odachi, Aiko Sonoda, Kota Horikoshi, Hiroko Nobuto, Kaori Yoshida, Tatsuma Takeda, Satoshi Mimura, Kaede Nakano, Ai Shimada, Mai Takagi, Yujiro Uetake,

Miki Amemiya, Akane Koide, Yukiko Oyama, Fumiaki Yoshida, Yukari Motoyama, Toshiyuki Maeda, Mai Sone, Yasuko Eto, Chigusa Kondo, Chifumi Kobayashi, Masaki Sato, Takuya Kumagai, Marina Isawa, Yusuke Toda, Takanori Ishii, Seisuke Momono, Haruka Tokita, Wataru Yasuda, Masao Hieno, Maki Kurata, Genya Ito, Yuka Wakabayashi, Ami Fujiki, Shiho Ito, Sayoko Yoshizawa, Yuri Fukaya, Serino Yamaguchi, Ryo Yanagisawa, Sena Nagata, Satomi Uchida, Aki Sumida, Syohei Hayashi, Haruko Soma, Sakurako Iida, Maki Fukai, Akinobu Tsukamoto, Satomi Uchida, Takuya Watanabe, Akiho Hijikata, Yuri Yonemoto, Chihiro Shimzu, Miharu Yamamoto, Sena Nagata, Misa Hiramatu, Yudai Ohara, Yuki Daimon, Kanako Ikeda, Miki Hayakawa, Noriko Takeda, Asami Koyano, Kentaro Yokozeki, Miki Sasaki, Kinu Morita, Mao Maeda, Kyoko Miyamoto, Nanae Mochiduki, Hikaru Nakase, Junpei Matsue, Takashi Fujimoto, Shion Oguchi, Ayumi Hayasaka, Akeno Yamamura, Haruka Nizeki, Misa Hiramatu, Etsuko Sugawara, Motoki Ikeda, Minoru Ishida, Ayaka Takenoshita, Rentaro Murachi, Emi Nakamura, Akiha Simizu, Monami Ono, Tomomi Shimaoka, Maroki Yagisawa, Junichi Umedu, Koki Omae, Mizuki Eguchi, Ayane Shiraishi, Yurika Hatori, Keiko Tosabayashi, Aiko Sonoda, Takayuki Ishii, Kozue Kitayama, Ippei Kimura, Kai Murakami, Yuriko Matsuo, Gakudai Kawasumi, Hirono Yamakage, Setutagugen—**Scout Caravan**—Maki Momono, Maika Kozu, Kazuko Suzuki, Yutaka Sugiyama, Taizo Sugimoto, Gaku Shimogaito, Masaki Sato—**Painting Administrative Director**—Koichiro Endo—**Art Handler**—Jun Tagawa—**Studio Manager**—Mitsuru Oguma, Mariko Ueda—**Artist's Assistant**—Shoko Suzuki—**Studio Administration**—Toshiko Wada, Ayumi Hashimoto, Eriko Murakami, Hideko Takeuchi—**Studio Maintenance**—Aiko Hamahira, Chinatsu Okamoto, Chifumi Okumura, Natue Hirayama, Kunie Tozawa, Ritsuko Yamaguchi, Keiko Shino, Taizo Moriya, Tomoko Akimoto, Kayoko Komine, Makiko Kodayashi, Yoshio Maehara, Machiko Kurauchi, Ritsu Aikawa, Mitsuko Murakami, Yoshihiko Hirano, Masataka Ochiai—**Over Drive Co., Ltd.**—Atsushi Saga—**Kaikai Kiki Gallery Taipei**—Chiang Ming-Yu, Guan Tseng, Mikan Kuo, Sophie Tseng—**Kaikai Kiki New York, LLC**—**Administrative Director**—Masako Iida—**Installation**—Shinichi Kitahara, Sayaka Toyama—**Project**—Nao Tazaki, Bradley Plumb, Alan Seise, Kentaro Ikegami—**Painters**—Ivanny A. Pagan, Germaine Chang, Kristen Leone, Jan Descartes, Yohei Watanabe, Siho Yoon, Katherine Korns, Jeb Long, Guillaume Ziccarelli—**Lucky Wide Co., Ltd.**—Hirohisa Yoshizawa, Hiroki Iijima, Makoto Dohi, Tsukasa Morohashi, Hironori Ushio, Chikahiro Yamada, Tomoyuki Arai, Yohei Naito, Takeshi Nagata, Nao Saito, Ryo Kakinuma, Morimasa Shimizu, Terumi Fujimori, Shotaro Niikura, Ryota Kawauchi, Yuji Kinoshita, Yusuke Yokozawa, Keita Kunizuka, Tsuneto Baba, Hiroaki Iwauchi, Seiko Kikuchi, Shiho Fujimoto, Miyako Ito, Shinobu Hasegawa—**Curatorial Assistants**—Jenny Moore, Gary Carrion-Murayari, Marguerite Lauras, Quentin Beun—**Atelier Zeus**—Seiji Miyamoto—**Uchida Co., Ltd.**—Tadahito Ogino, Kazuhiro Yokota, Junpei Ochiai, Hideo Toyofuku—**Takibi Kikaku**—Yoshihiro Miyashita, Shingo Amakata, Shin Takaoka, Takashi Inukai—**Kobayashi Kogei**—Shinji Kobayashi—**Koko No Shokunin**—Tomohiro Yamamoto—**Creation Kikaku**—Shigeru Aoki, Fumiko Yaguchi, Satoru Tozawa—**Izawa Kougyoujo**—Masatoshi Izawa—**Kenshi Art**—Kozue Higurashi, Takeo Shintani—**Kurotani Bijutsu**—Munehiro Kurotani, Akinobu Oosawa, Yoshiharu Nishida, Masahiro Kushida, Susumu Kuse, Tsuyoshi Kobayashi, Kazutaka Terabayashi, Ryo Hori, Kazuo Utsunomiya, Michio Watanabe, Taku Takaghi, Ruriko Shimasaku, Eiji Shima—**Sano Douki Chakushokujo**—Shigeru Sano—**Aerotech**—Yasuhiro Osone, Okimitsu Osone, Masaru Soeda, Junya Ichihashi, Kazuko, Atsuta, Riri Ito, Risa Hoshina, Teruko Tomita, Akiko Nakajima, Tomomi Nakabayashi—**Jiyuro—Jiro**, Katsumi Numasaki, Takeshi Ukita, Minoru Nakajima, Tateo Mitsuwa—Tetsuya Tamanoi—**Sun Arrow Co., Ltd.**—Masaaki Seki, Satoru Matai, Mizuki Konno, Satomi Toyonaga—**Shaco Co., Ltd—Earth Work**—Hisoka Miyauchi—**Sun Ad Balloon**—Yasuro Kiribe—**Rediaworks**—Fumito Kobayashi, Teruyoshi Higuchi, Seiko Ogasawara—**Kosakusha—Lucius Hudson—Tokai Shoji Co., Ltd.—Seripack Co., Ltd.—Eguchi Kohan Co., Ltd.—Tokyu Process, Ltd.—Holbein Works, Ltd.**—Takashi Konuma—**OLM Inc.**—Toshiaki Okuno, Syukichi Kanda, Tokuhiro Matsubara, Shoji Ota—**OLM Digital Inc.**—Misako Saka, Megumi Kondo—**Studio Jack Co., Ltd.**—Katsuyoshi Kanemura—**Geek Pictures Inc.**—Tamotsu Kosano—**Melody Punch Inc.**—Toru

Midorikawa, Eiko Sakurai, Azumi Inoue, Hana Takamizawa, Shizuka, Tatsuya Osabe, Junko Takeuchi, Mahito Tsujimura, Kanye West—**Universal Music Group**—Def Jam Recordings, The Island Def Jam Music Group, Pharrell Williams—**Think Corporation**—Hiroaki Takeuchi, Nozomi Seike—**Studio Poncotan**—Mebae—**Tyo-Animations Inc.**—Satoshi Yamaguchi, Junichi Sato—**Cinegriot Inc.**—Masashi Sakamoto, Yuetsu Murakami—**Love & Light**—Mayumi Gojo, Osamu Kobayashi, Takashi Yamashita—**Nishimura Eizo**—Yoshihiro Nishimura, Mana Fukui, Takeshi Wada, Nanae Yoshida—**Studio Buckhorn**—Tsuyoshi Kazuno—**Studio Higemegane**—Taiga Ishino—**Office Hara**—Nori Fukuda—**Incs Toenter**—Kz, Ryo Uchiyama, Jun Tsugita, Jun Shiozaki, Yasutaka Nagano, Jun Kojima, Kazuki Yunoki, Chieko Shimizu, Yuji Saito, Isao Karasawa, Takuto Sueoka, Himeka Asami, Takumi Saito, Mayu Tsuruta, Asuka Kurosawa—**Hasenkamp**—Hans Ewald Schneider, Uwe Hoehne, Massimiliano Lodi, Joerg Kuester, Stefan Glade, Michael Bissot, Robert Schneider, Rudi Beran, Michael Winters, Theo Buettgenbach, Udo Pfotenhauer, Reinhard Moeller, Günter Rech, Mike Engelmann, Ortwin Schieb, Valentin Geck, Frank Neumann, Andy Herde, Patrick Kliem, David Reinwald, Ralf Wedekind, Robert Jaenisch, Florian Endres, Torsten Fricke, Rob Saamena, Jelmer De Porto, Sander Huiberts,—**Yamato Logistics Co., Ltd.**—Shinobu Taniguchi, Shizuka Hayashi, Masaru Shono, Takuya Ichiyama, Takeshi Miyashita, Takahiro Inoue, Isao Sakamoto, Hiroshi Okuma, Koichi Deguchi , Hajime Takayanagi, Kenji Iwasaki, Hidejiro Kudo, Akihiro Fukuzawa, Takahiro Hirano, Kaoru Ohashi, Fumio Murata, Miki Hirose—**KGL**—Amal Mustafa, Hassan Mokthar—**Qatar Airways**—Akbar Al Baker, Mohammed Azim, Roopesh Shetty—**Qatar Customs**—Ahmed Ali Almohandi, Ahmad Almass—**Bruening und Schubert**—Michael Schubert, Sandra Schaefer—**Interspace**—Kevin David White, Robin Paul Drakestone, Marais Gerhaud Smit, Jothikumaran, Srinivas Raju, Majumdar, Agnel Mordom, Claudio Natalio, Kularathna Agalawatte, Gyanendra Raiman, Naresh Ram, Dinesh Ram, Parikshit Golder, Vishwanath, Roy Abhimanya, Prasad Durjan, Ram Guddur Navik, Albert Yesuvadiyan, Subash Chand Nagar, Priyanath Biswas, Ram Samujh Prasad, Ramesh Prasad, Manik Chand, Surendra Rama Shankar, Ramachandra Chowdary, VAdan Kumar, Chakyar Kuzhiyil, Rajeev Kanakamma, Robinson Appavu, Esakkimuthu Jaganathan, Dennis Gabriel, Sohan Kumar Sahni, Upendra Singh, Anjaya Pitla, Deeplal Prasad, Karuppu Panja, Gangadhar, Lalith Kumar, Sanil Kumar, Gurnek Singh, Rambhadur Subedi, Neelam Kumar, Magar Singh, Bharat Biswas, Matrika Prasad, Dinesh Kumar Ram, Subash Narayanan, Binod Kumar, Narasimalu, Ravindra Kailash, Deepak Ghosh, Karthik Rama Murthy, Ravindra Rajbar, Rakesh Singh, Rajesh Dharma Rajan, Pittambar Yadav, Padam Narayan Raj, Rajabanshi, Ashok Chauhan, Sarvesh Chauhan, Senthil Rathinam, John Mathai, Muthuswamy Ramaya, Subash Sharma, Ravindra Shah, Jitendra Vishwakarma, Ram Ashish, Eshwar Misthri, Ram Suresh, Chandip Rajkumar Shah—**Macy's Parade and Entertainment Group**—Amy Kule, Stephanie Logan, John Piper, Fobert Pfitzenmeier, Jim Artle, Danny Jones—**Lumatron**—Talal Wehbe, Henry Silva, Salim Abilmona, George Tellos, Luisa Valenti, Brenn Barretto, Albert Celen, Mamuka Natchkebia, Neil Eballar, Carlo Acolea, Ian Aaron Anarna, Nomer Nungay, Mariel Inosanto—**Goto Design**—Takaya Goto, Lesey Chi—**Brownbook**—Rashid Bin Shabib, Ahmed Bin Shabib, Vanessa Purcell, Christopher Read, Jerry Balloch, Matthew Russell, Alma Kamal, Danielle Simpson, Nahda Suleiman, Anna Seaman, Jack Taylor—**Urban Way**—Erik Ranieri, Didier Melouk, Olivier Mazau, Limay Tonguet—**Radici**—Antonio Gallo, Saul Guio, Savoldelli Francesco, Laura Mottalini, Isabella Zammito, Paolo Pozzi, Luciano Moro, Claudio Moro—**Neon Circus**—Dom Ellis, Mike Harradine, Mark Wade, Dan Shaw, Vlad SHotropa, Antony Williams—**The Darkroom**—Bruce Ferguson, Emma Wolf—**Photography**—Ambroise Tezenas, Gion, Chika Okazumi, Guillaume Ziccarelli—**Digital and Post-Production**—D-Factory—**Production**—Art Department Europe—**VSO/BHD**—Fabien Legrand, Martine Teil, Joël Beziat, Jocelyne Badet, Francisca Castagnet, Yannick Champagne, Mostefa Ghanmi, Didier Mohsen Banan, Bernard Moncourrier, Bruno Sansfacon, Loic Thillet, Sébastien Thillet, Maryse Trochon, Philippe Jaffredo, Sylvain Lobet, Nicolas Gely, Bruno Hervy—**Logyline**—Théophane Langlais—**BHD IN**—Fabrice Amprino—**ST-IC**—Alain Dessard—**Anceschi**—Umberto and Samantha Anceschi—**Hemaya Security Services Co.**—Mohammed Al-Ansari, Mohammed Al-Sharshani

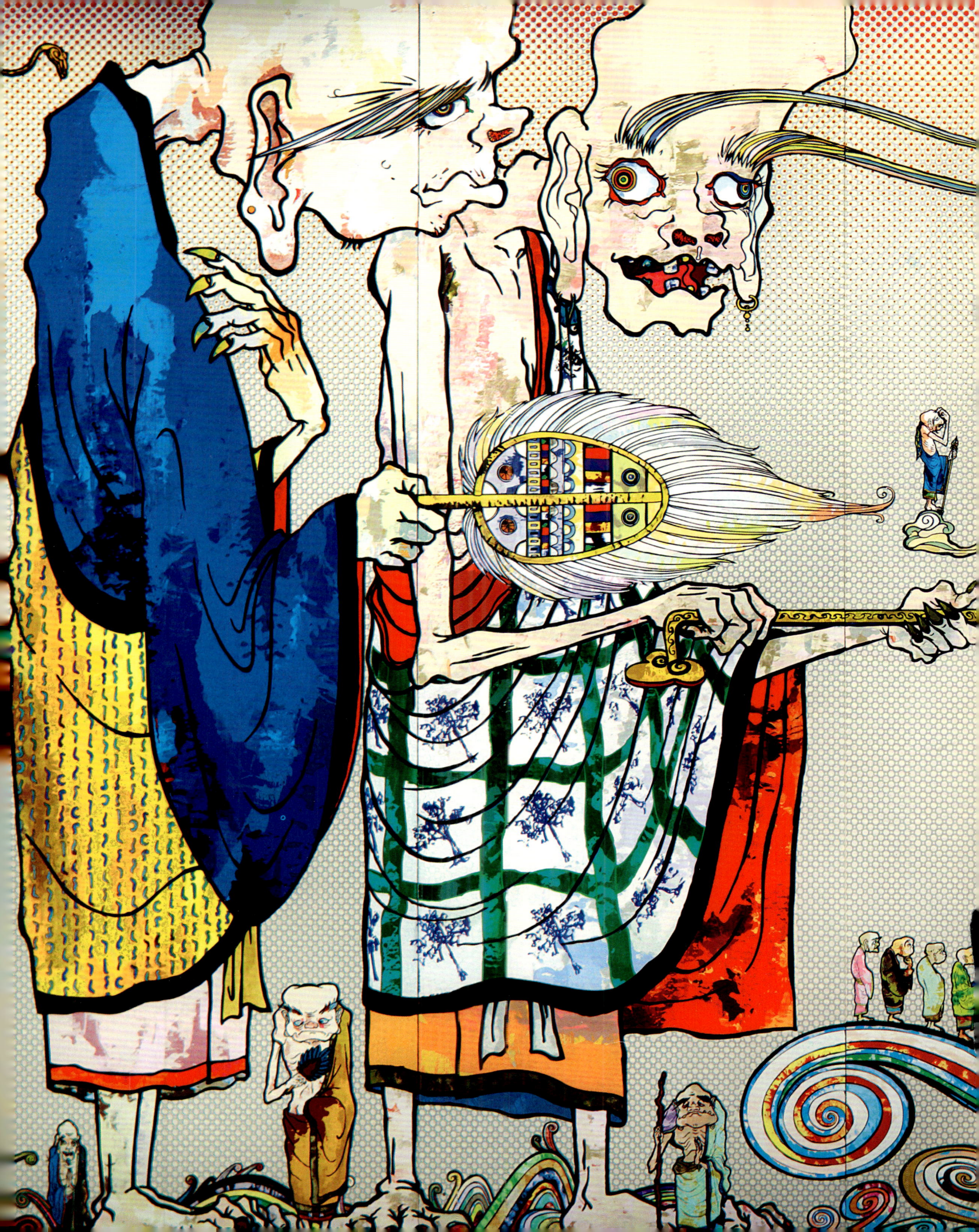

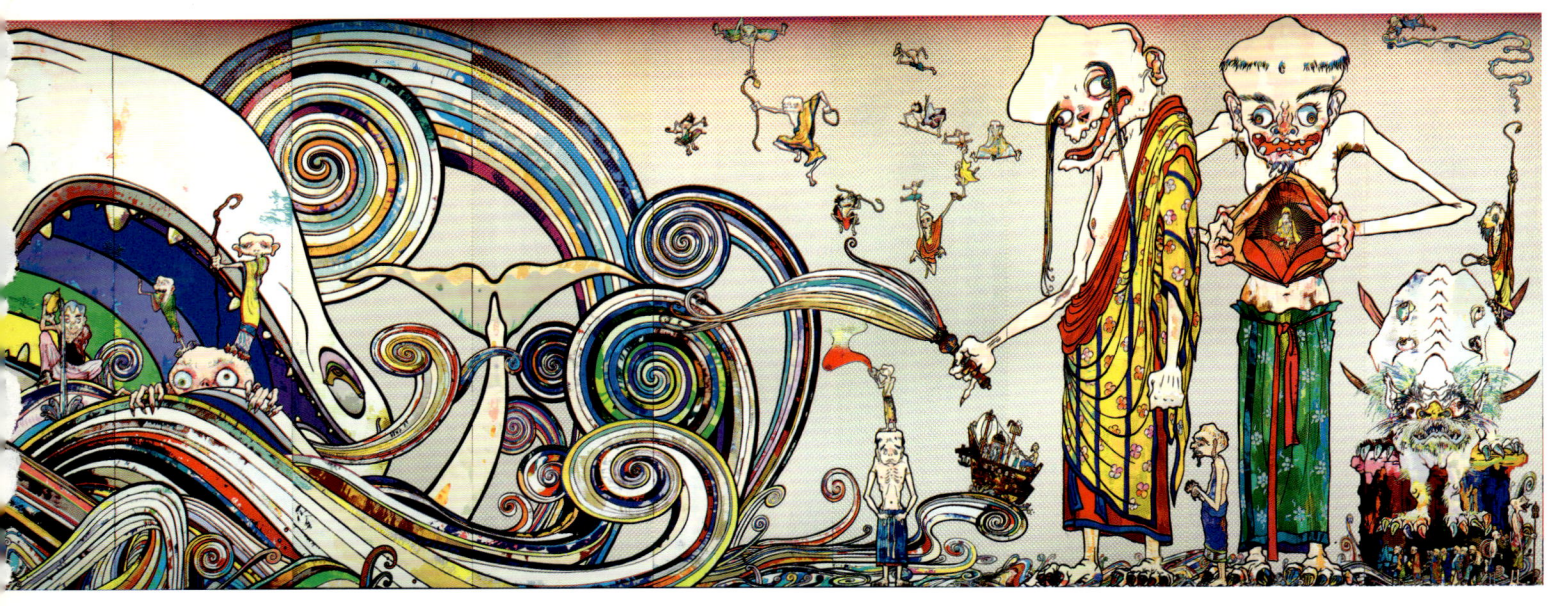

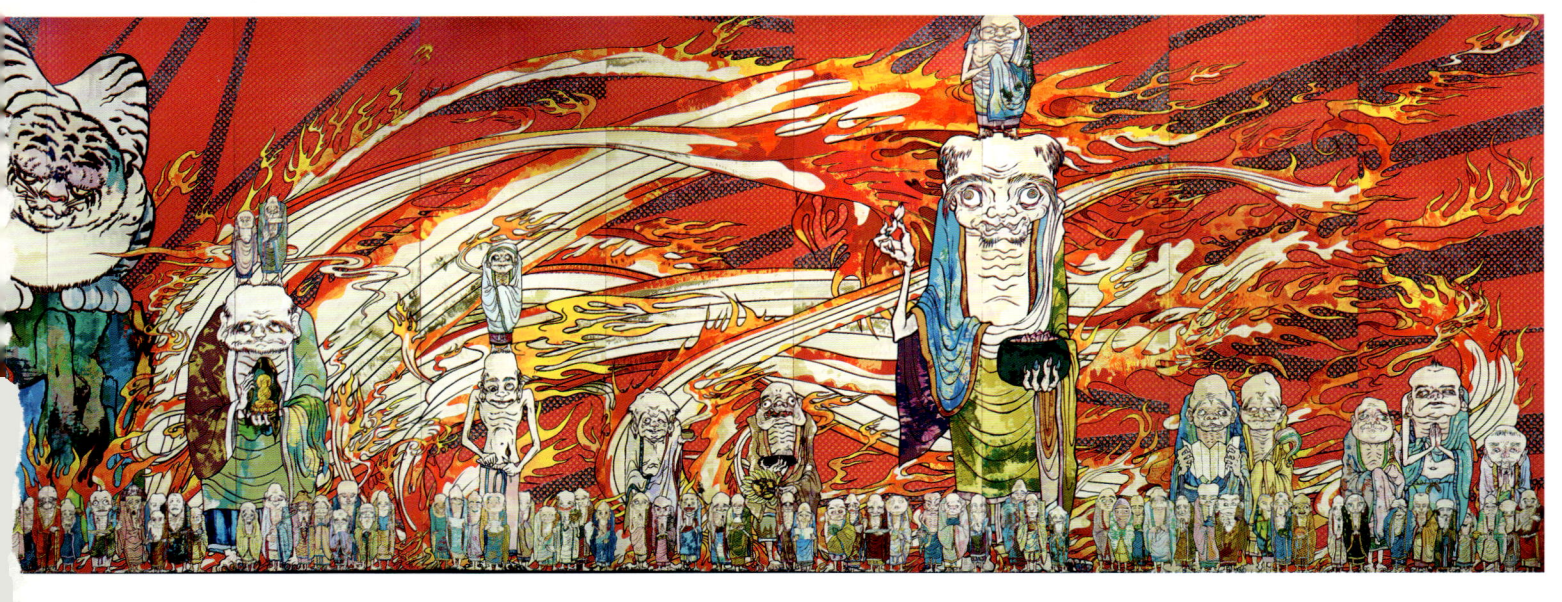

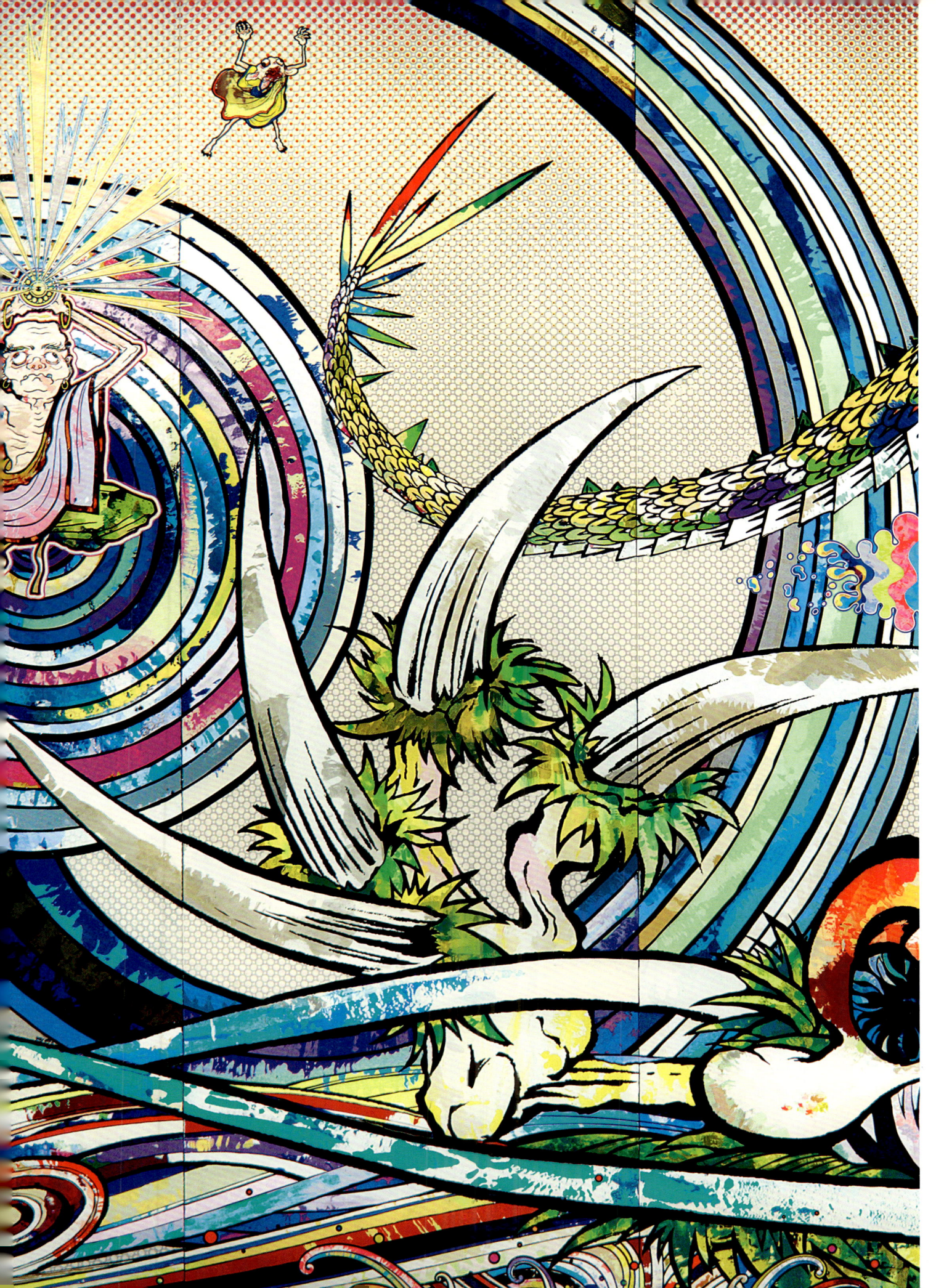

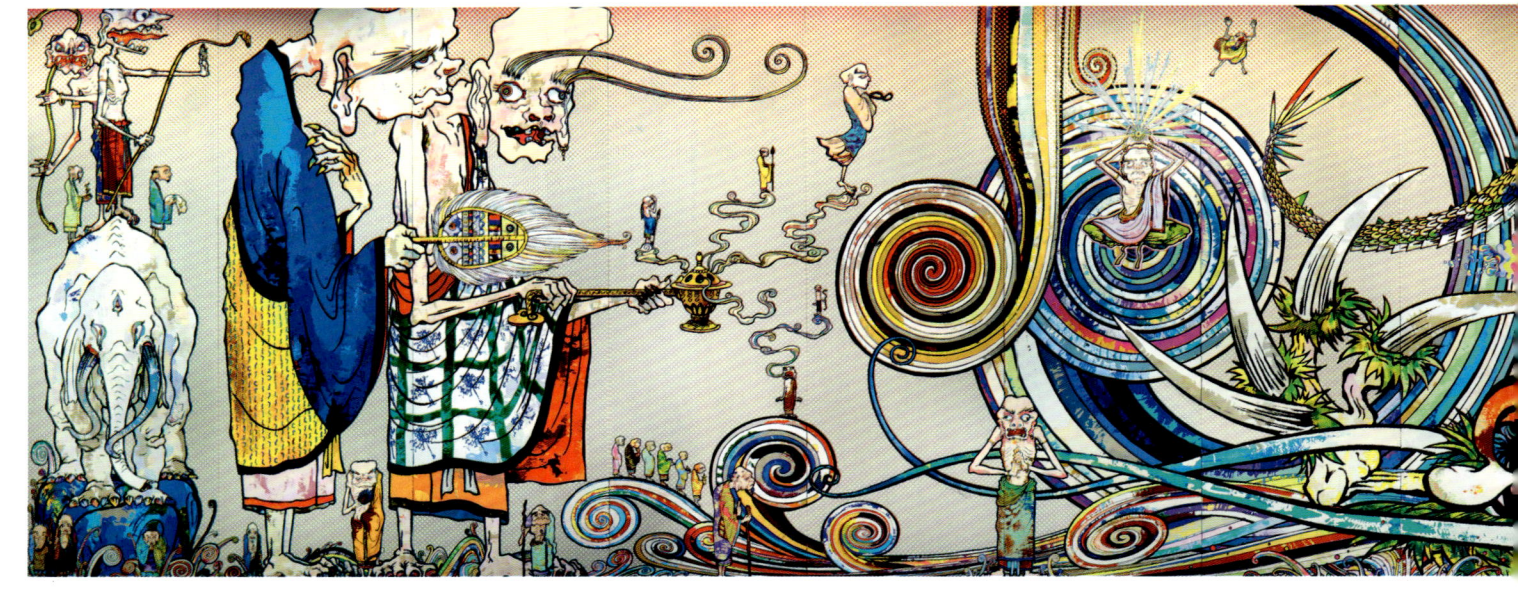

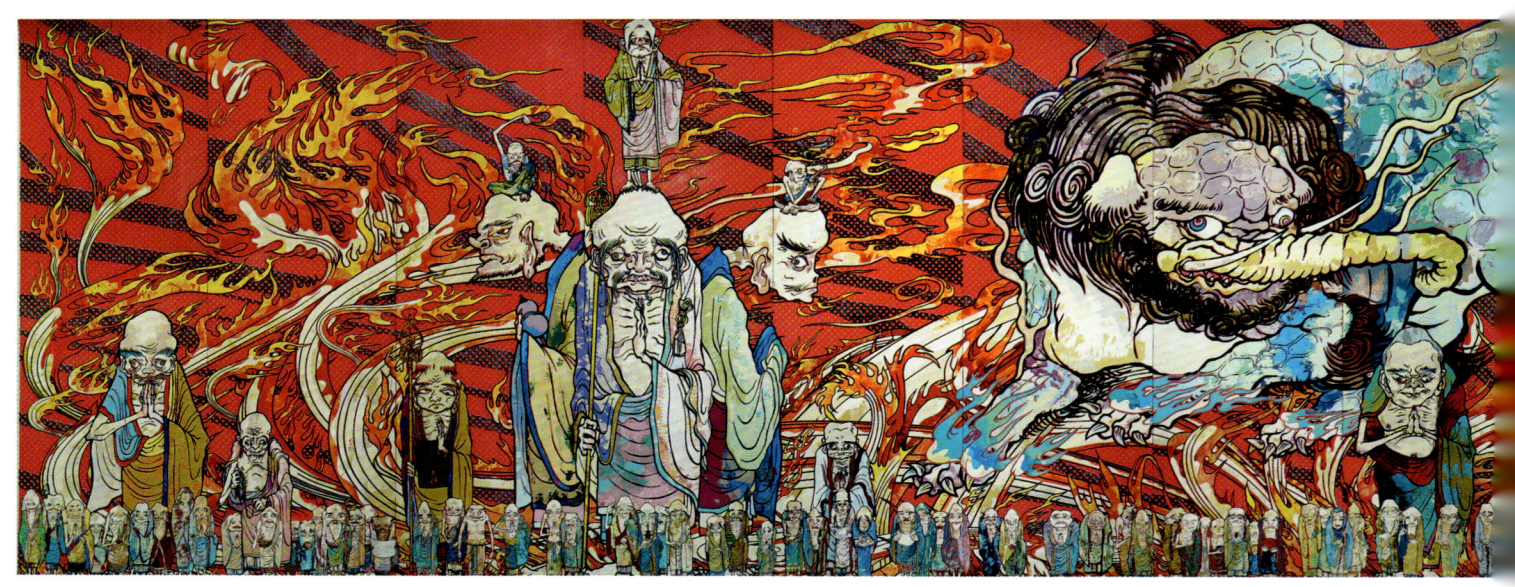

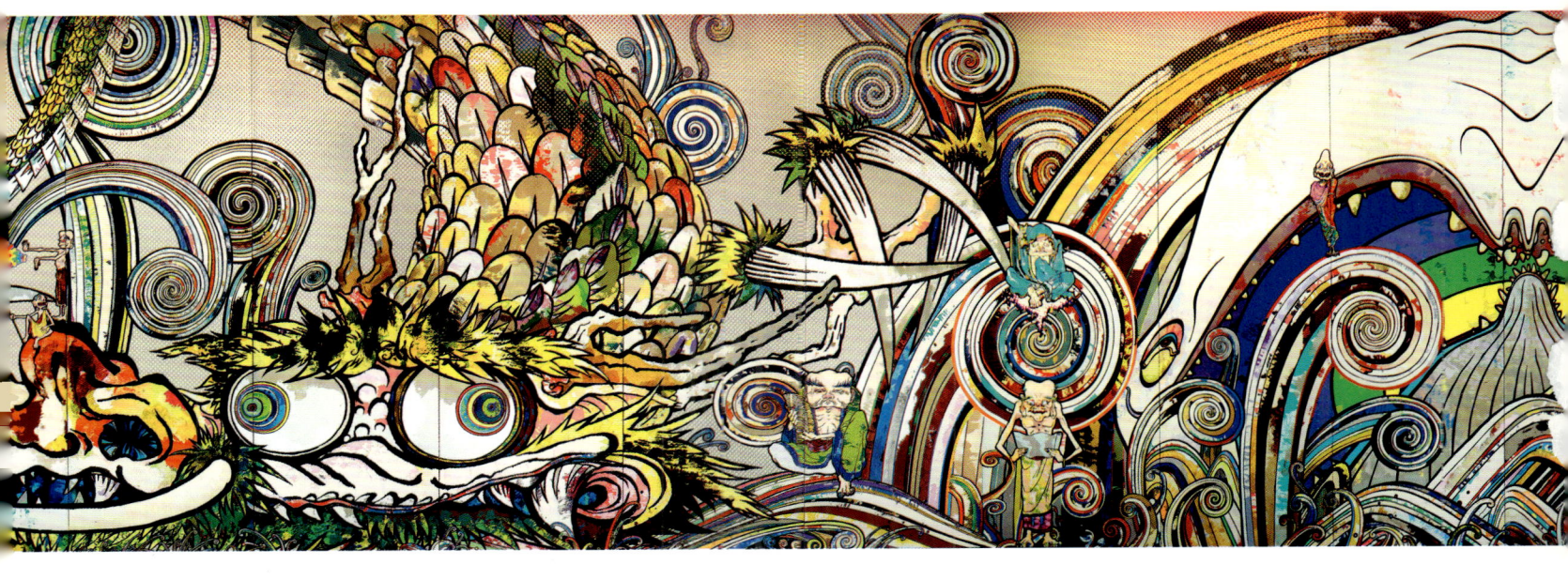

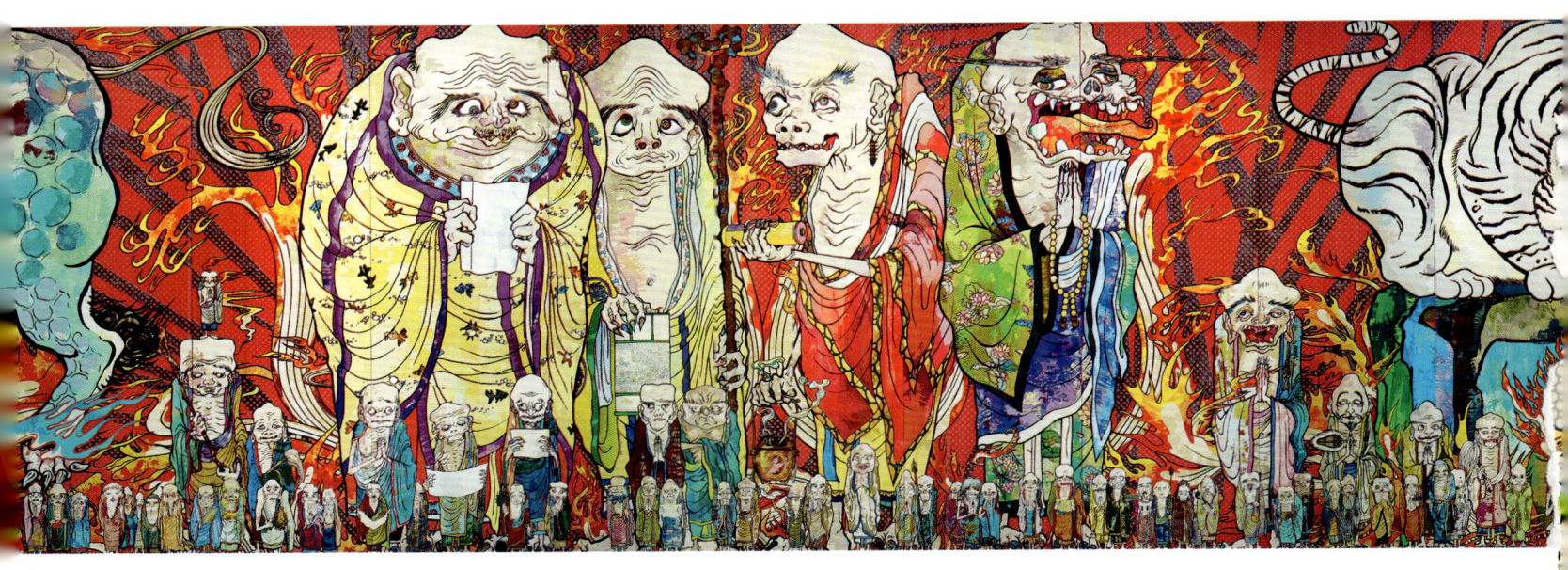

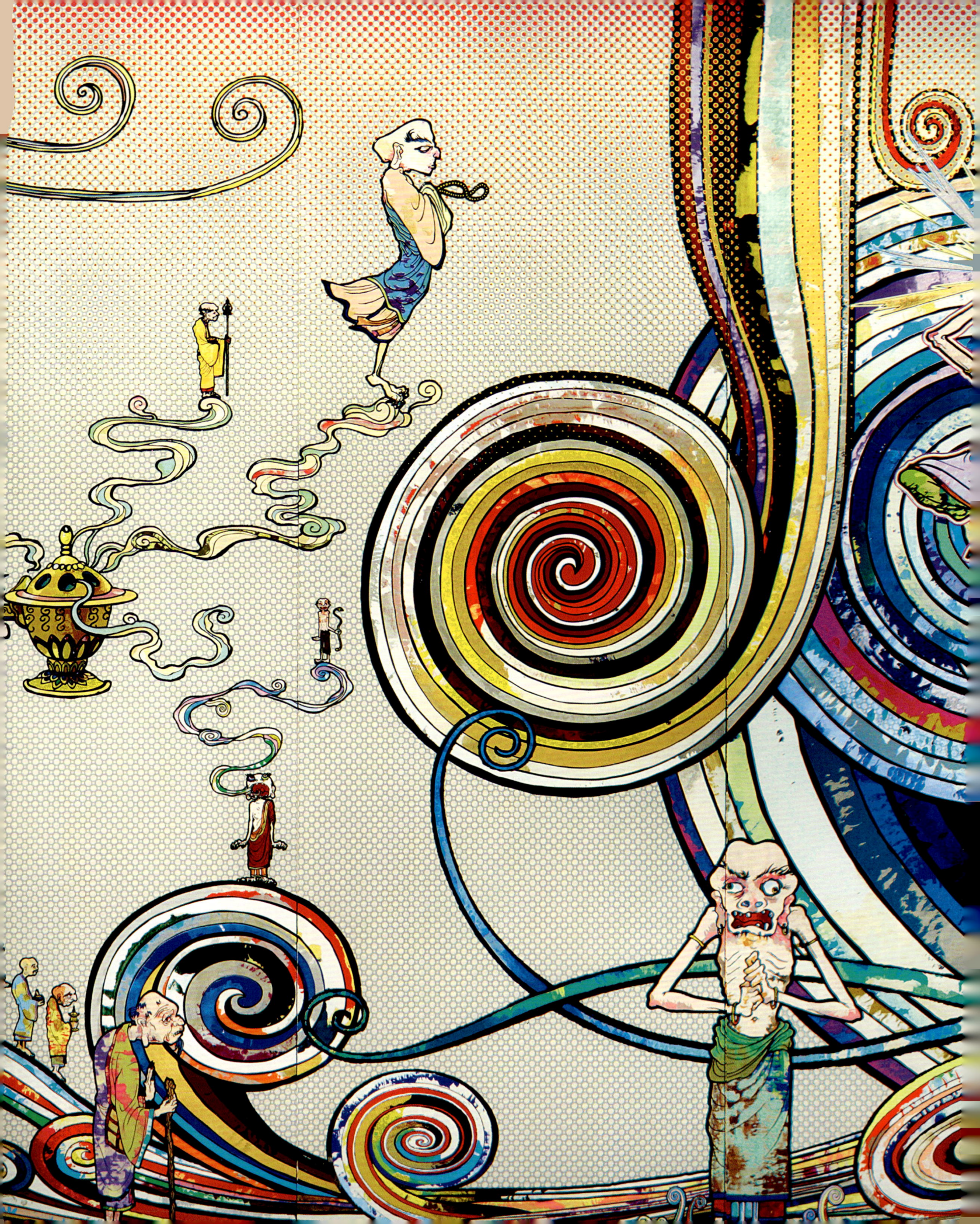

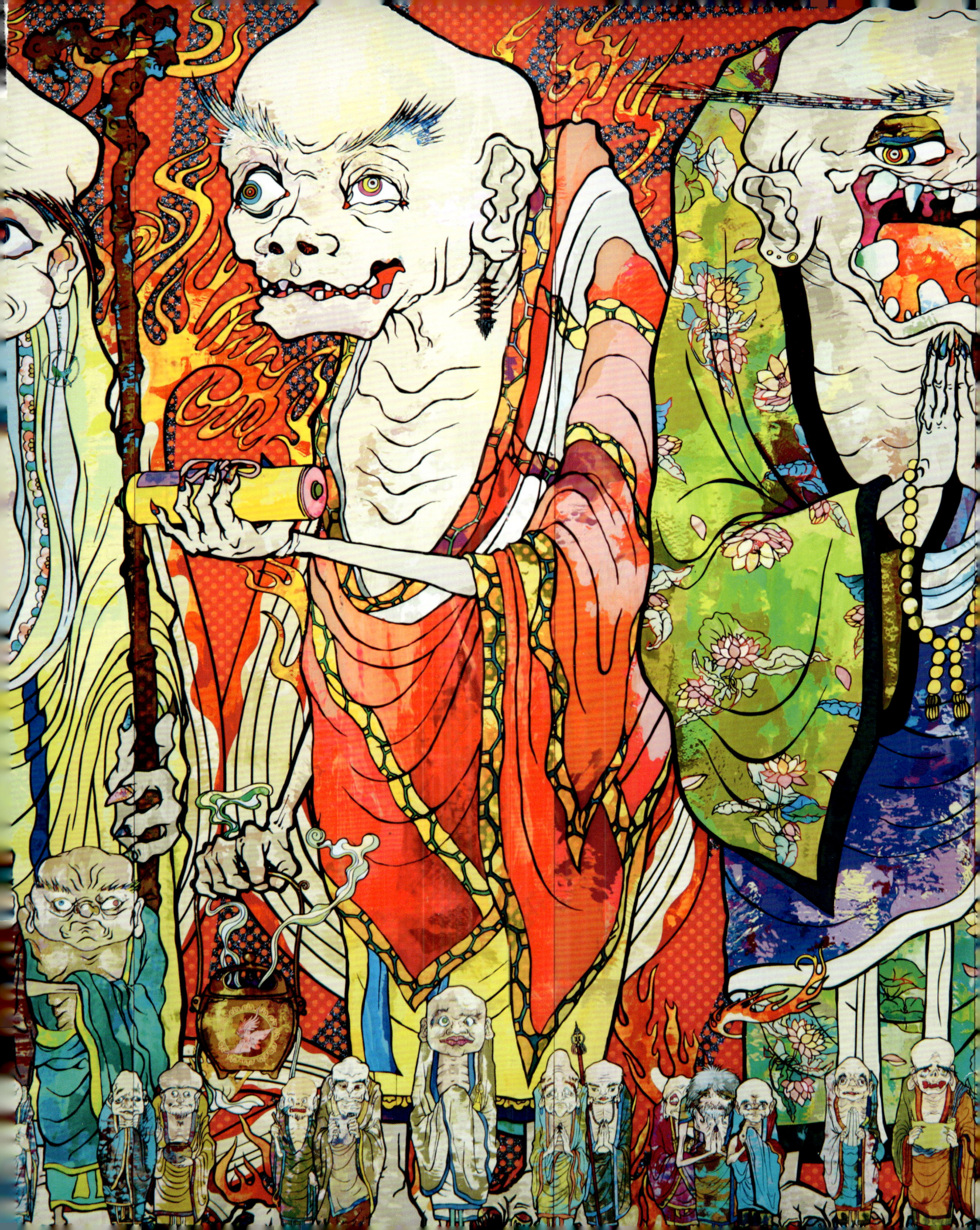

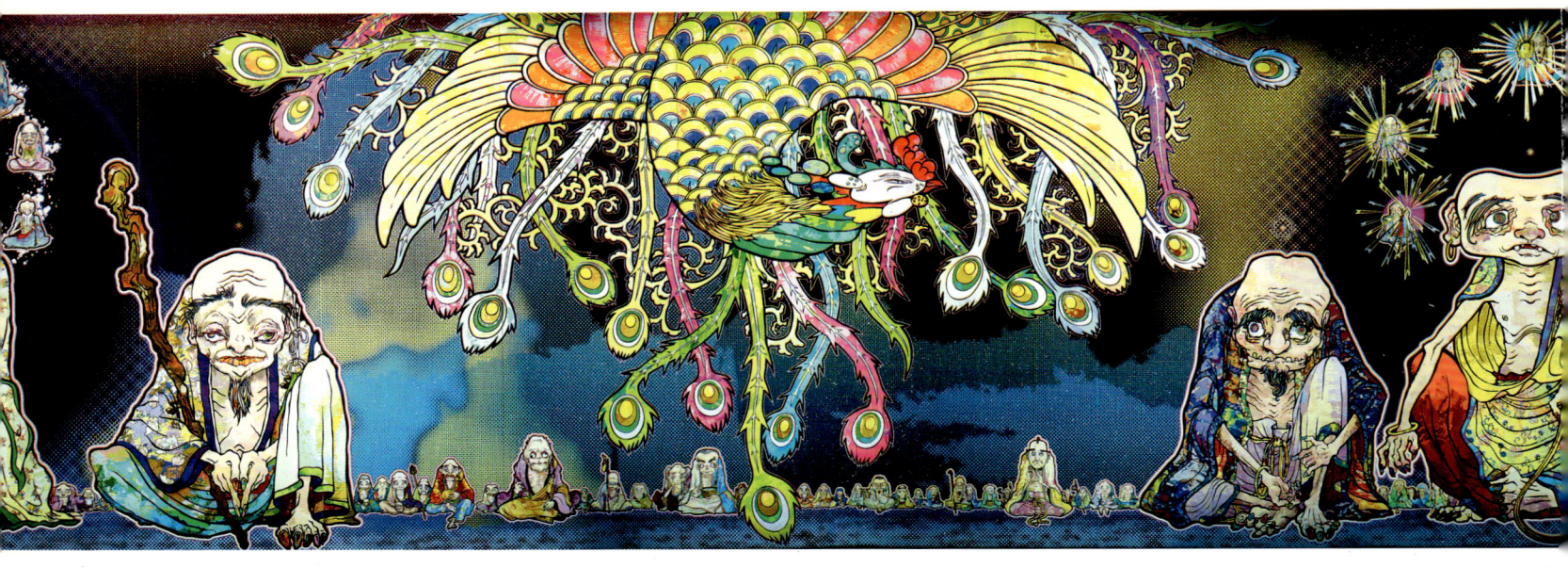

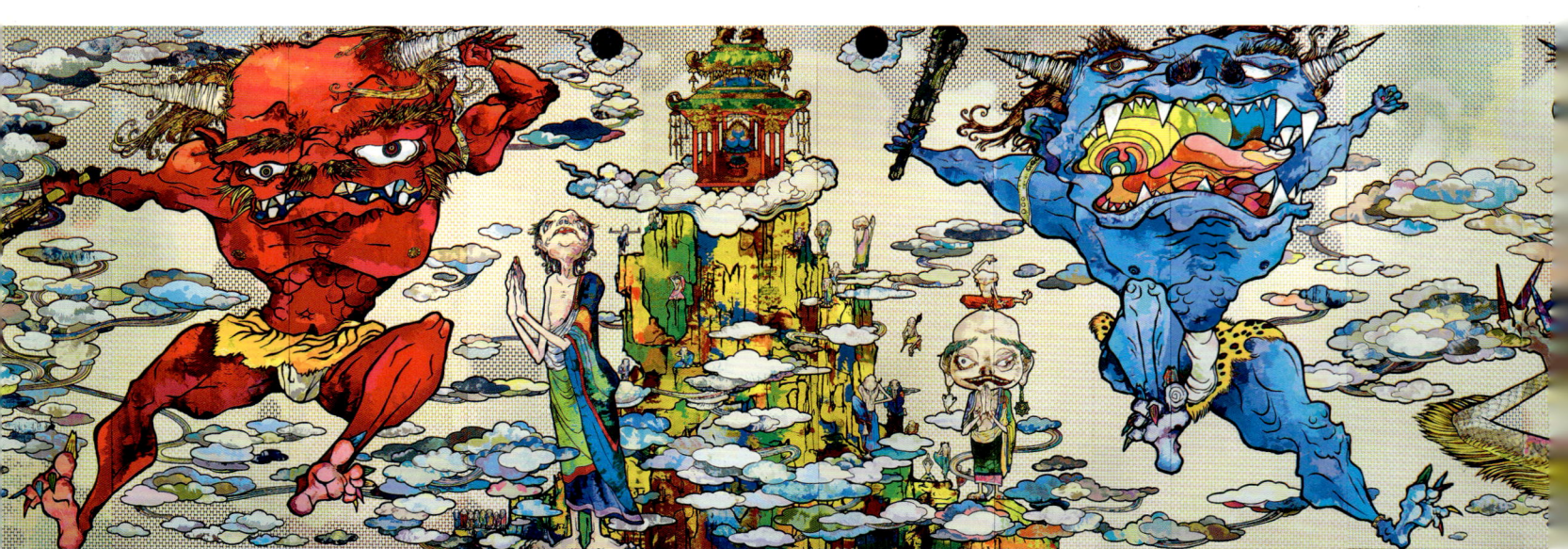

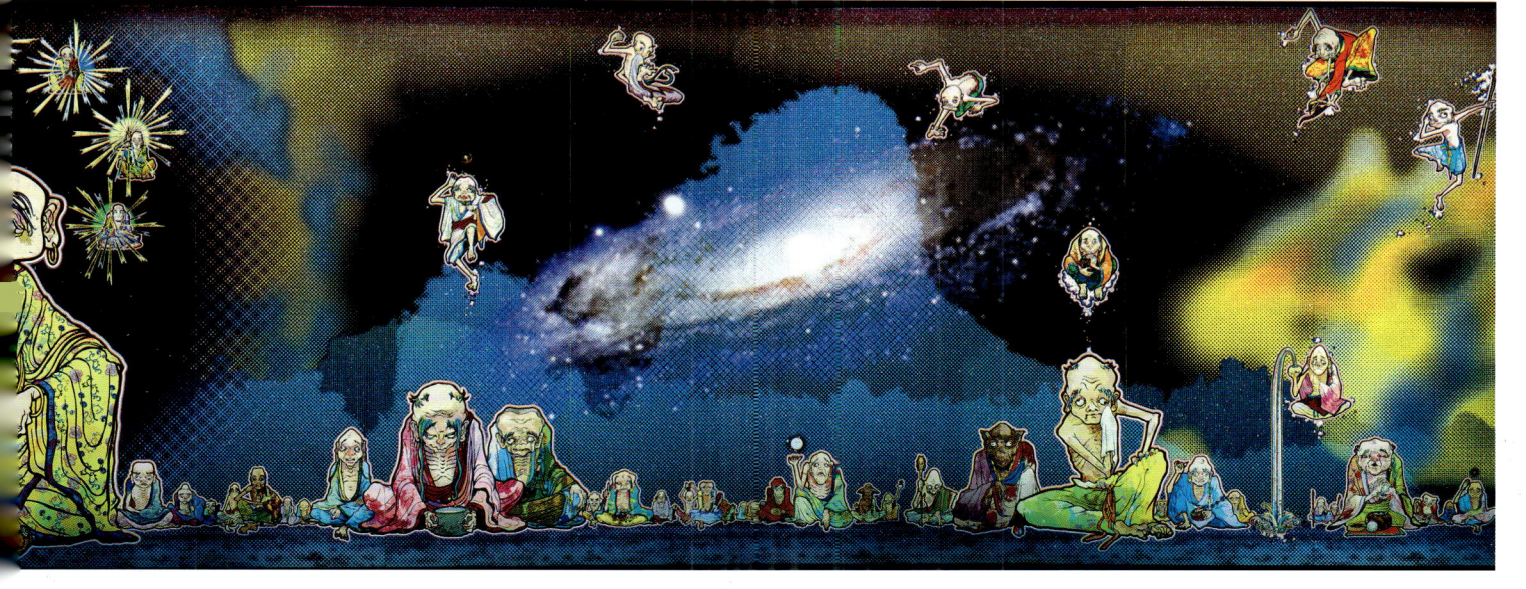

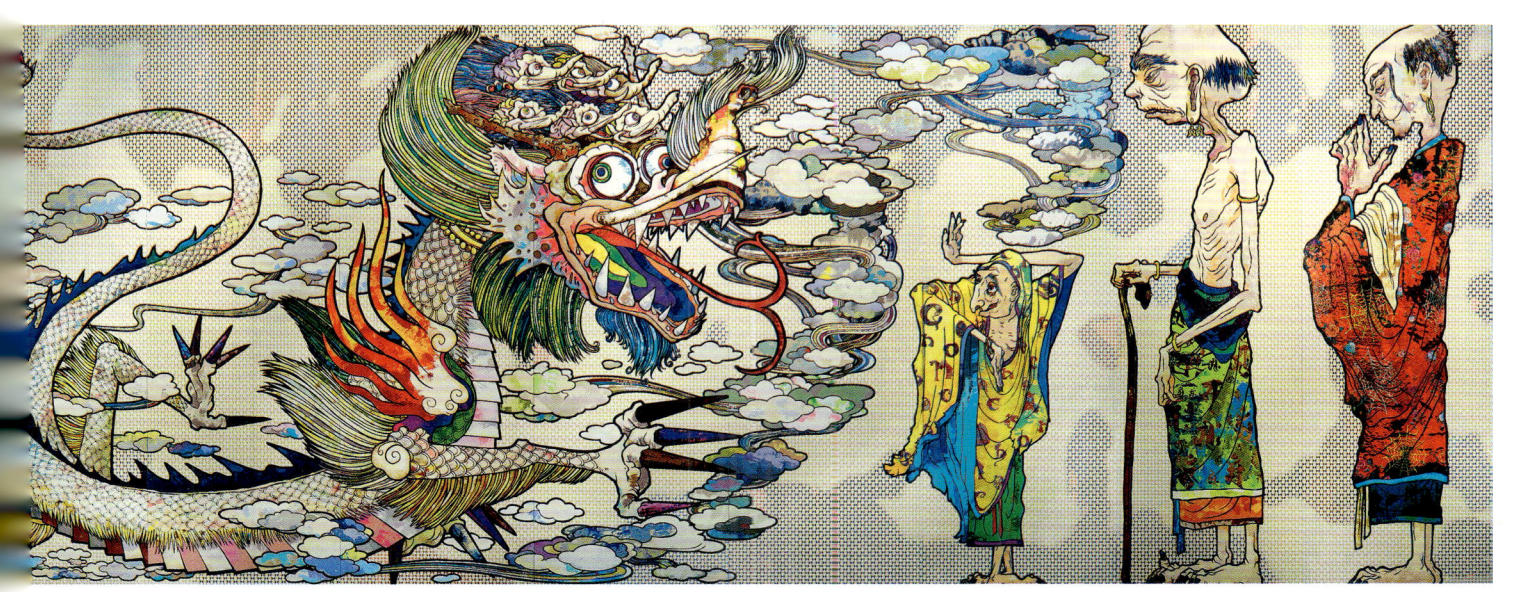

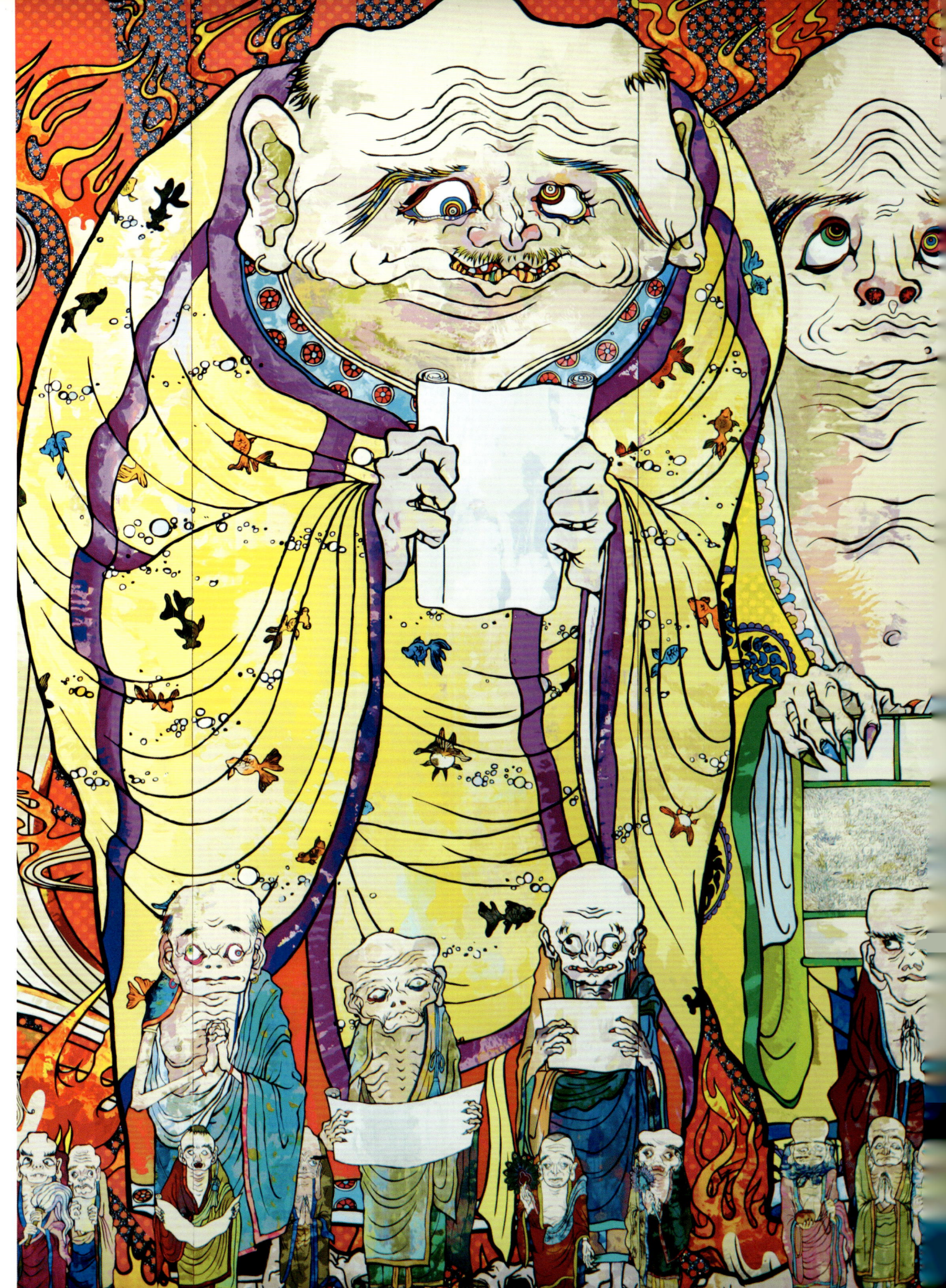

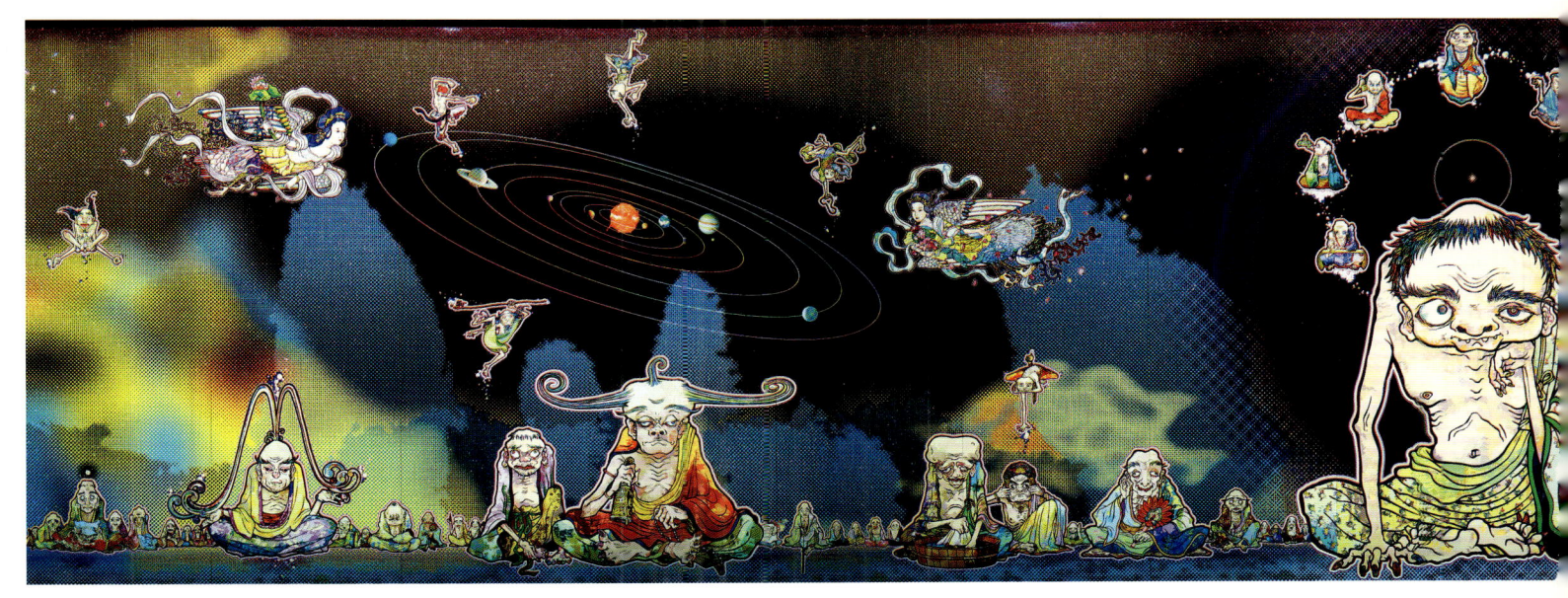

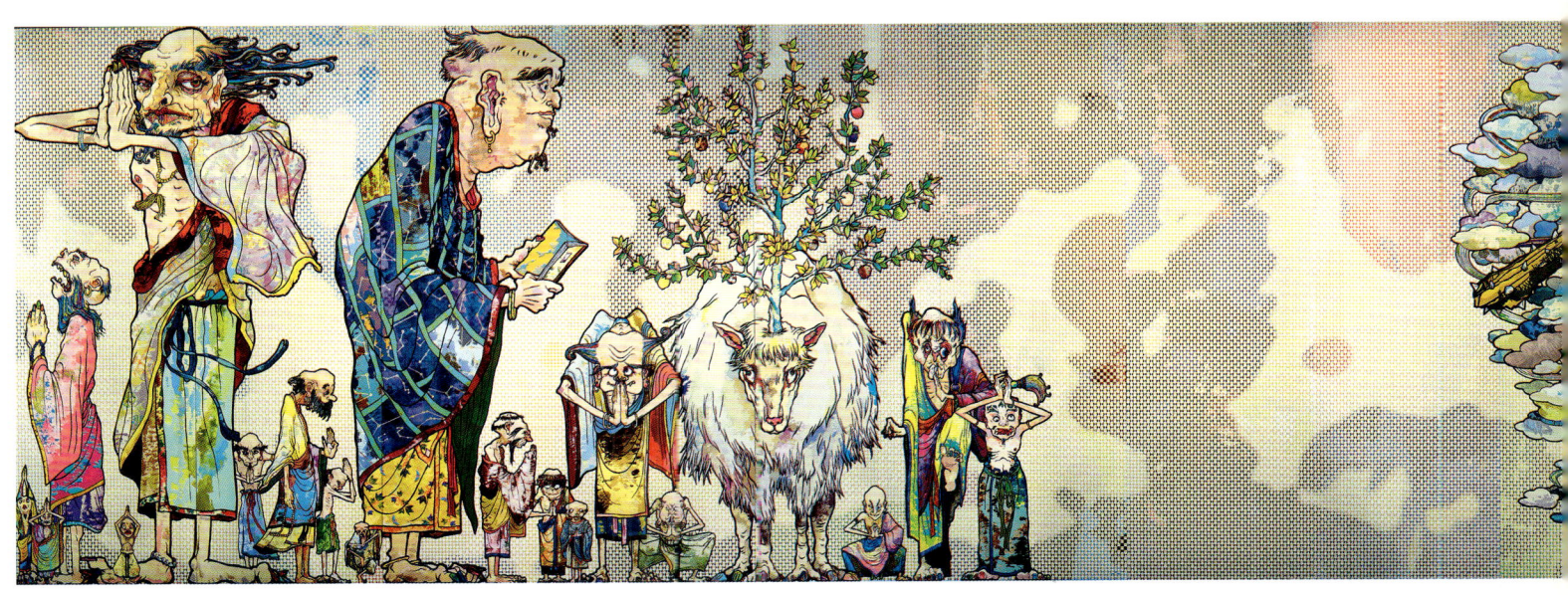

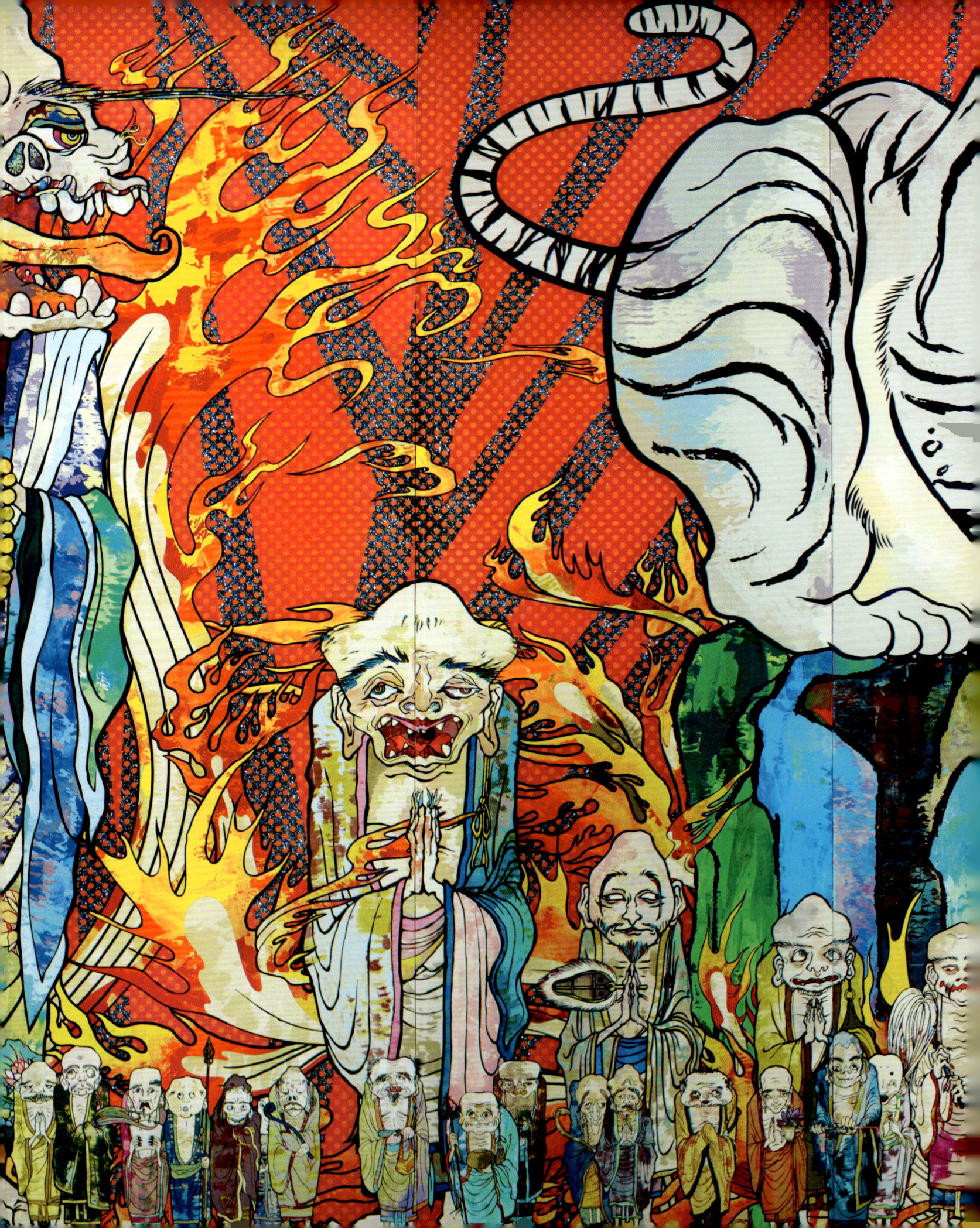

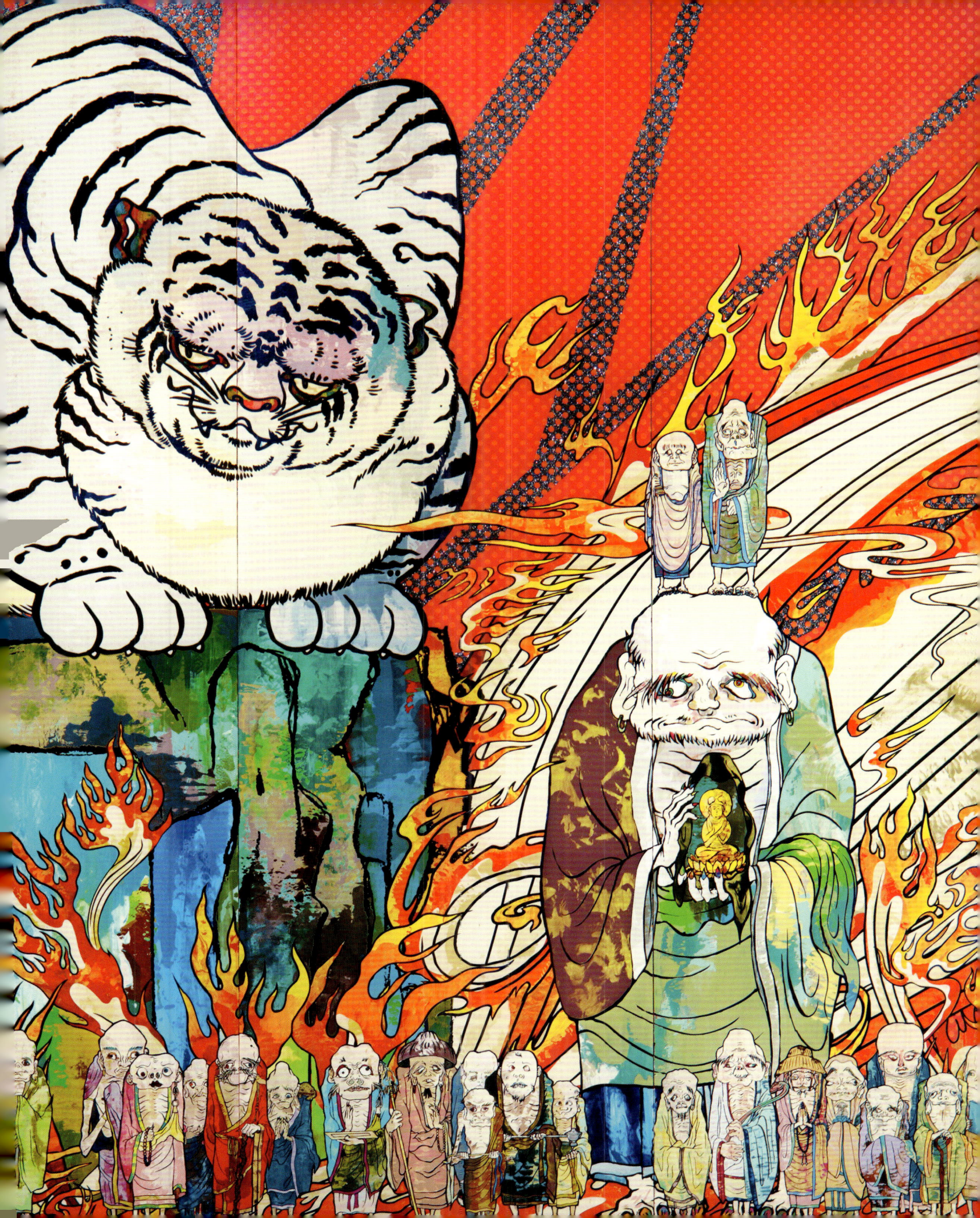

The 500 Arhats was conceived after 3/11—the Japanese earthquake in 2011.

In the old days, when there was a disaster, the monks had paintings made that they used to promote religion among the people who were suffering. I consider *The 500 Arhats* to be an equivalent of those historical works. It's a consolatory painting—it's my *Guernica*, perhaps.

IT'S A WAY FOR ME TO UNDERSTAND MY PLACE IN NATURE AND IN HISTORY.

The 500 Arhats is a big window open onto the forest: It's an image agitated by fires, by huge waves and tall mountains. In the painting, the Japanese environment is portrayed in a catastrophic state.

From early on in my career, I felt that the greatest moments in art history are the ones in which people really need images, when they really need art. So I've always thought about the relationship between war and art. The greatest period in Japanese art history was six hundred years ago, when Japan was divided by many wars and torn by earthquakes and tsunamis. A very dark moment, but a splendid time for art.

Six hundred years ago is also the time when many religions came into being in Japan: This is when our version of Buddhism was finally formalized. After the 2011 earthquake, Japan witnessed a return to religion, which to me seemed like a return to the atmosphere of Japan six hundred years ago.

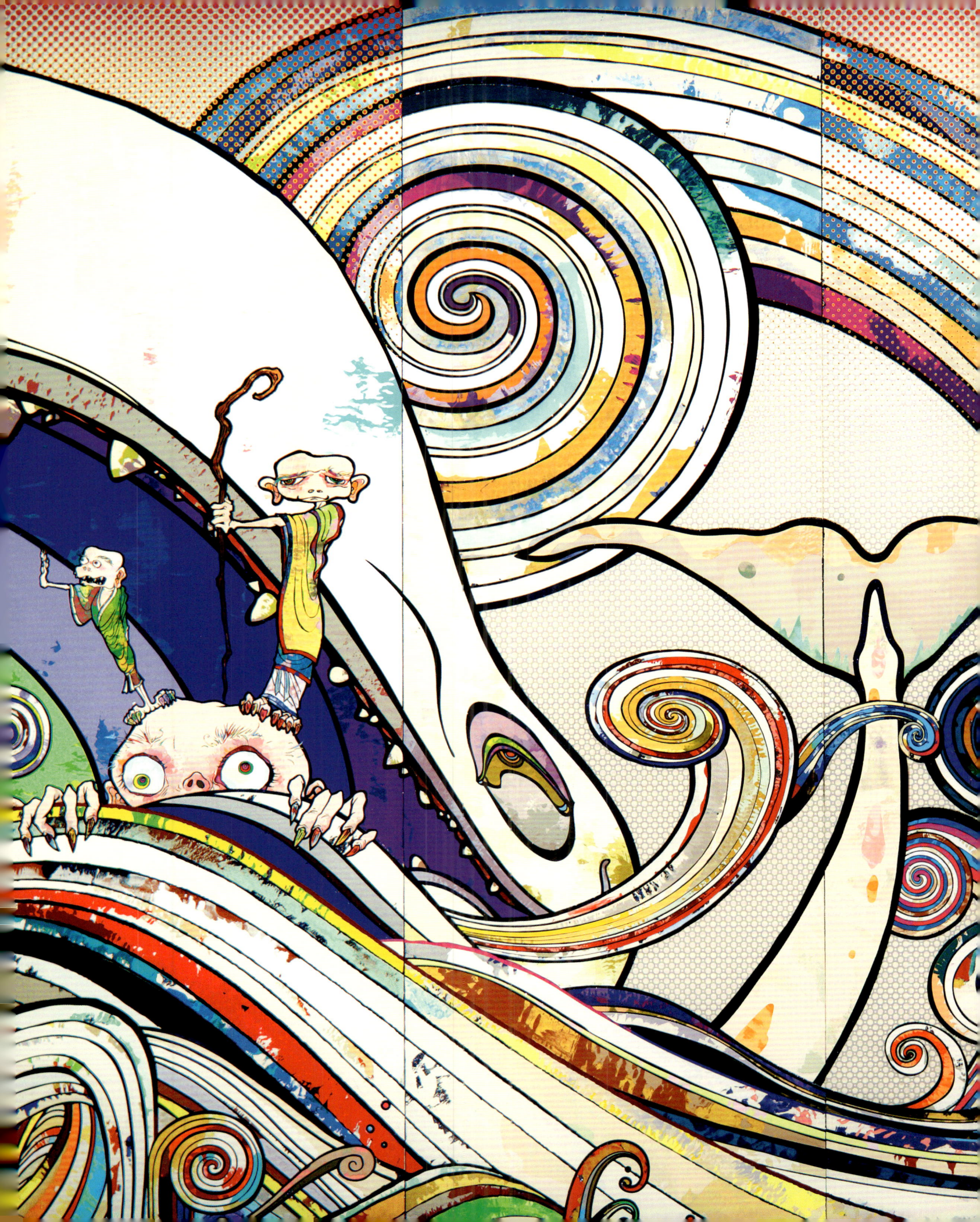

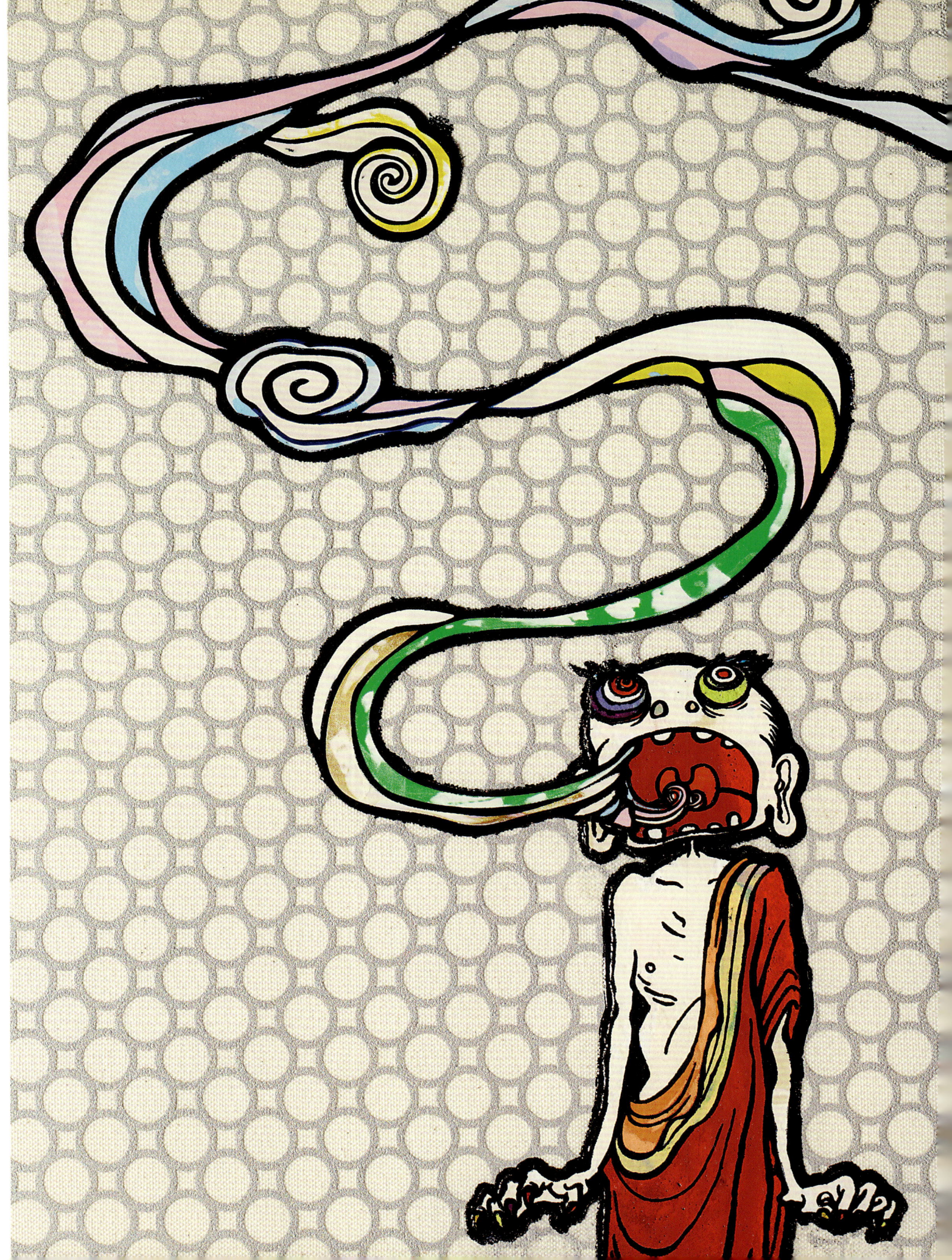

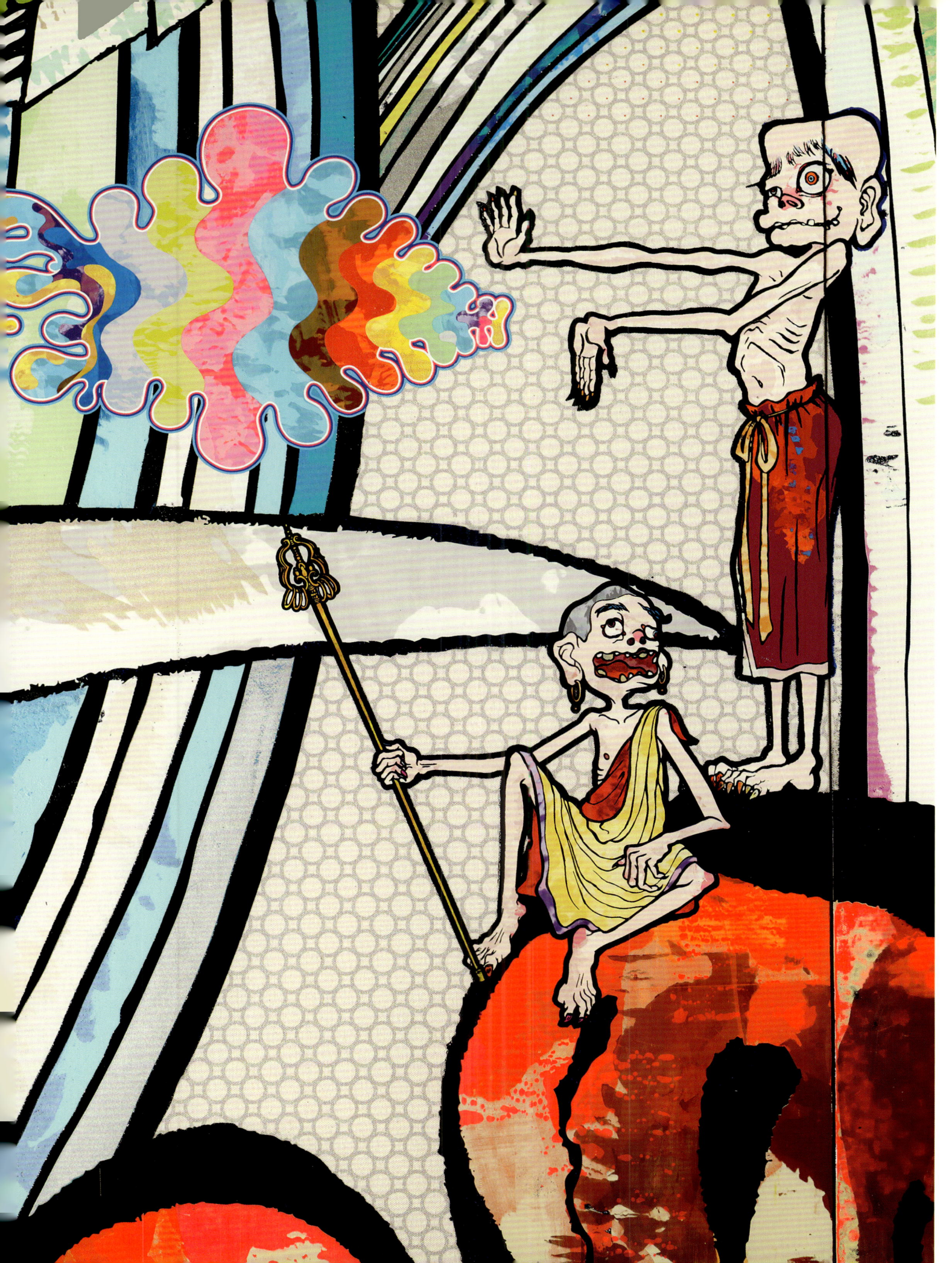

The 500 Arhats (detail) 2012

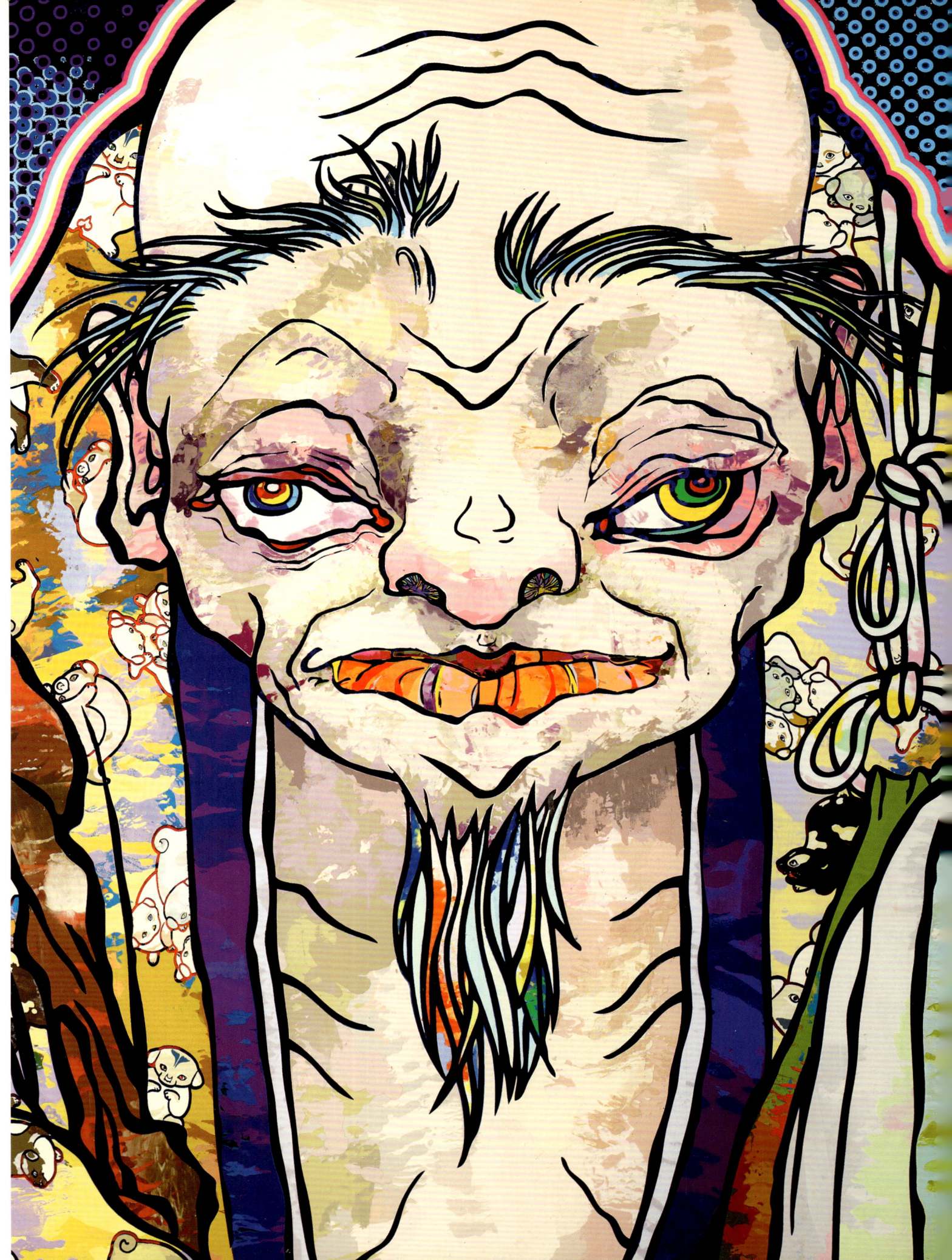

The 500 Arhats (detail) 2012

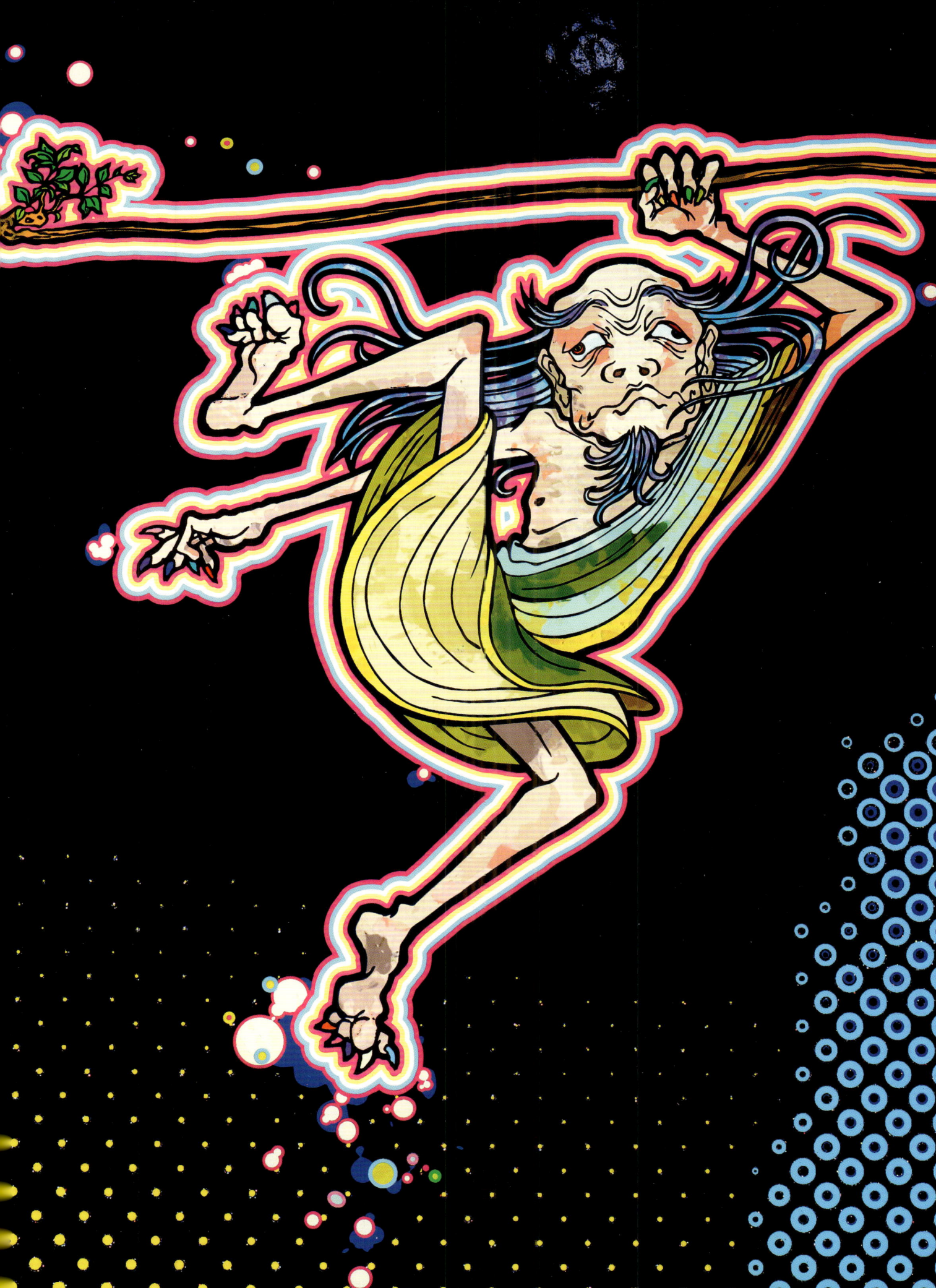

The 500 Arhats (detail) 2012

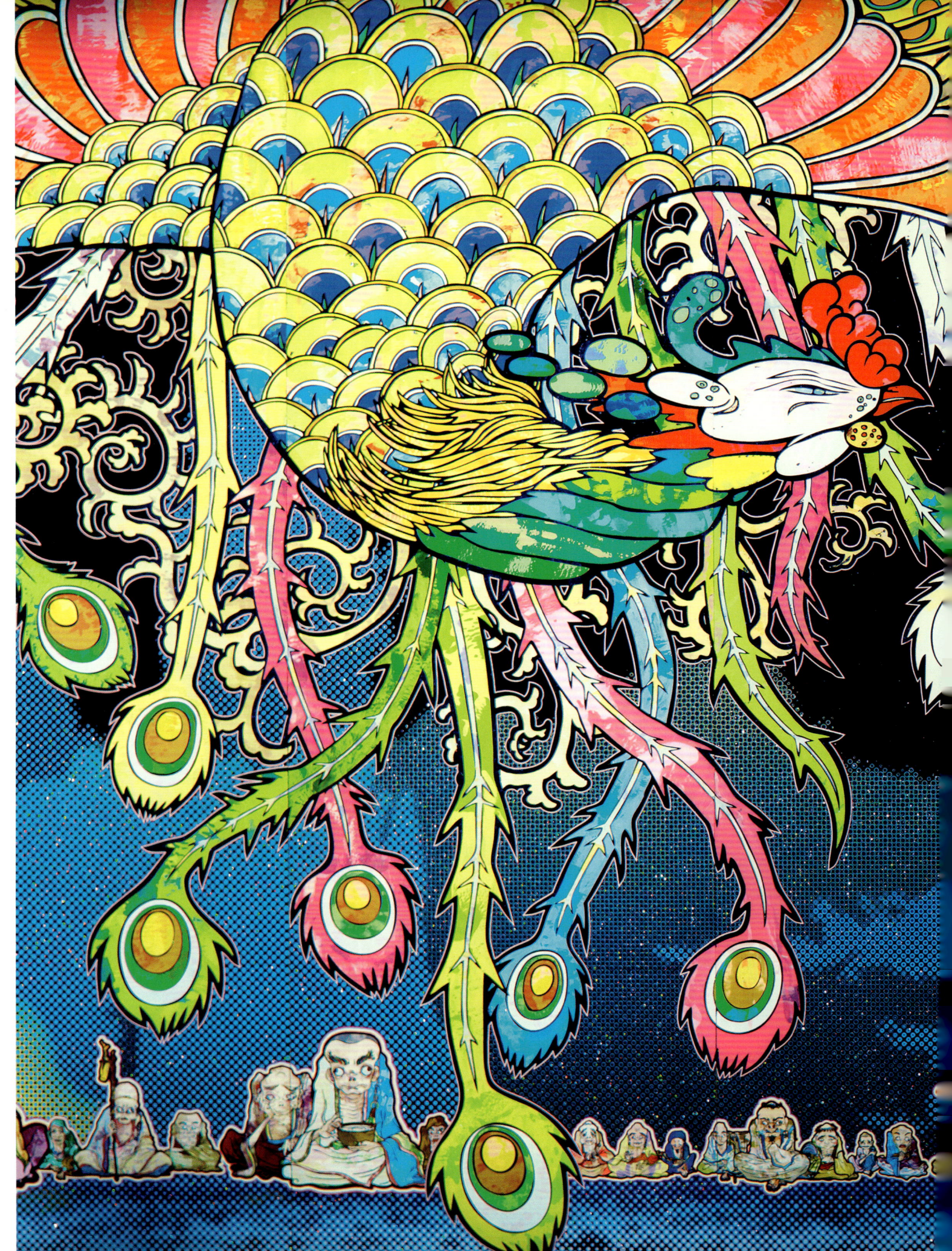

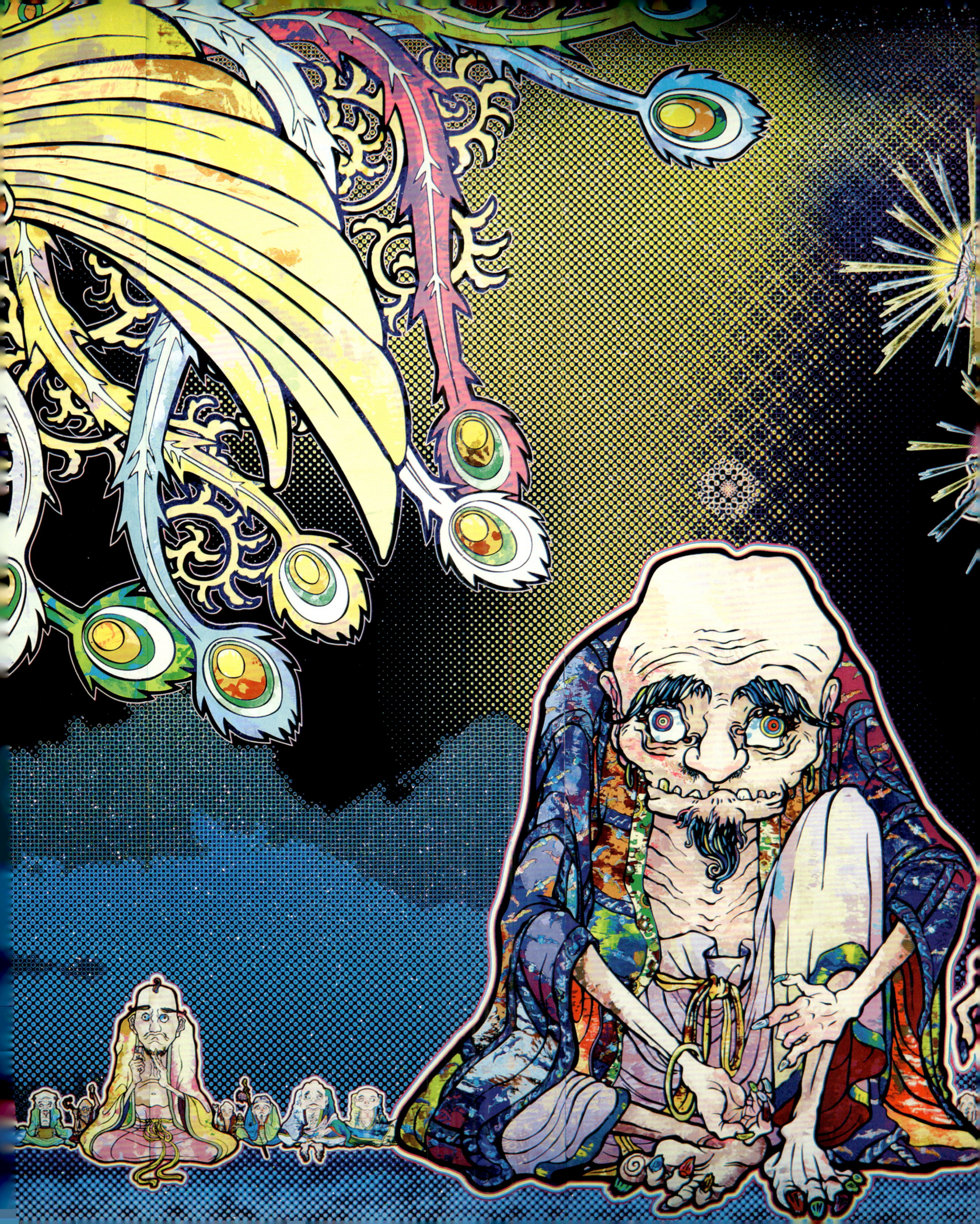

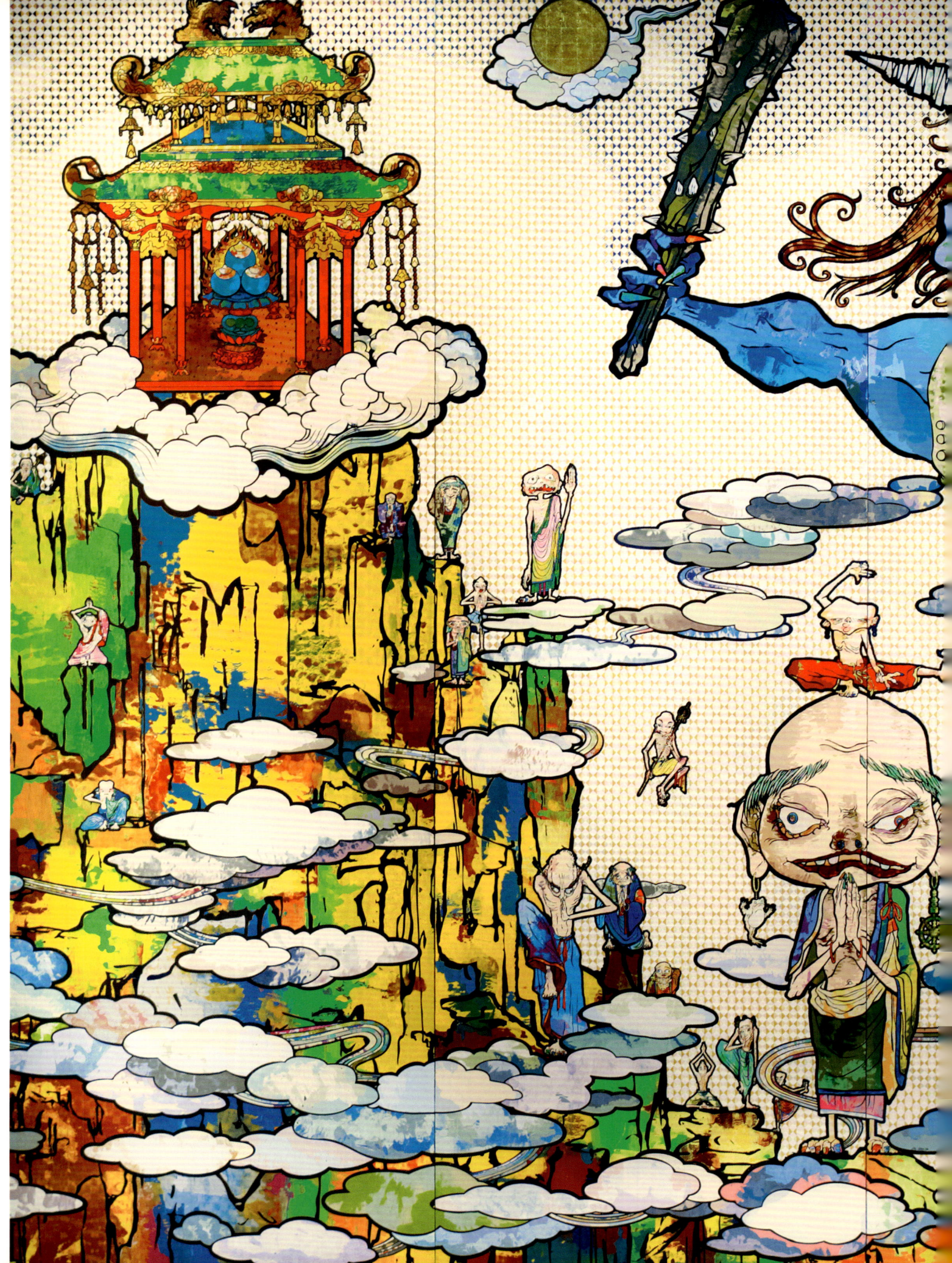

The 500 Arhats (detail) 2012

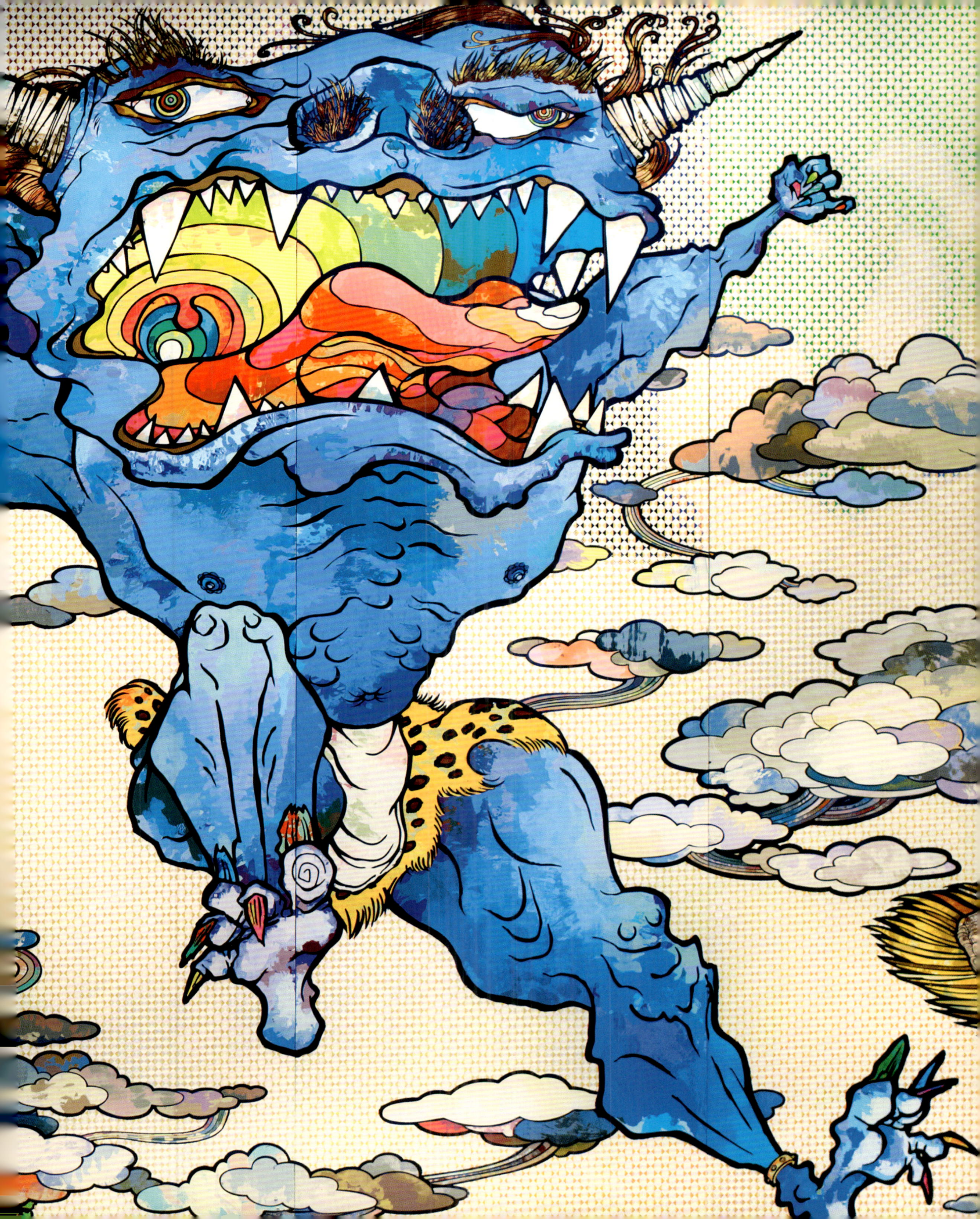

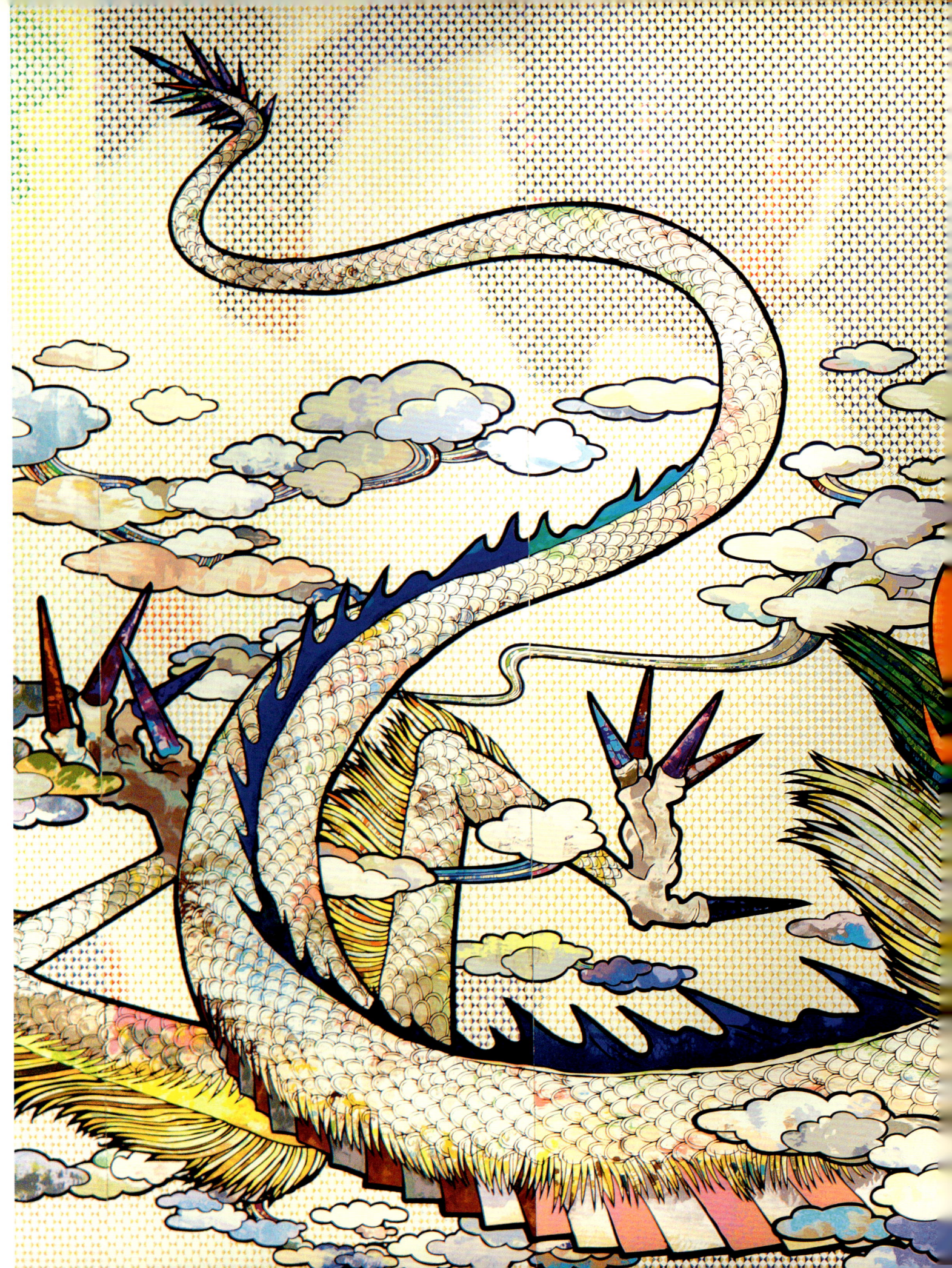

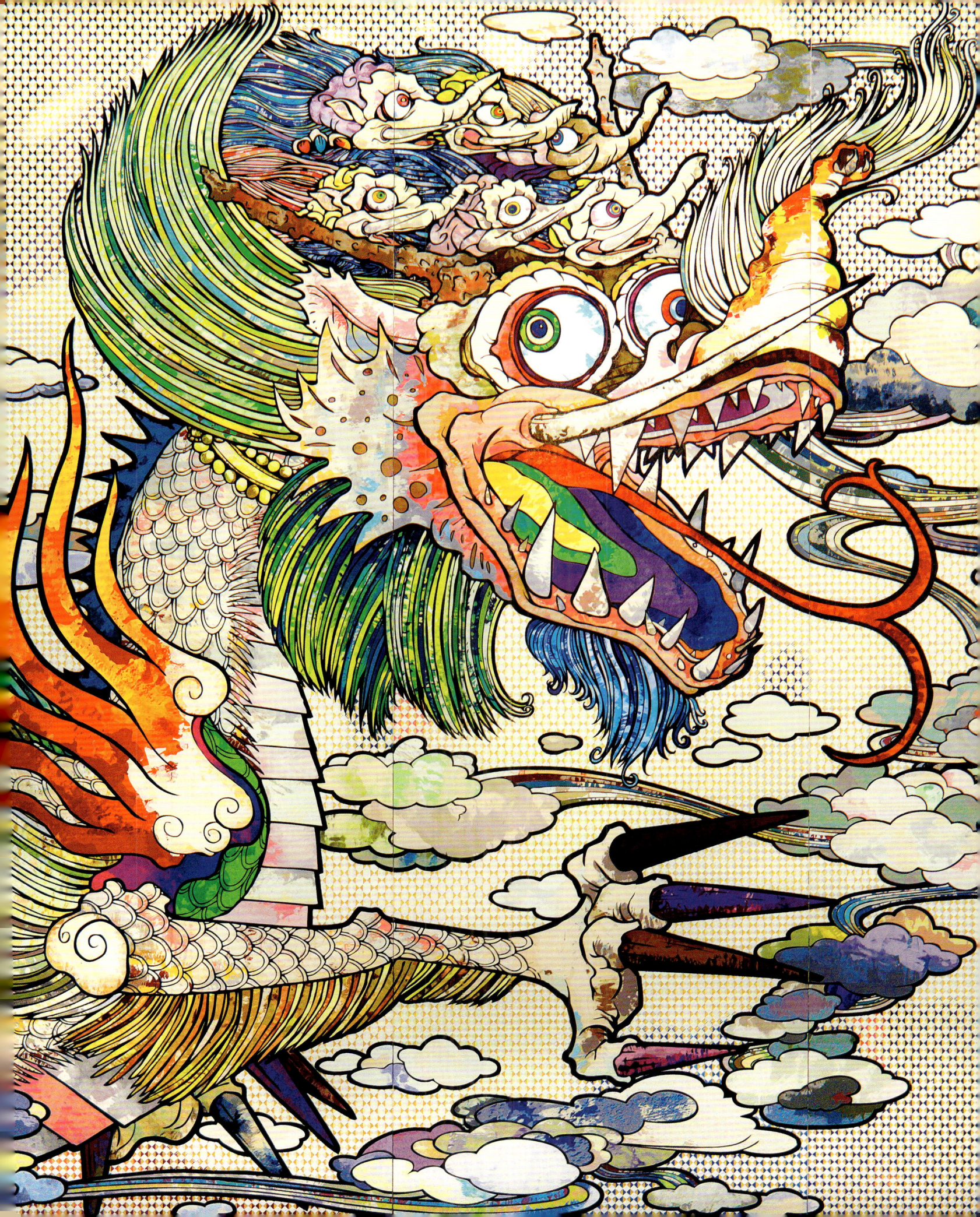

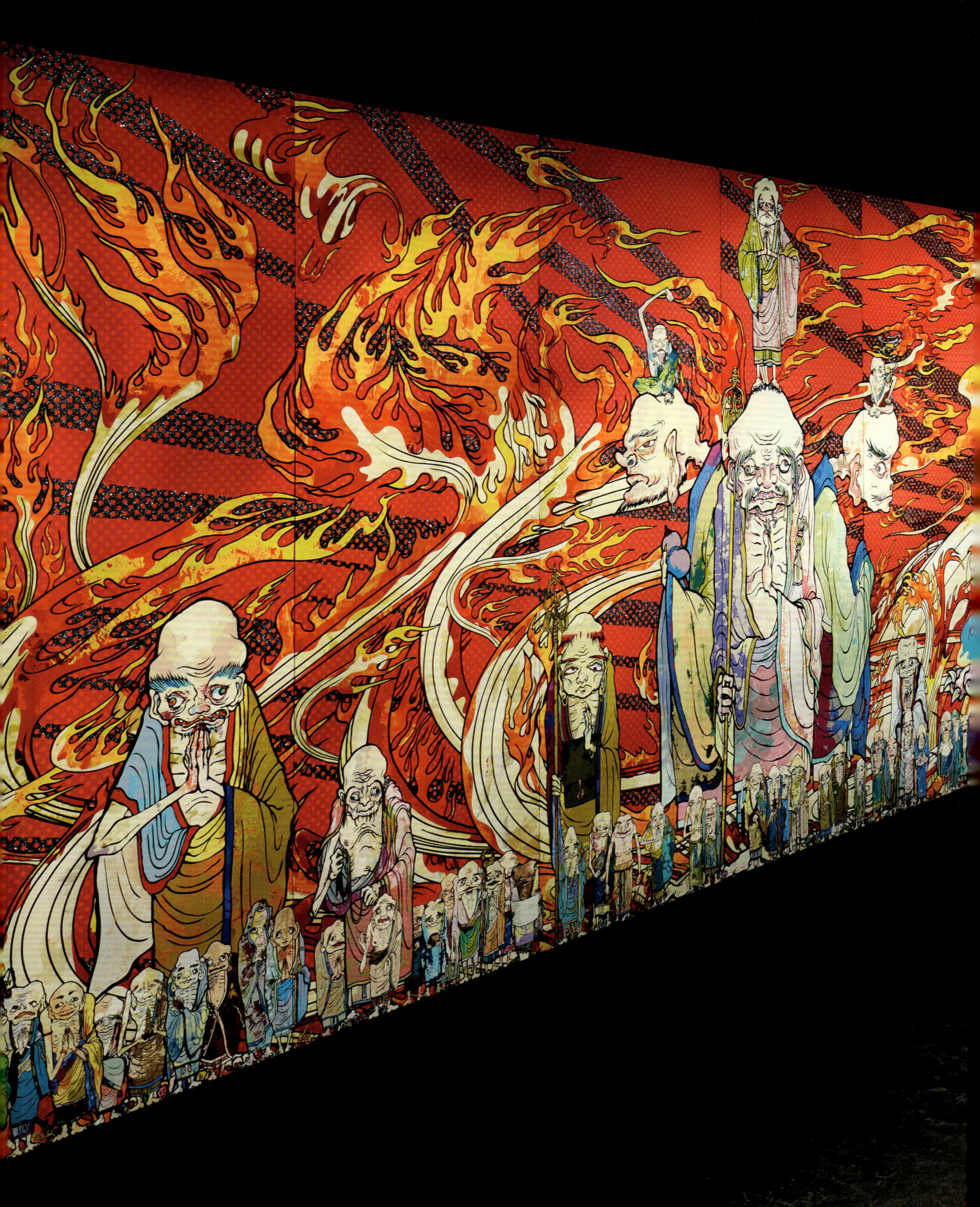

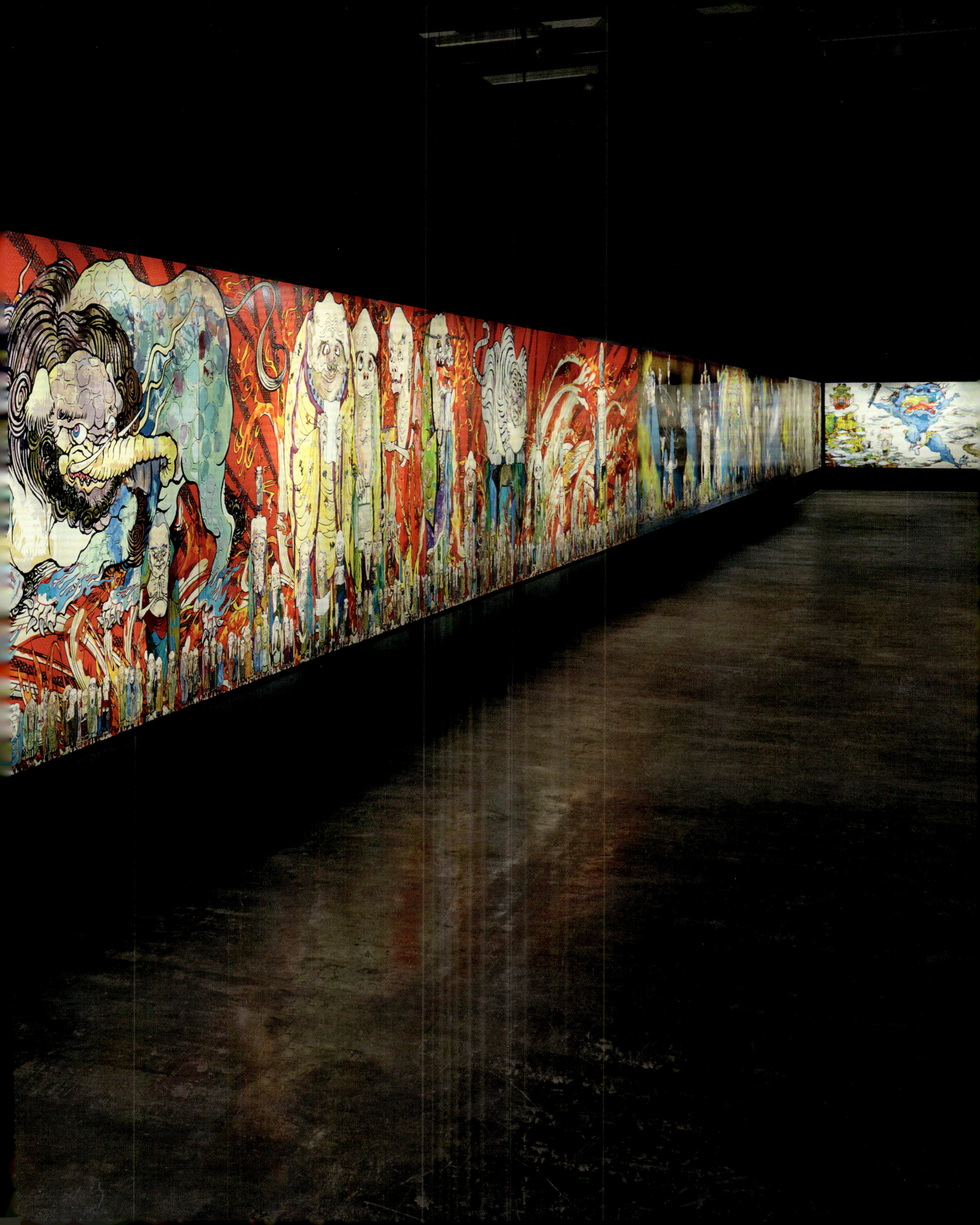

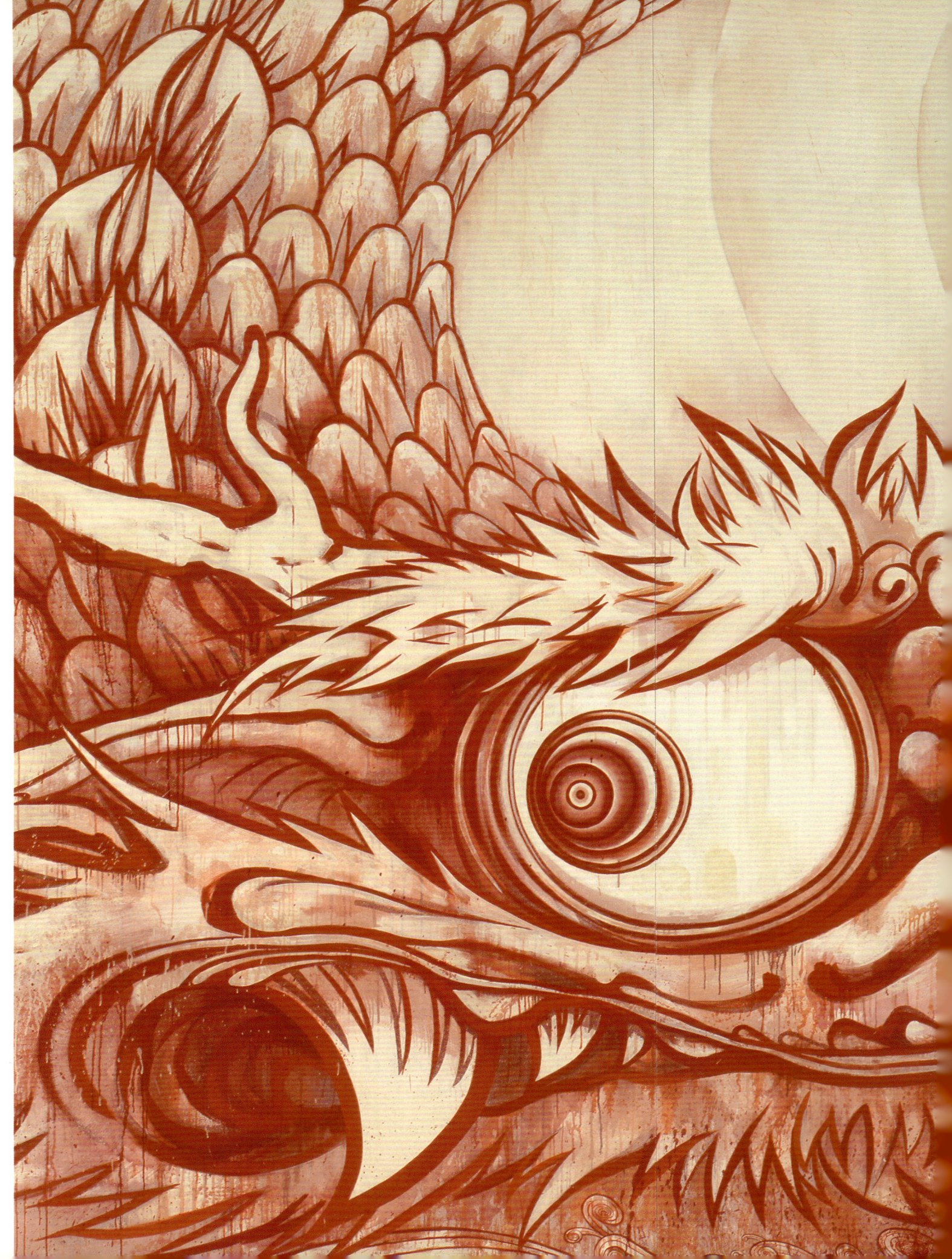

Dragon in Clouds – Red Mutation (detail) 2010

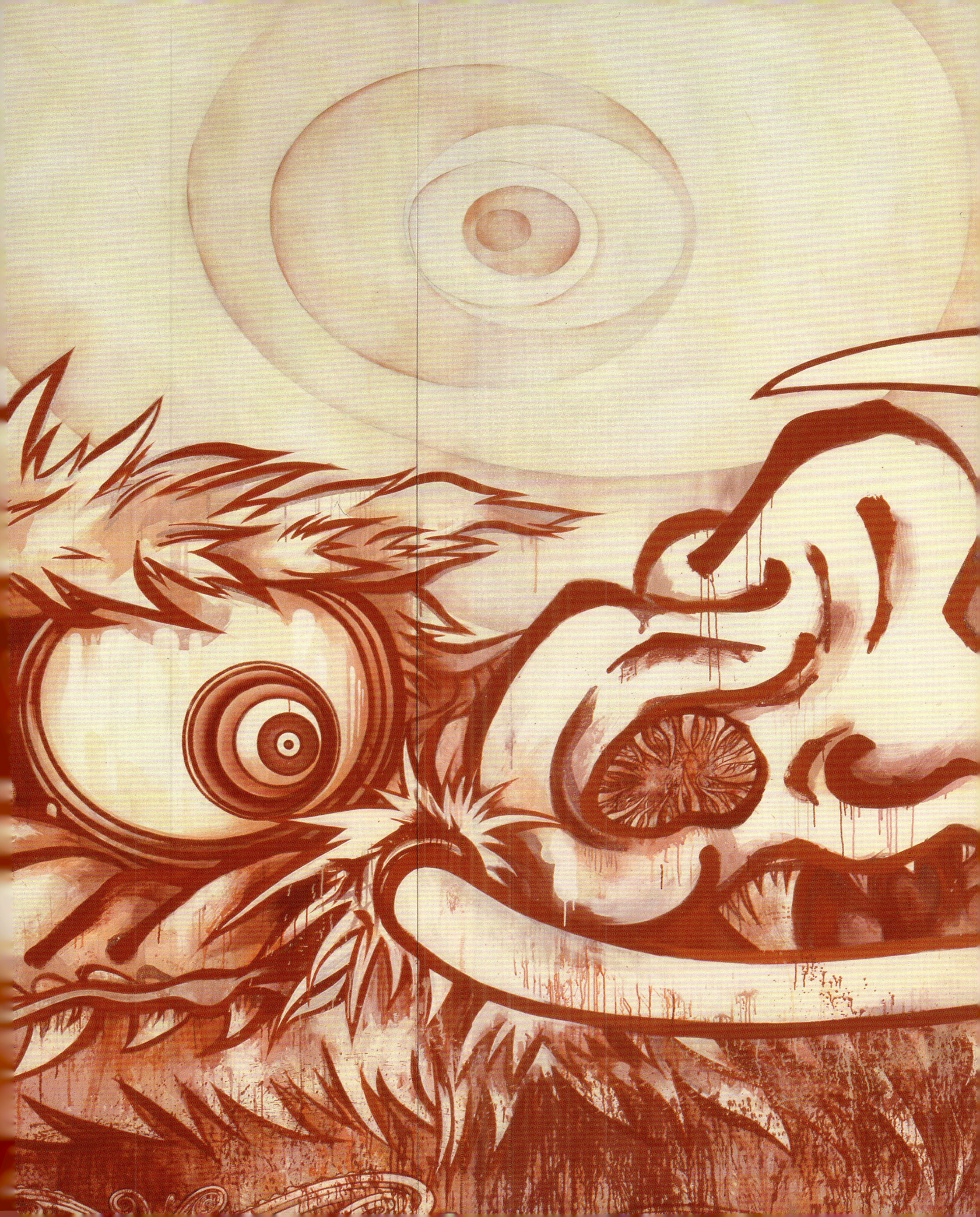

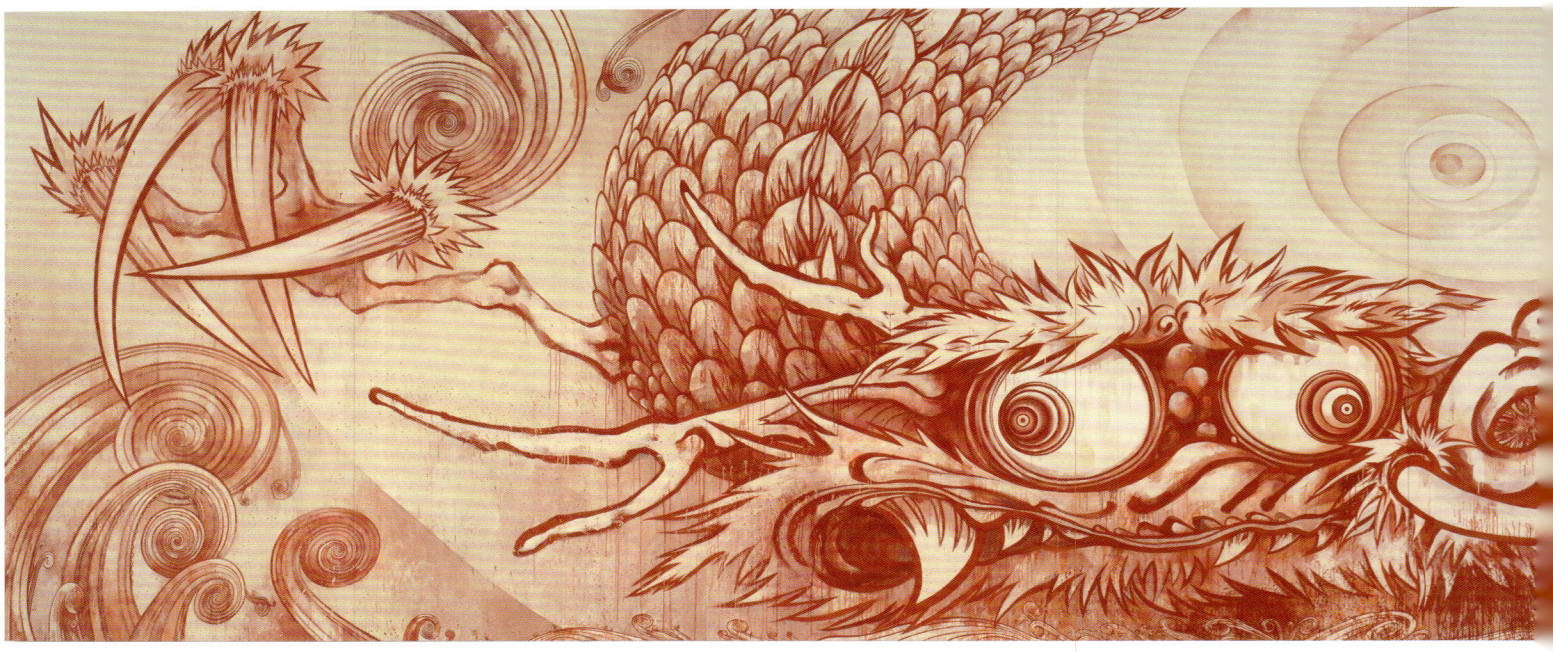

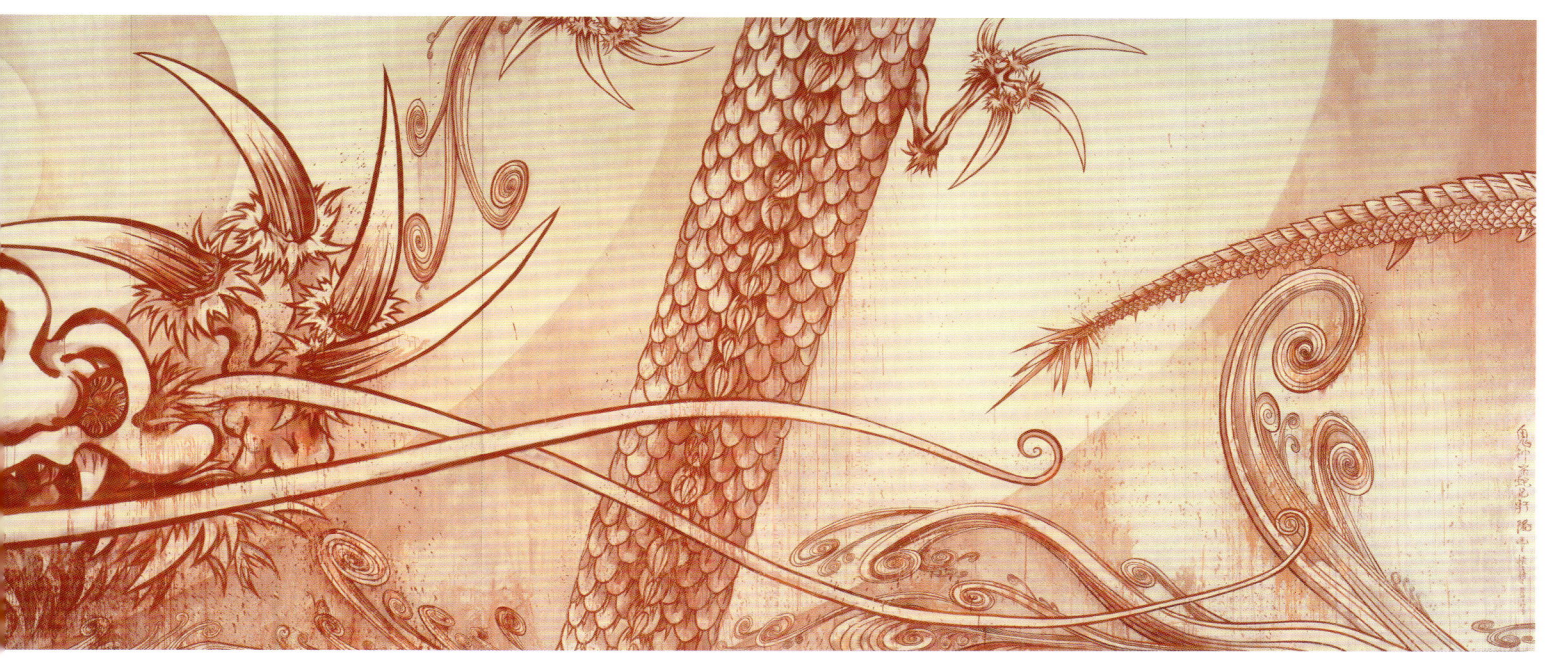

Dragon in Clouds — Indigo Blue 2010

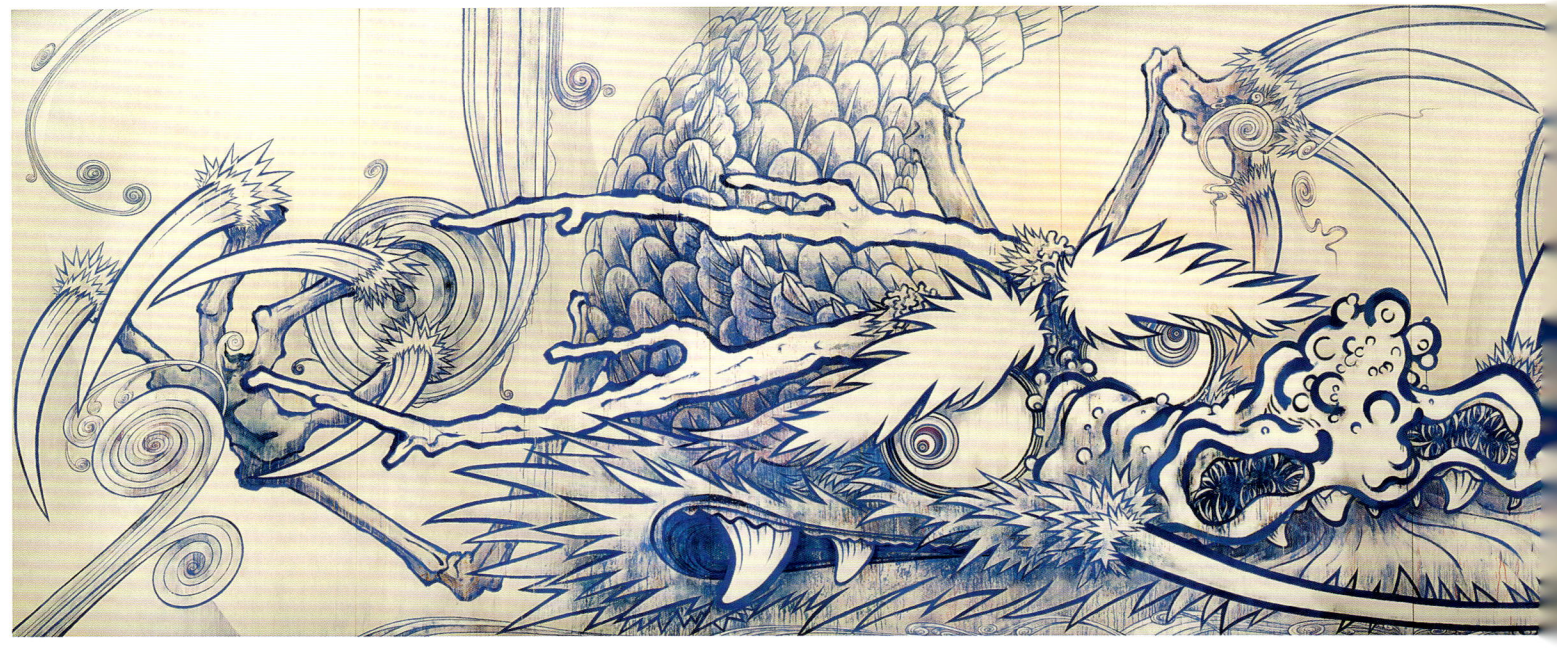

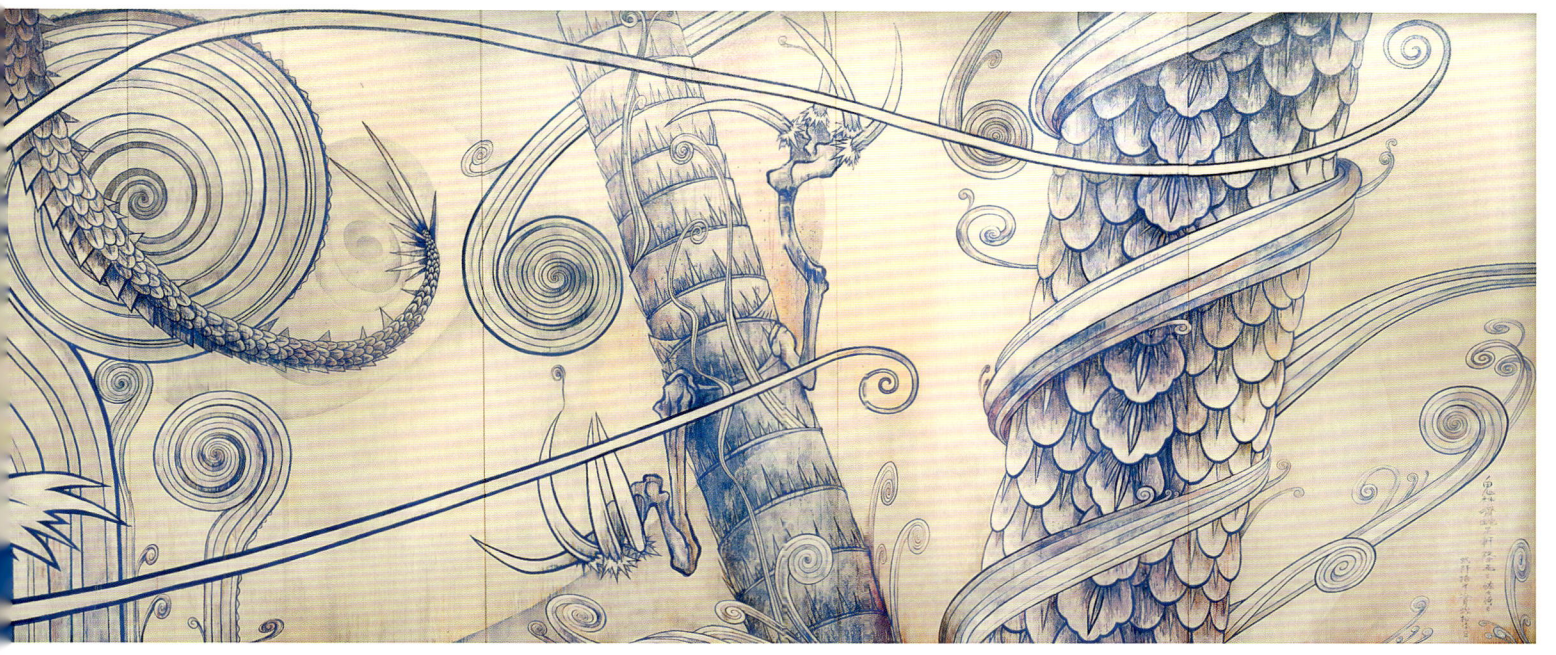

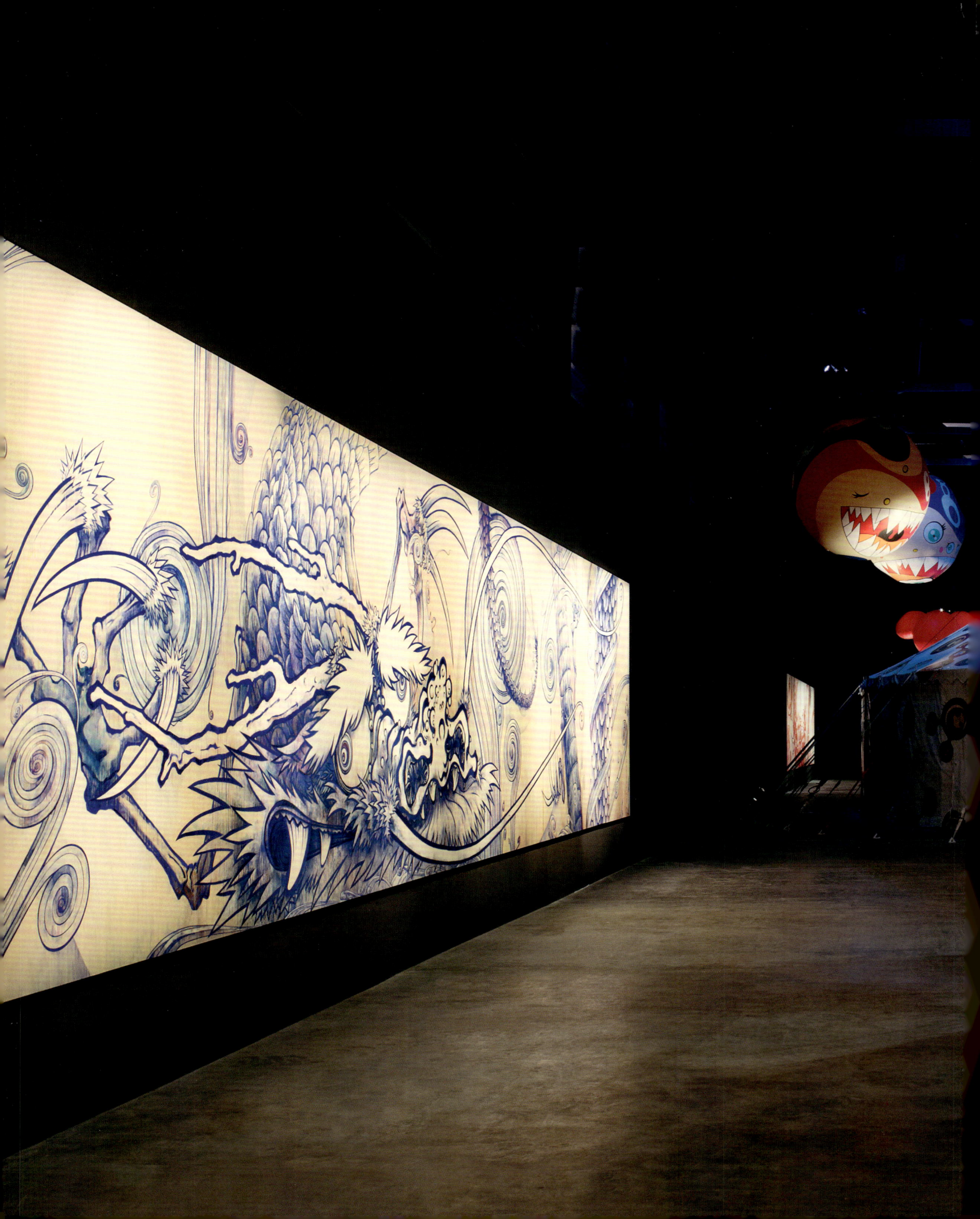

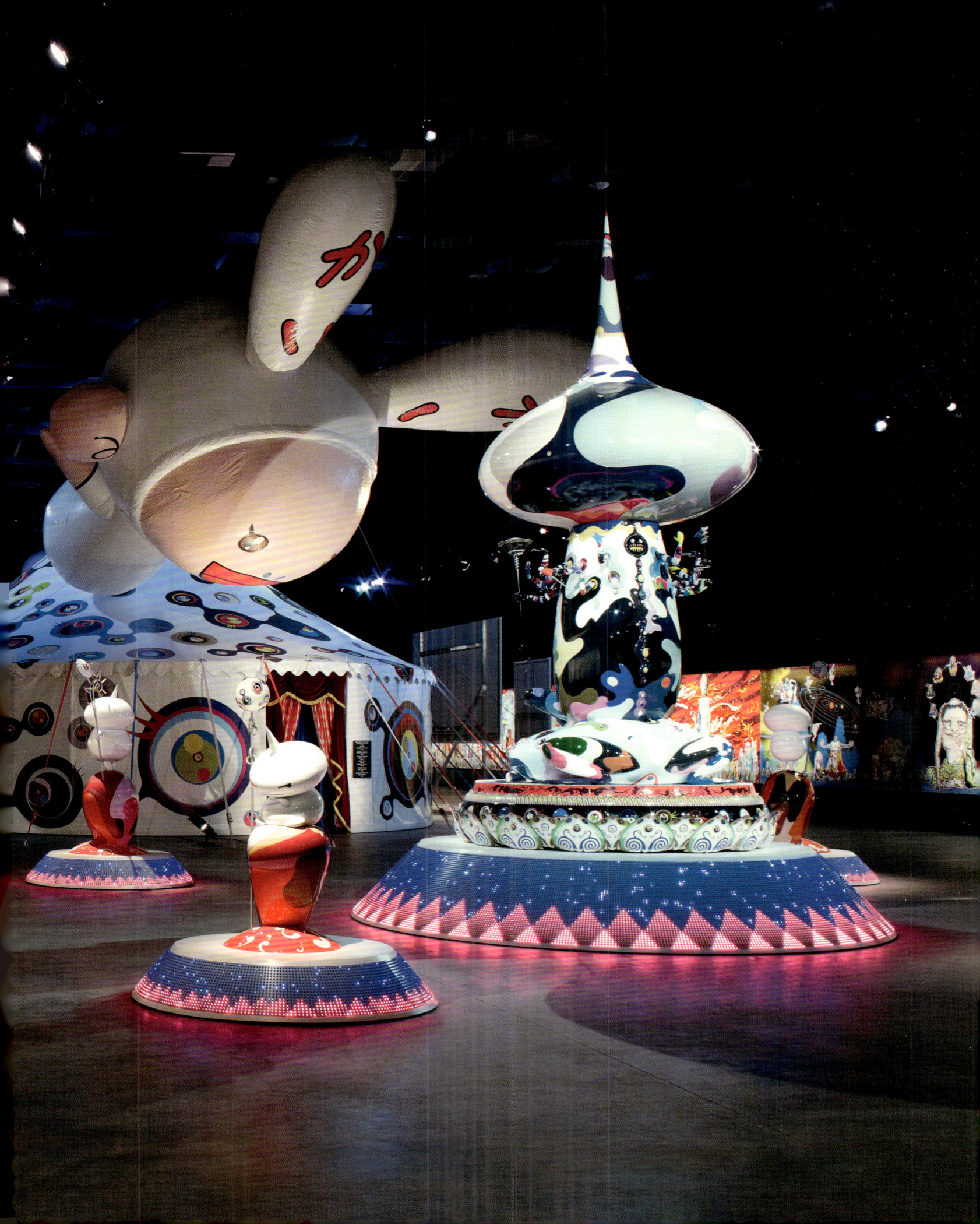

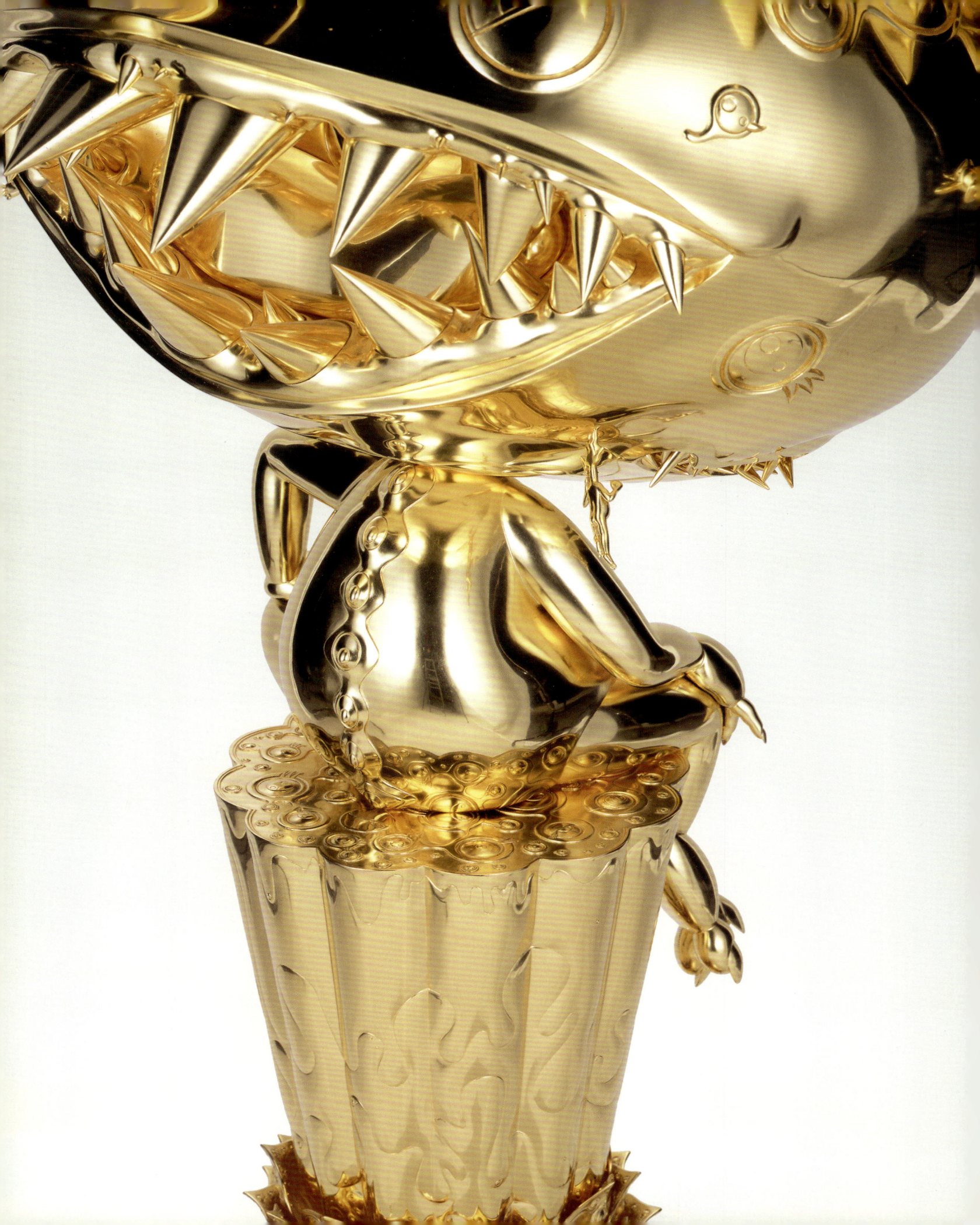

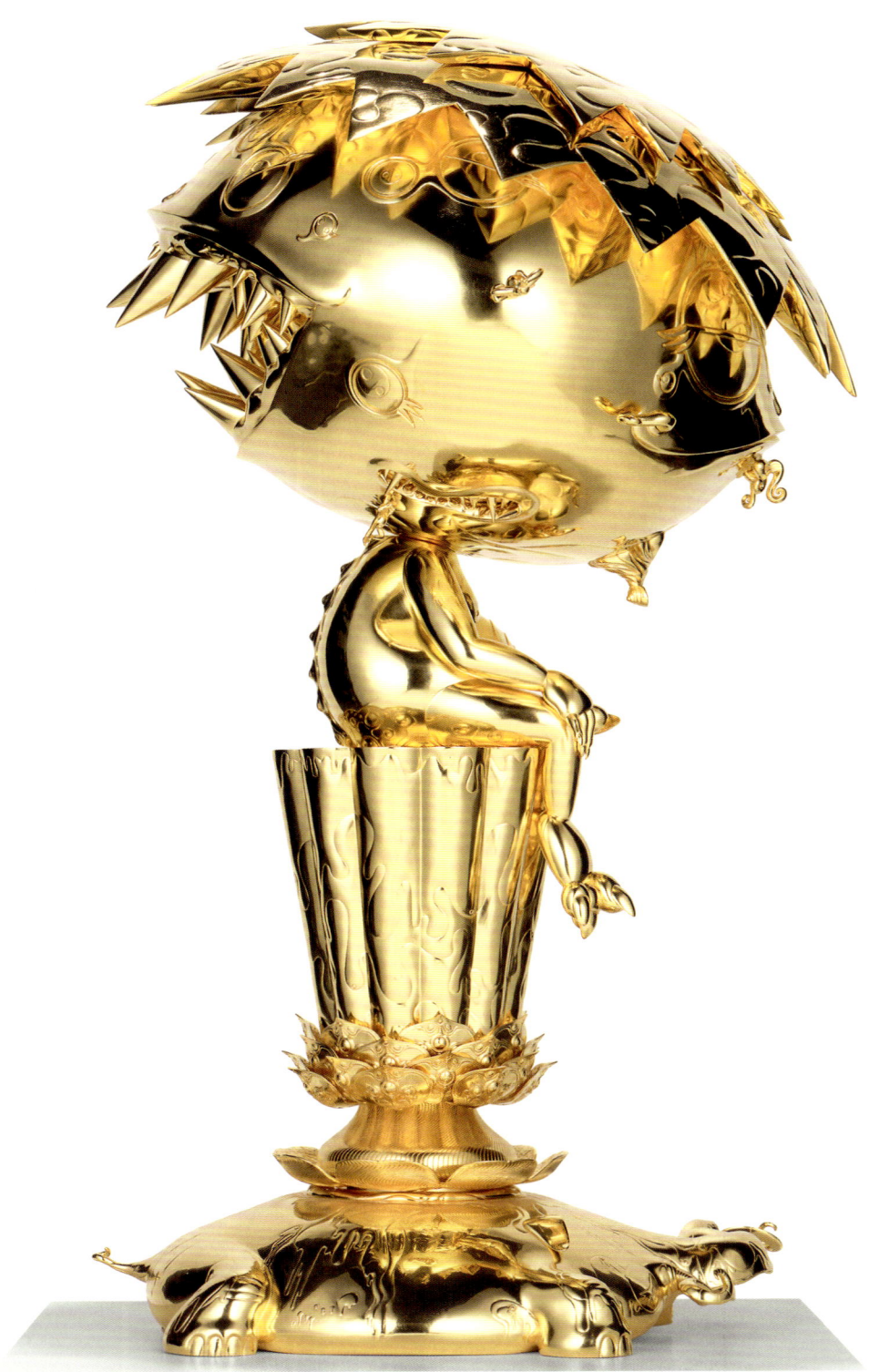

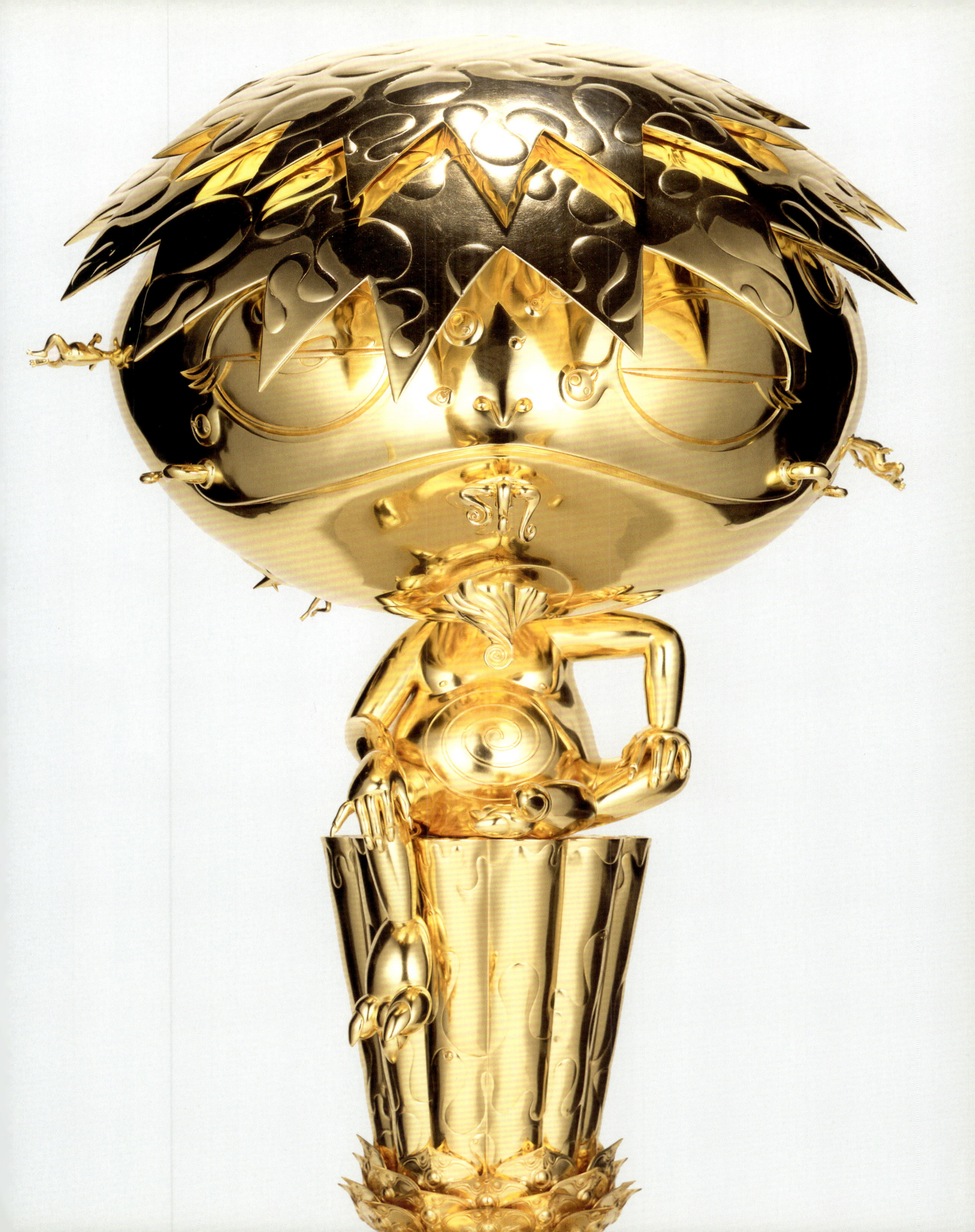

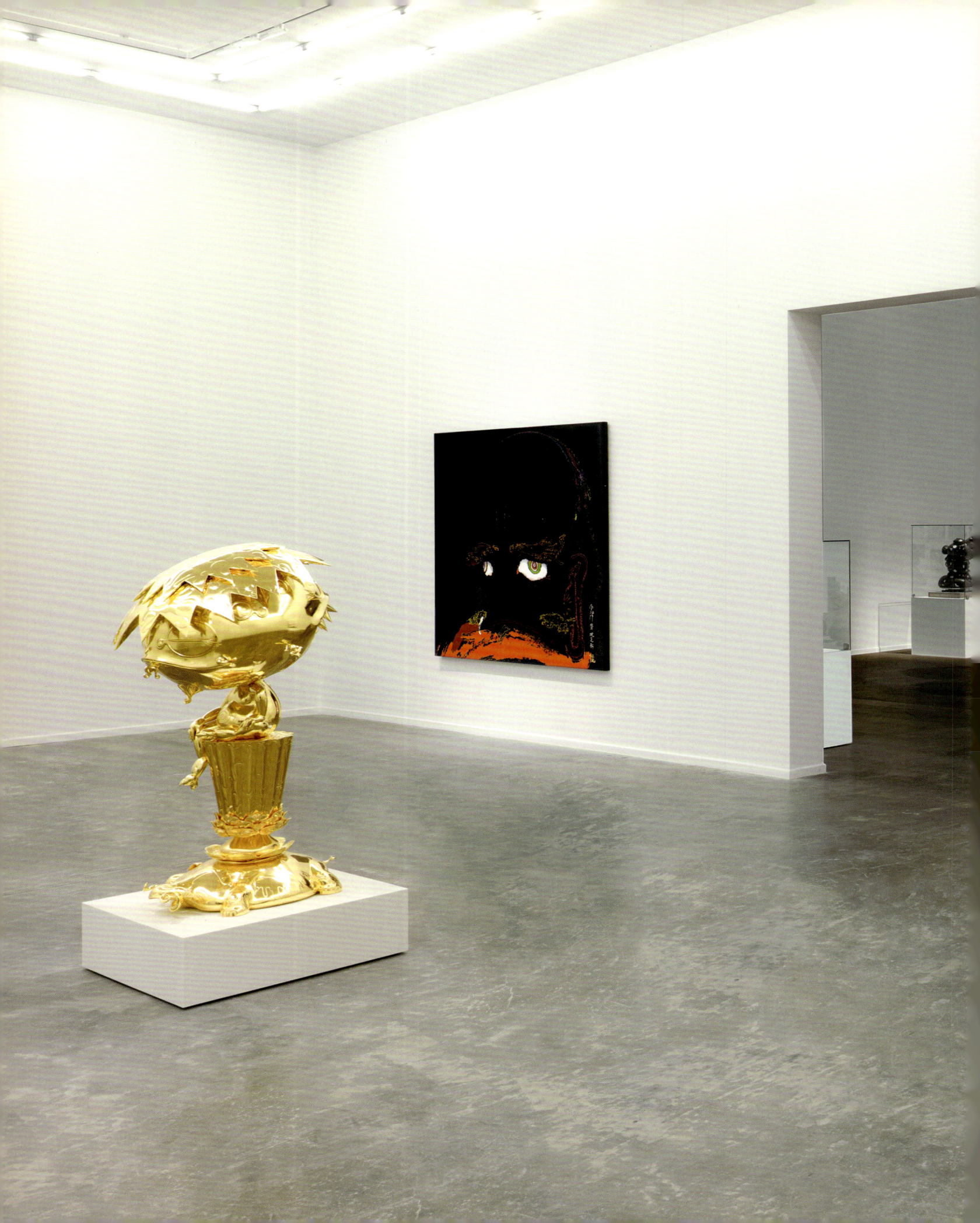

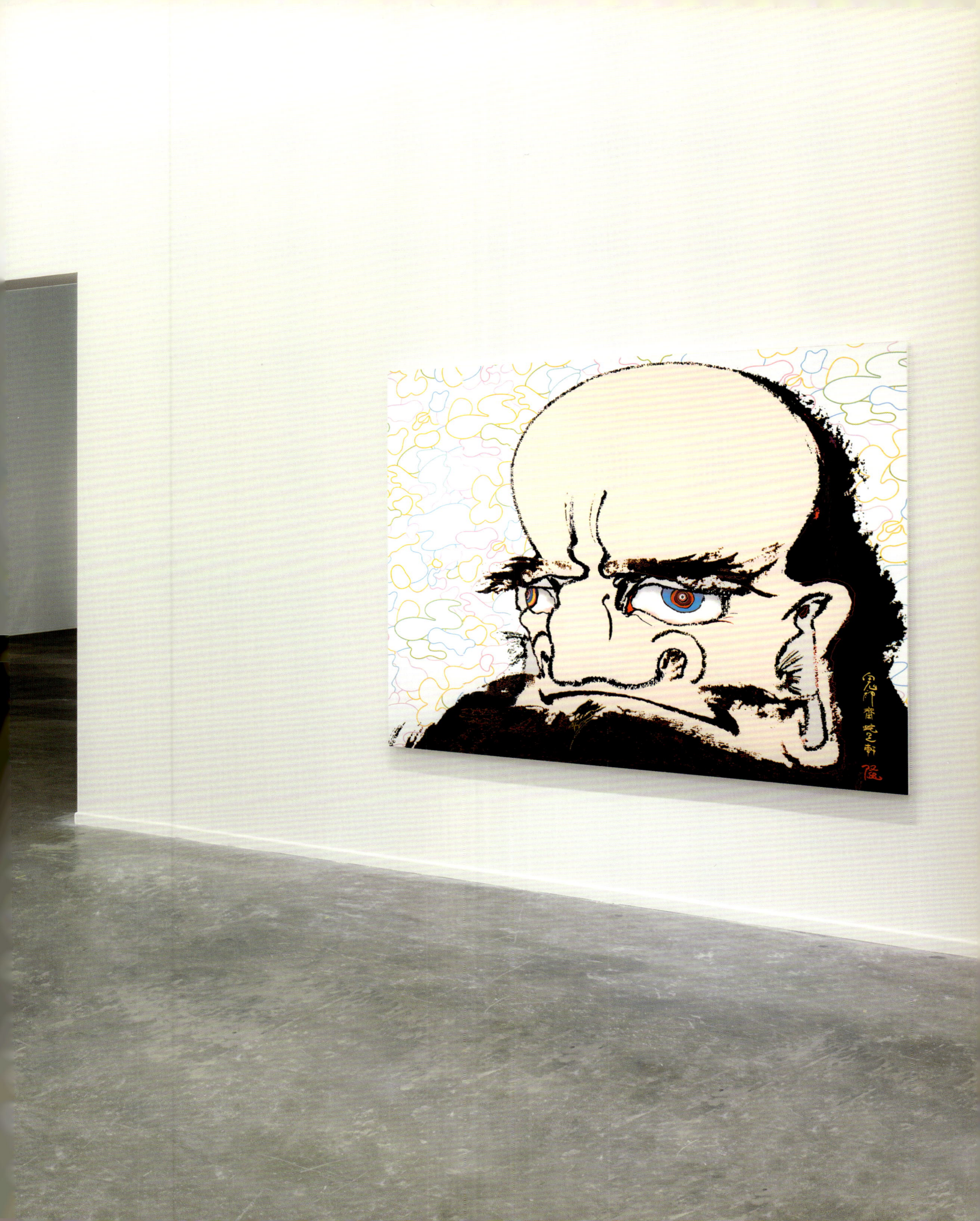

In my work, I have always wanted to create beautiful things.

I have the misfortune of having been born in Japan. As a direct result, after only two days spent overseas, I start craving Japanese food. I have tried various ways to appease my imprinted urges, but lately I just give in to my desires and dig in. My vision of beauty is based on my desires, my body, my memories—it can't be helped if it stinks of soy sauce.

Japanese contemporary art has a long history of trying to hide the soy sauce. Perhaps they'll strengthen the flavor to please the foreign palate, or perhaps they'll simply throw the soy sauce out the window and unconditionally embrace the tastes of French and Italian cuisine, becoming Westerners and following their model of contemporary art. We've been eating out for years. Although it might be easier, that path is not for me, I think. No matter how much trouble it takes, I see the need to create a universal taste—a common tongue—without cheating myself and my Japanese core. I prefer to trust my own taste buds and use them to guide me as I continue to blend seasonings, not cheat myself with something else. I have kept this thought in mind during my years of work in Japan. To follow the metaphor, I have been creating my own Japanese kaiseki banquet.

My banquet knows where it stands. I may have mixed in the universal forms and presentations of French, Italian, Chinese, or other ethnic cuisines—I am vigilant in my search for their best ingredients—but the central axis of my creation is stable. At first glance, it may have looked like I was bent on making something that can only be called eccentric creation, and come to think of it, that might be the truth.

However, at its core, my standard of "beauty" is one cultivated by the Japan that has been my home since my birth in 1962. It is a core that is not easily shaken. The materials I have at my disposal are Japanese art history, manga, anime, otakudom, J-POP culture, postwar history, and imported accounts of contemporary art.

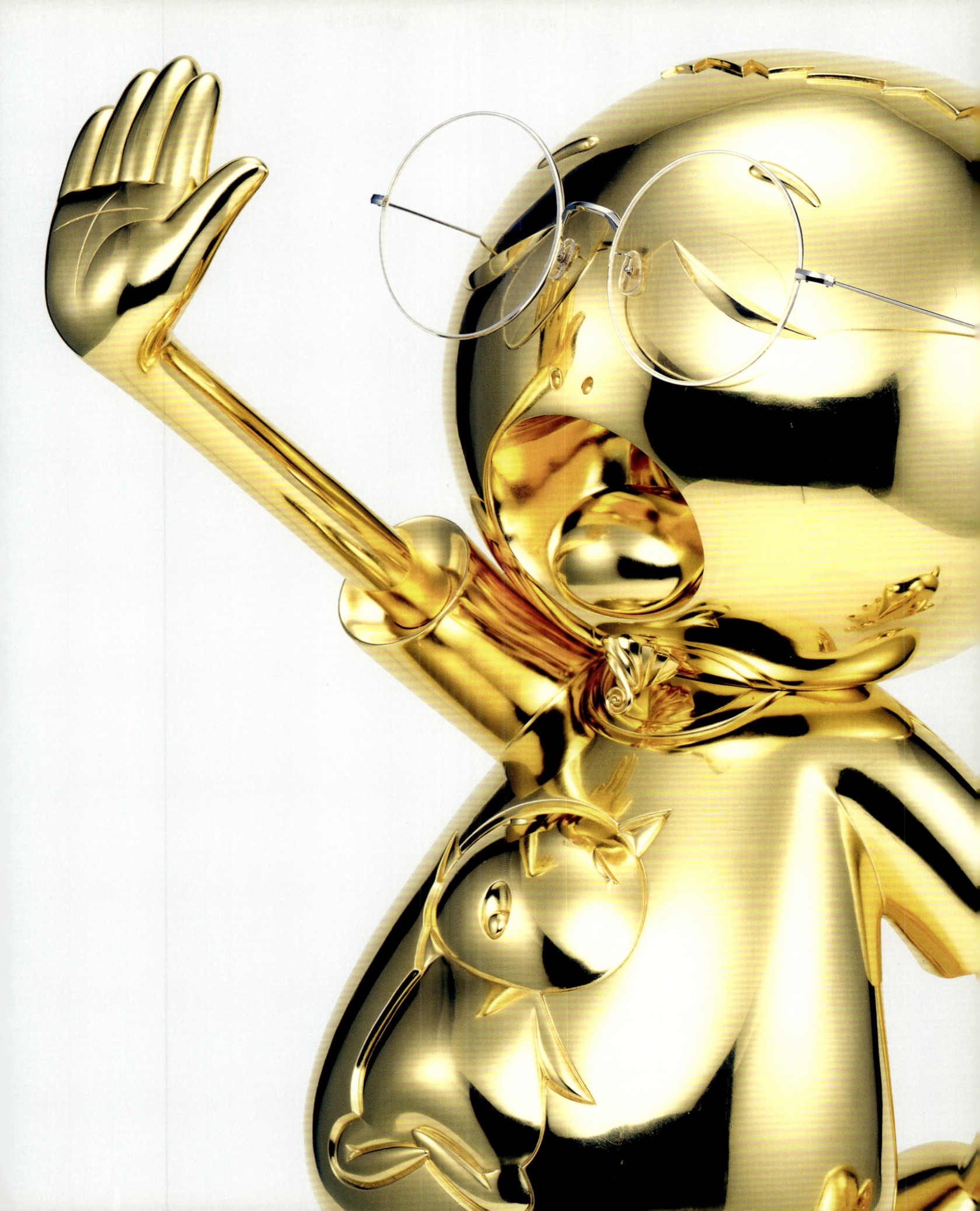

Pom & Me (bronze) 2009

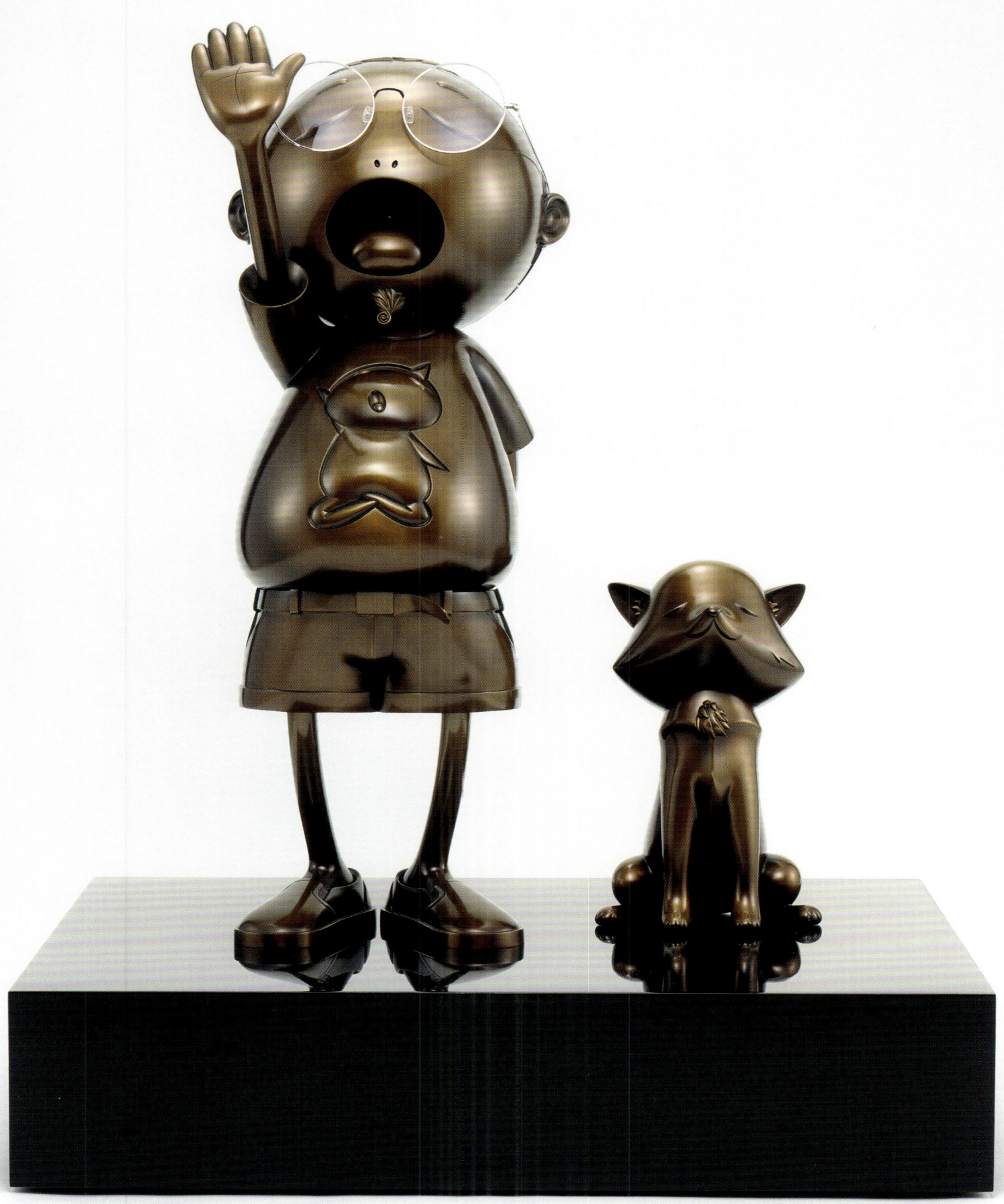

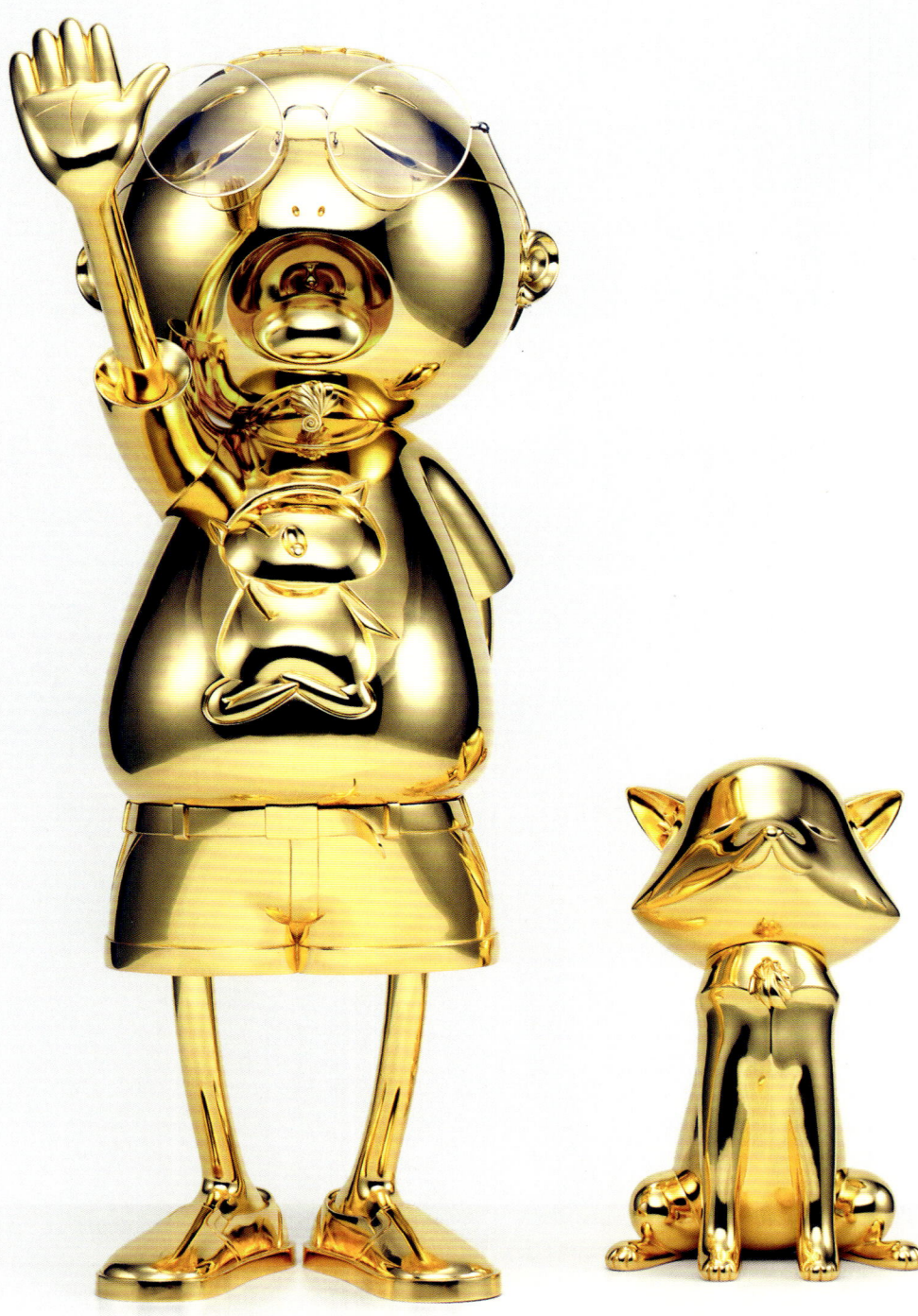

Pom & Me (gold) 2009

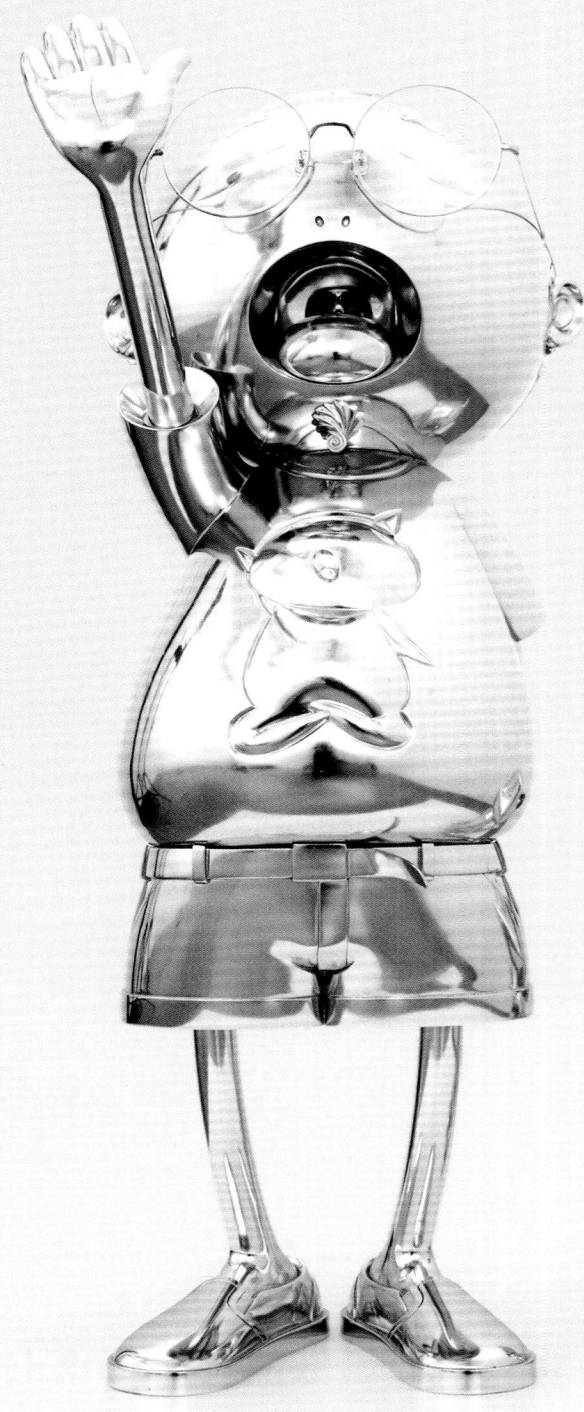
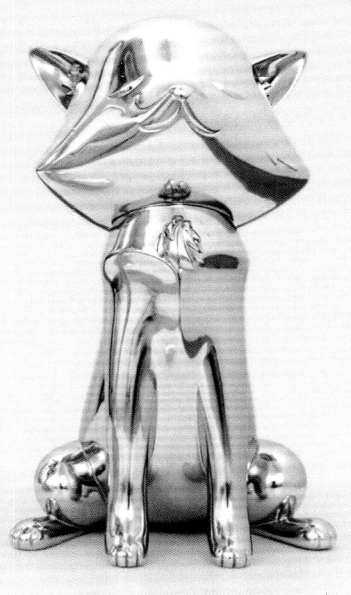

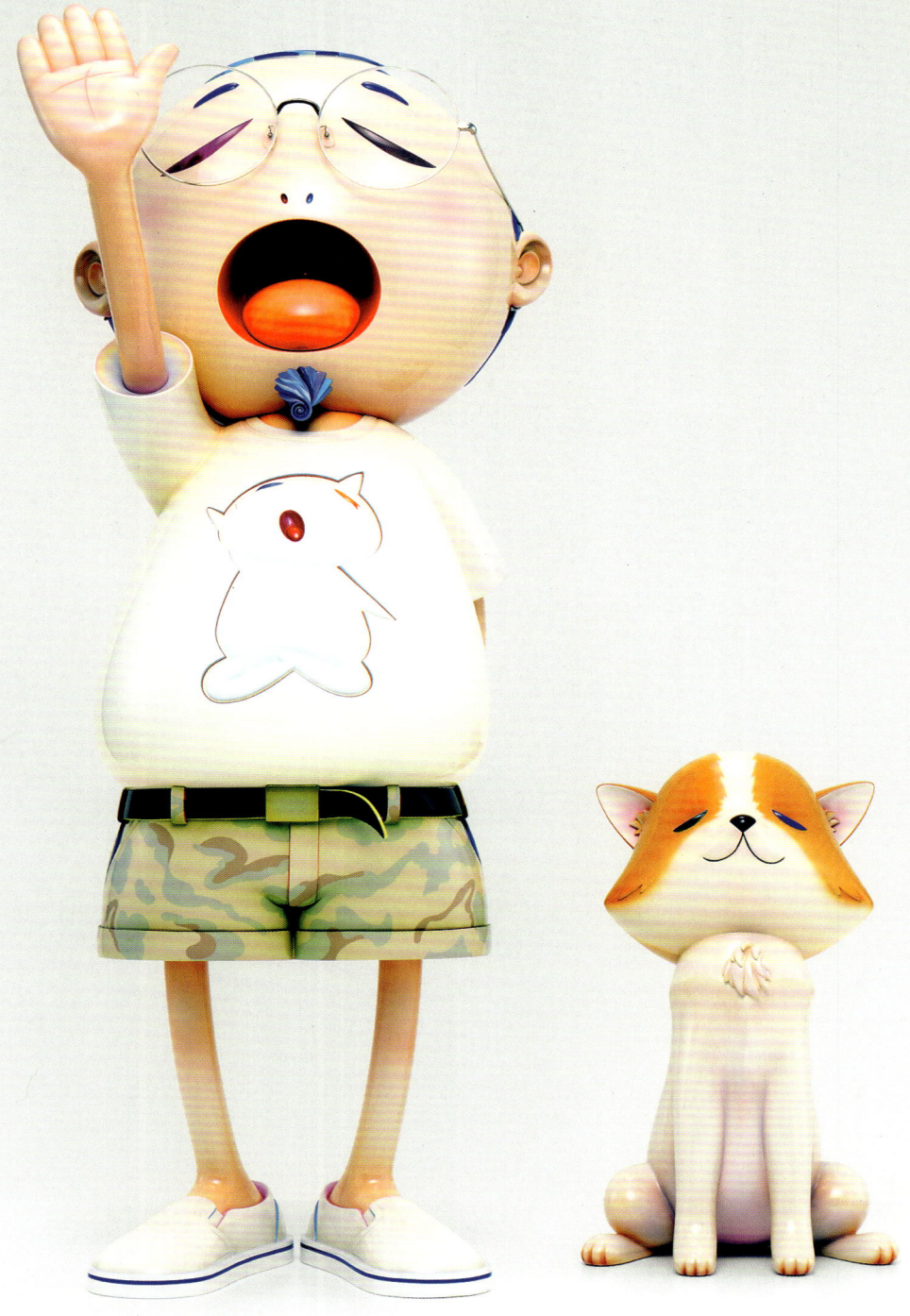

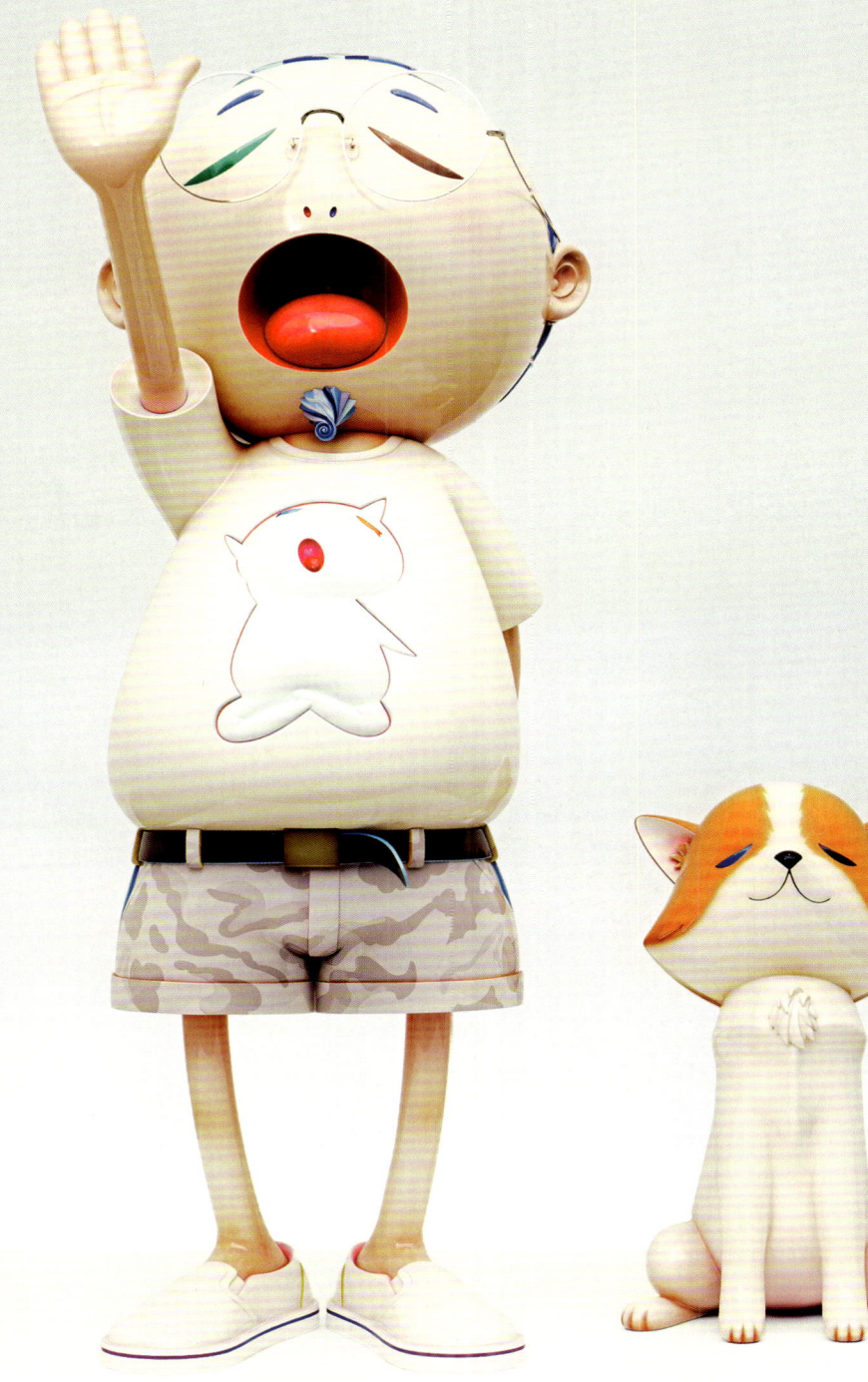

Pom & Me (carbon) Artist Proof 2009

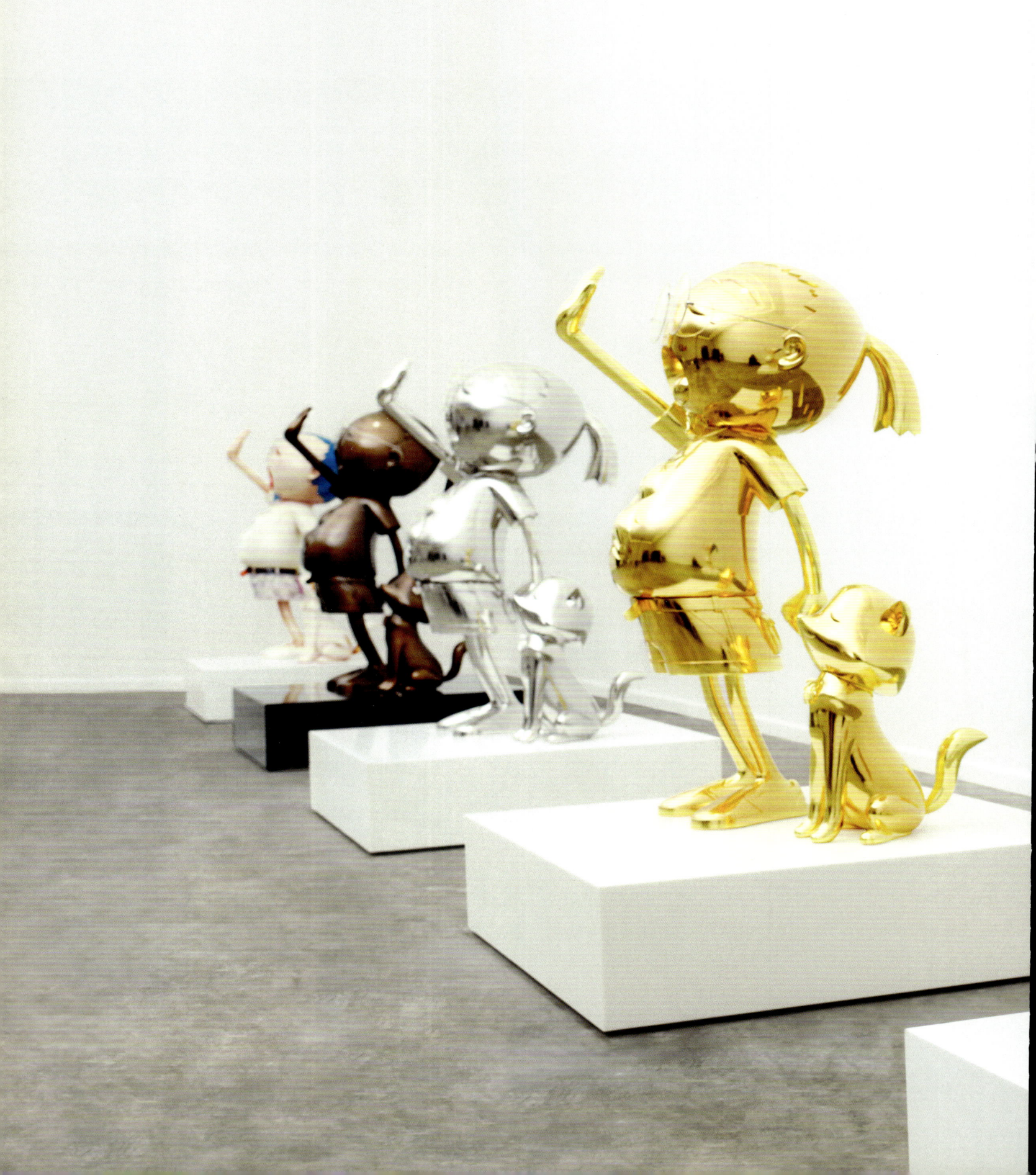

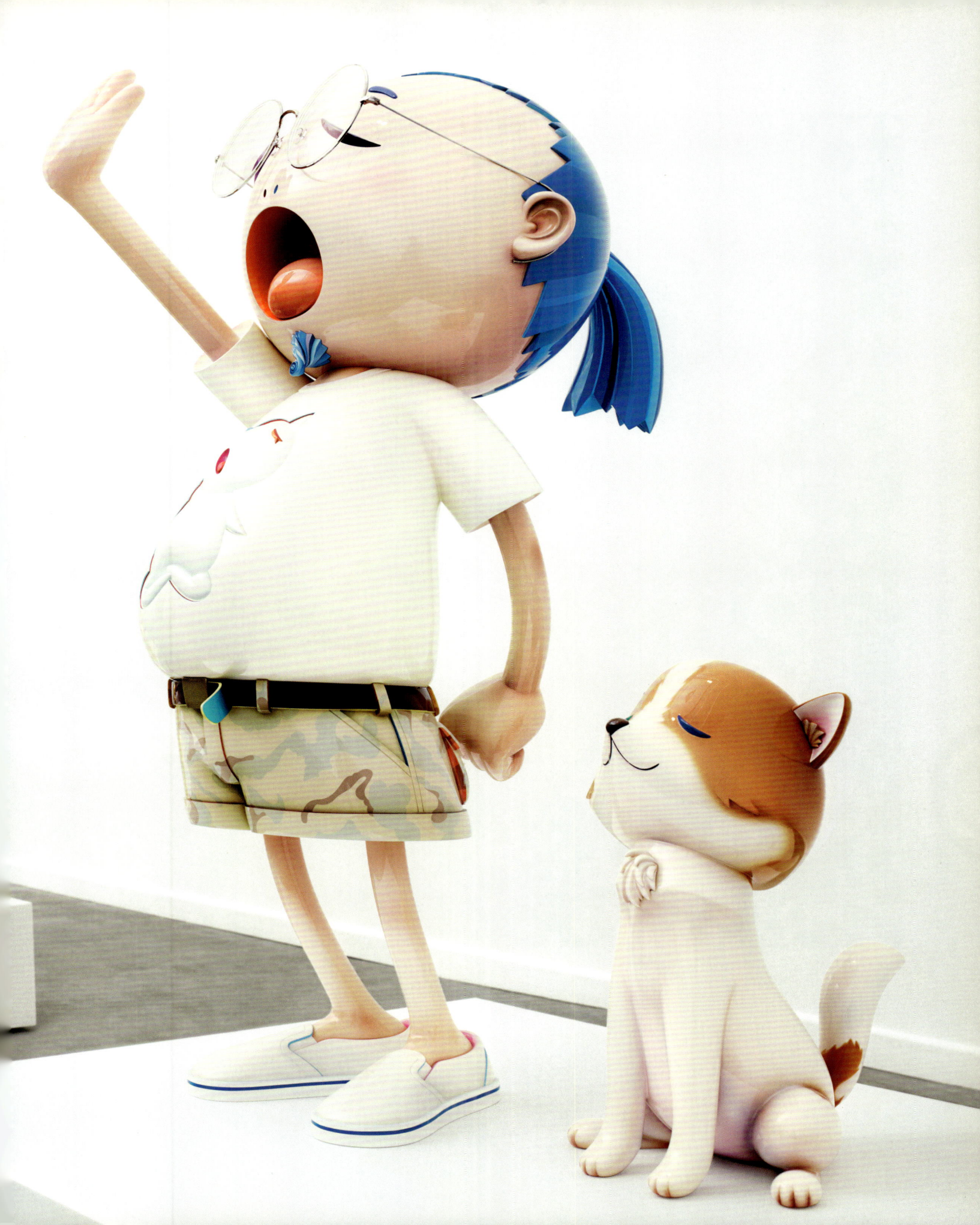

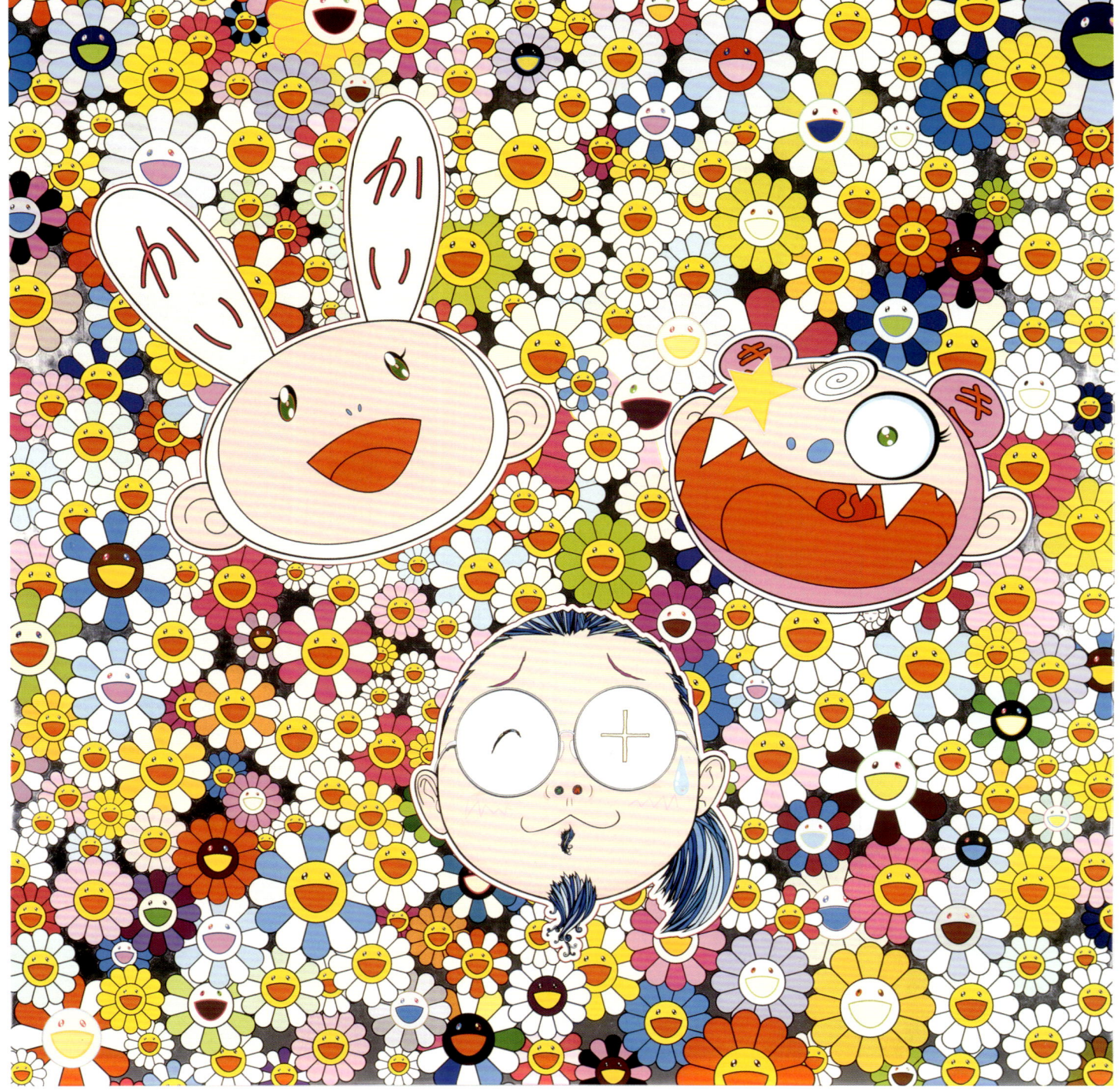

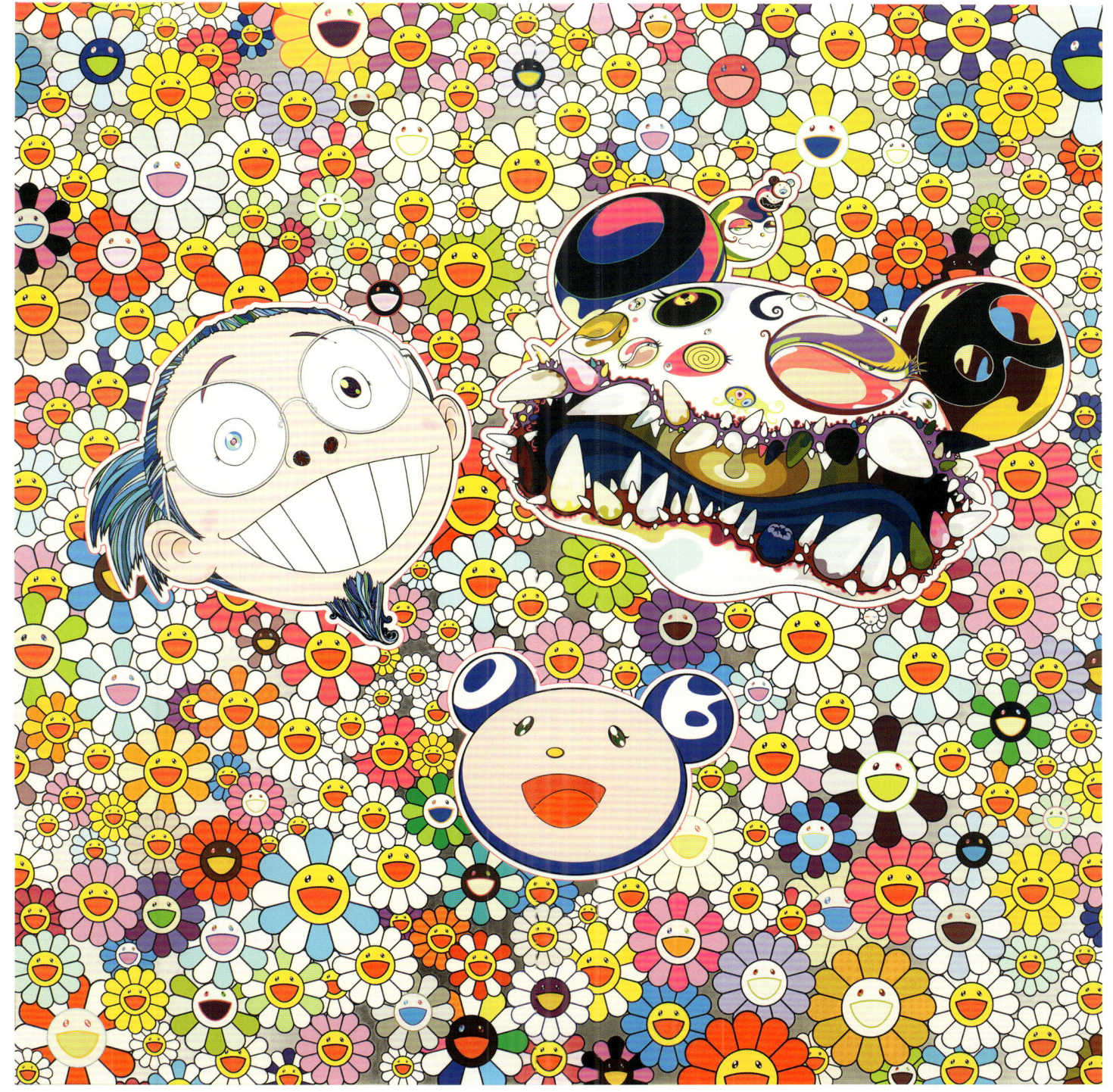

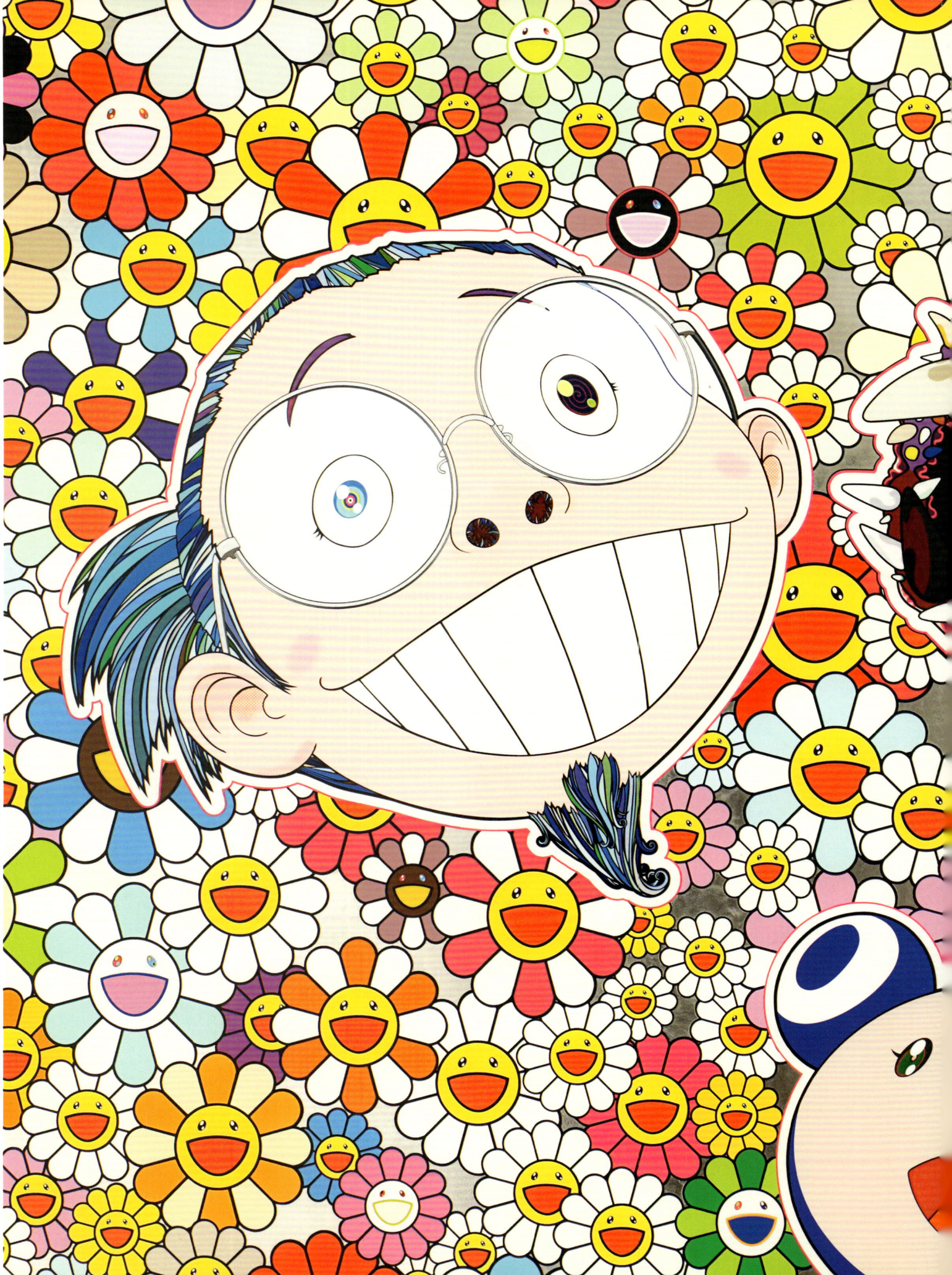

Me and Double-DOB (detail) 2009

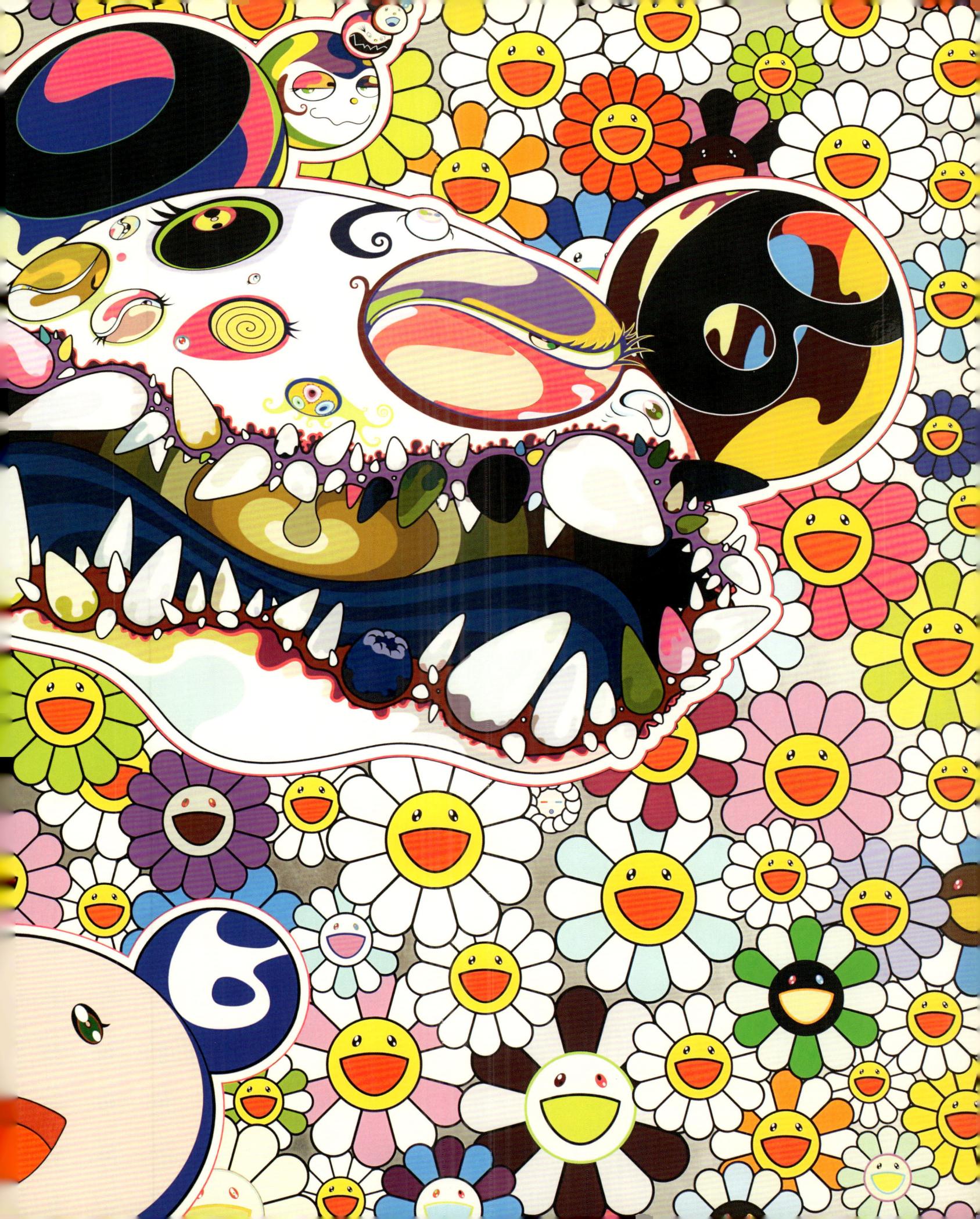

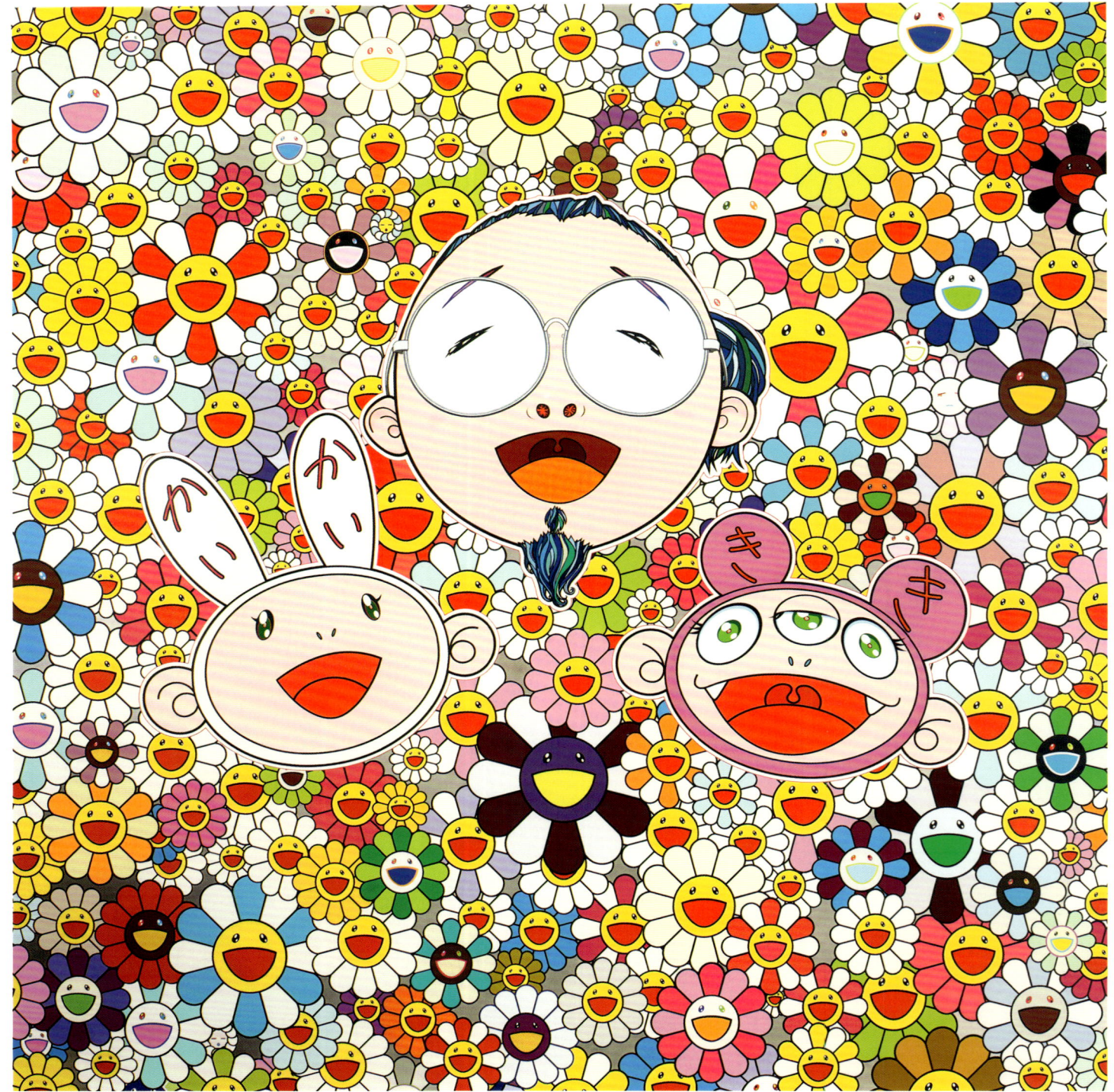

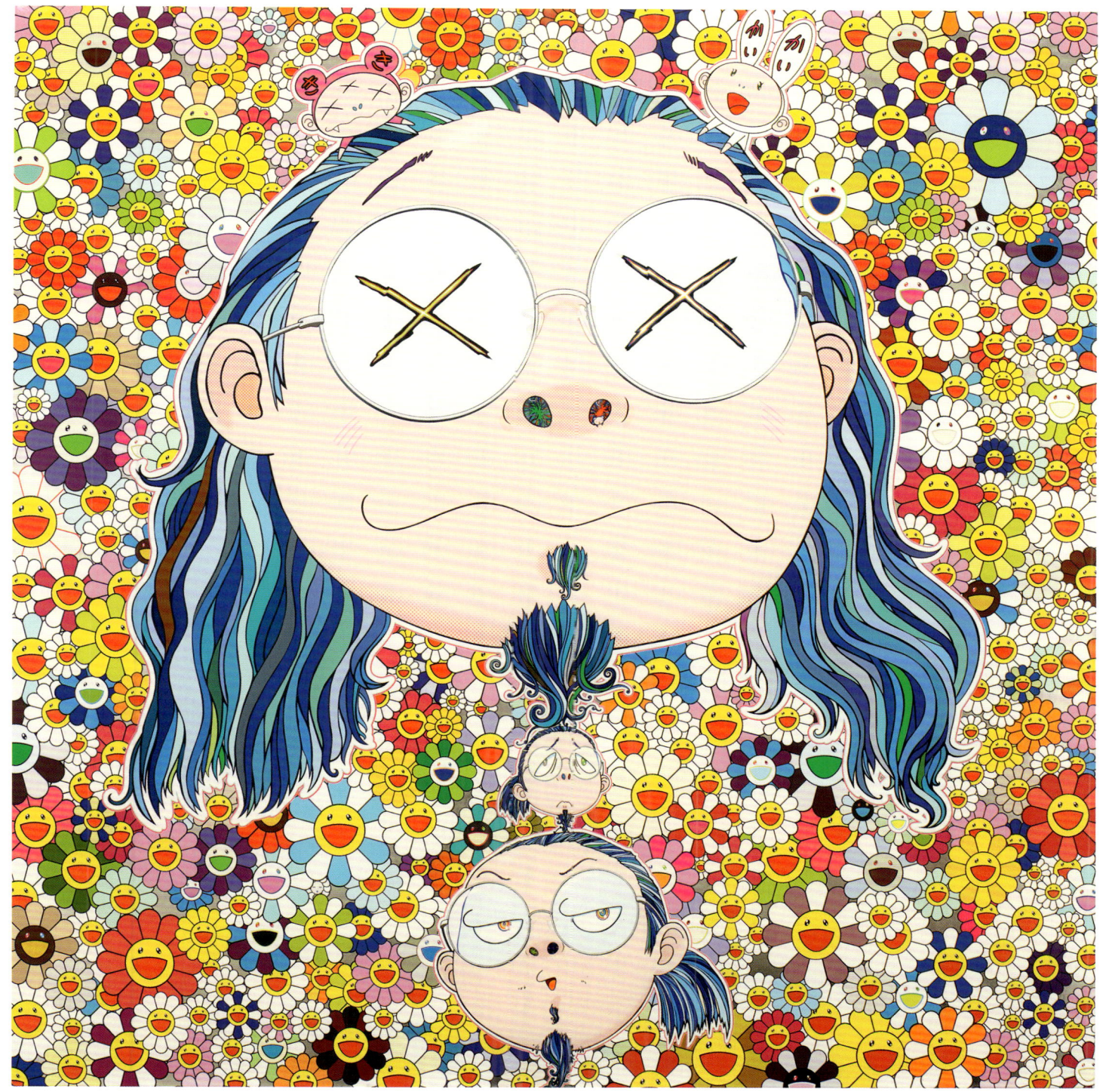

Self-Portrait of the Distressed Artist 2009

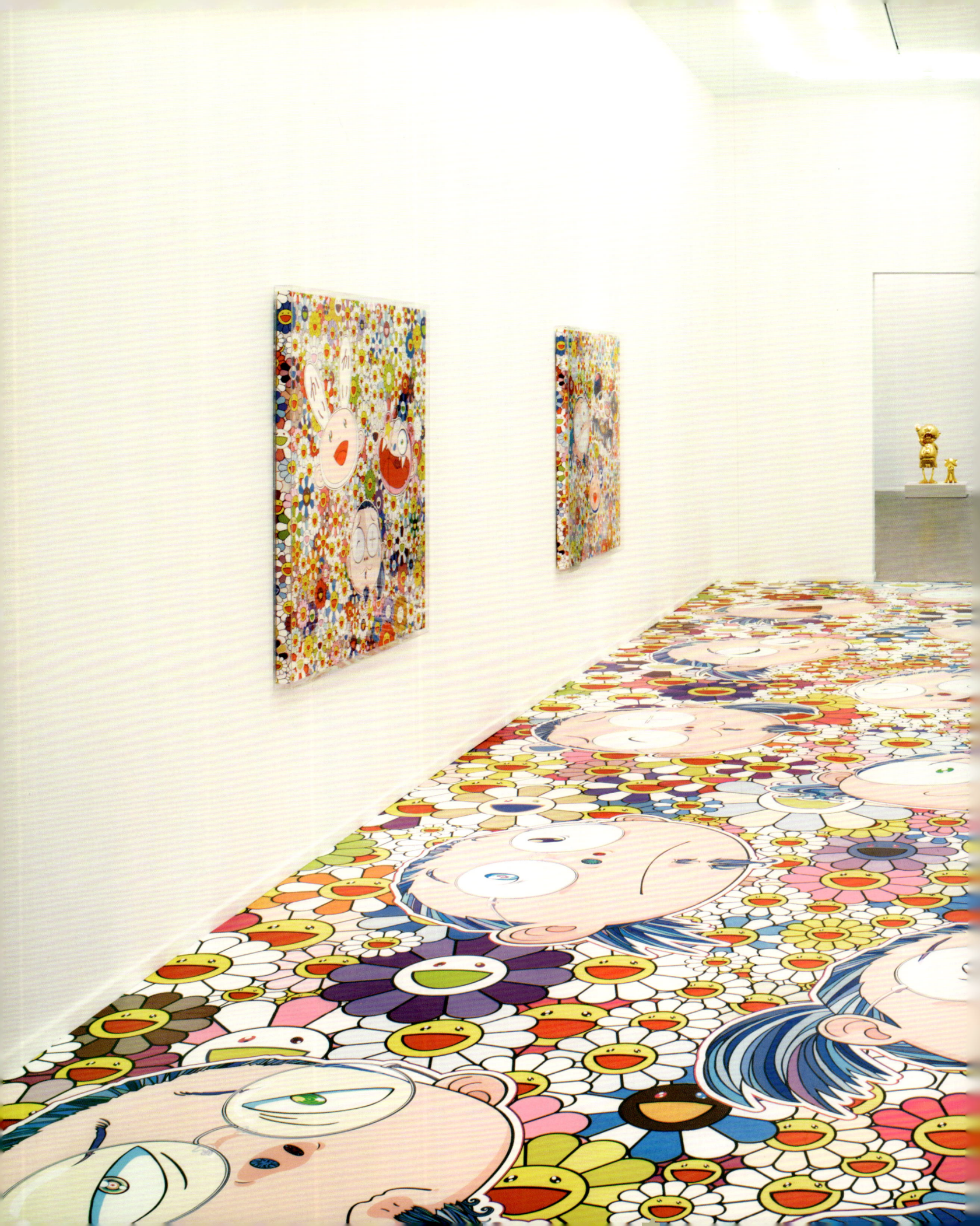

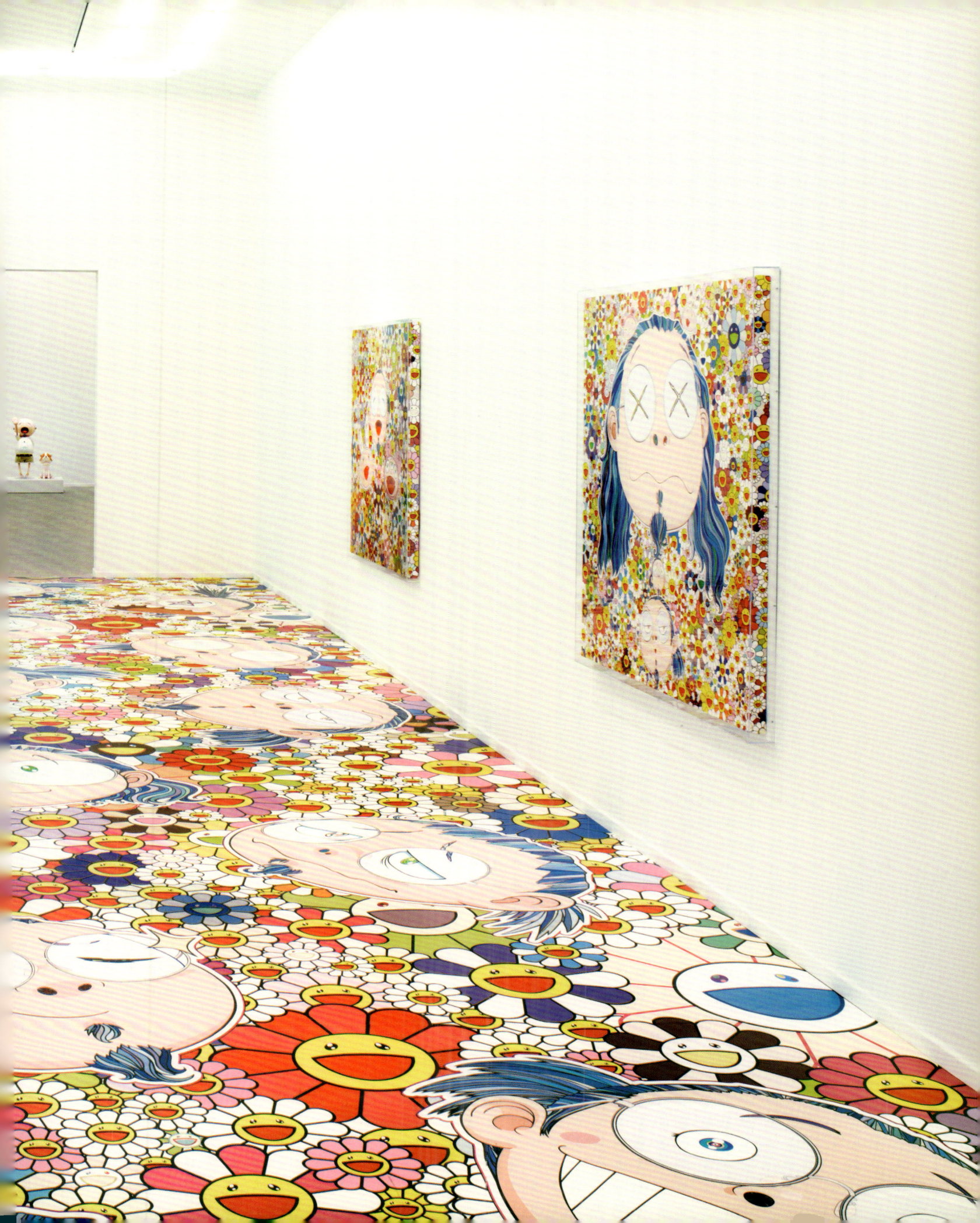

Welcome to Murakami Ego 2012

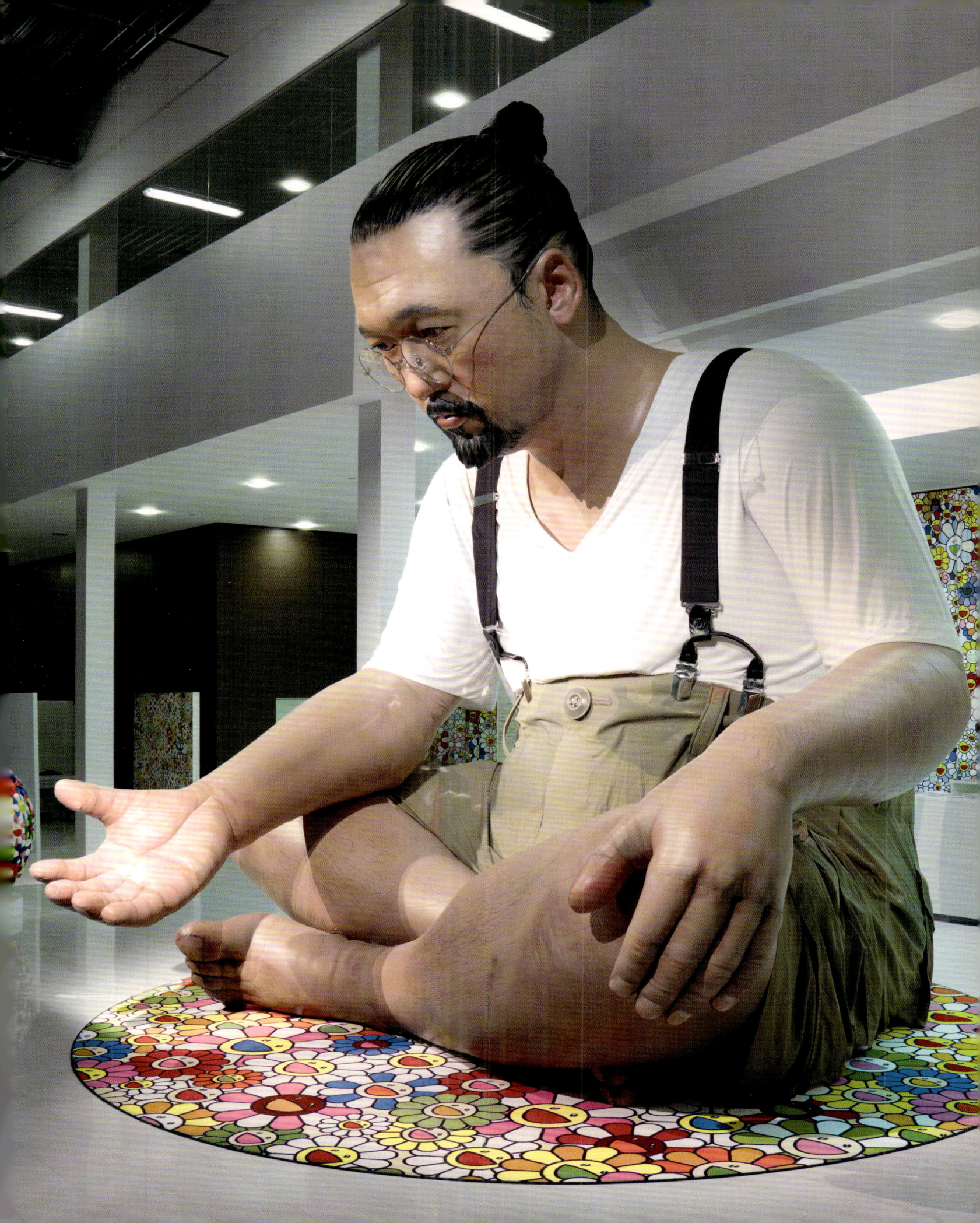

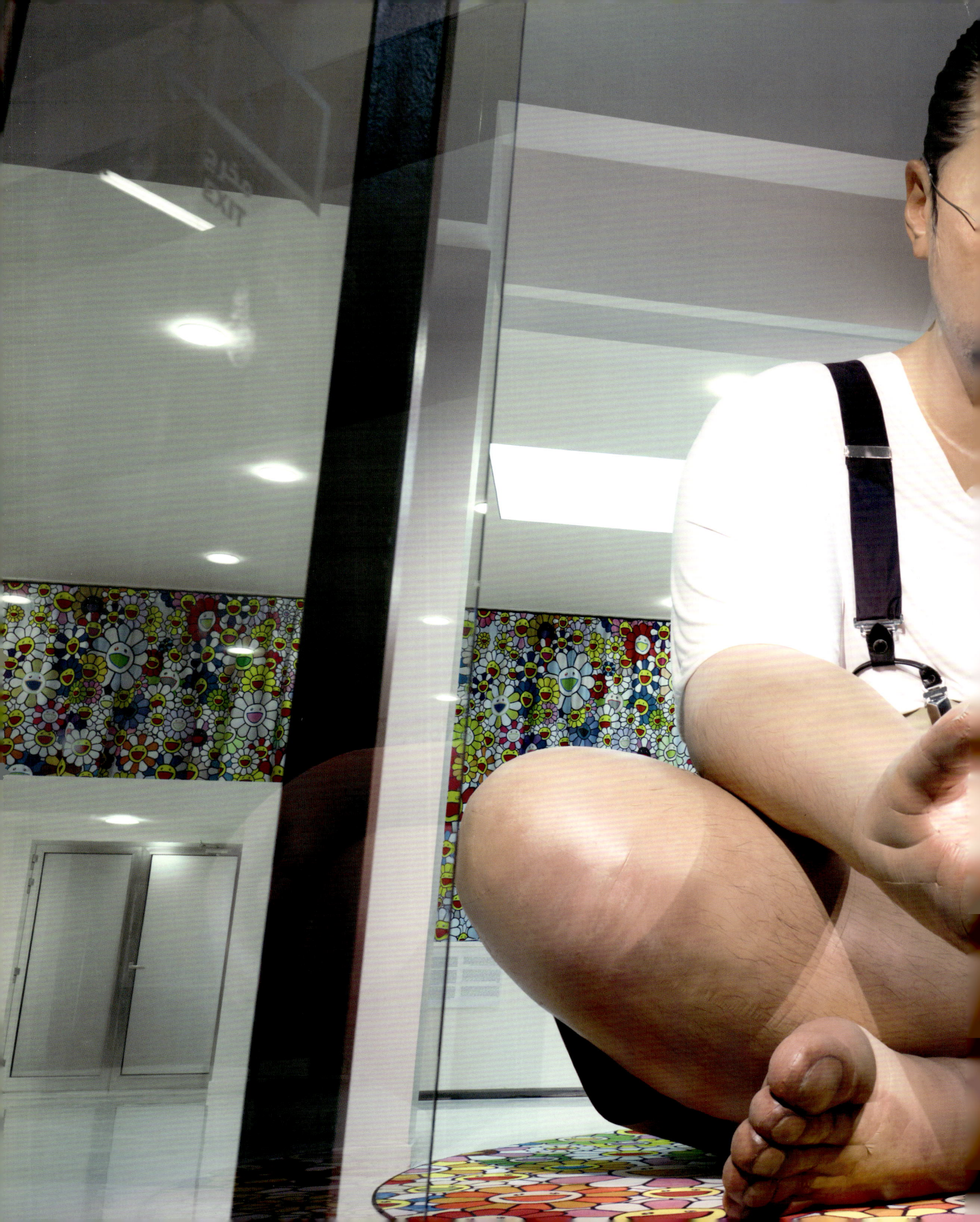

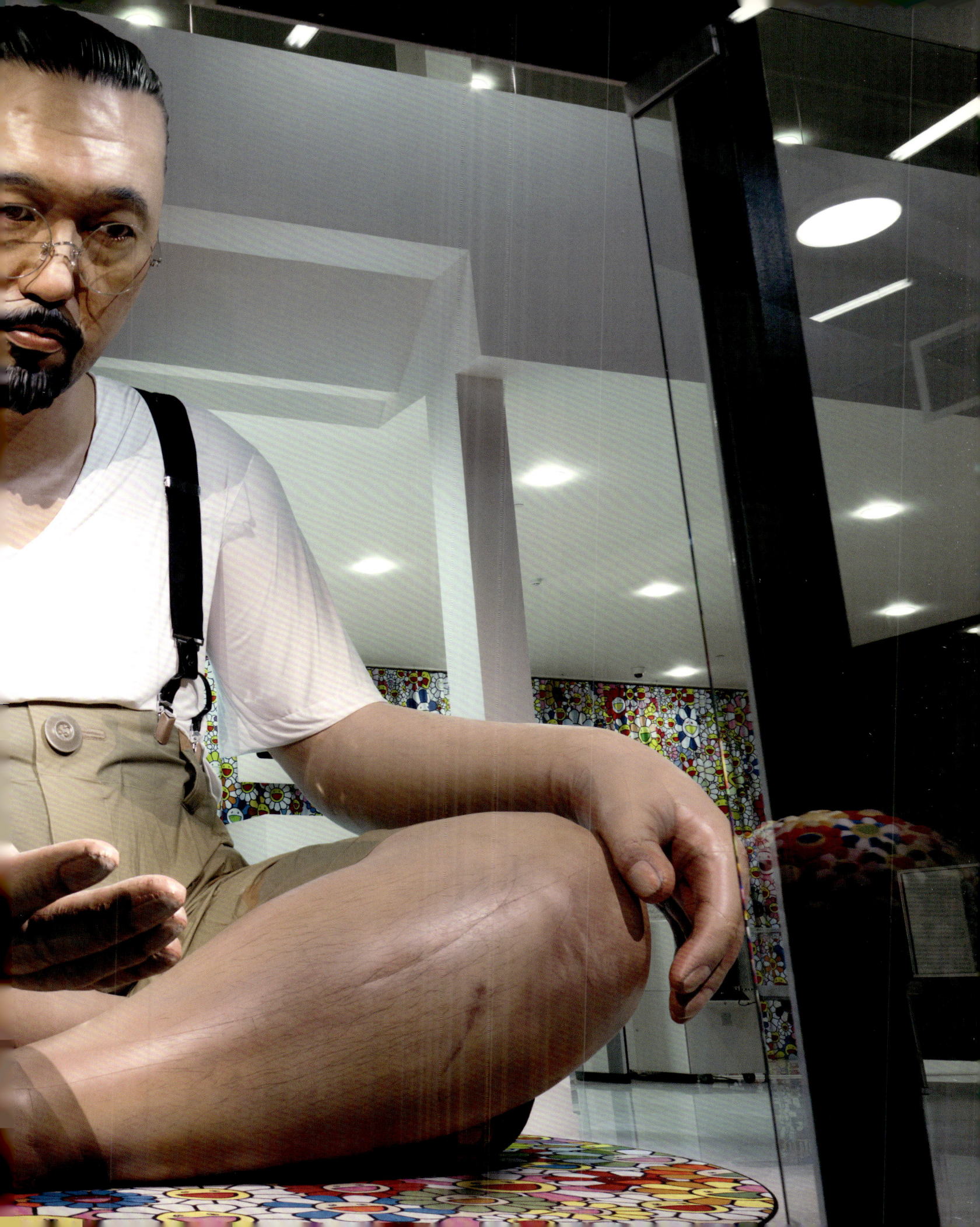

I WILL ALWAYS WORK FOR THE SAKE OF BEAUTY.

Whether I am in Japan or anywhere else in the world, I will create beauty and rejoice in her name. If I must start by tilling the soil, I will happily cover myself with mud.

It is because beauty brings reality to the fantasy that everyone is an equal before it, if only for a moment. It is the culmination of people's desire to simply understand one another.

This is what I work for. I pray every day that I can maintain this passion until I die, that I can live earnestly and fulfill my role as a disciple of beauty.

Beauty is something that will continue to change with the times. Art's role is to create a connection that goes beyond borders. When I stand before an artist's work—whether it is by Cézanne or Warhol or anyone else—and look at its finished state, I can experience whatever the artist was feeling at the time of its creation. This kind of experience is beautiful and beyond words.

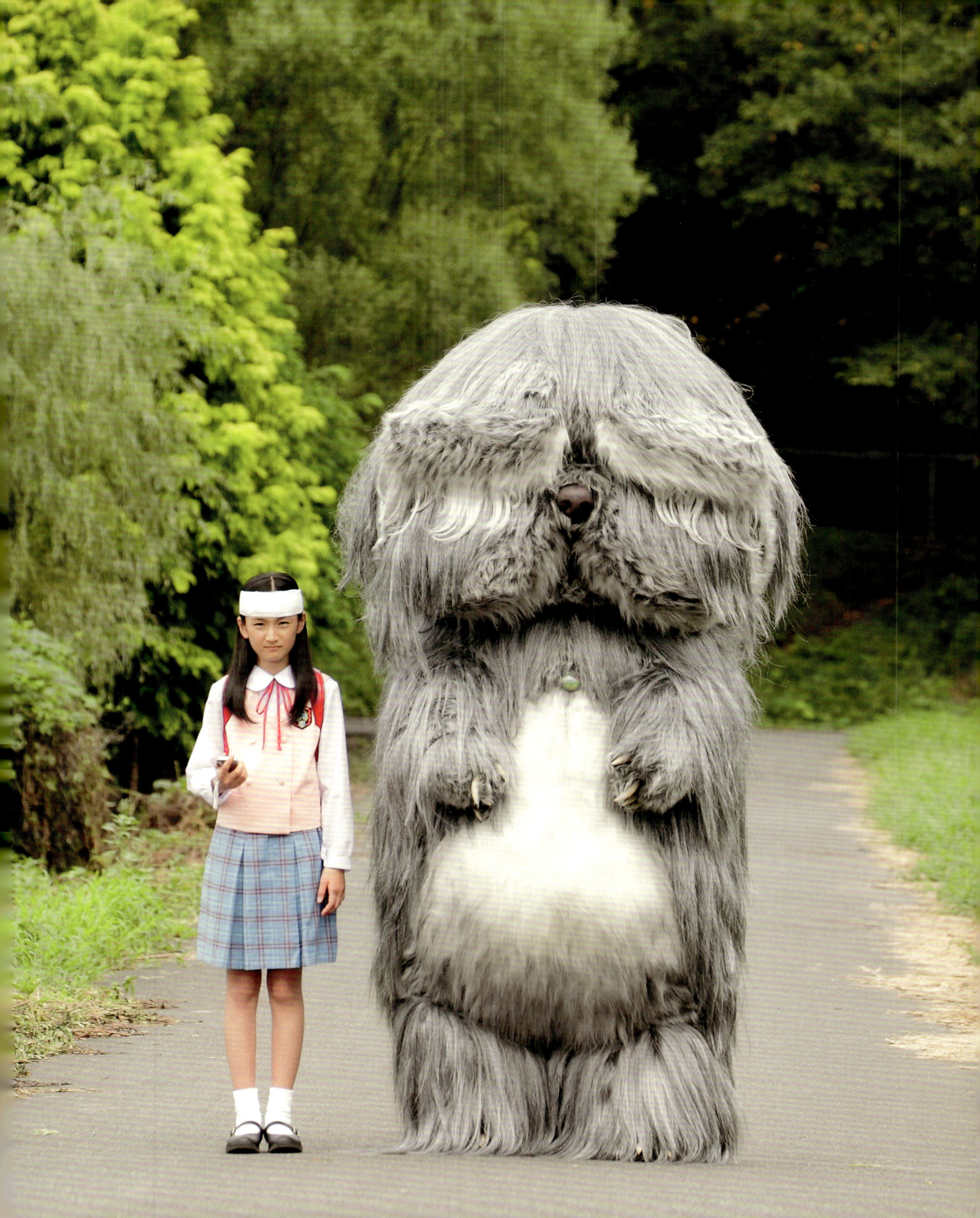

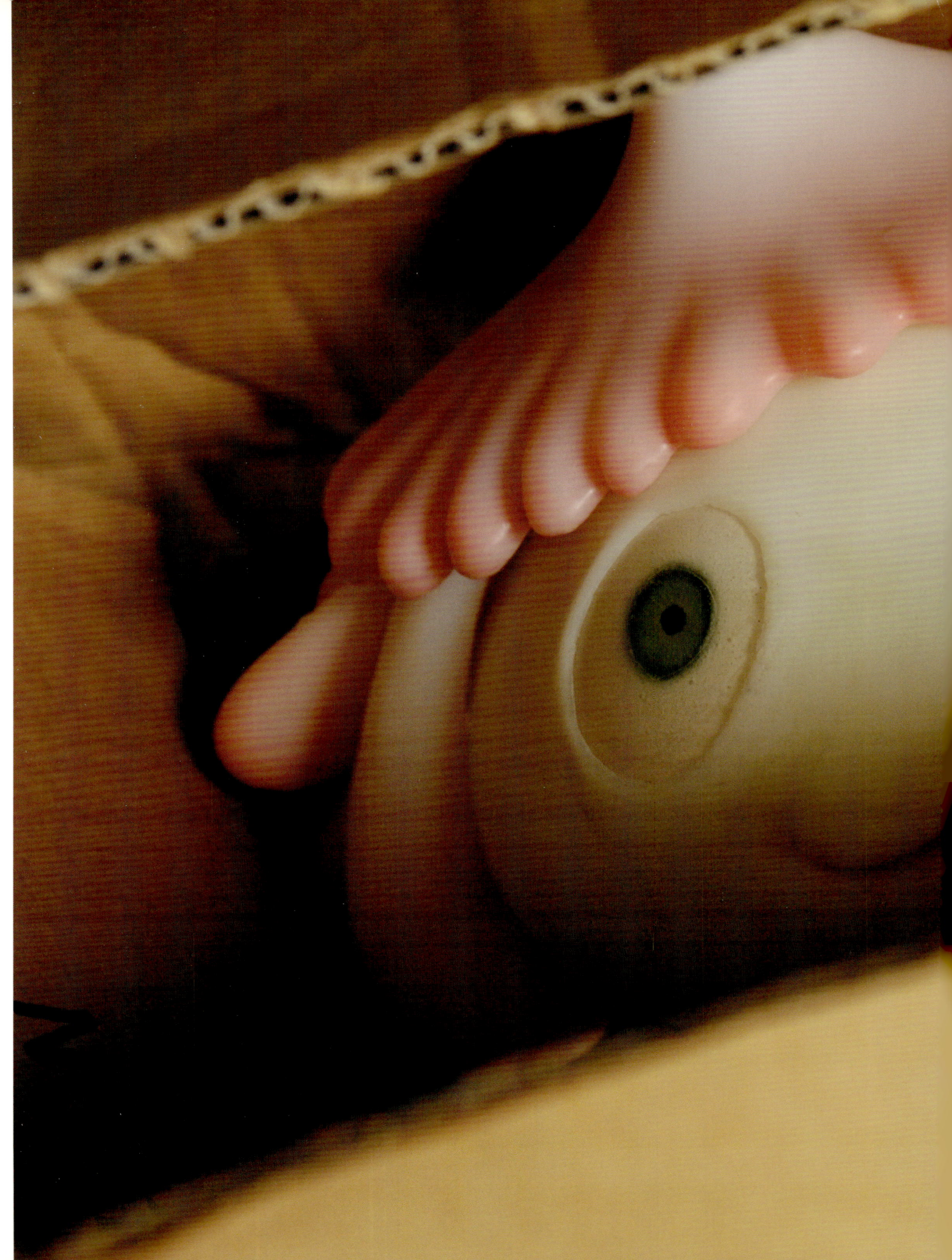

Still from <u>Jellyfish Eyes</u> 2011

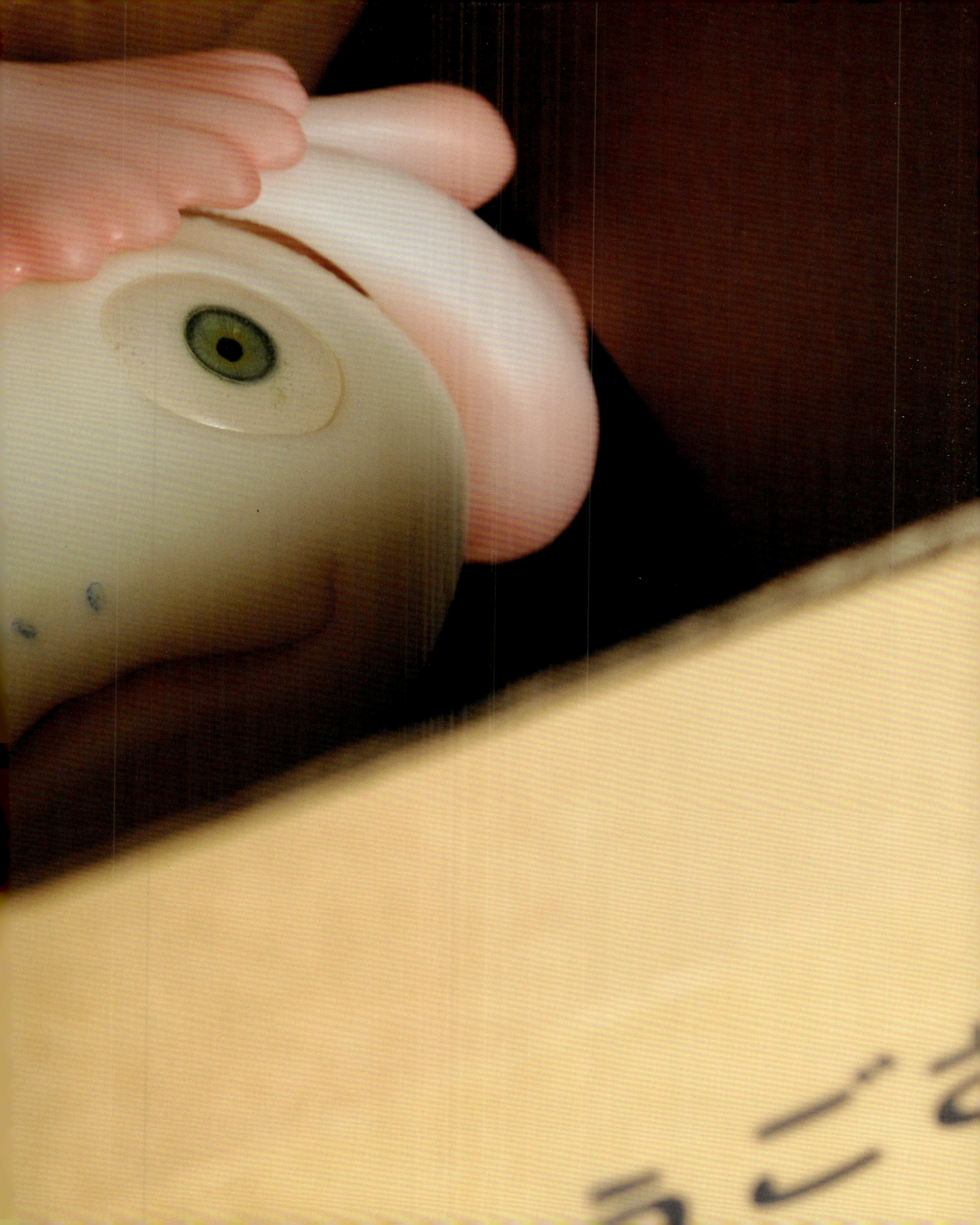

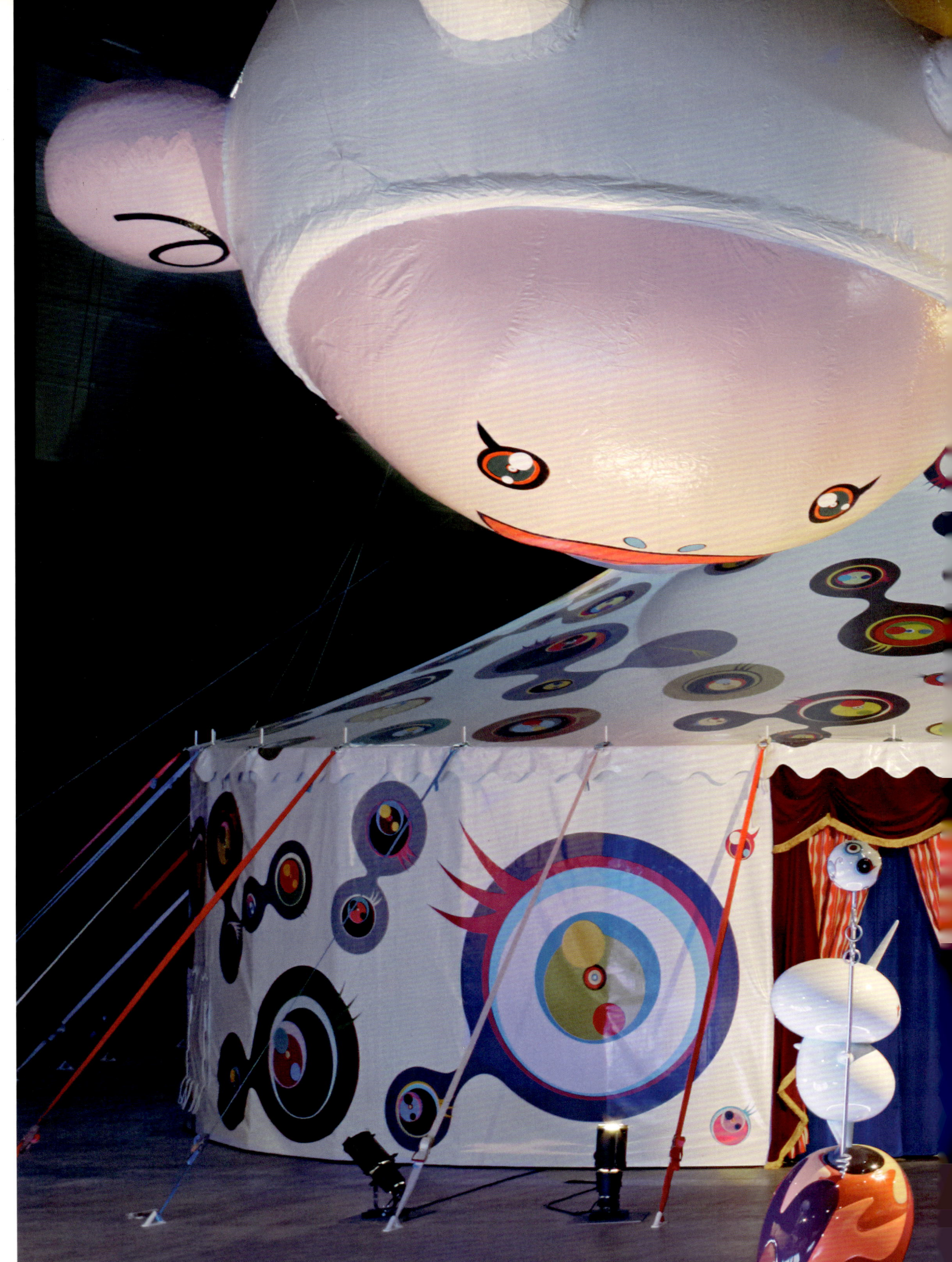

Murakami—Ego Monster (circus tent) 2012

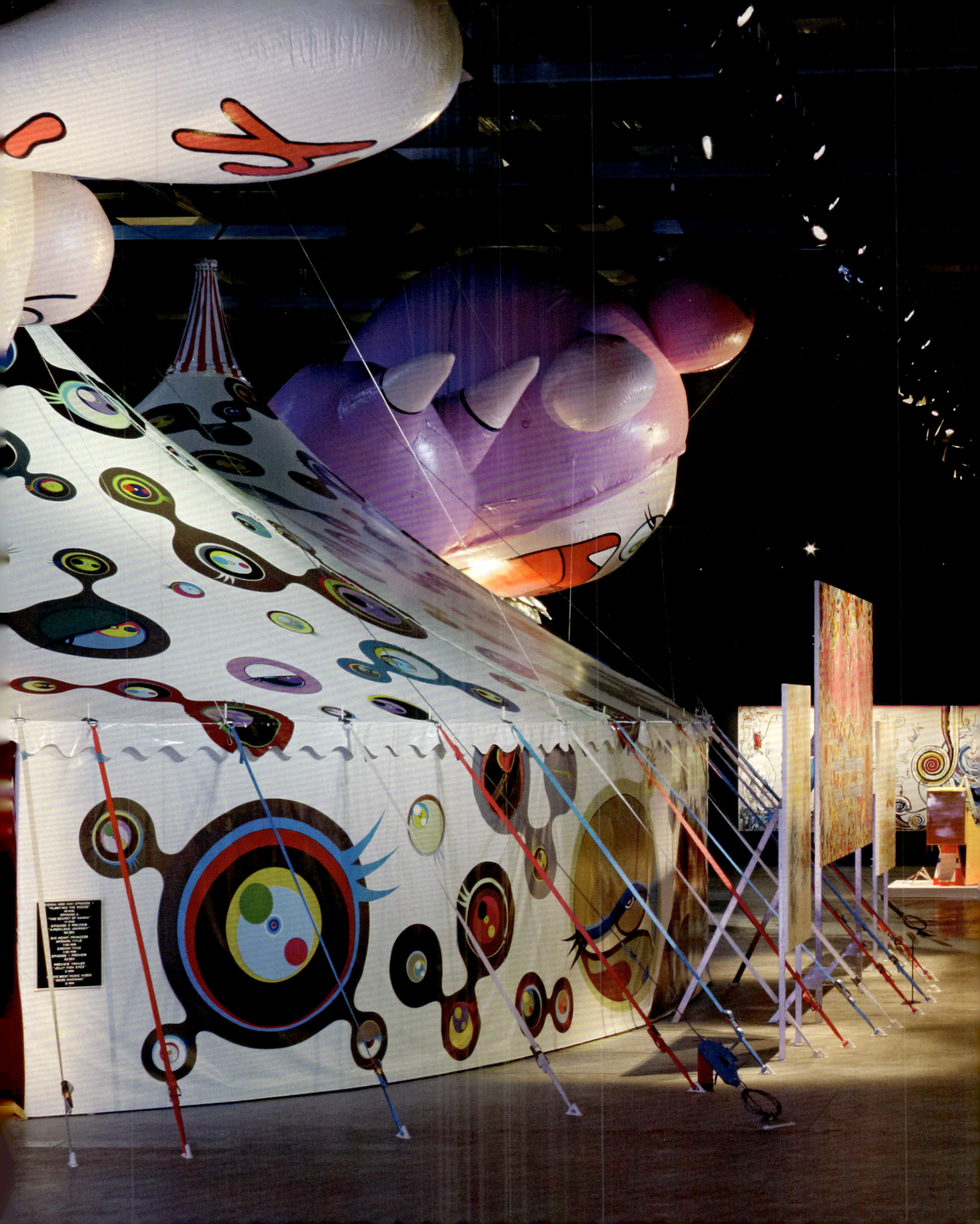

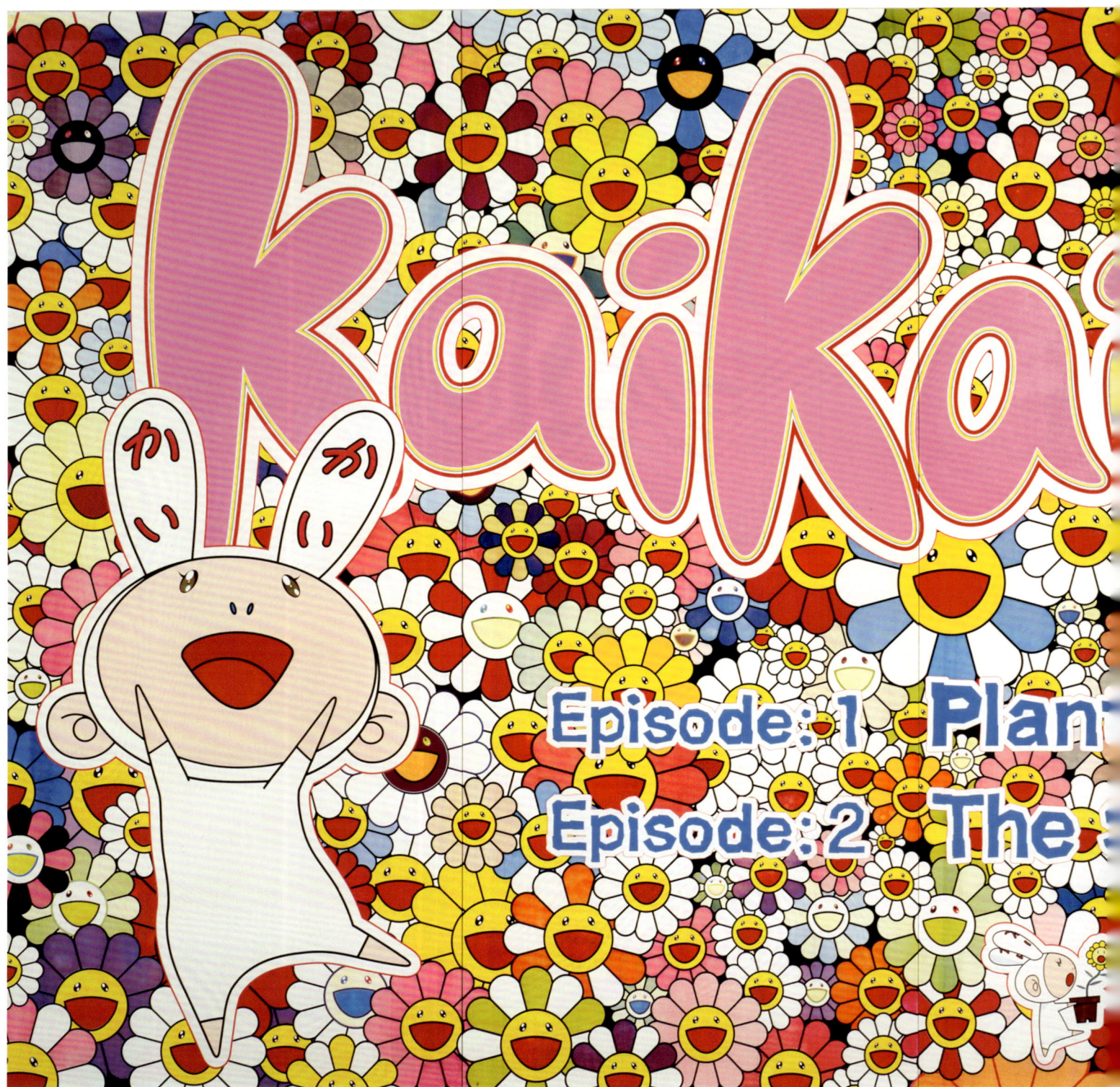

Episode: 1 Plan
Episode: 2 The

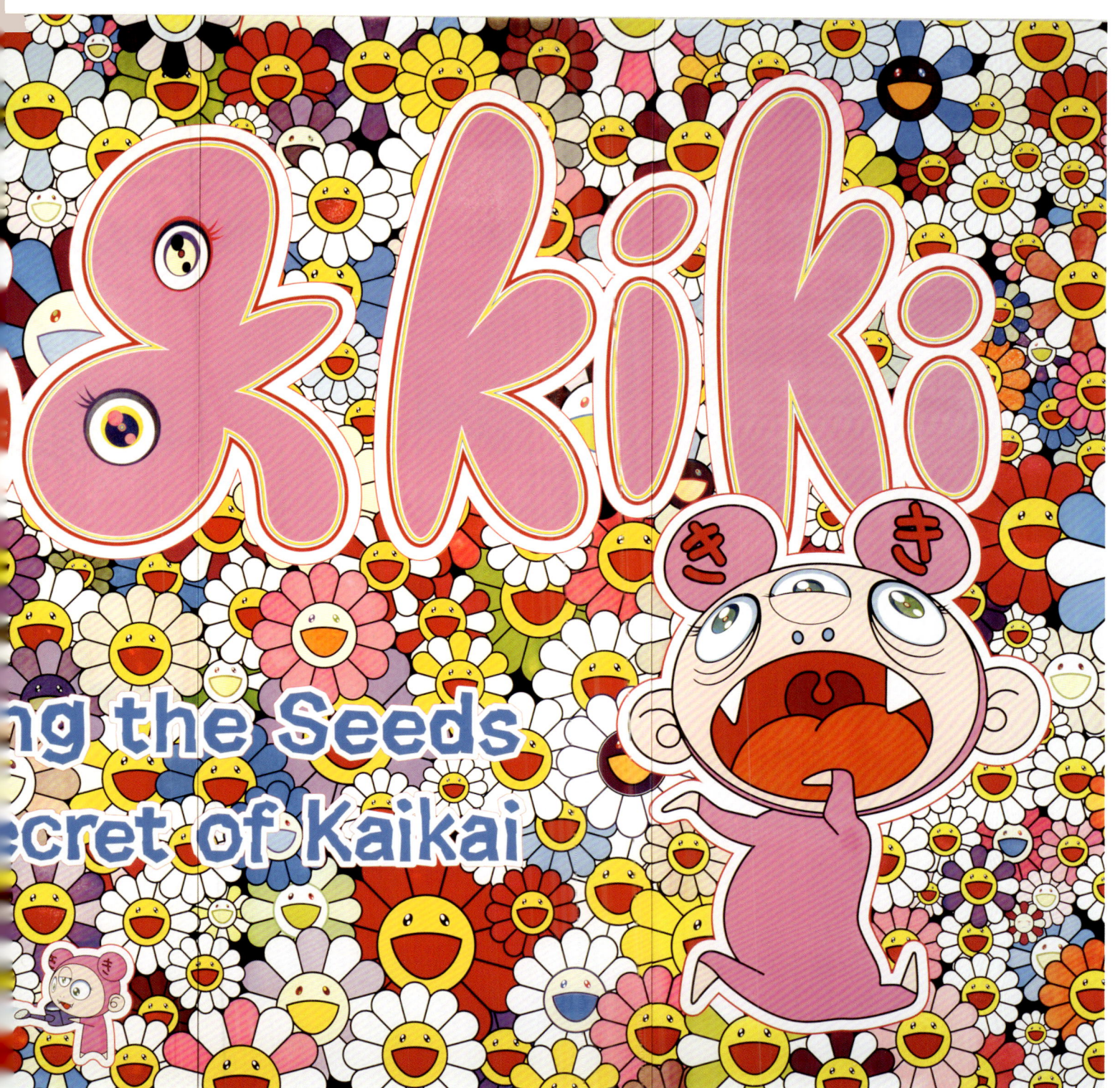

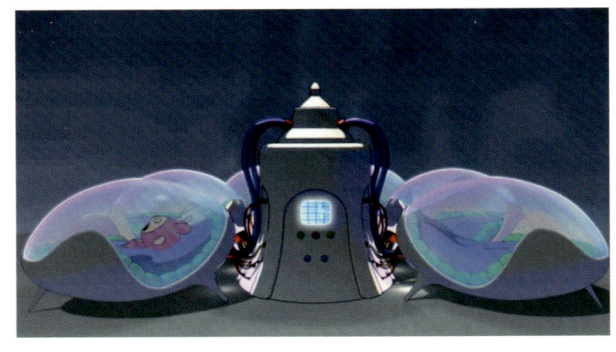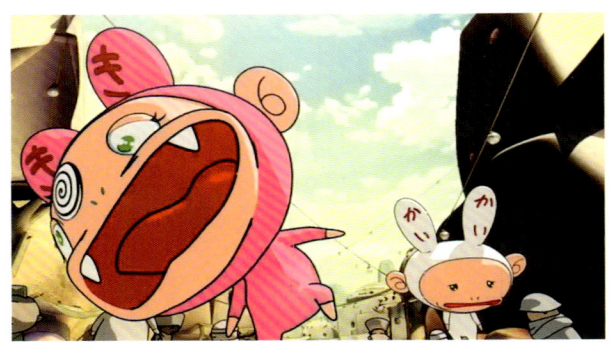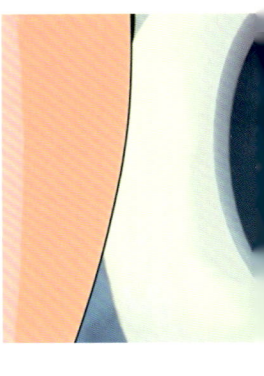

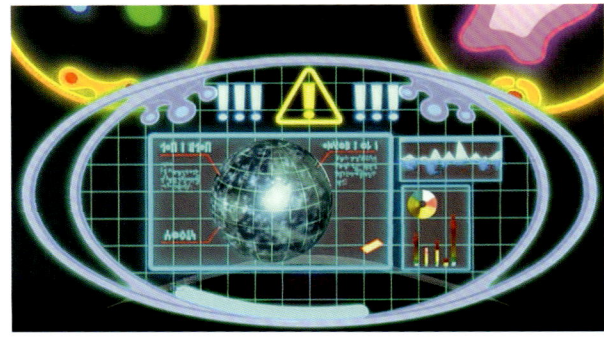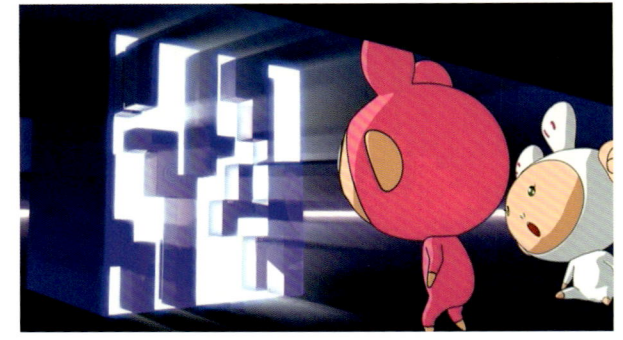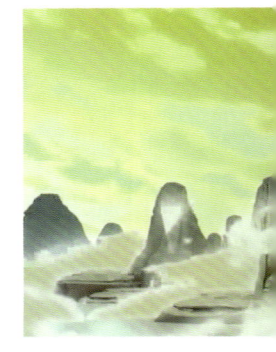

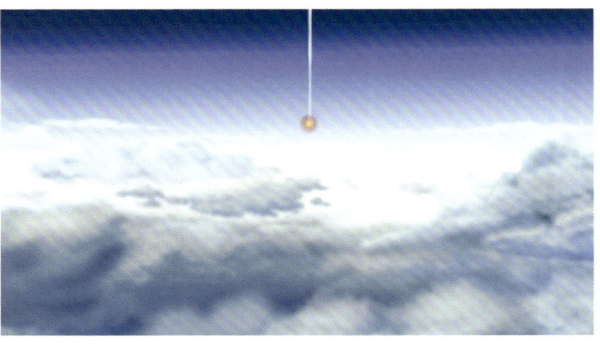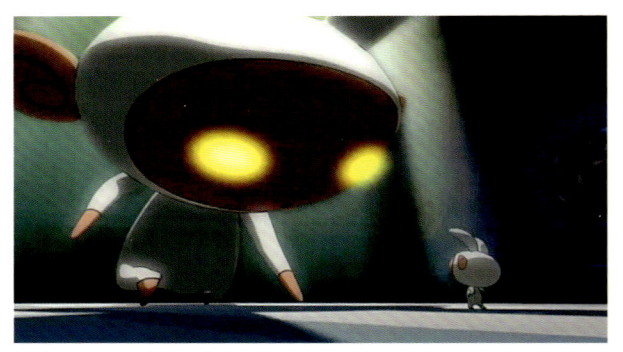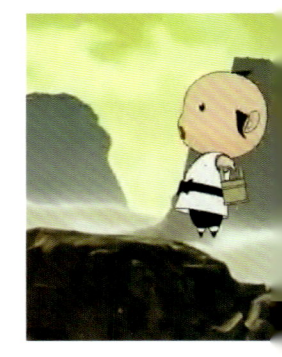

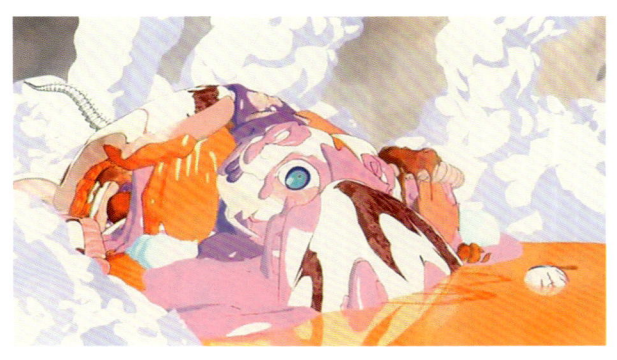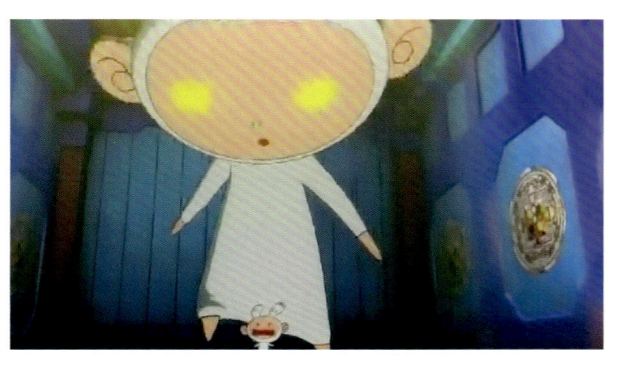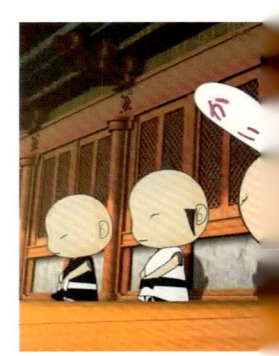

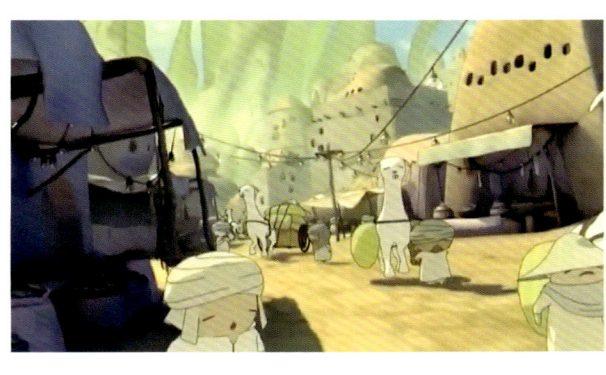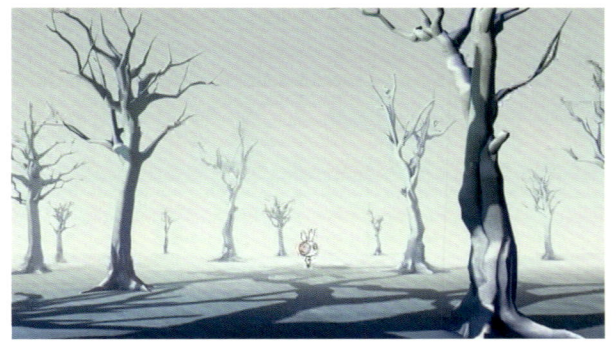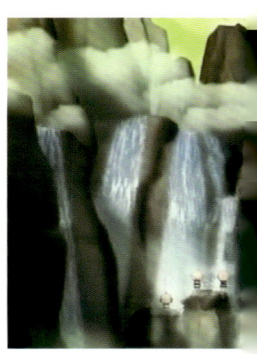

Stills from Kaikai and Kiki Animation Episode 3: A Perilous Journey 2012

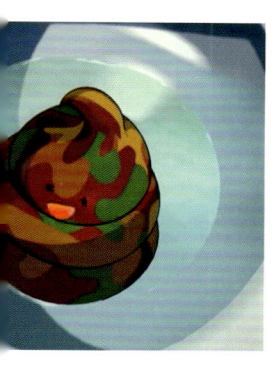
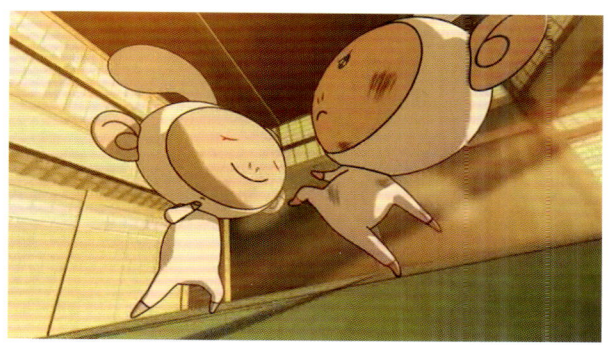
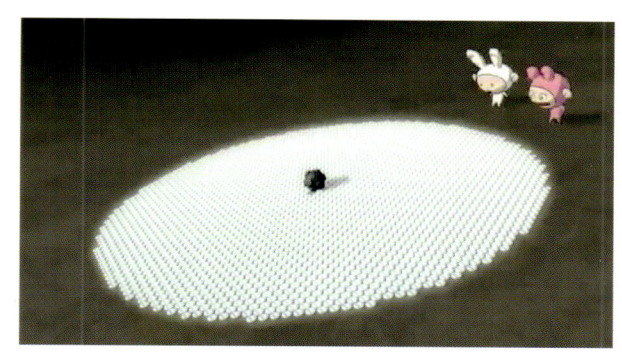
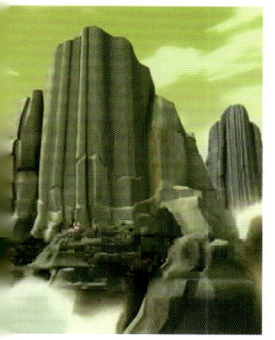
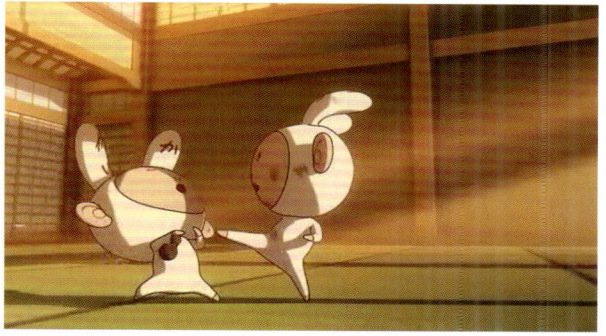
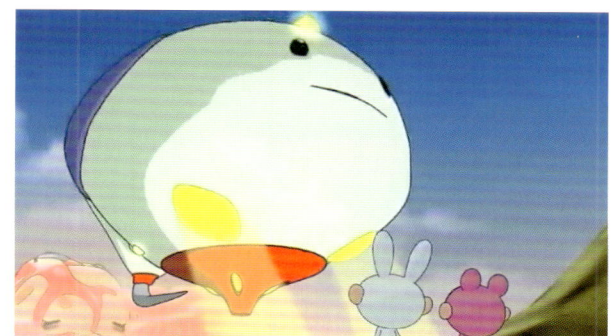
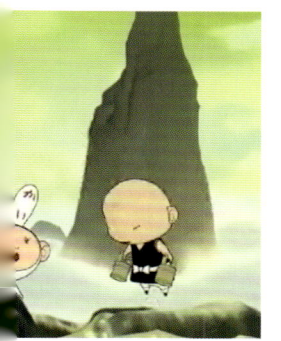
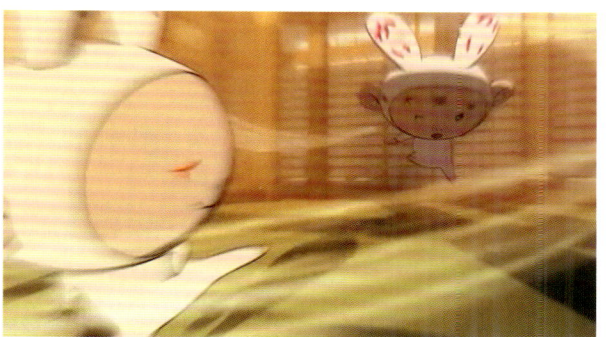
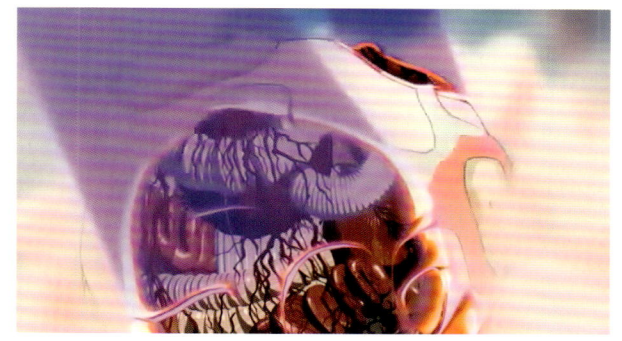
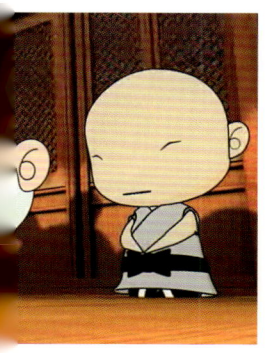
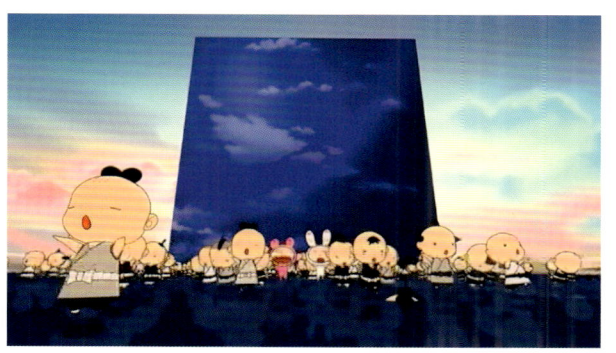
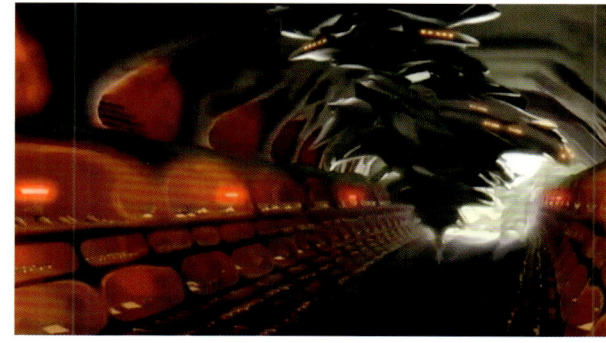
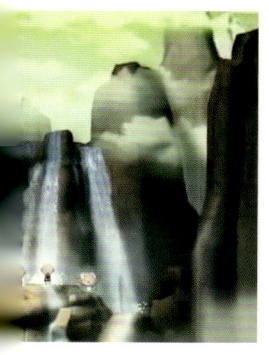
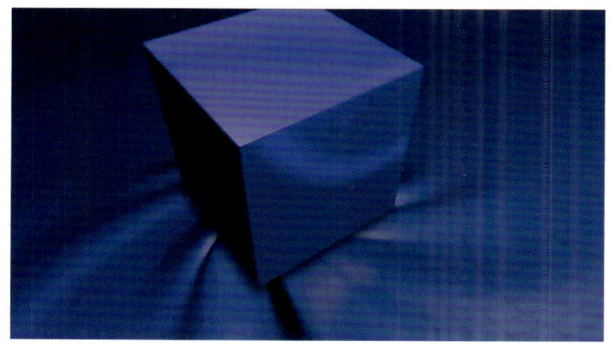
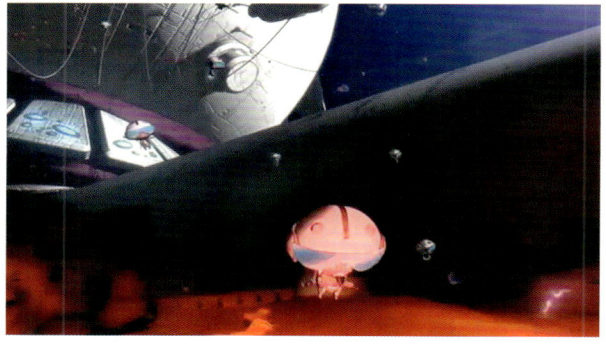

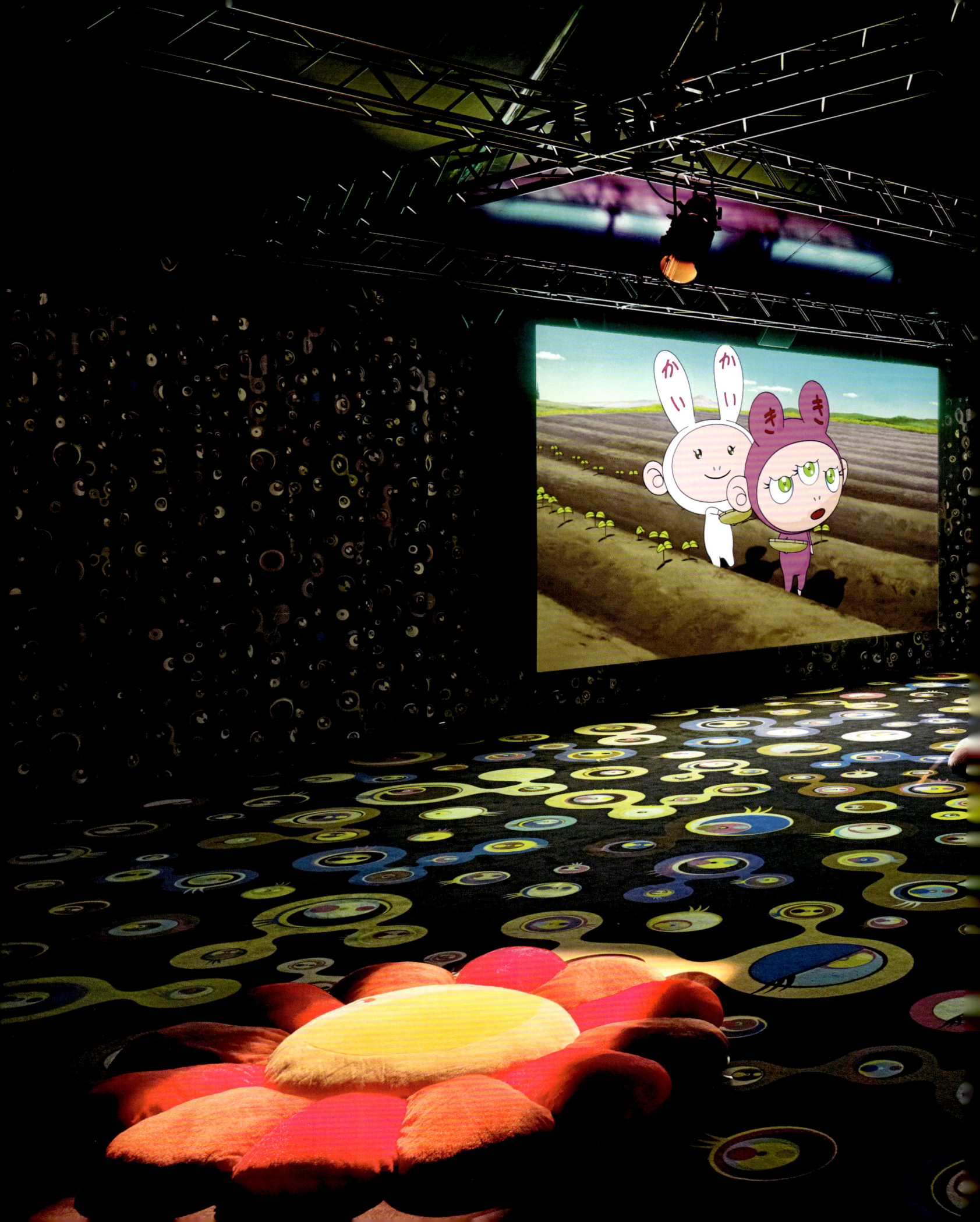

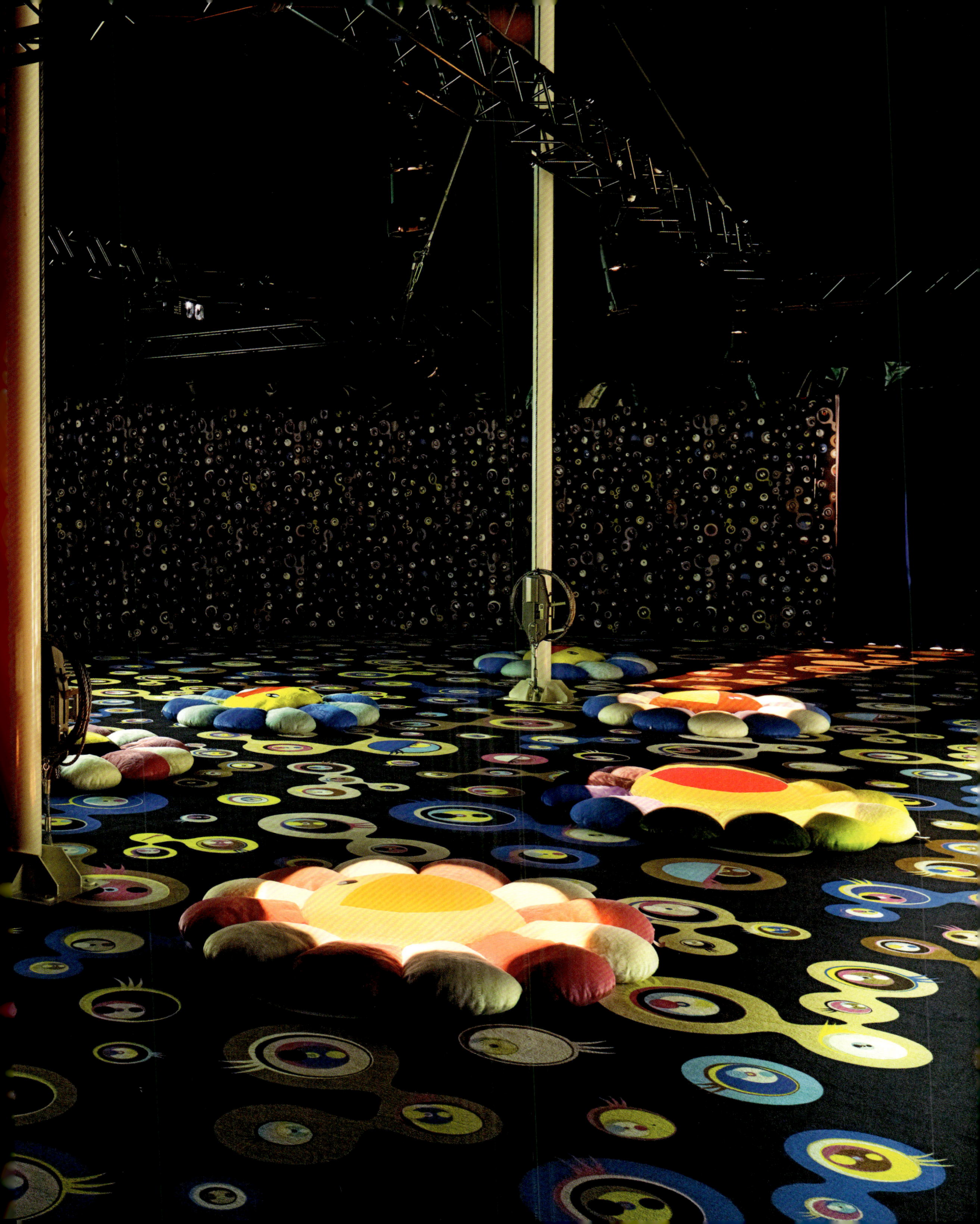

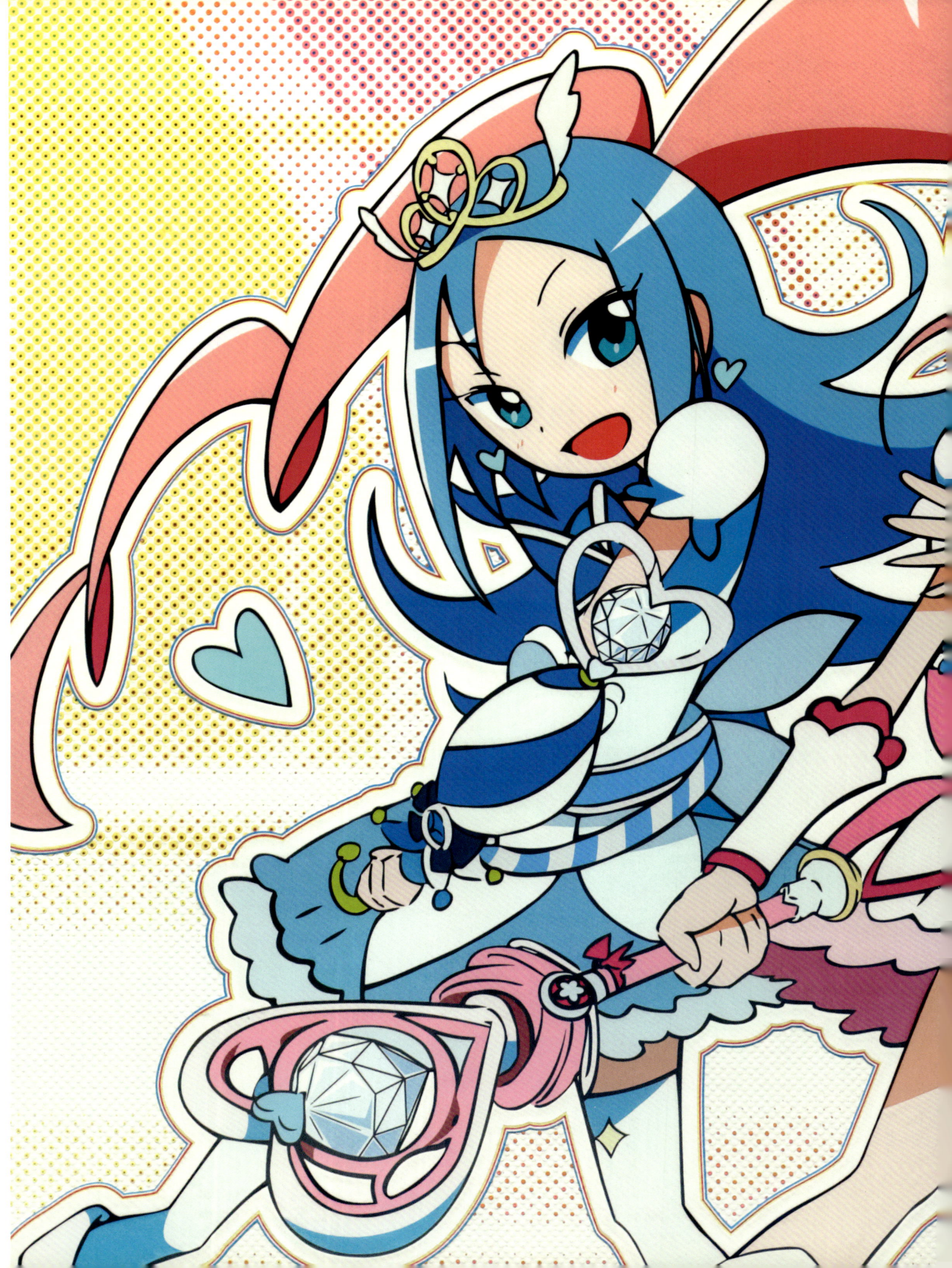

Six ♡ Princess: Battle Formation (detail) 2012

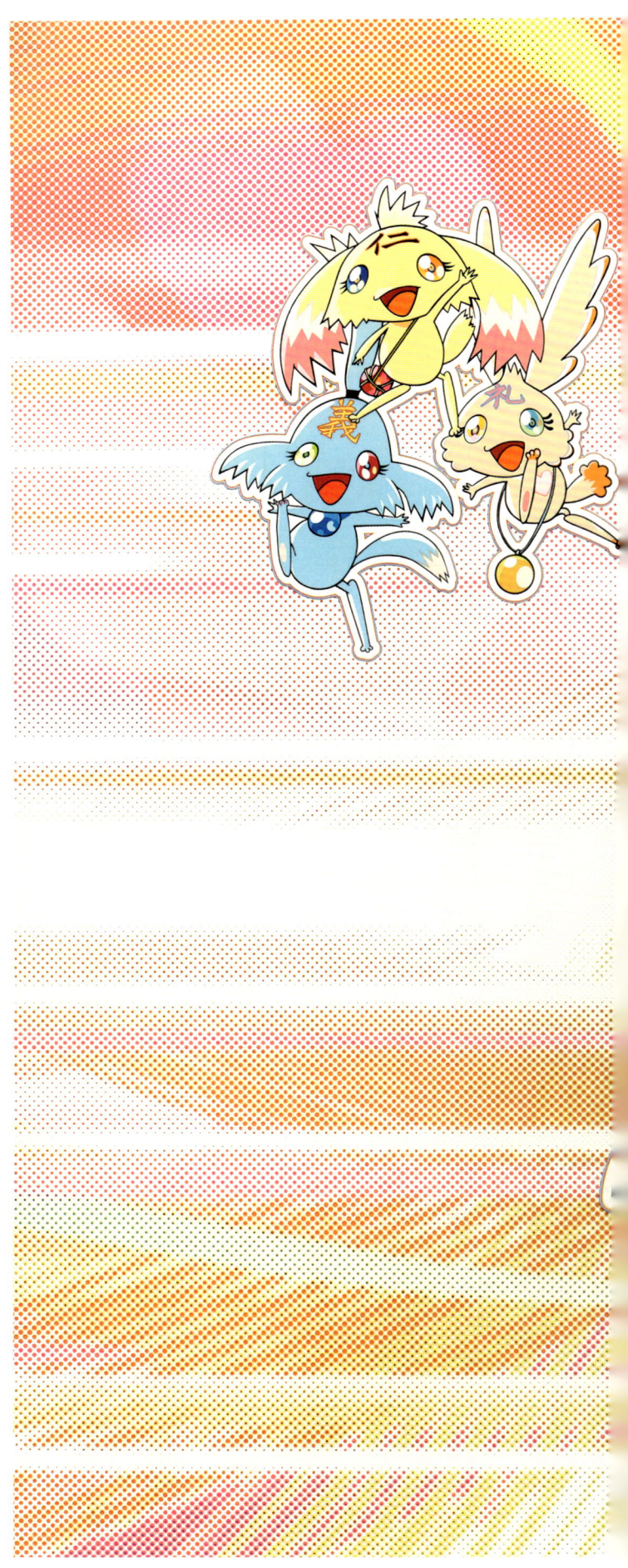

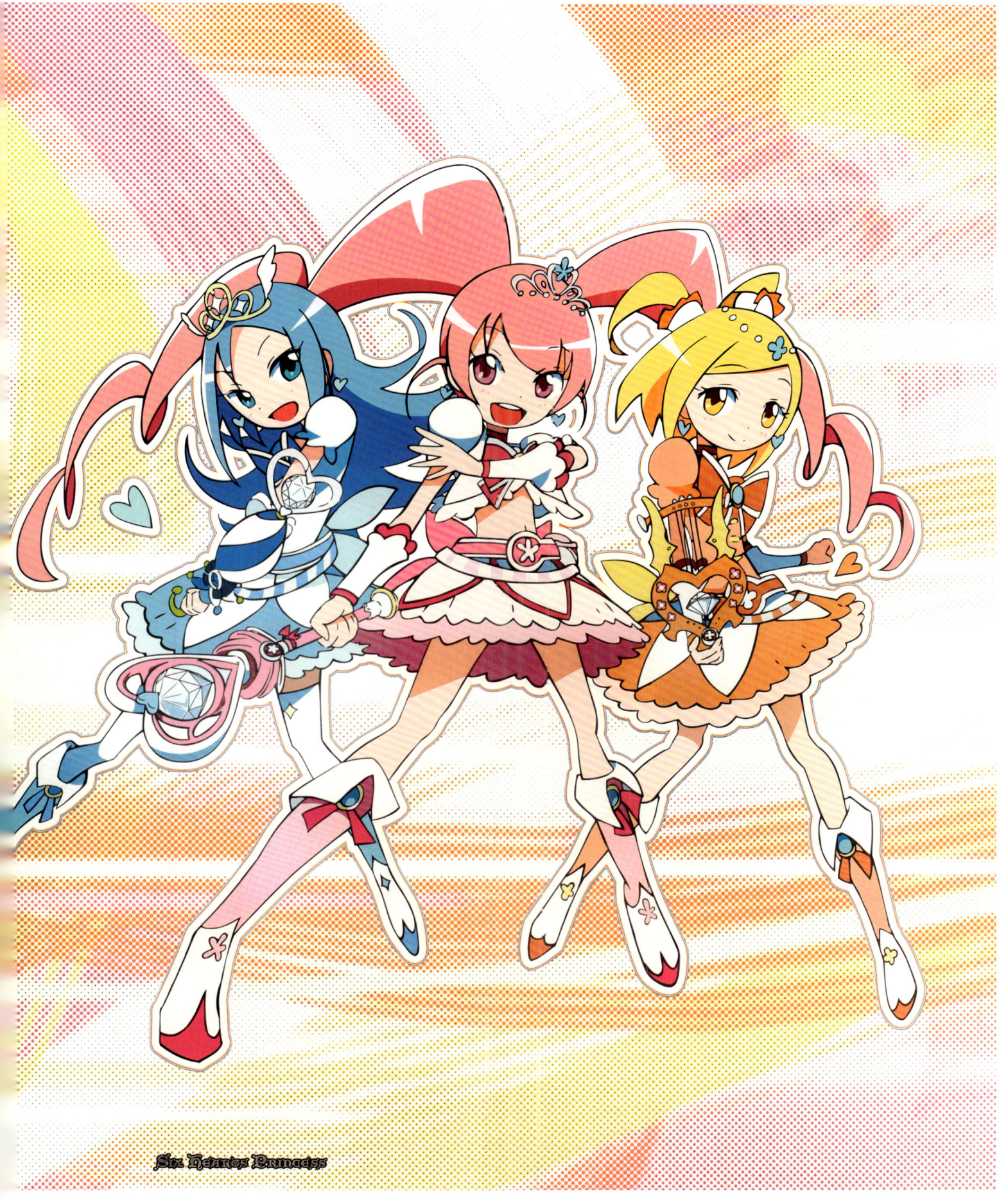

Six Hearts Princess

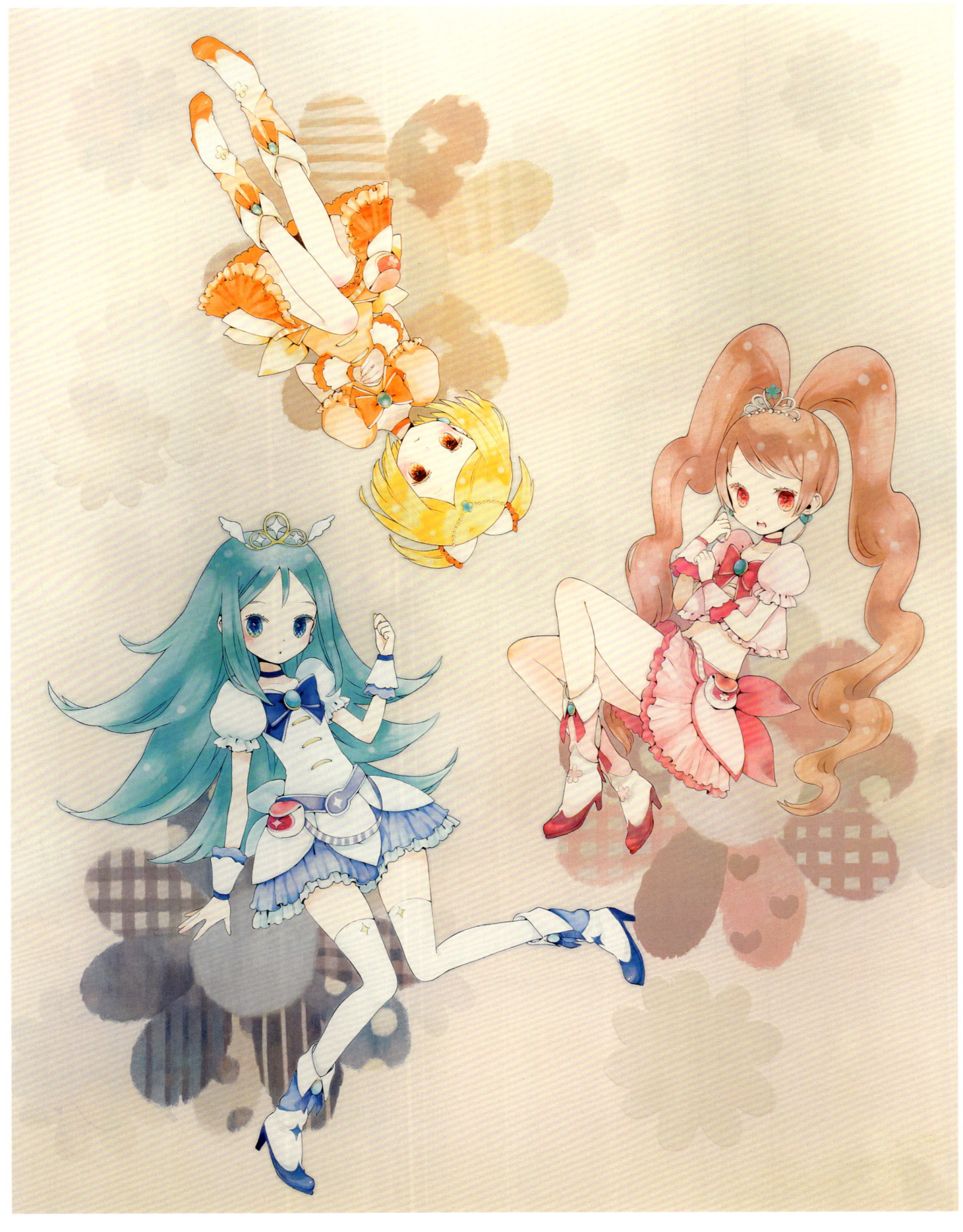

Still from Six ♡ Princess, Ending Title 2010

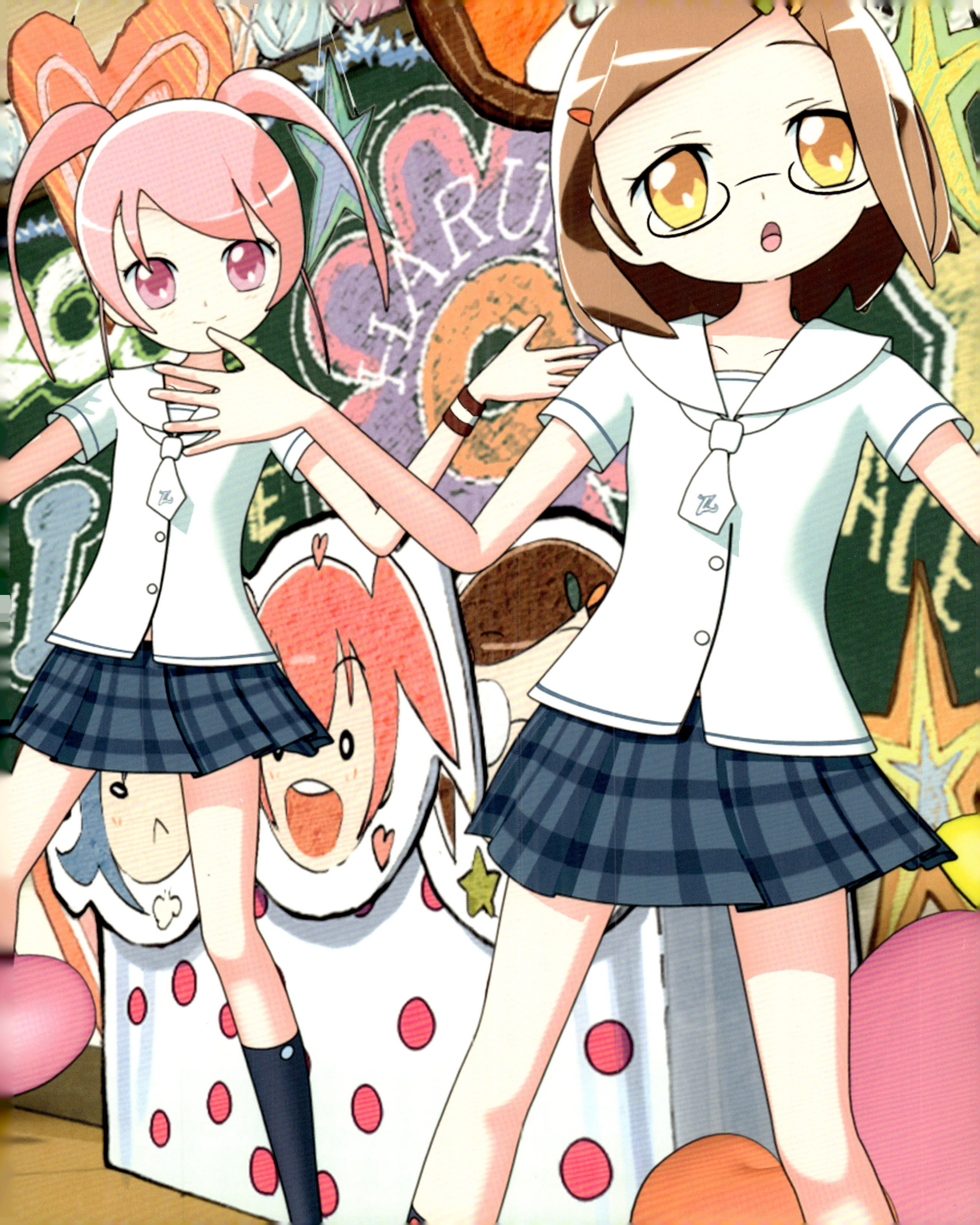

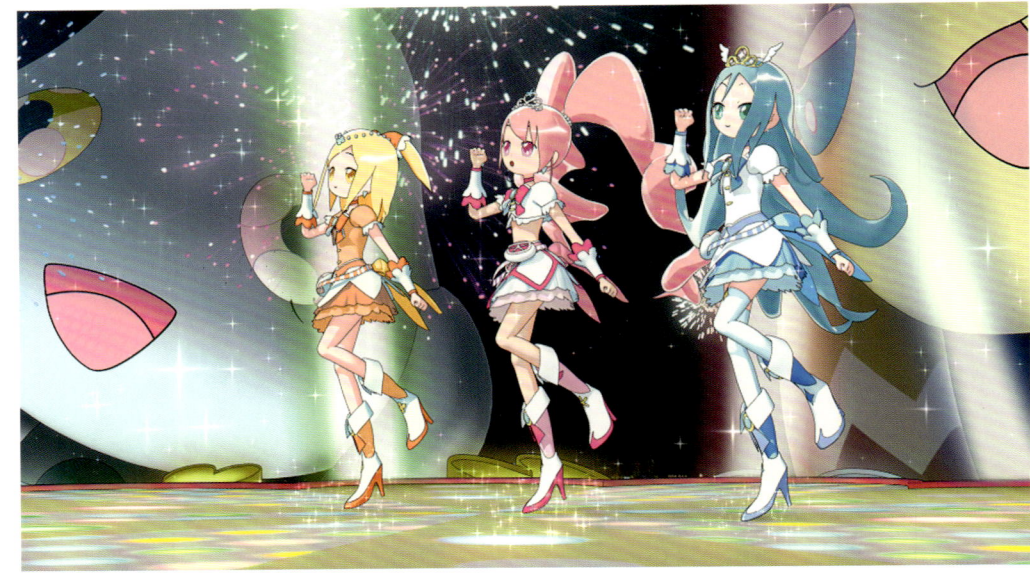

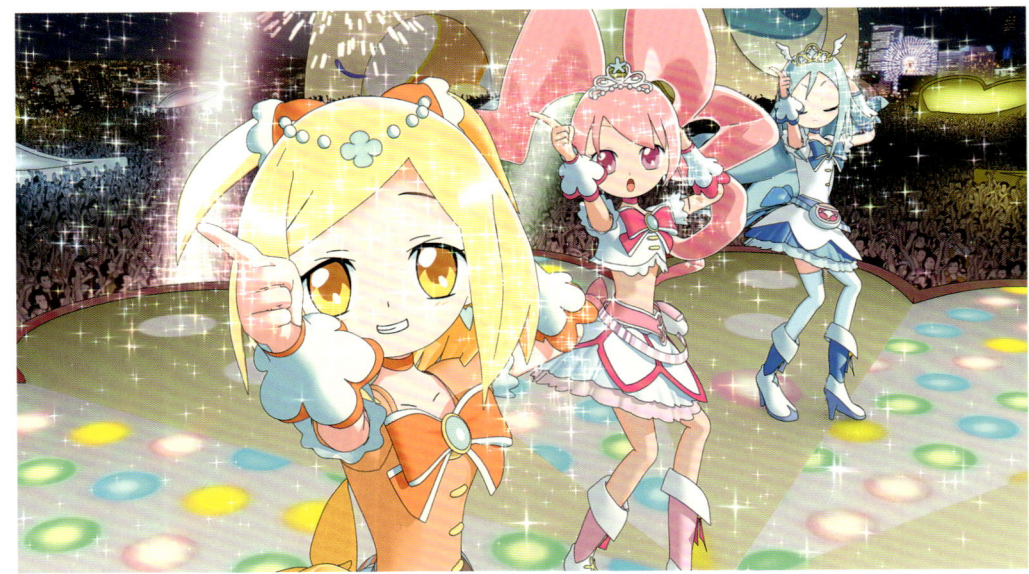

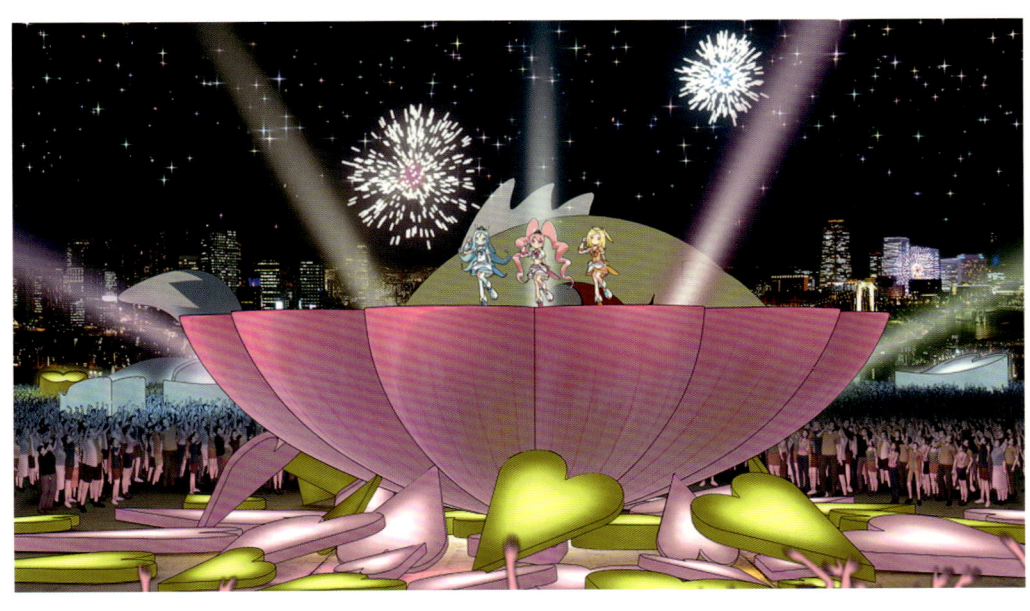

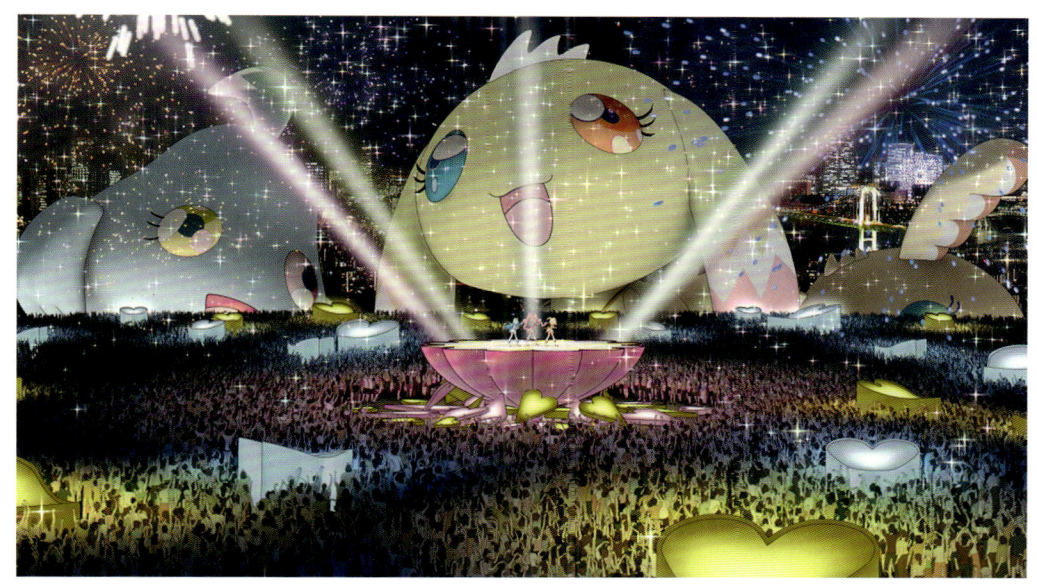

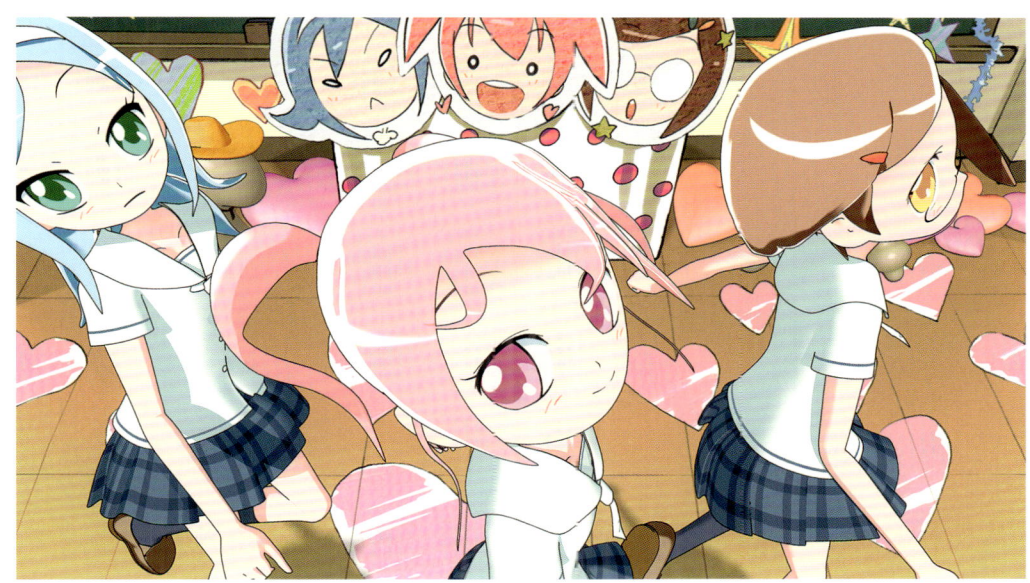

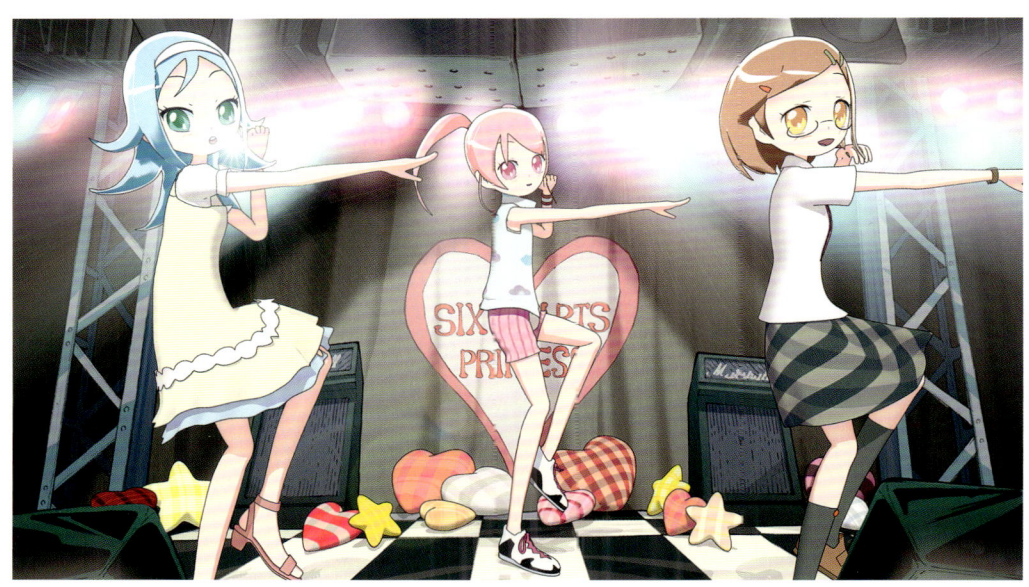

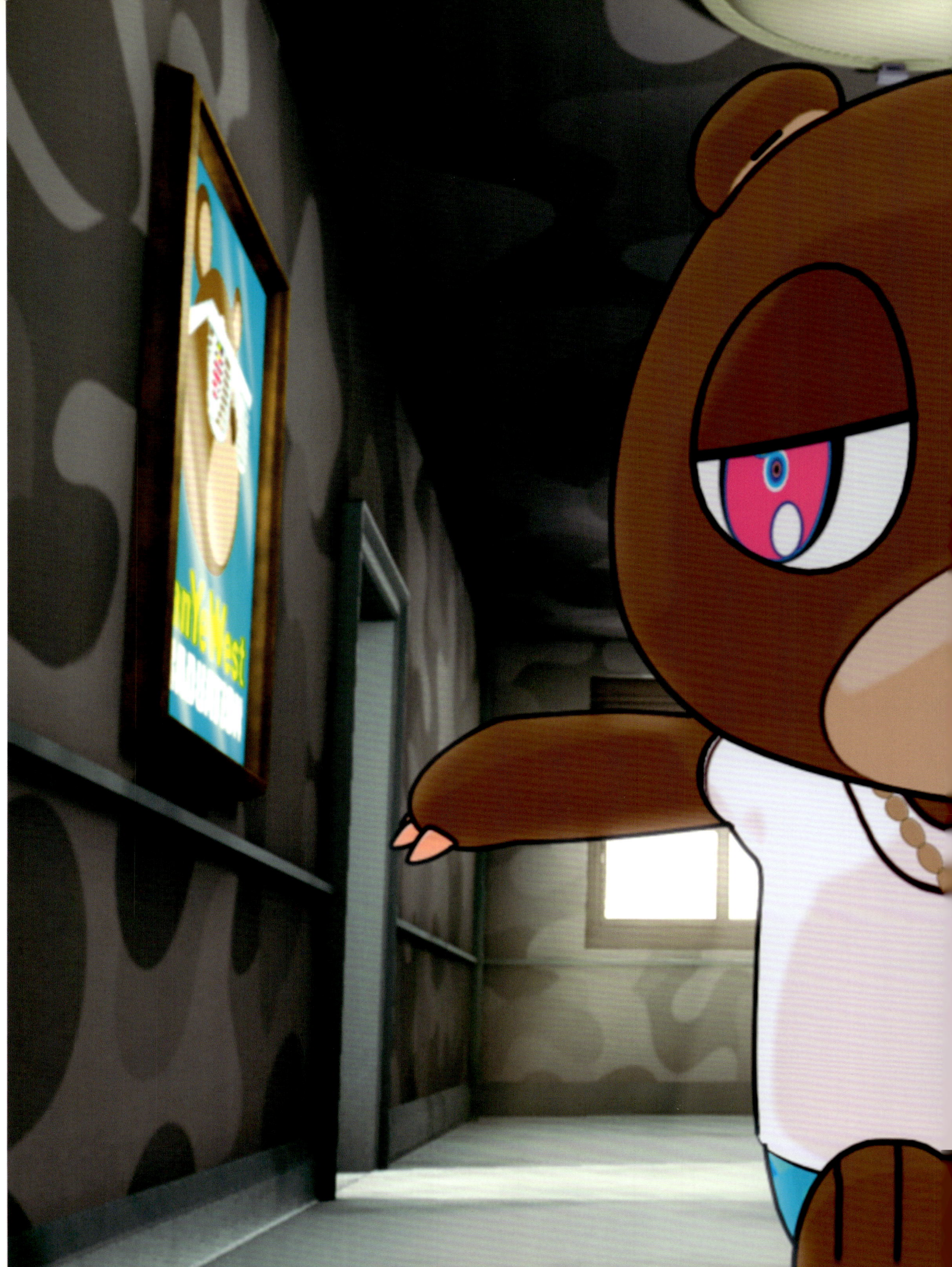

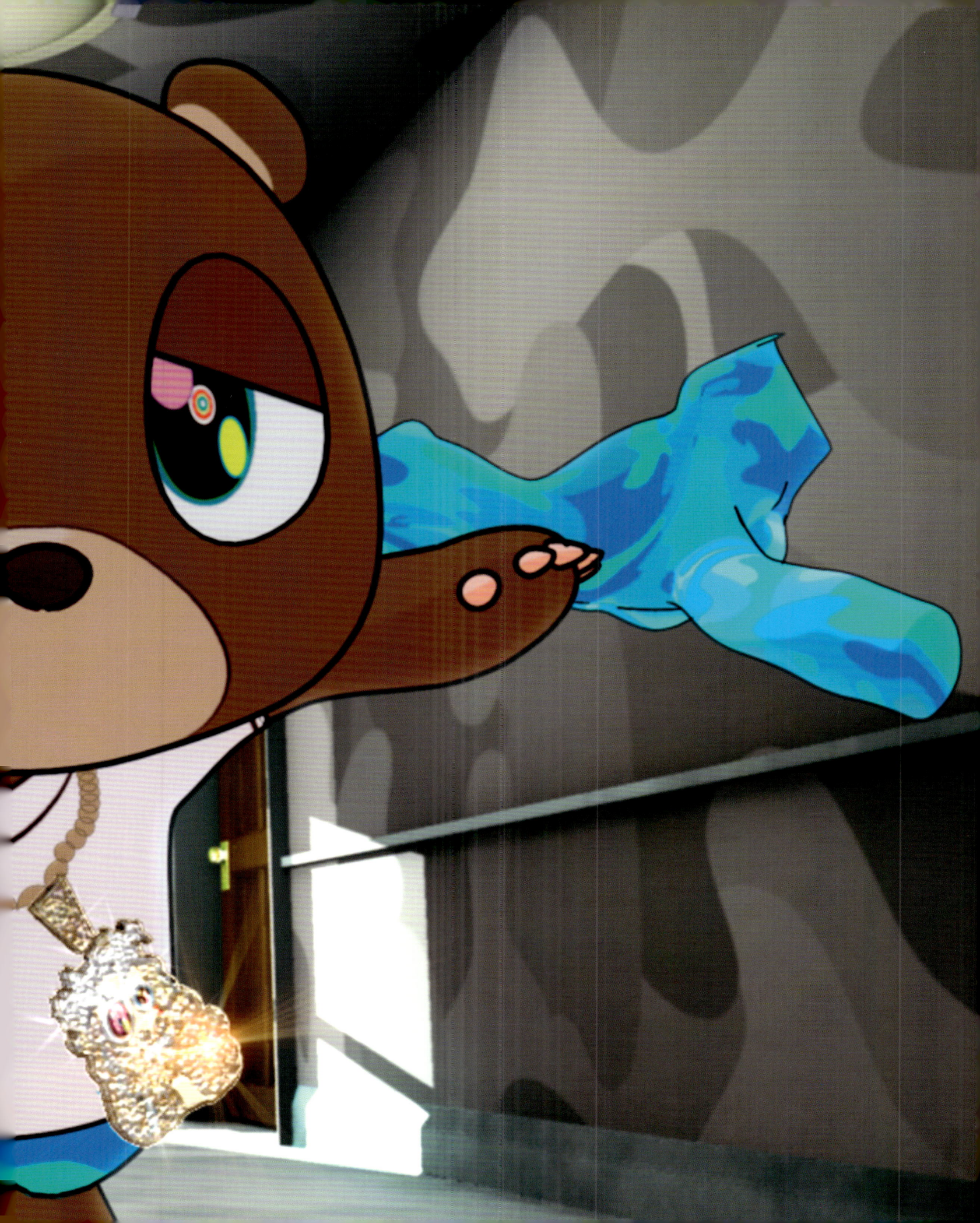

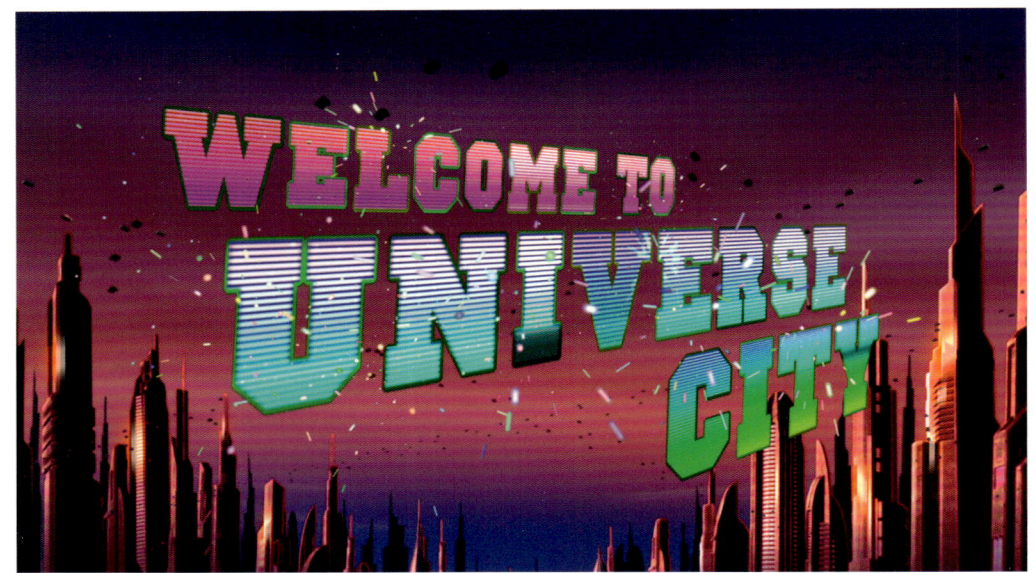

Stills from Kanye West Music Video <u>Good Morning</u> 2007

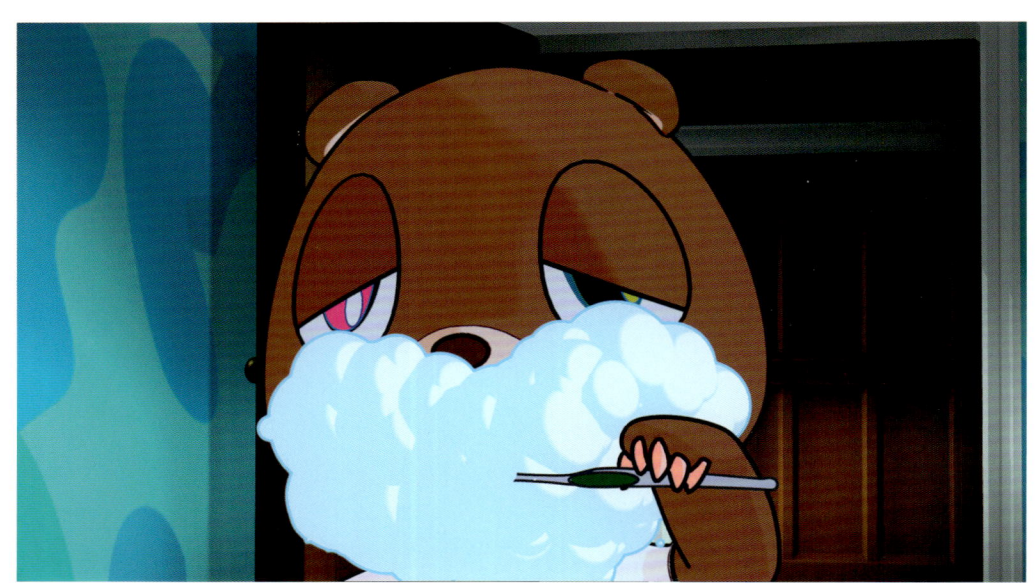

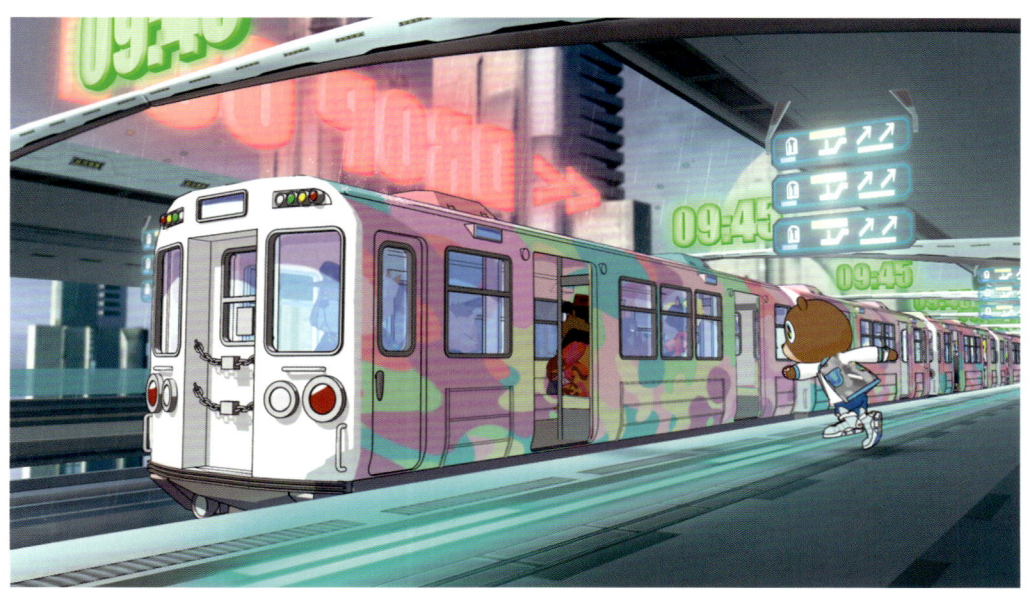

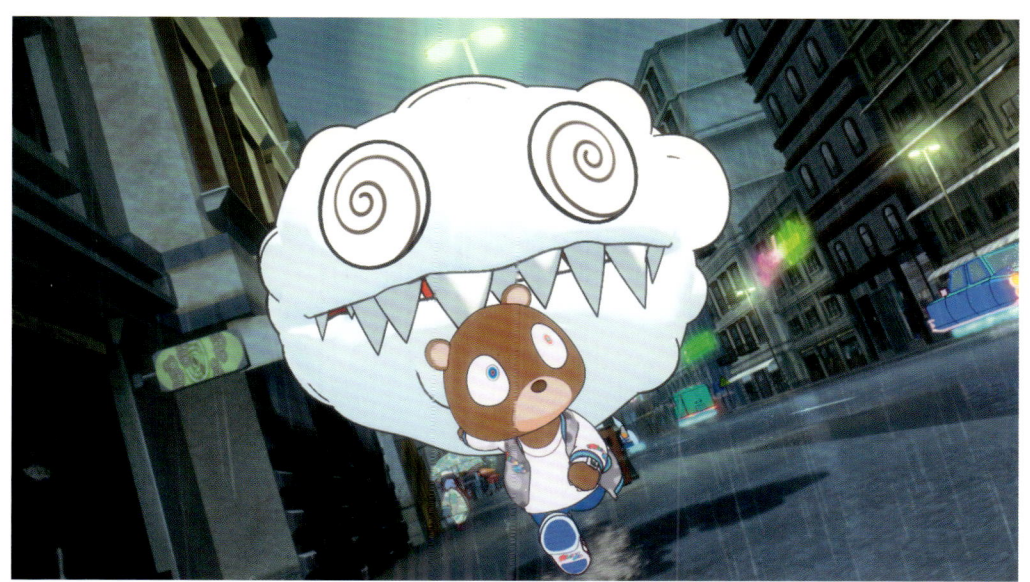

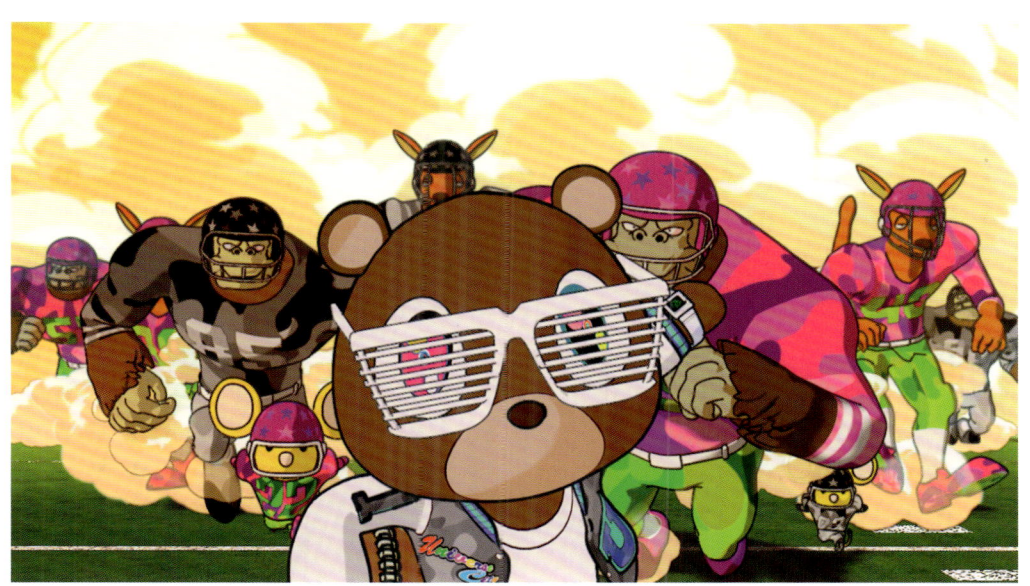

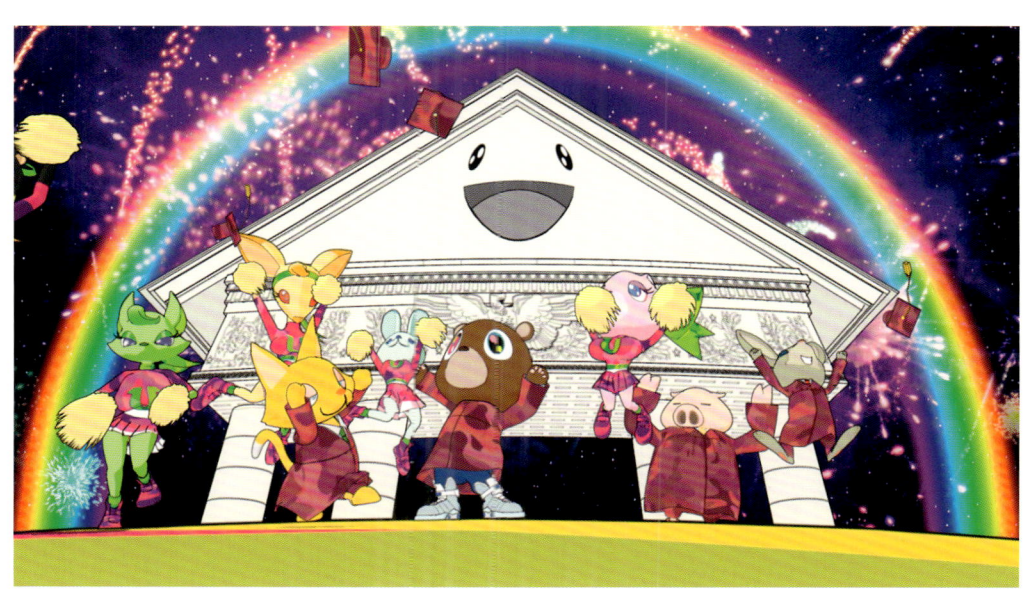

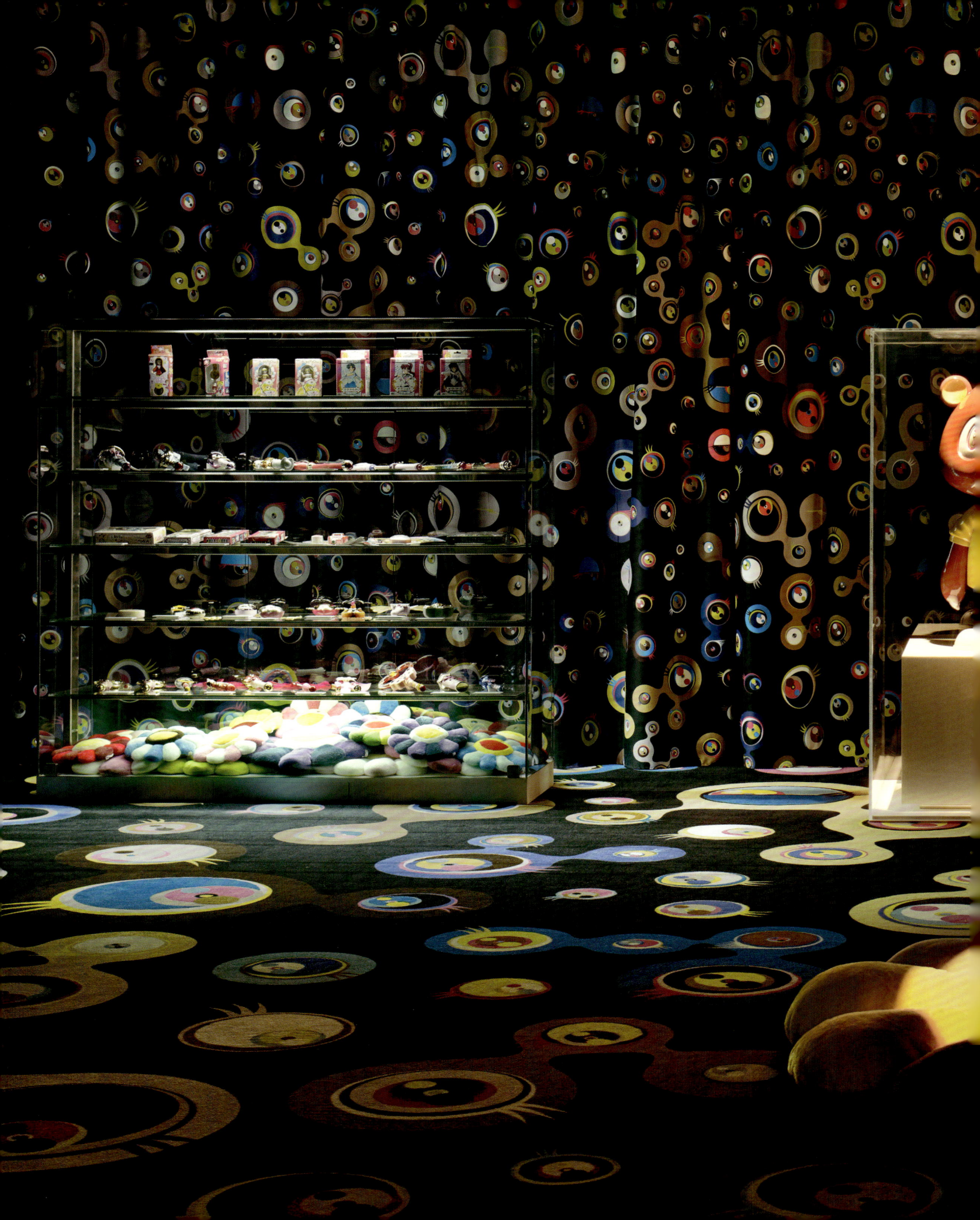

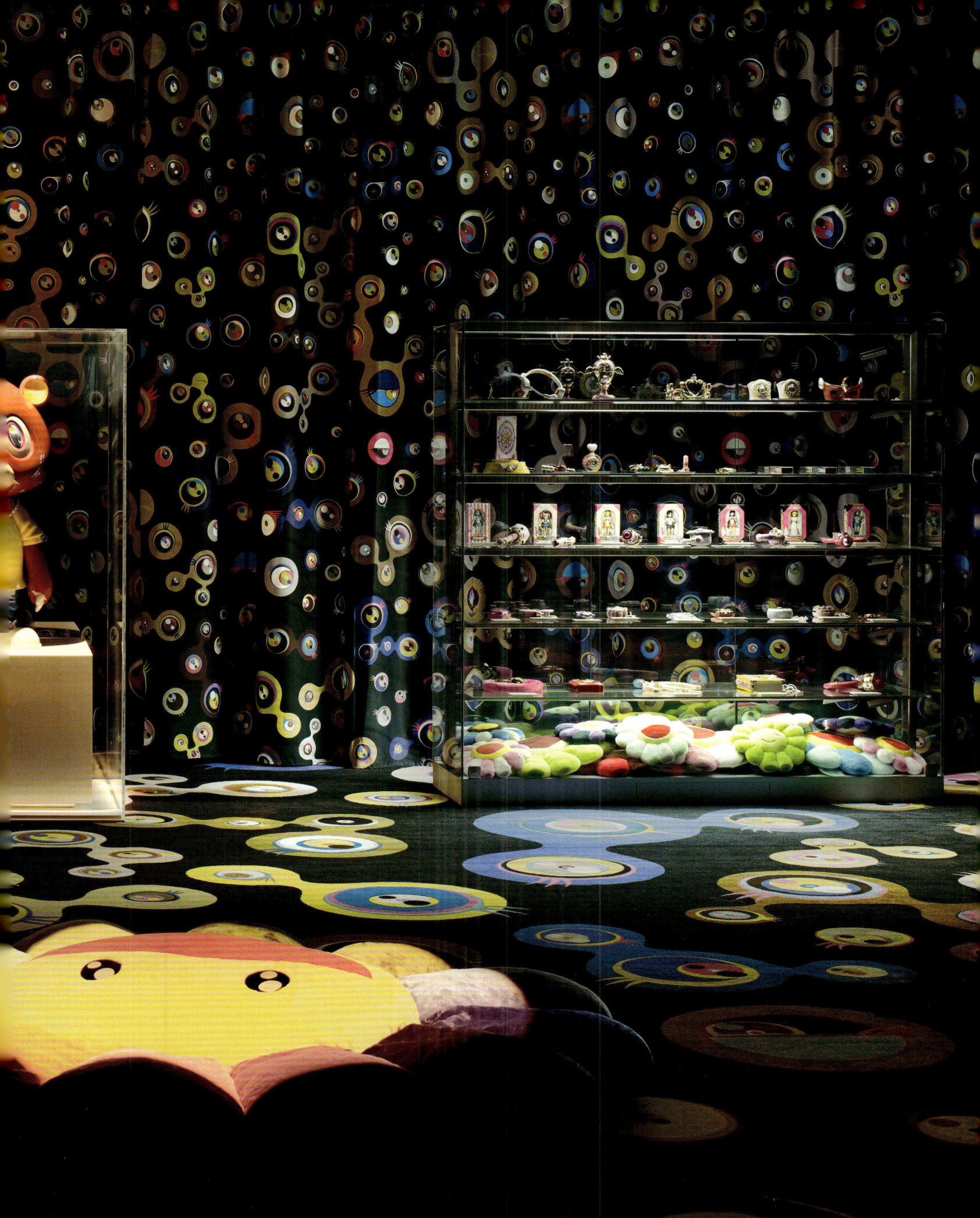

I don't think of it as straddling. I think of it as changing the line. What I've been talking about for years is how in Japan, that line is less defined. Both by the culture and by the post-war economic situation. Japanese people accept that art and commerce will be blended; and in fact, they are surprised by the rigid and pretentious Western hierarchy of "high art." In the West, it certainly is dangerous to blend the two because people will throw all sorts of stones. But that's okay—

I'M READY WITH MY HARD HAT.

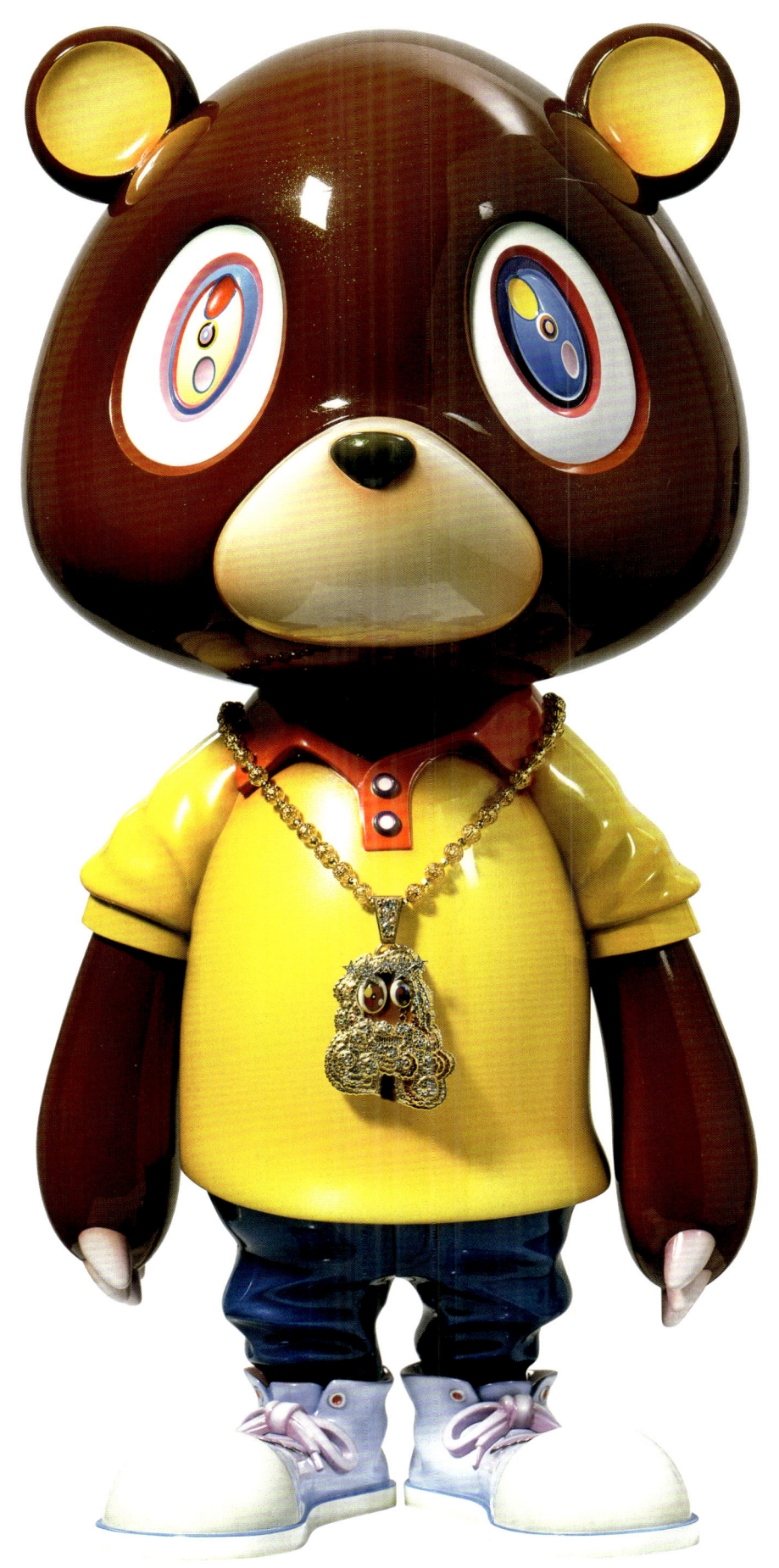

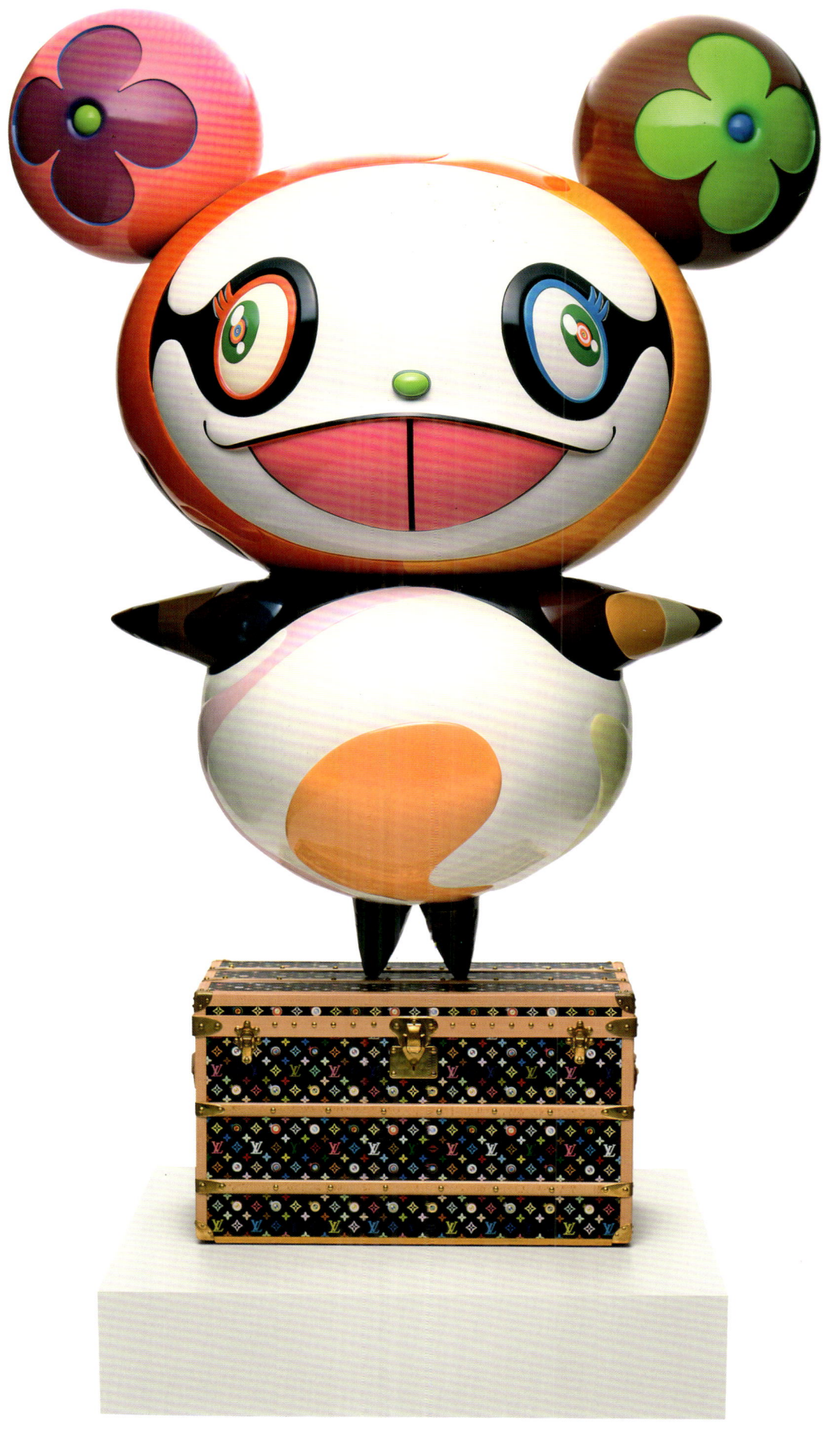

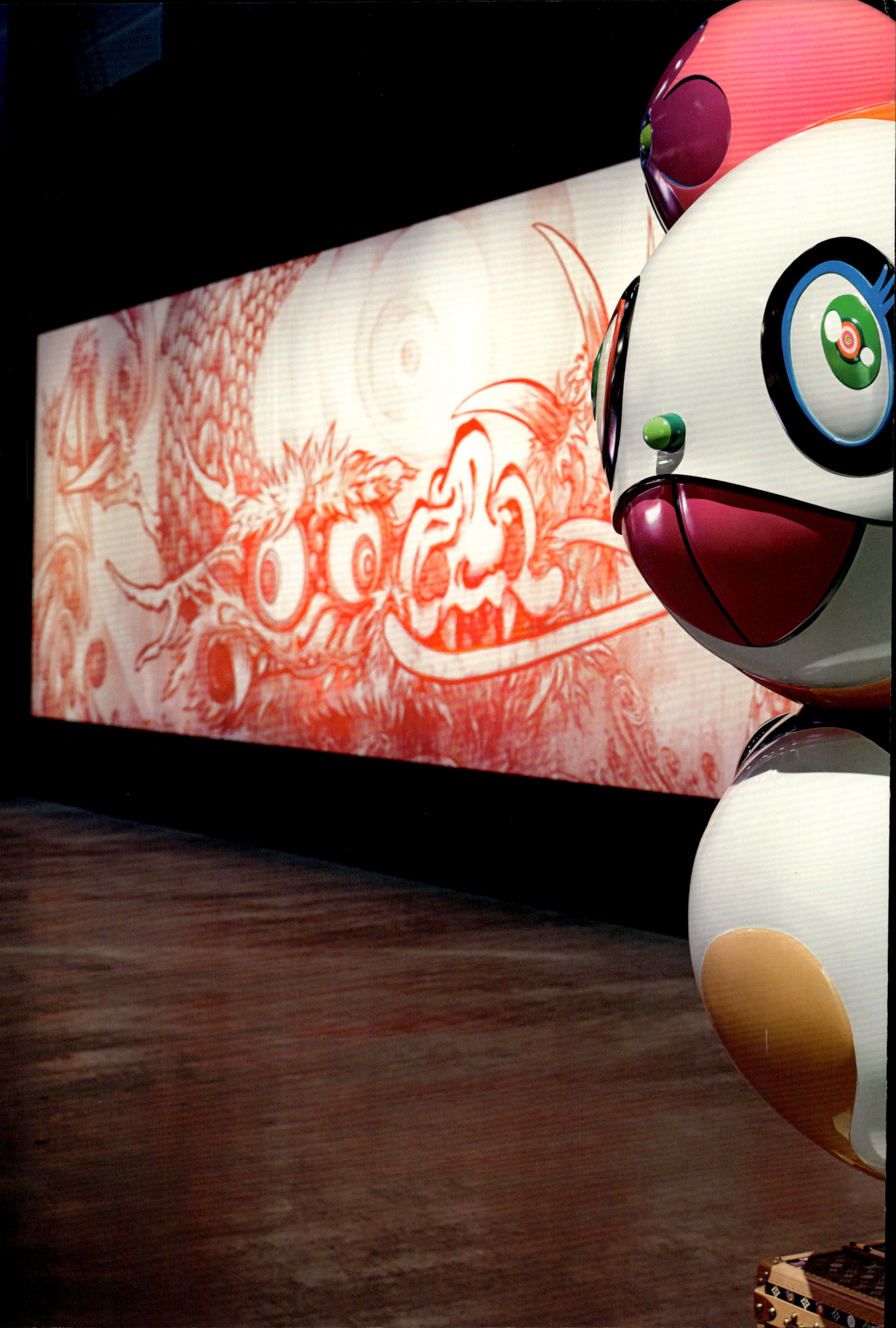

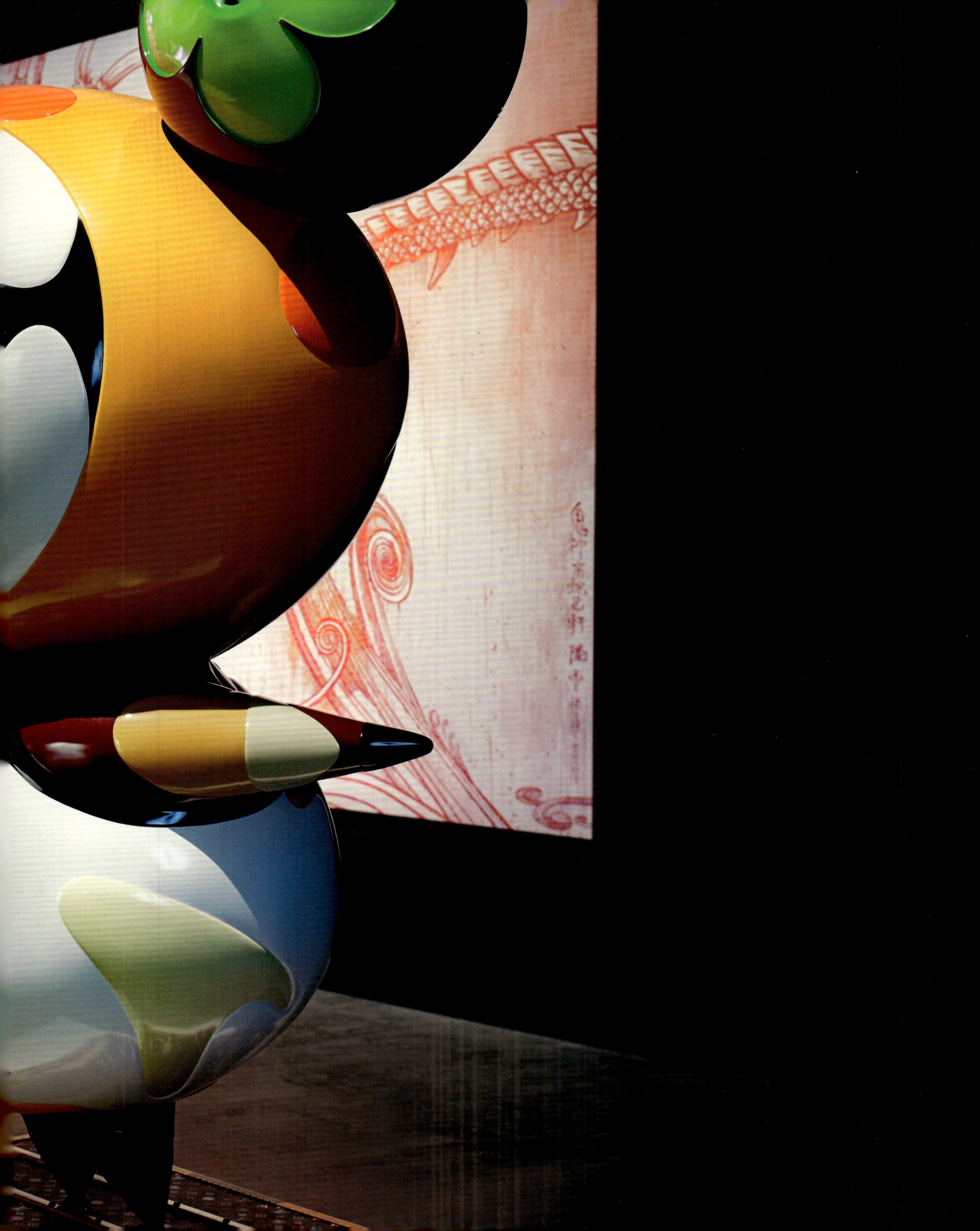

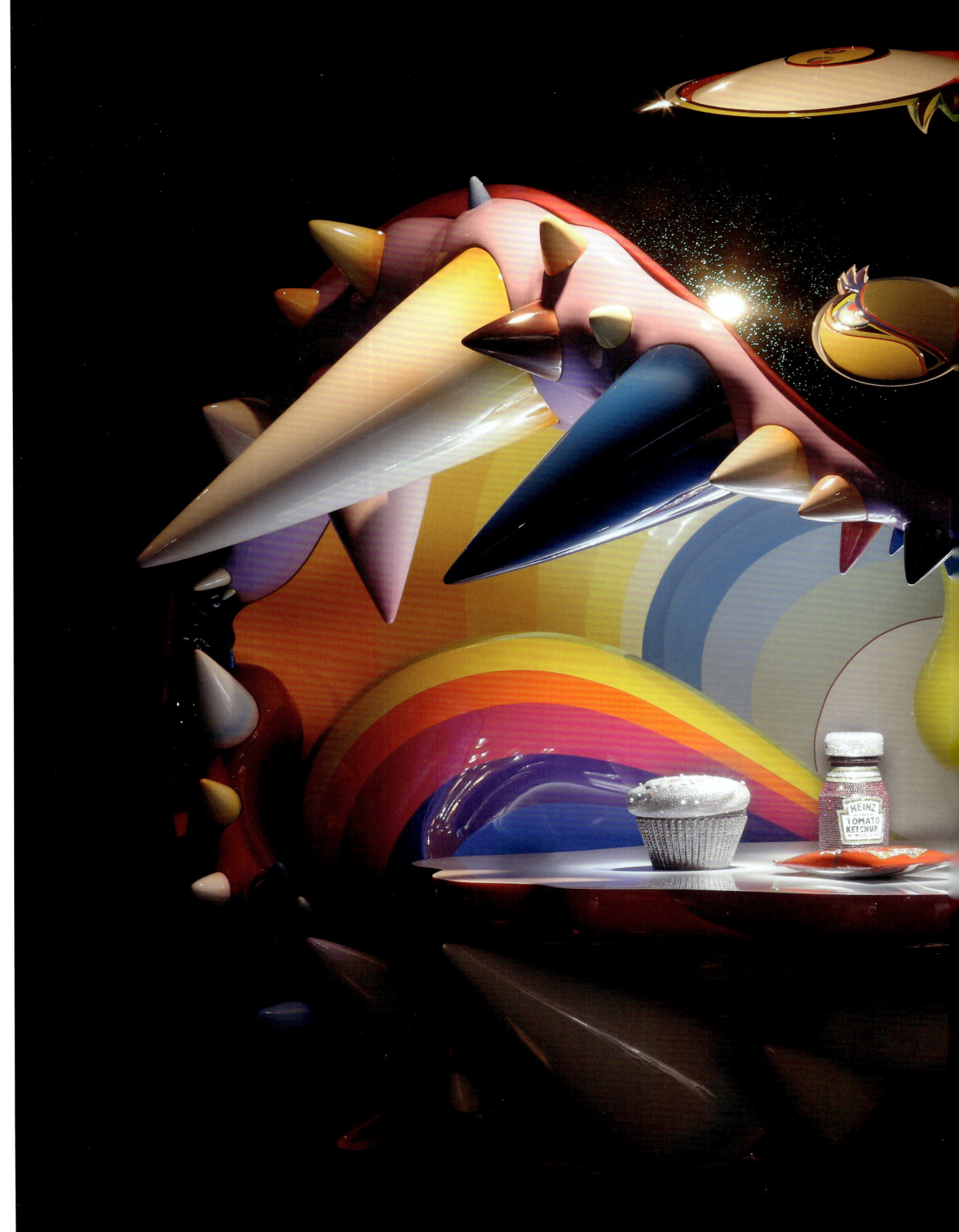

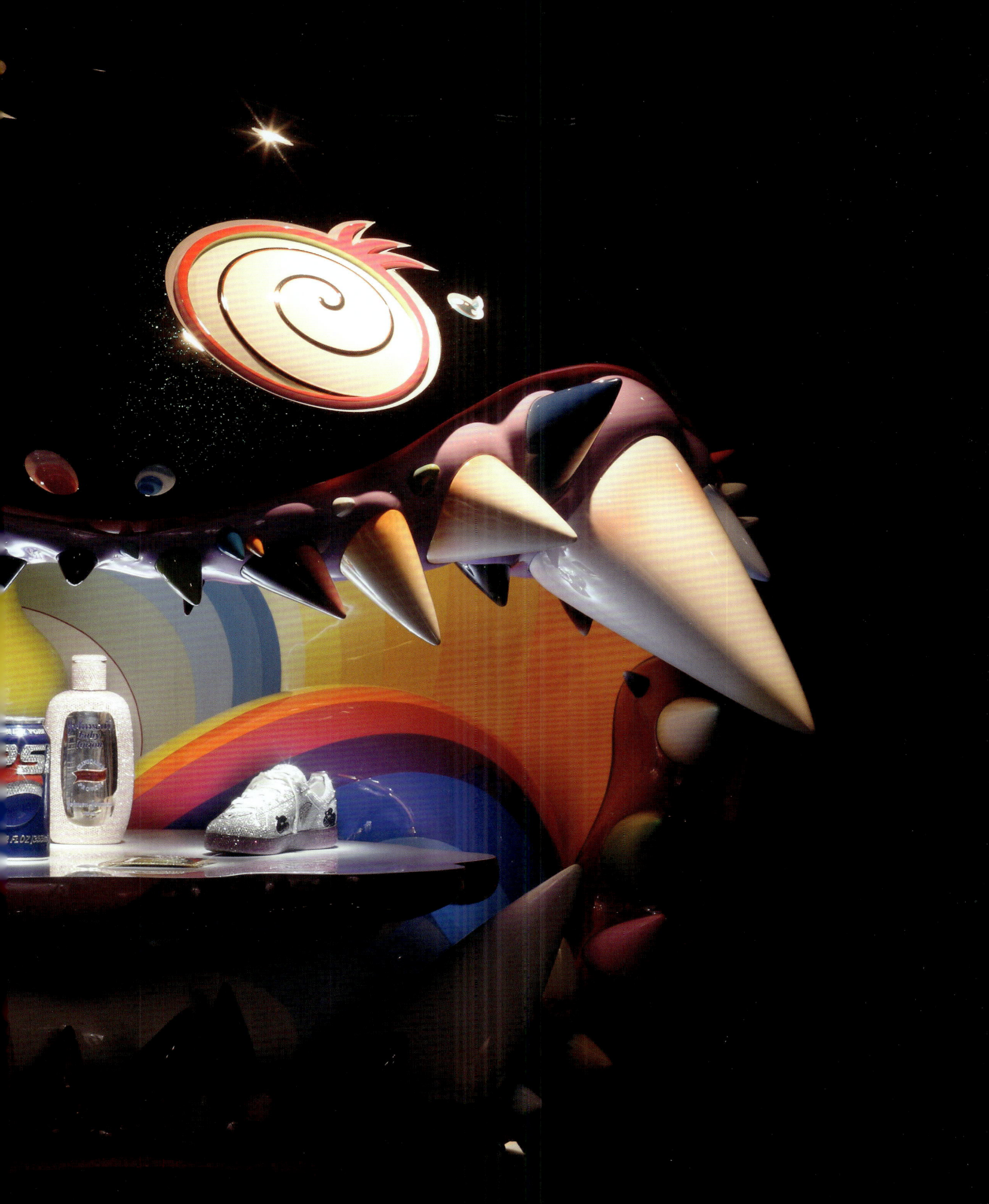

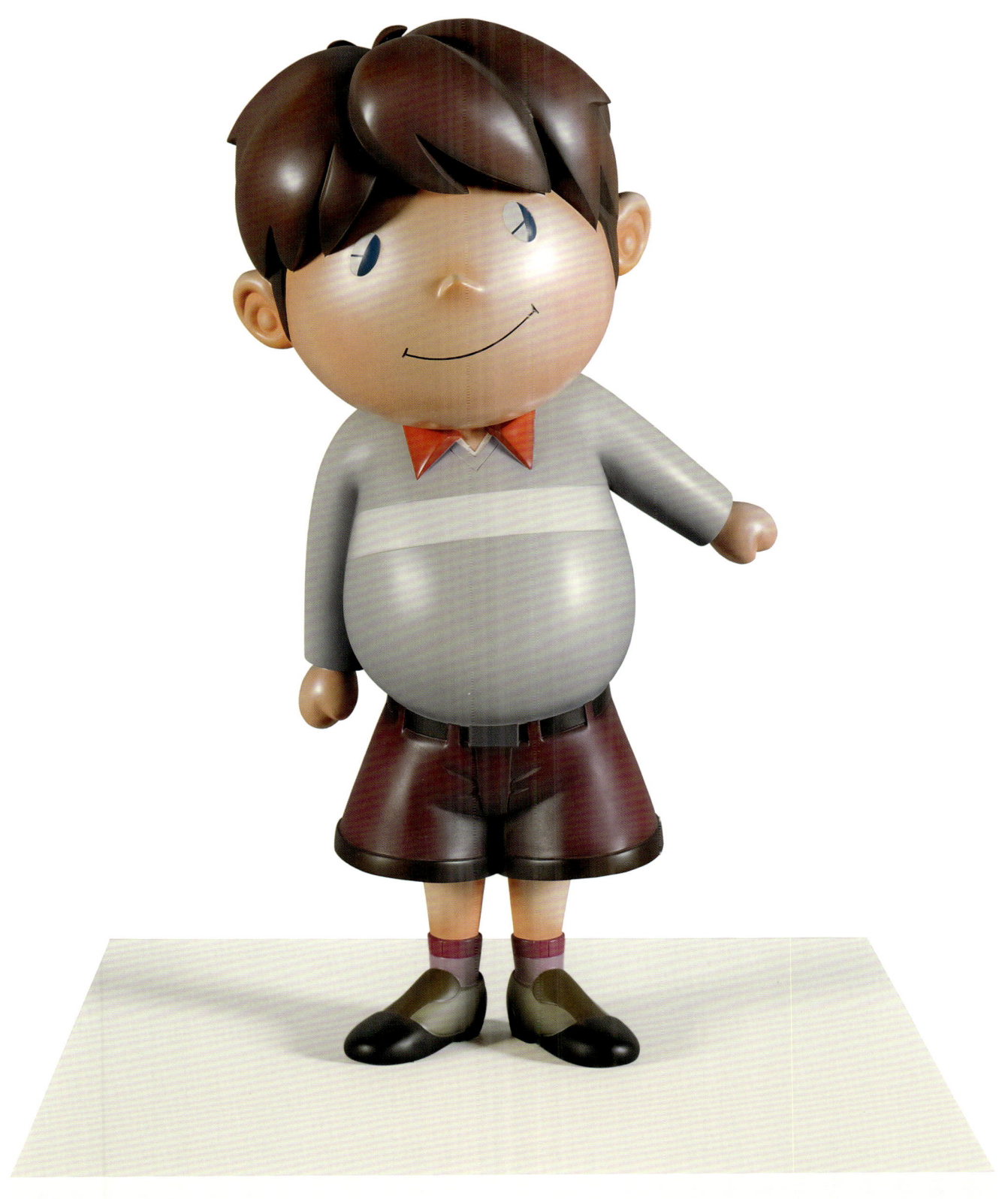

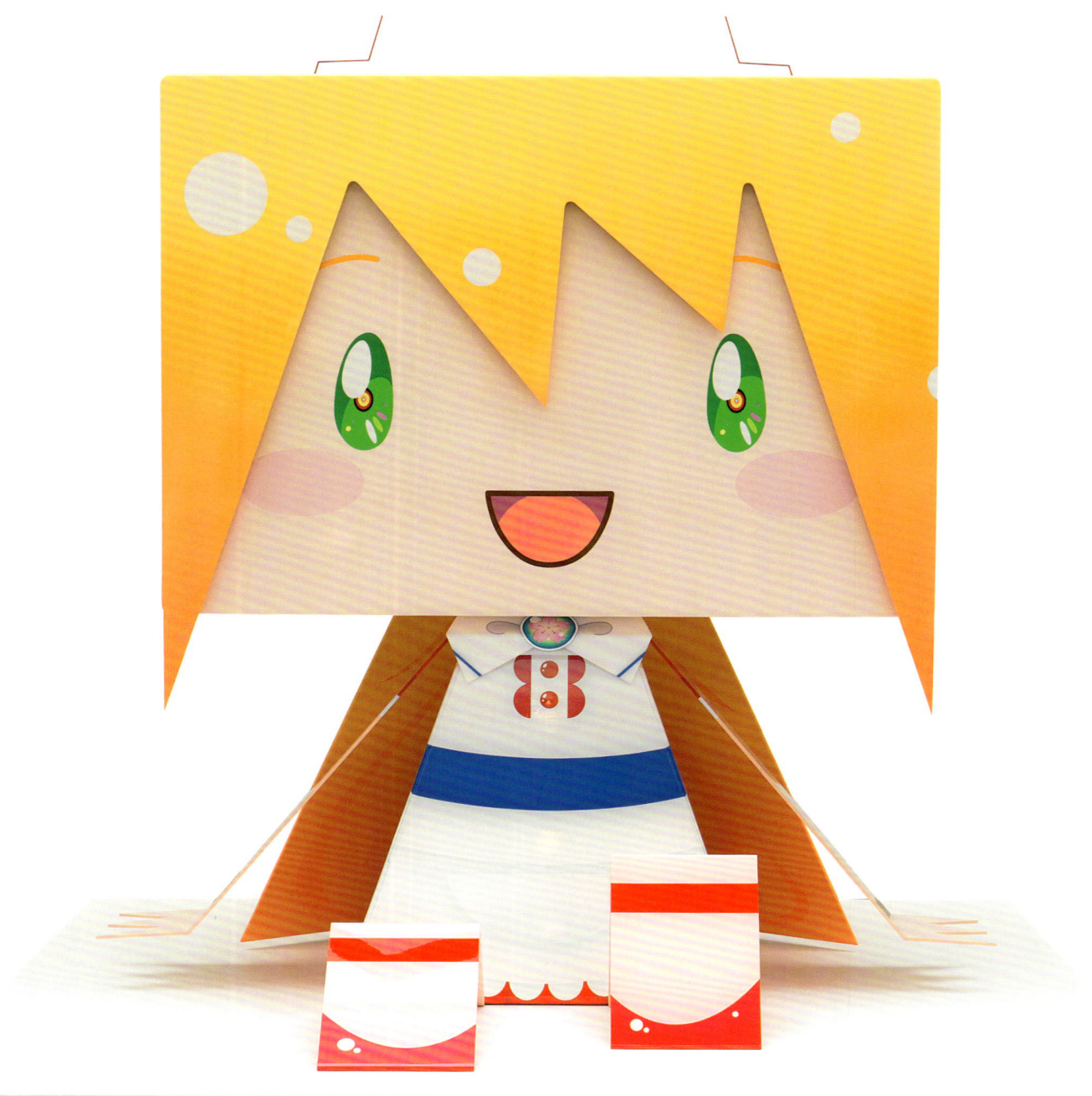

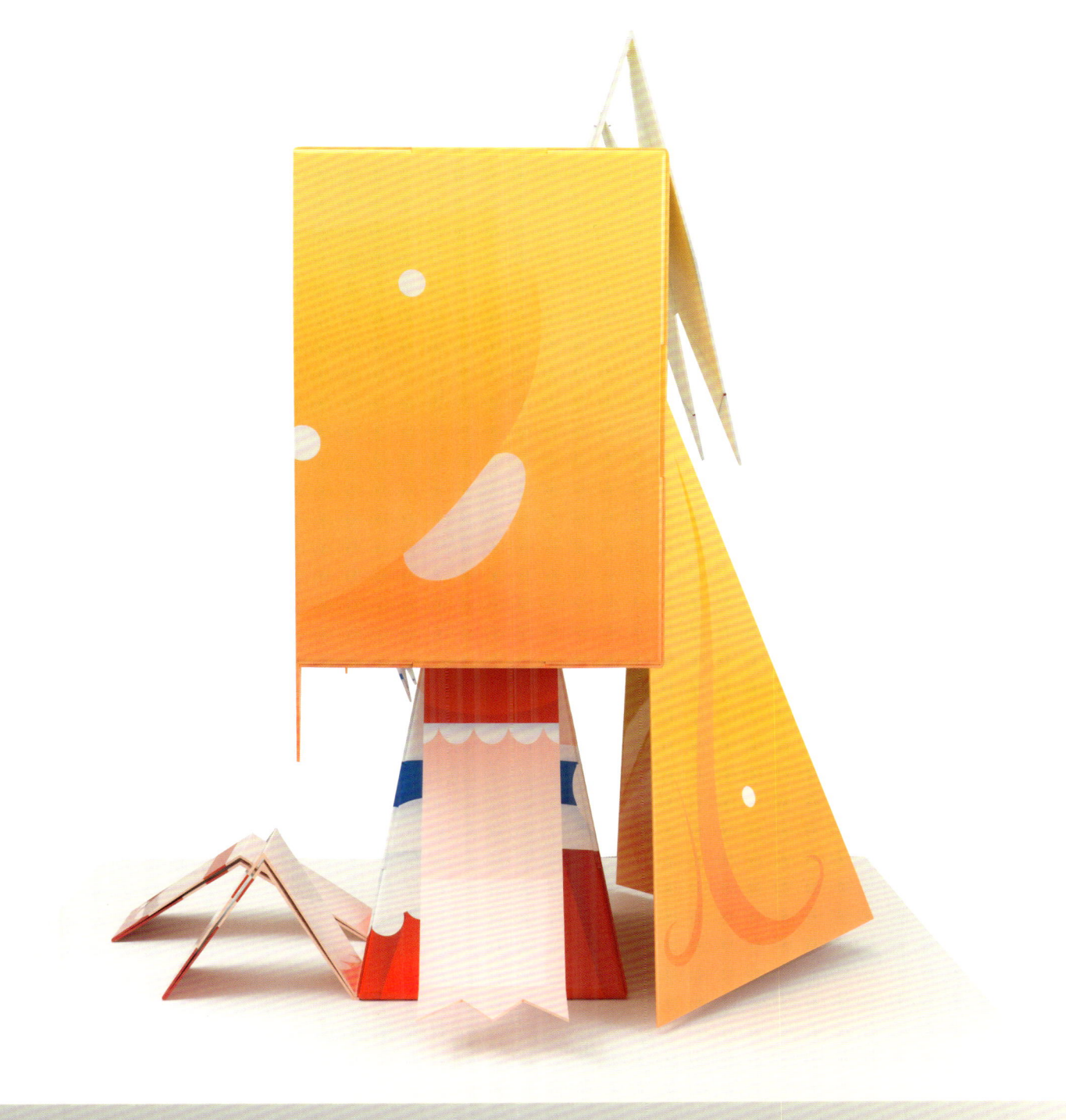

Yume Lion (The Dream Lion) 2009–10

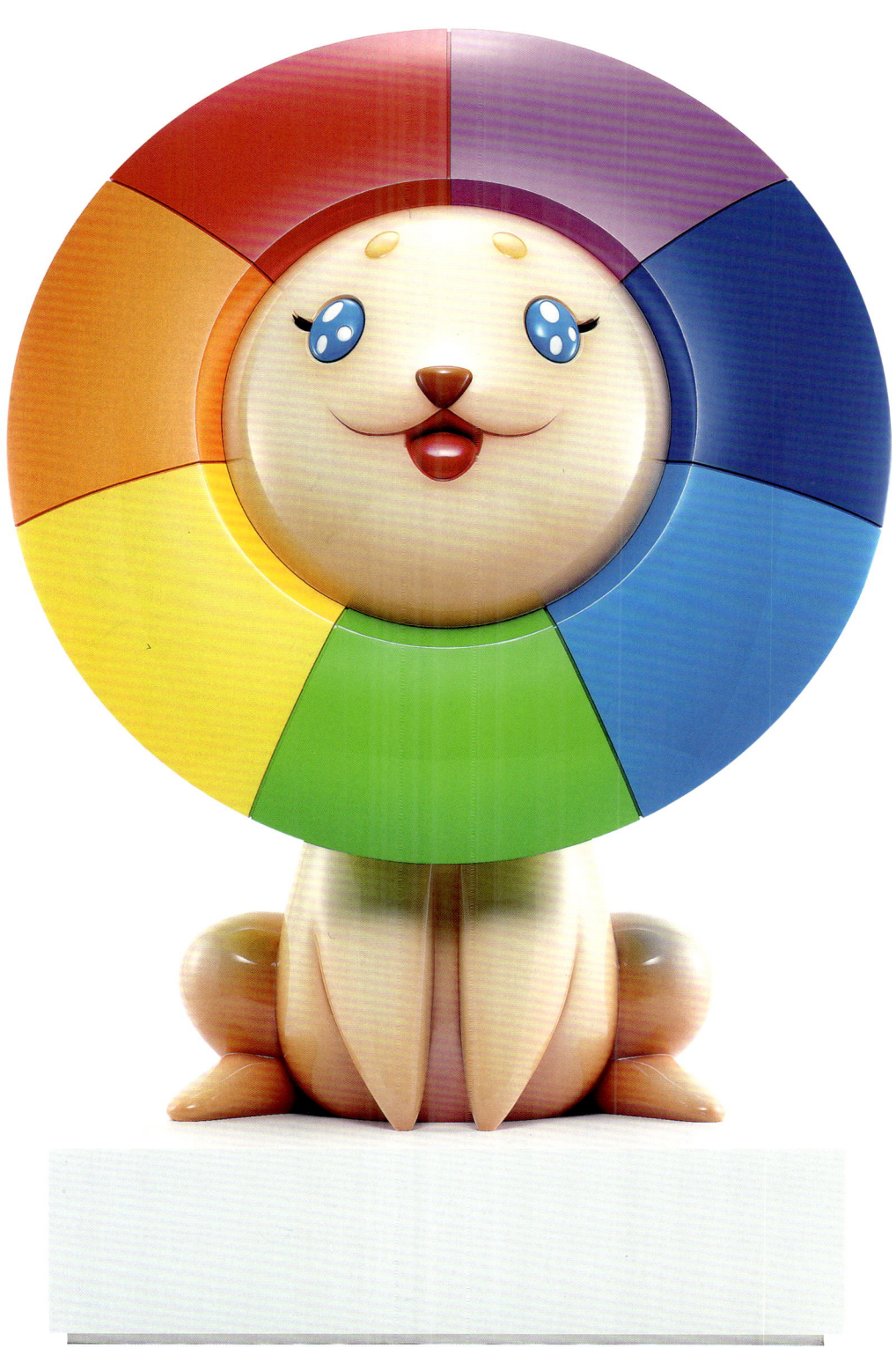

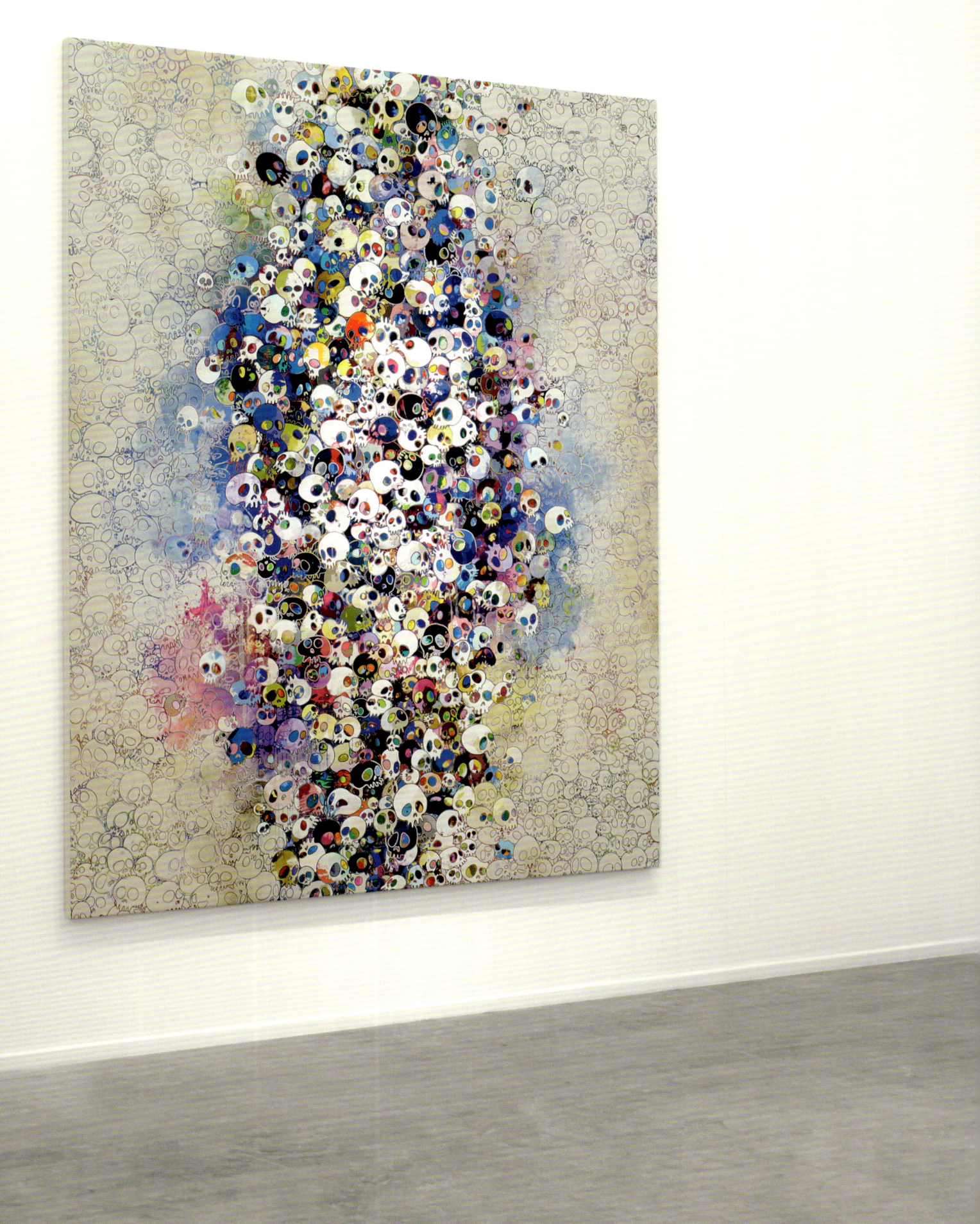

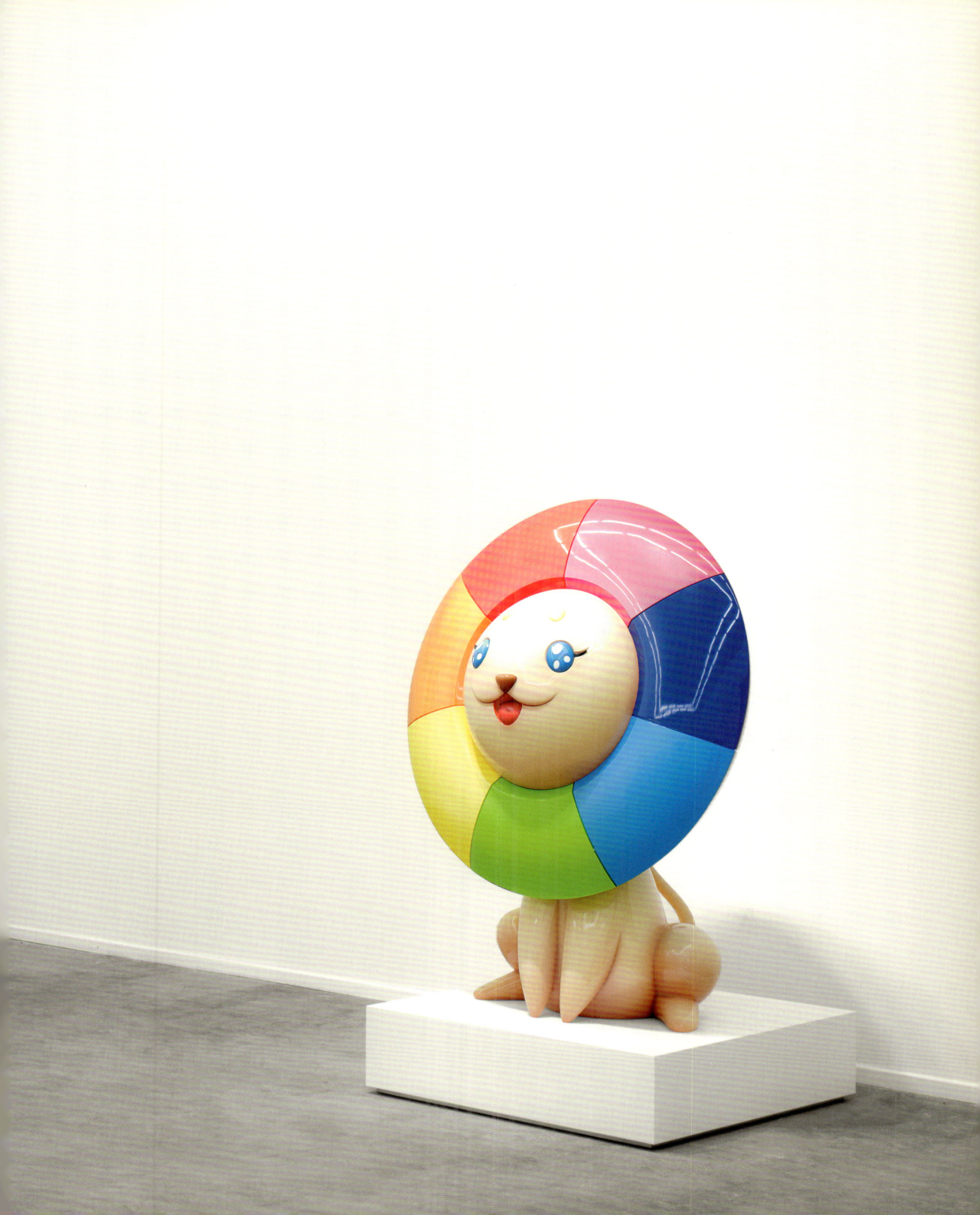

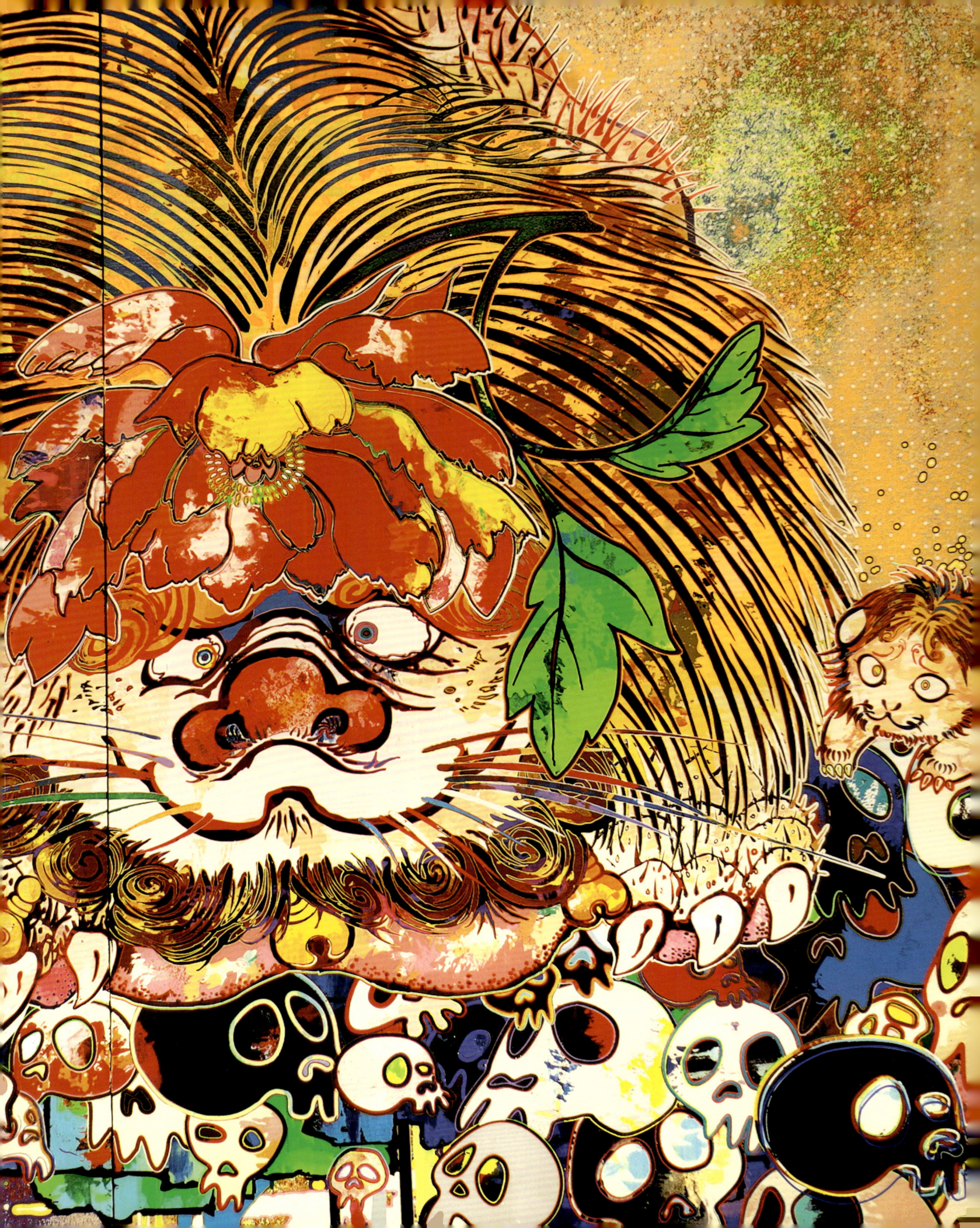

I HAVE BECOME MORE STOIC WITH MY PRODUCTION STANCE AND HAVE TRIED TO EXERT MORE CONTROL OVER THE FEELING IN MY WORK.

This is because my goal as an artist is for my work to survive after my death. I'm not trying to live the life of a rock star.

To continue shaping a world after your death is supposed to be like holing up in a temple for religious training. I have to work on creating art with strong enough content that it can continue after I'm gone. As a result, I try to remind myself not to get caught up in the assessments of the present world.

Reputation now, in today's world, is meaningless. Regardless of whether or not one thinks it's self-evident that art history can only be written after the artist has died, what's before our eyes is dark and unknown. Of course, sometimes I feel nauseous, like I can no longer go on. I would love to be an artist like Henry Darger, whose exploits are discovered posthumously, and who solves the mysteries of the human brain in its most profound state of creation.

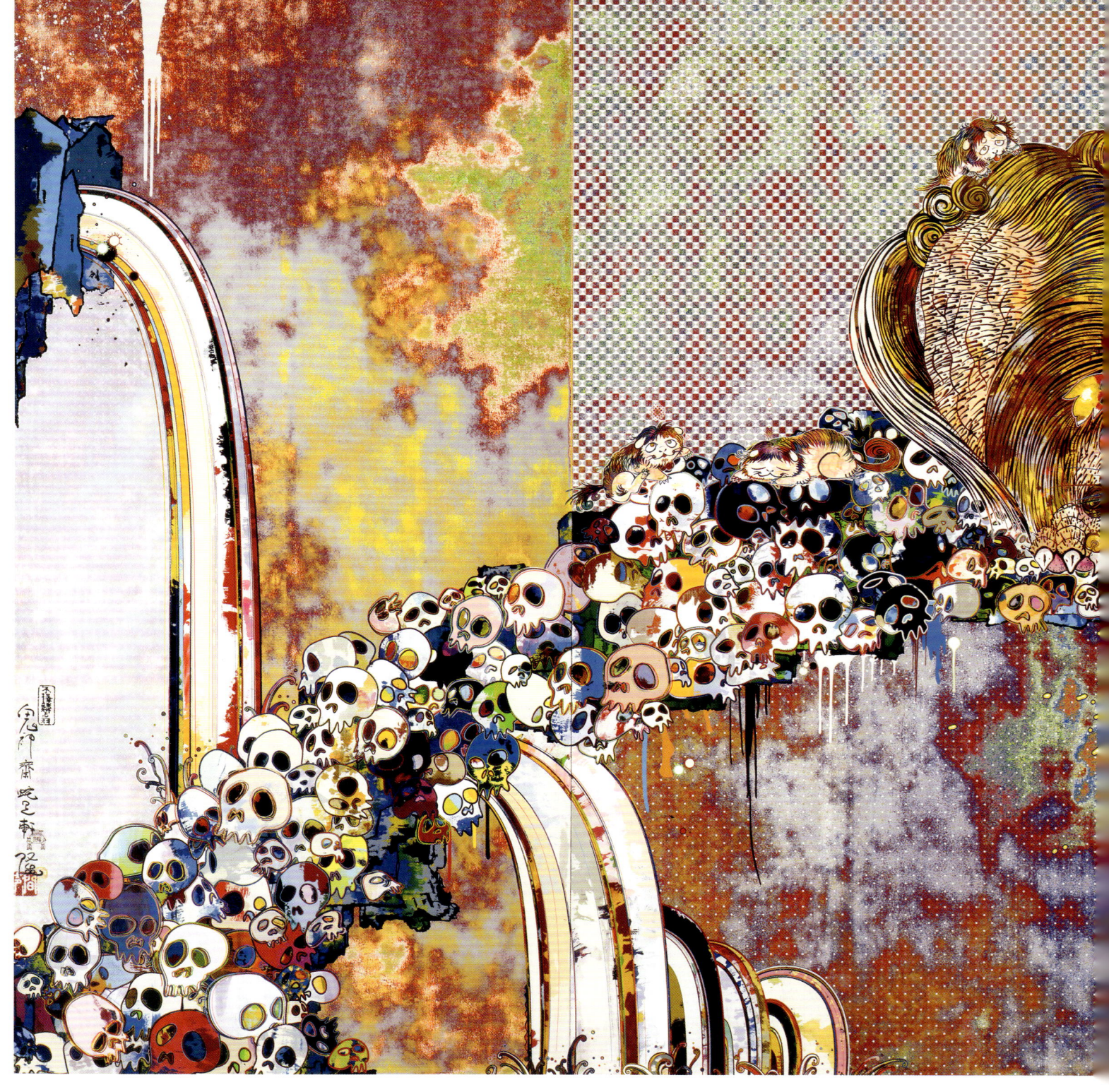

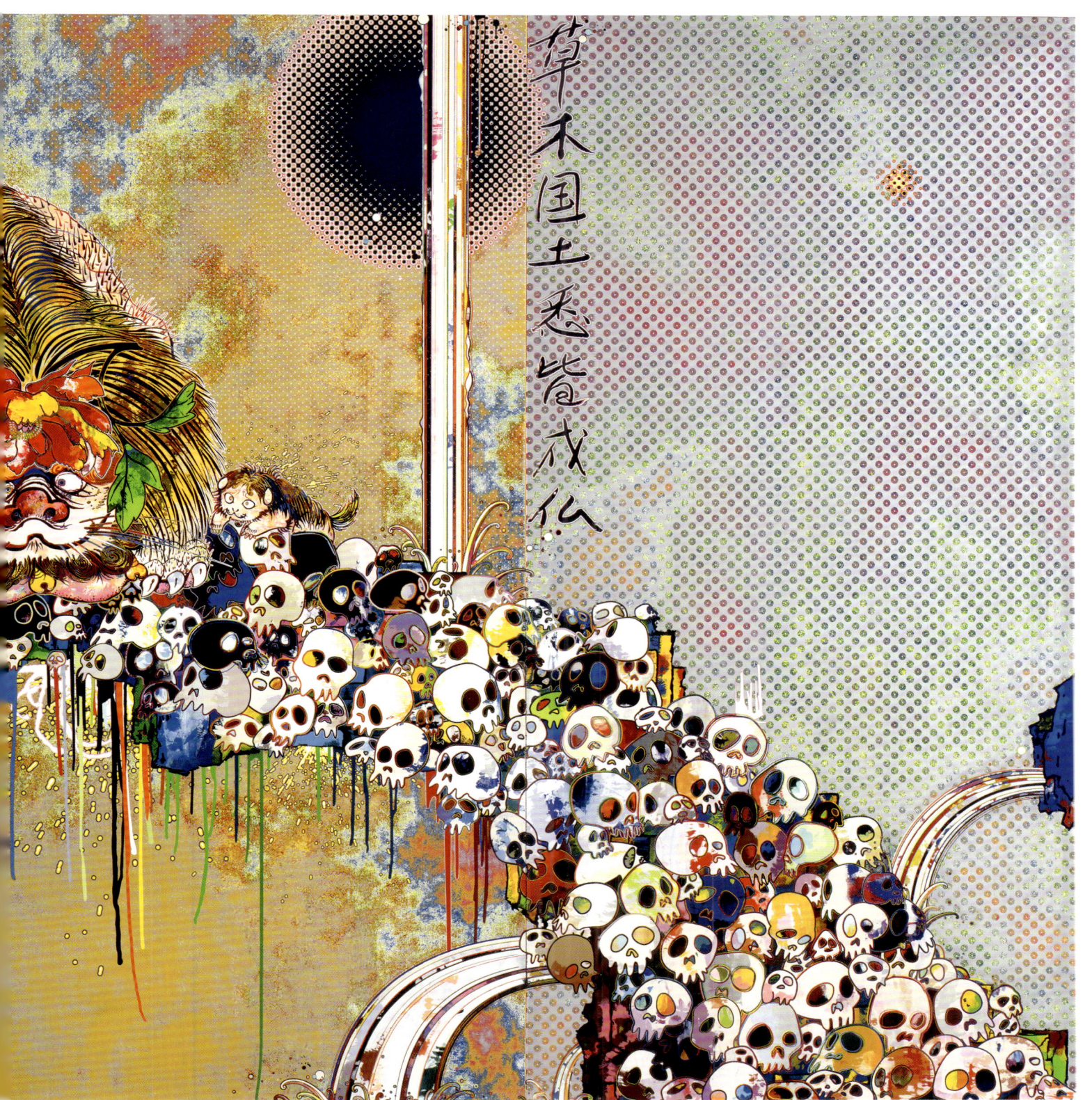

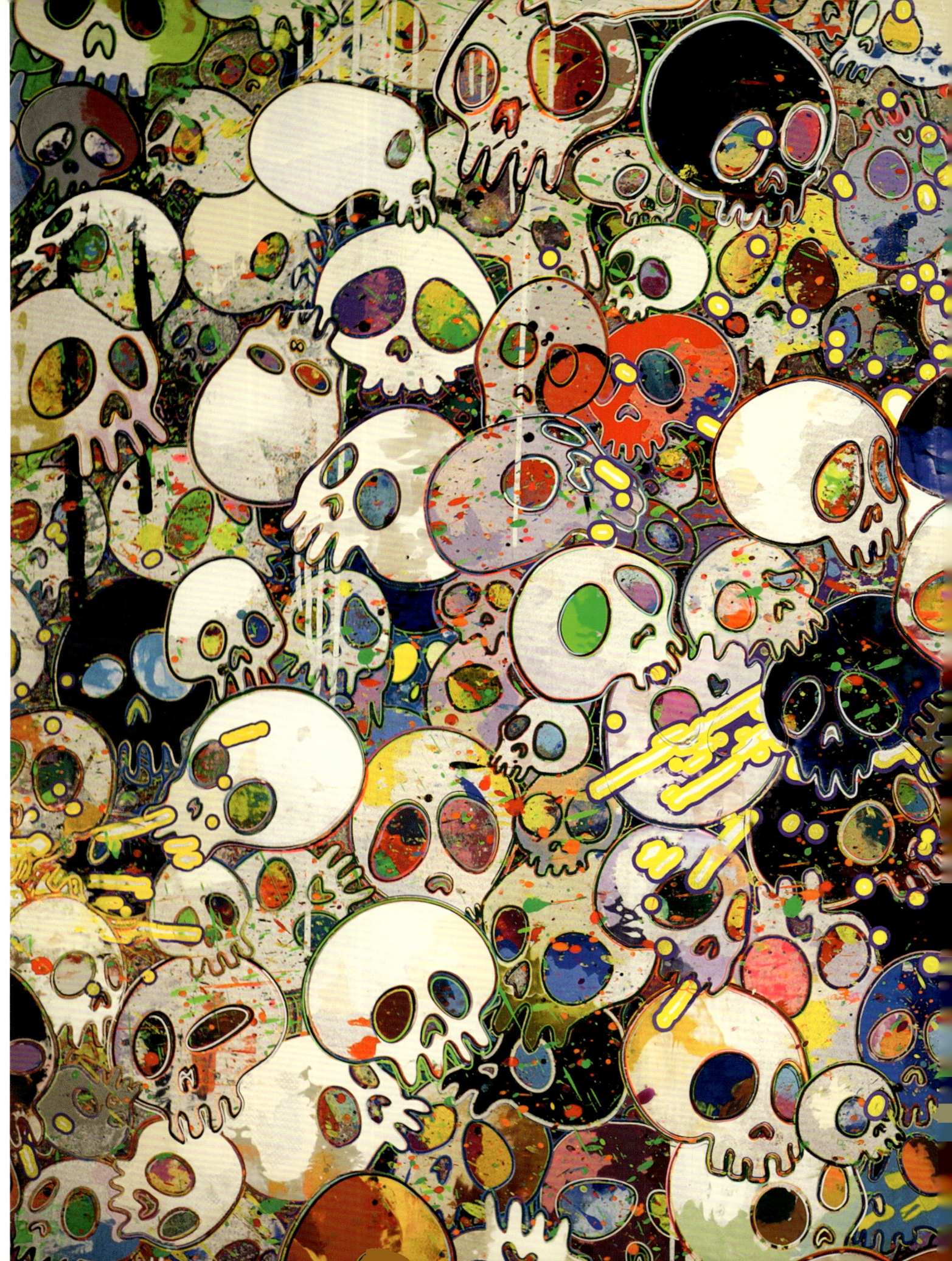

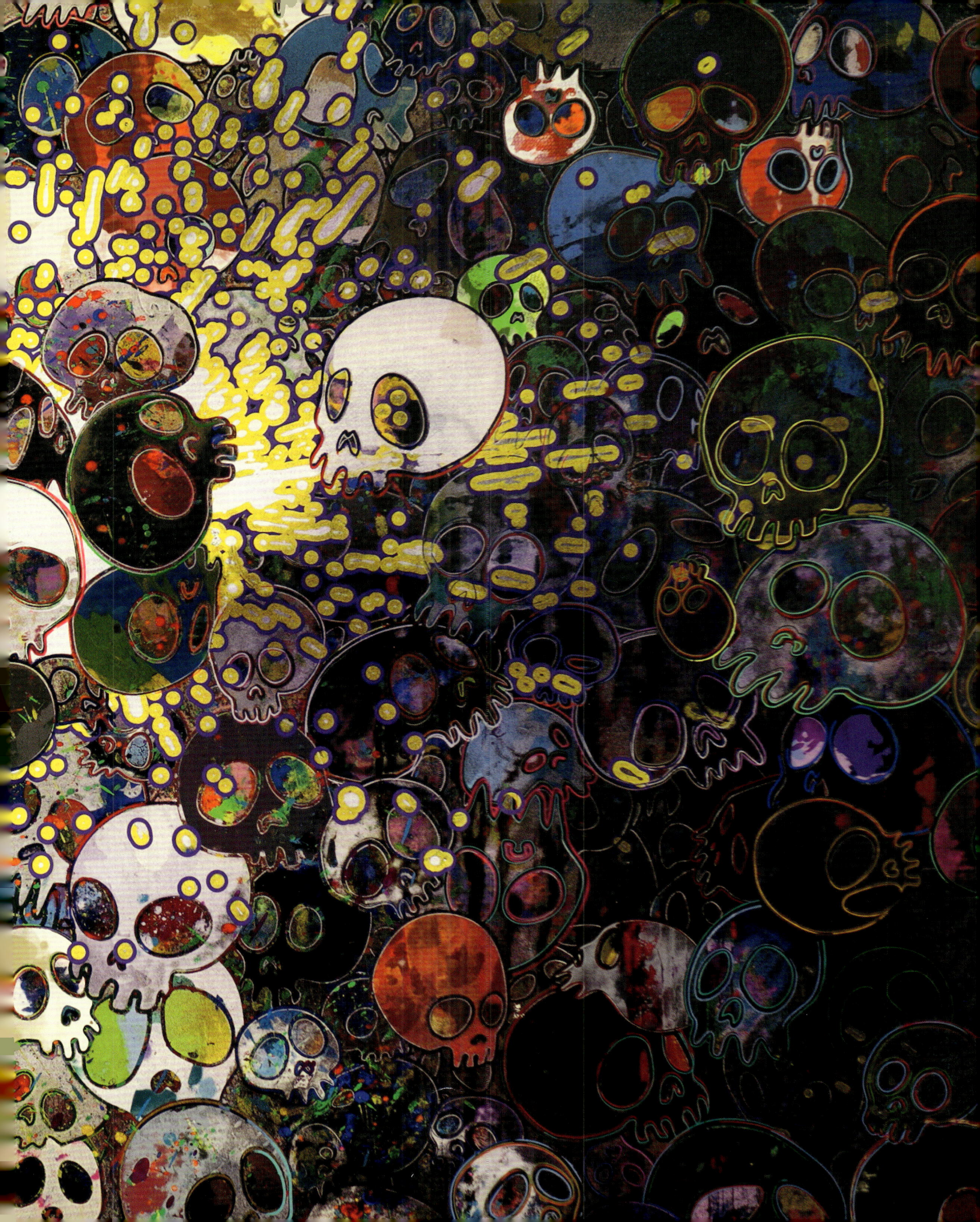

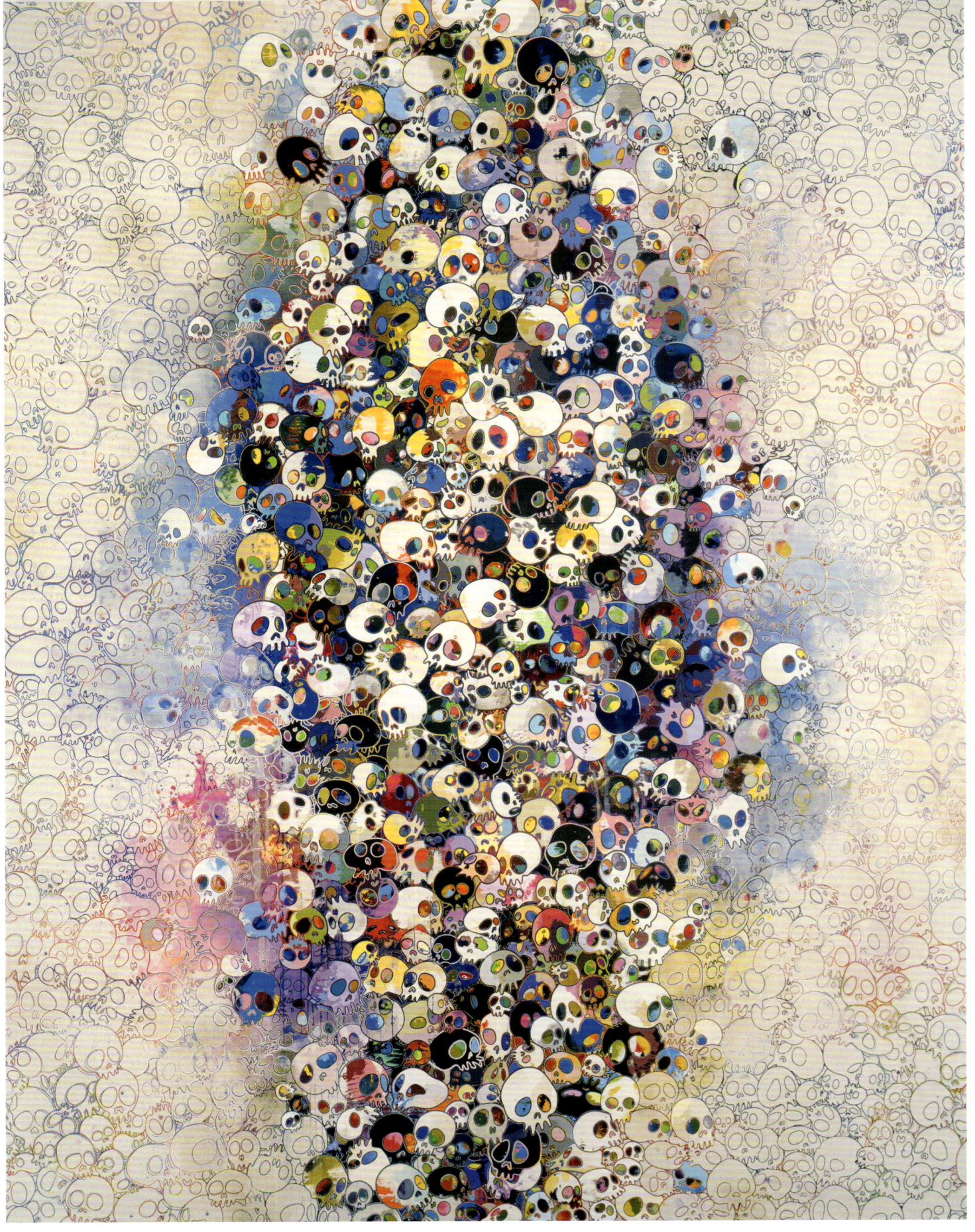

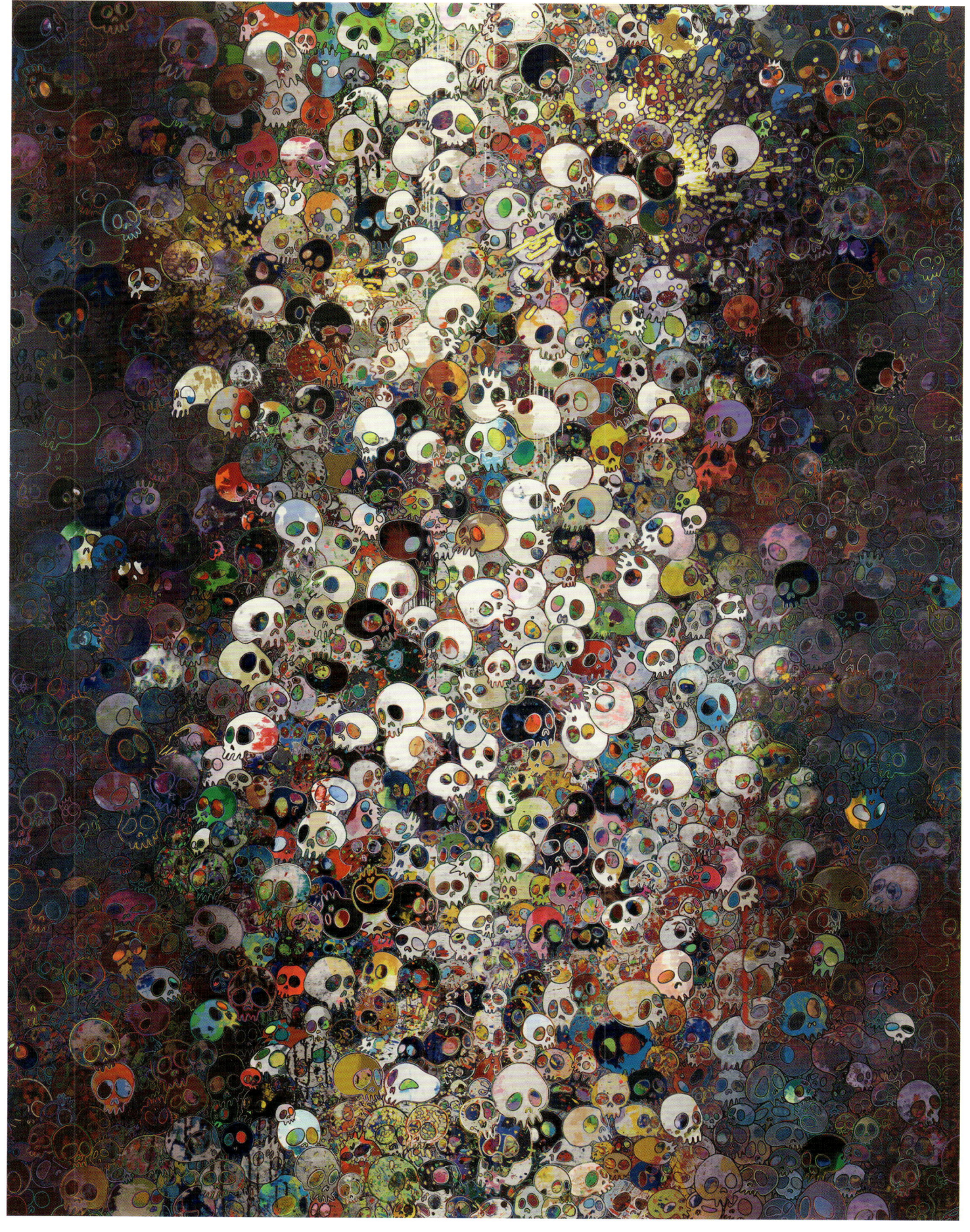

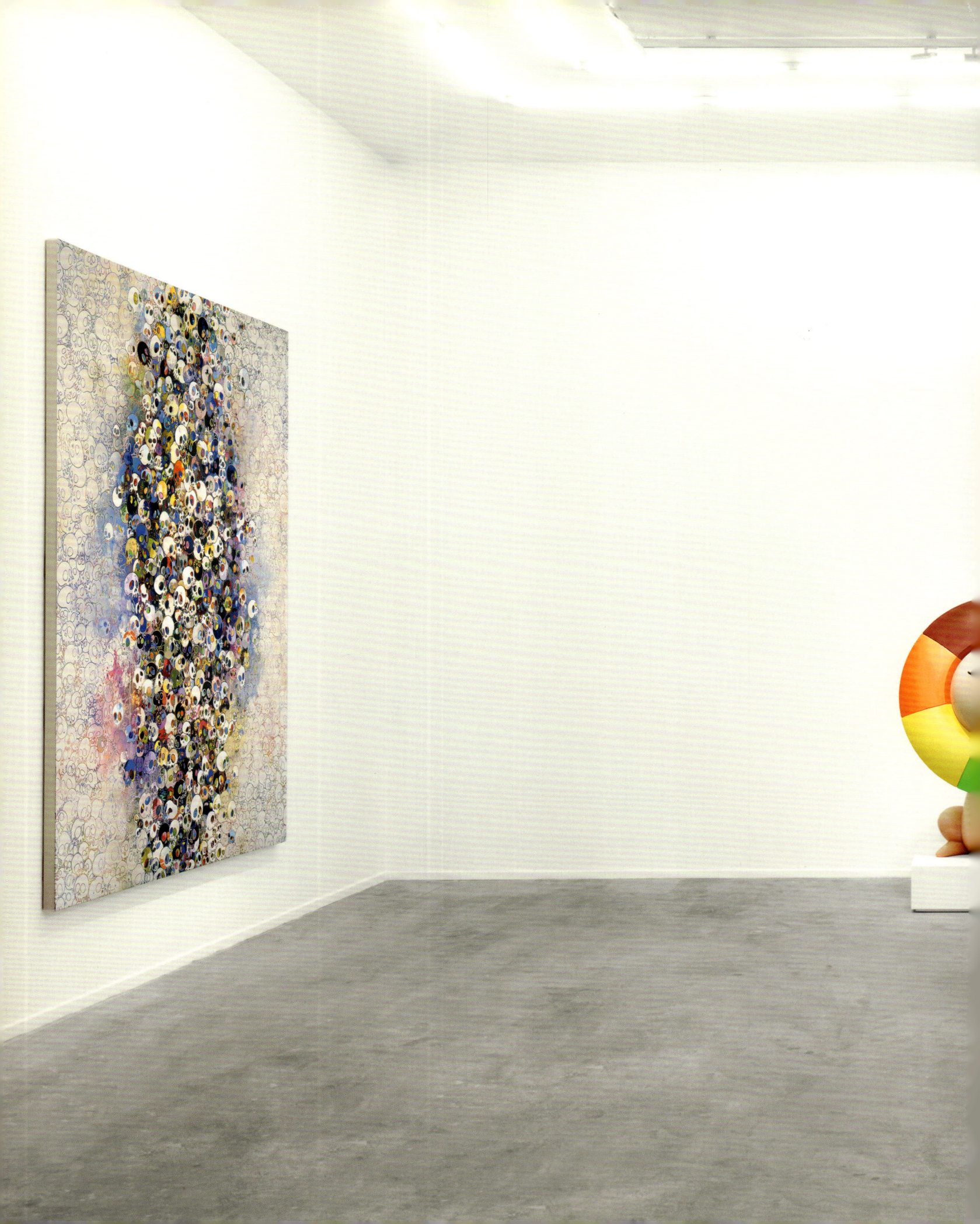

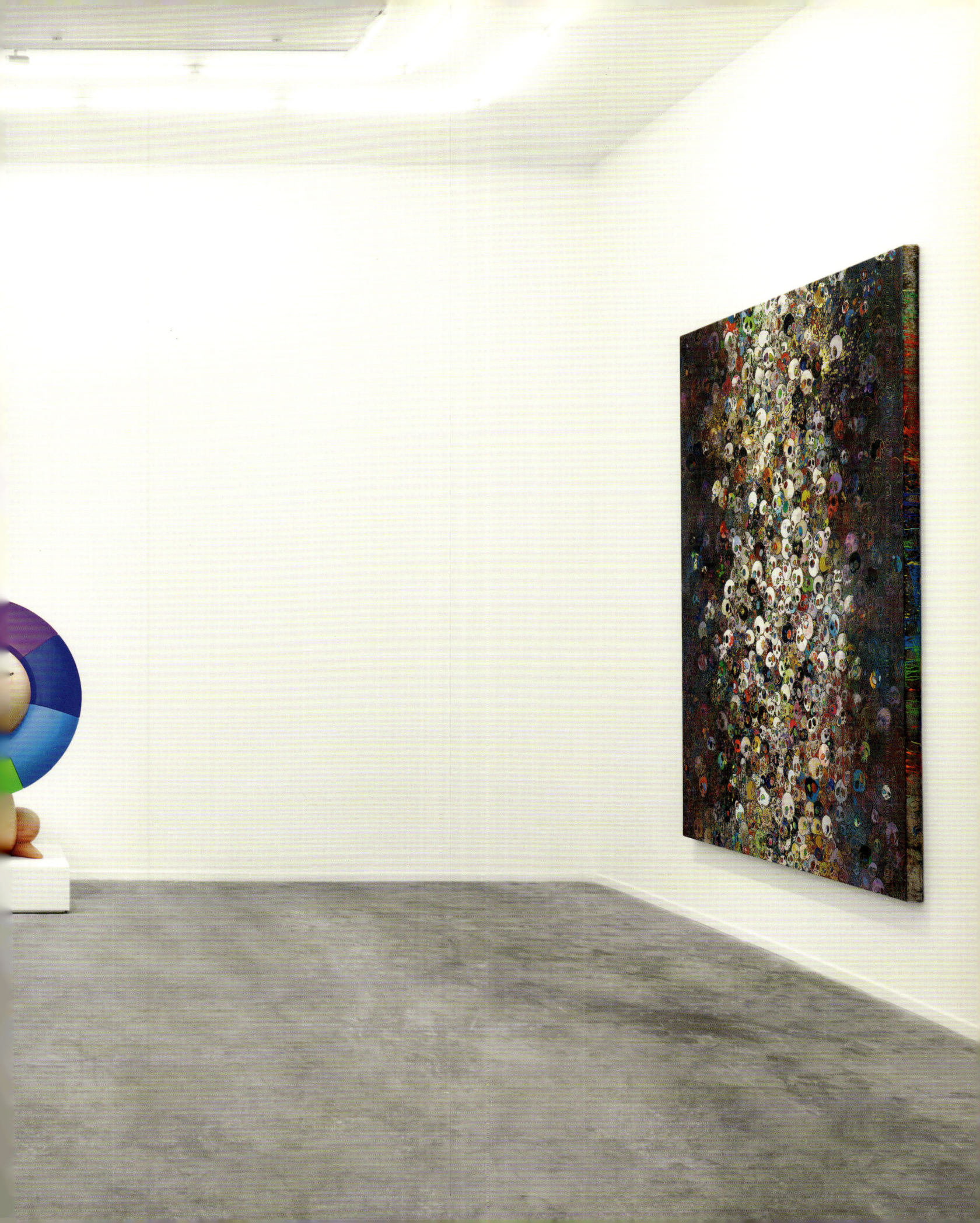

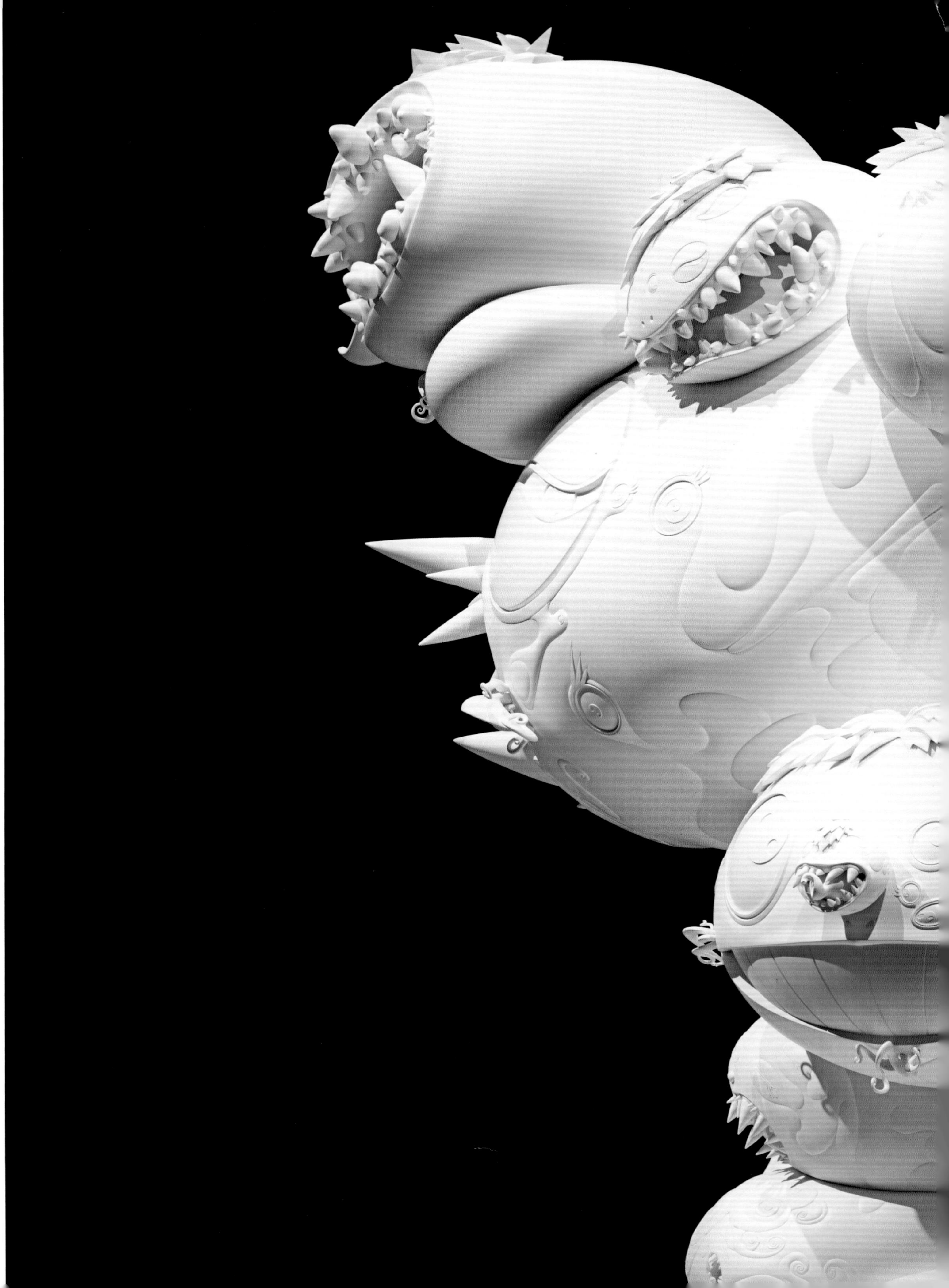

Daruma Scale Model (detail) 2009–11

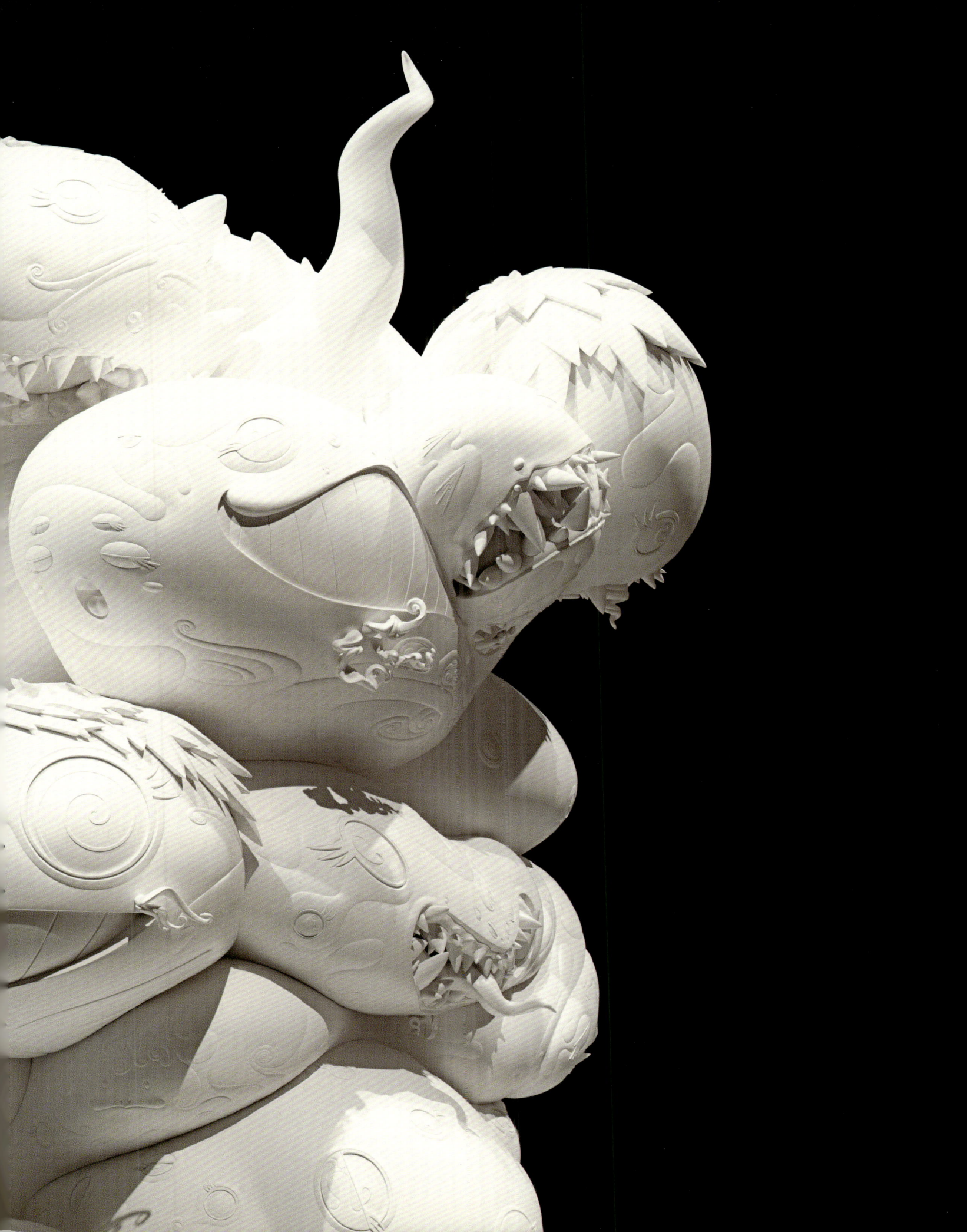

In the art world, critics always connect entertainment with guilt, amusement with superficiality. I think my work is the answer to that criticism. Which doesn't mean that I make work only to amuse. Taking architecture as an analogy, you could say that my paintings are like buildings: On the surface, they appear very light and flimsy, but they're actually made of very solid materials underneath. The depth is visual.

I get a sense of fulfillment whenever strangers buy my work or merchandise. It's a compliment that transcends words. Art is a constant give and take between cultural signifiers, and I'm constantly importing and exporting art as both merchandise and culture. I think there are a lot of people who take great pleasure from these transactions of the heart. Whenever I support or directly mediate this process to ensure that it goes smoothly

MY HAPPINESS IS IN DIRECT PROPORTION TO THE AMOUNT OF WORK AND EFFORT PUT INTO THE PROJECT.

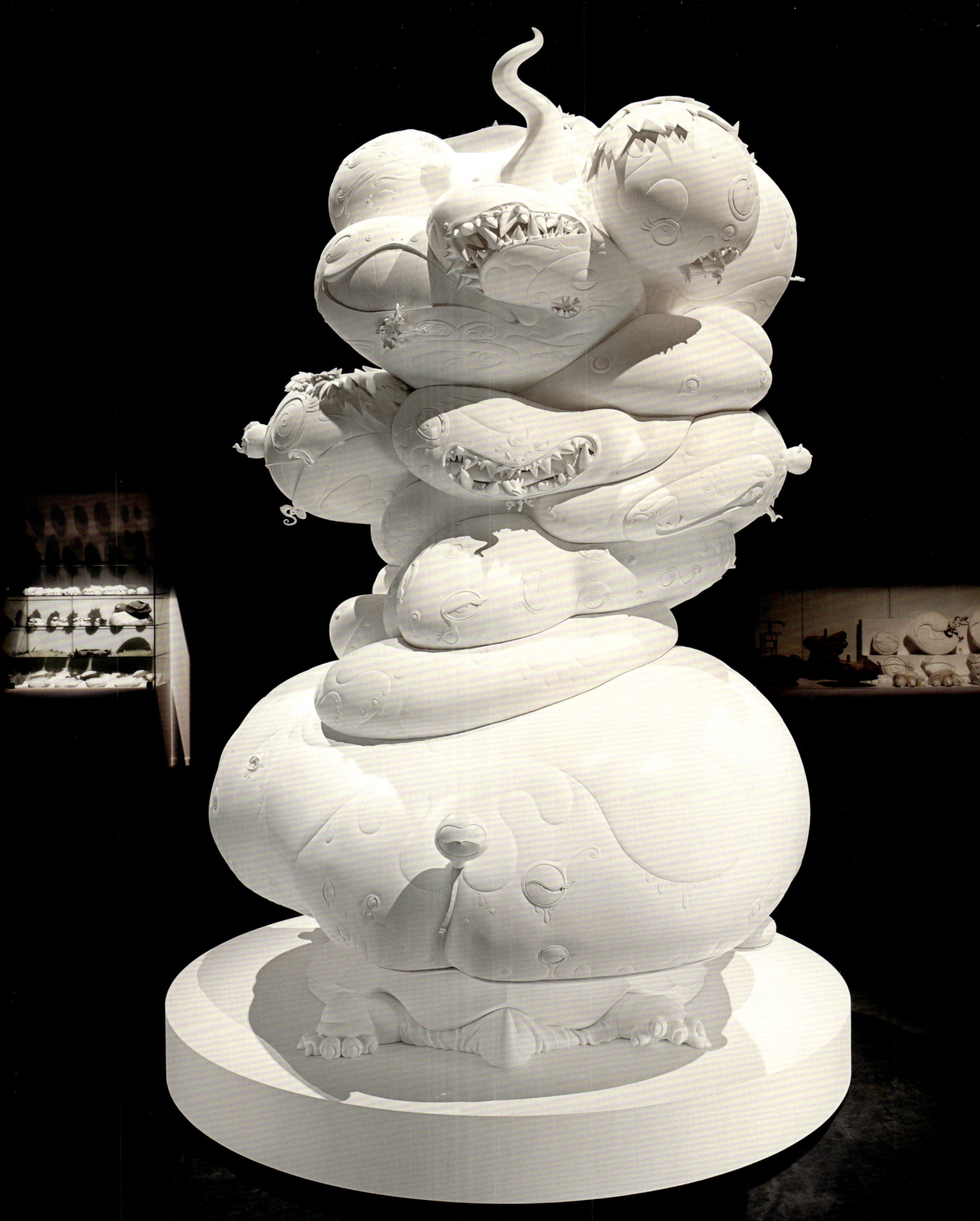

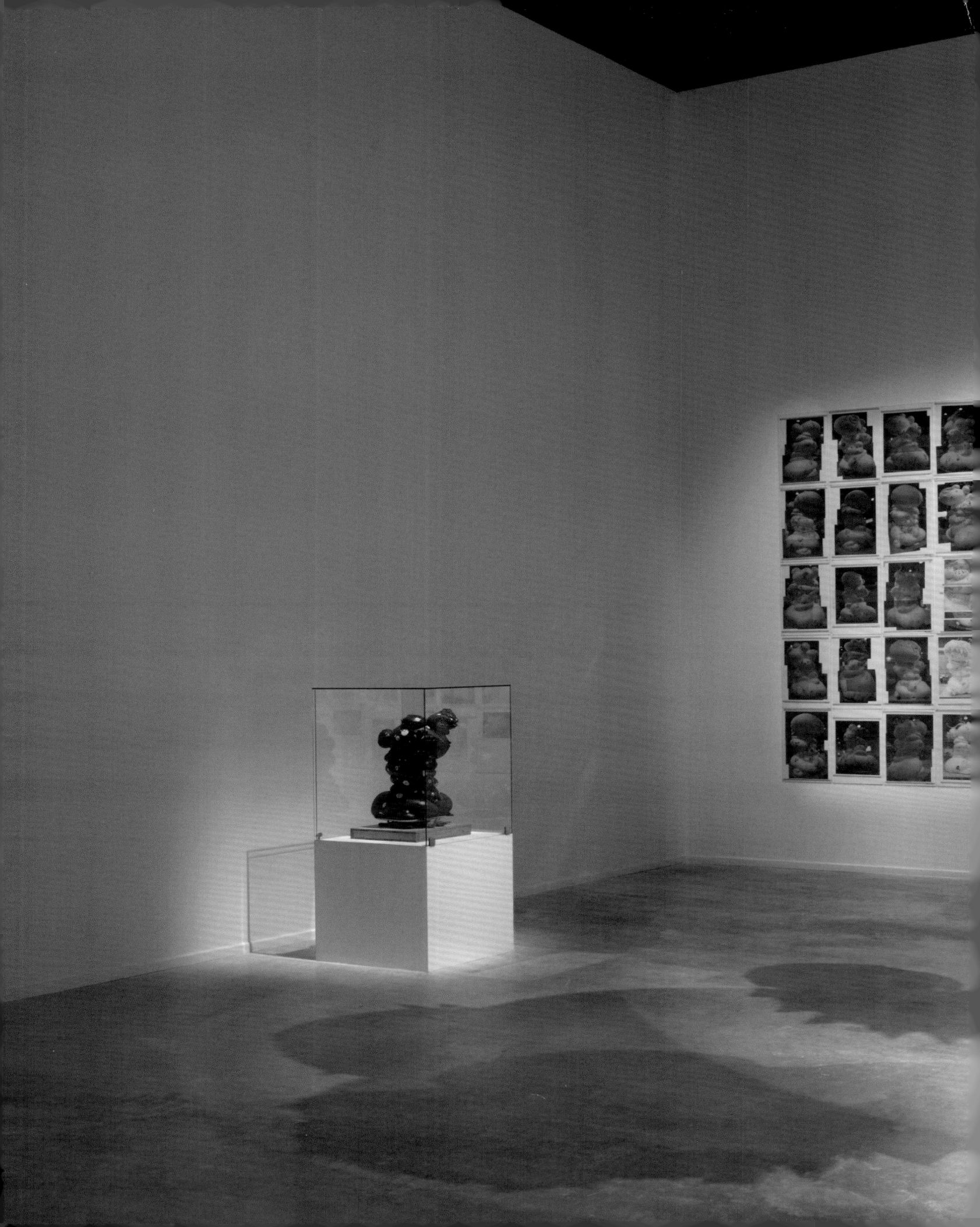

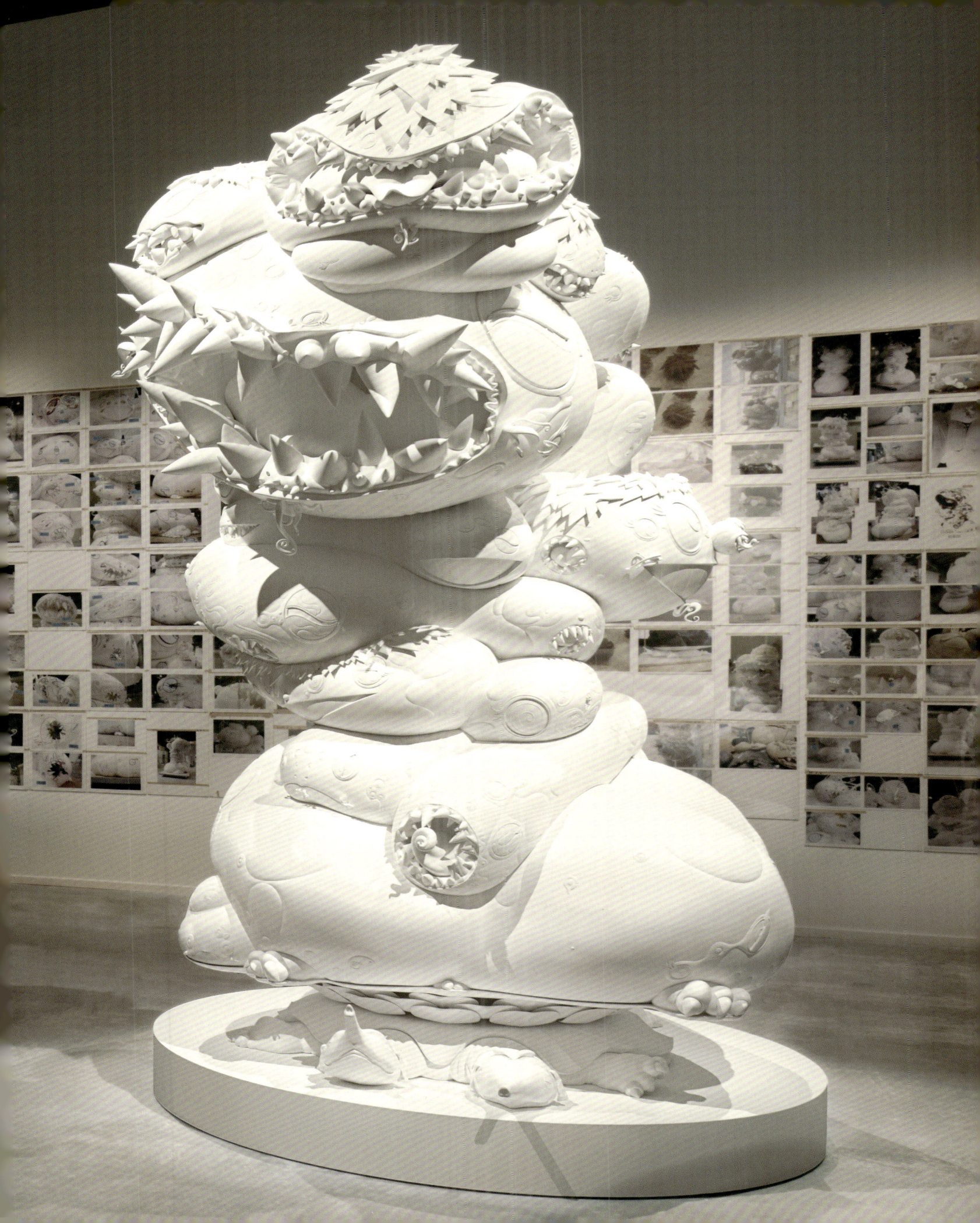

In the heart's eye, a universe 2007

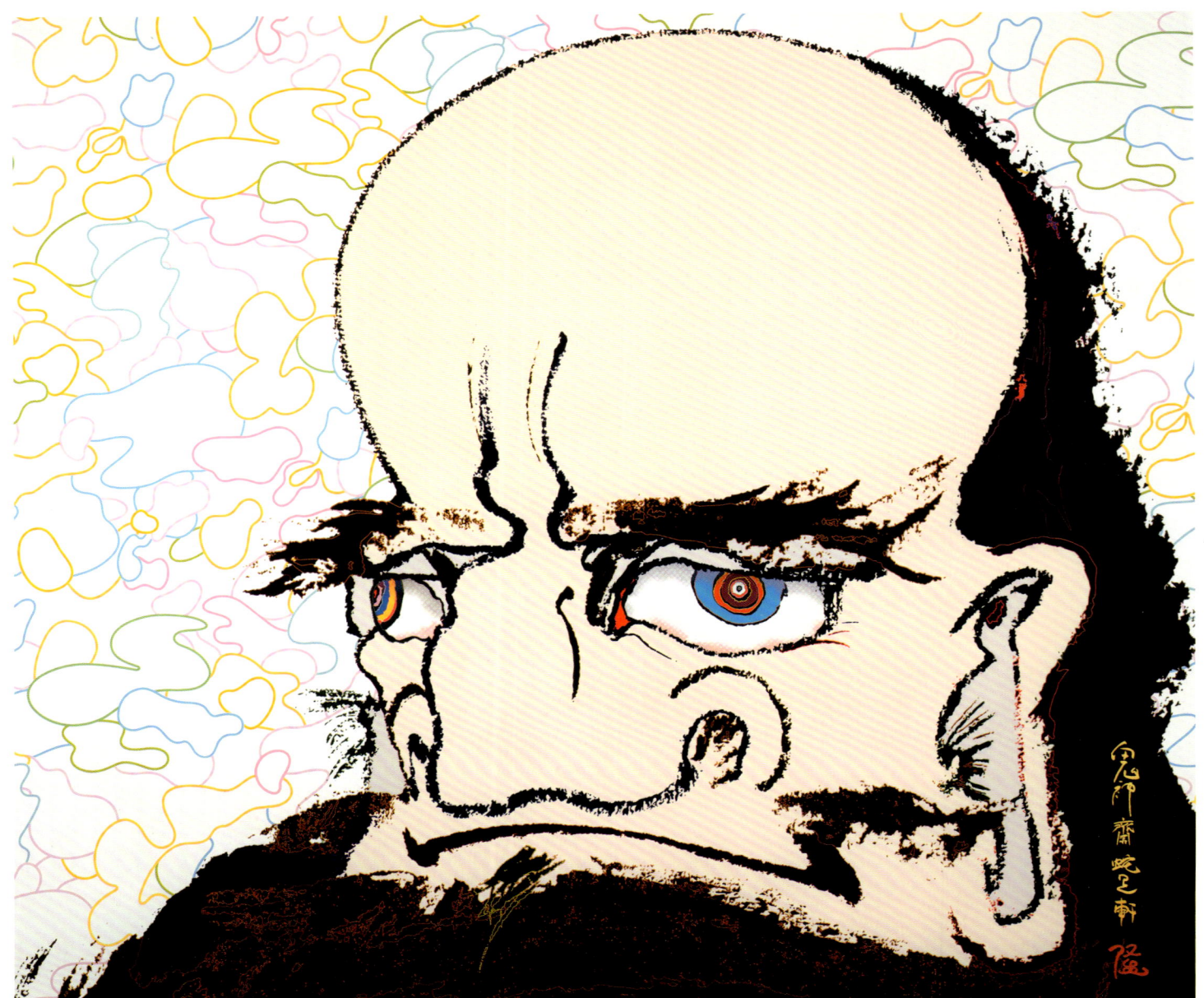

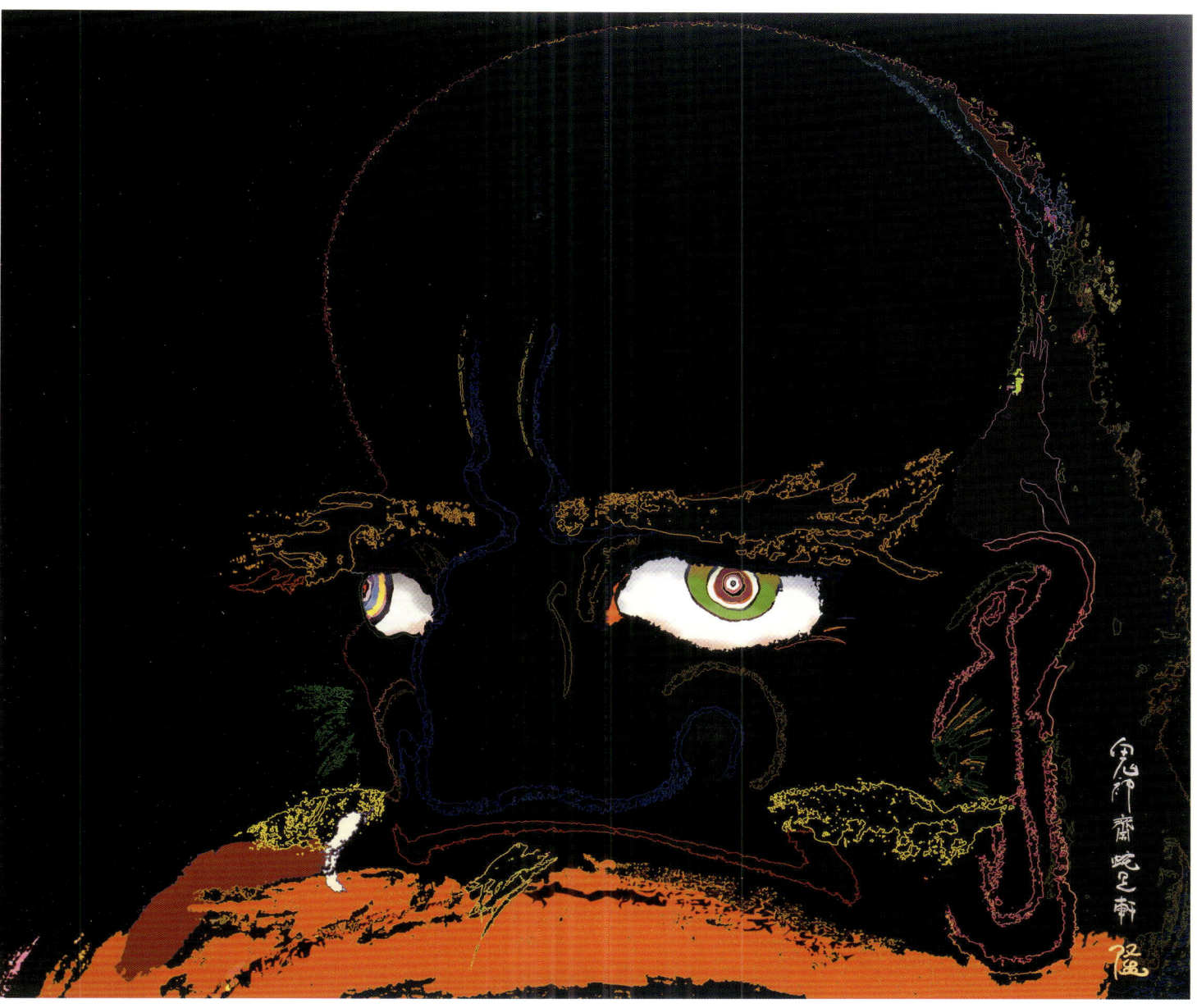

My arms and legs rot off and though my blood rushes forth, the tranquility of my heart shall be prized above all. (Red blood, black blood, blood that is not blood) 2007

Release Chakra's Gate at This Instant (detail) 2008

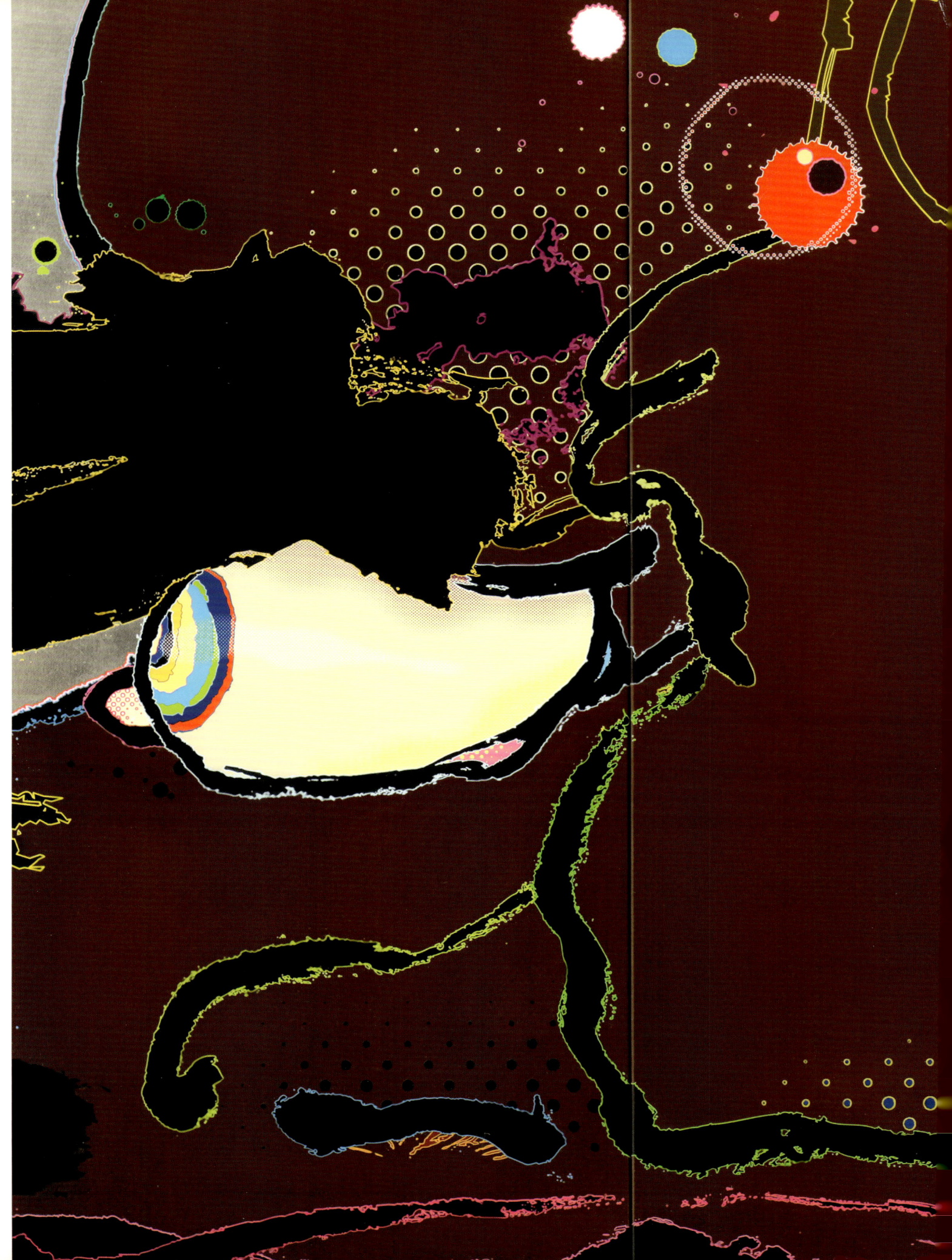

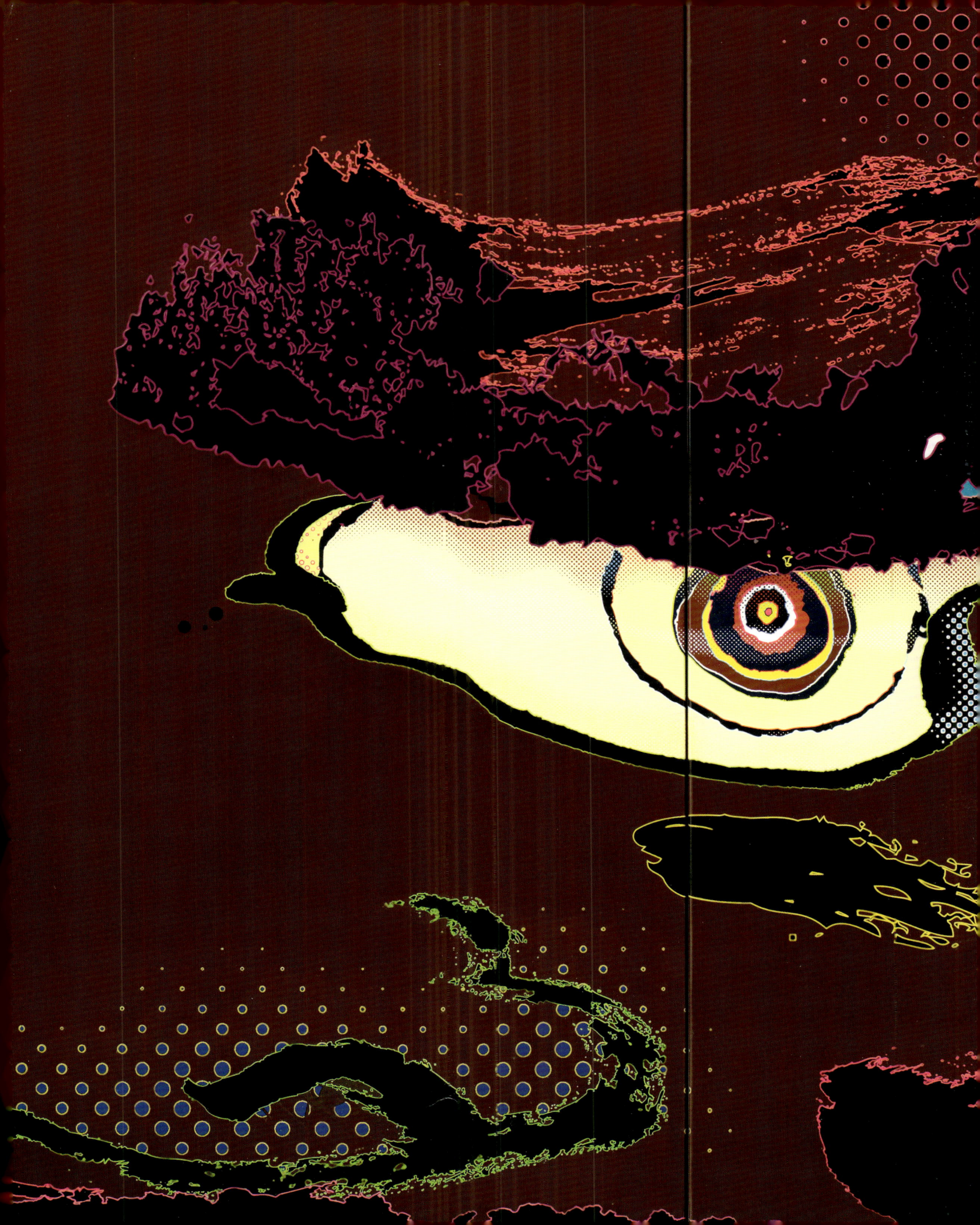

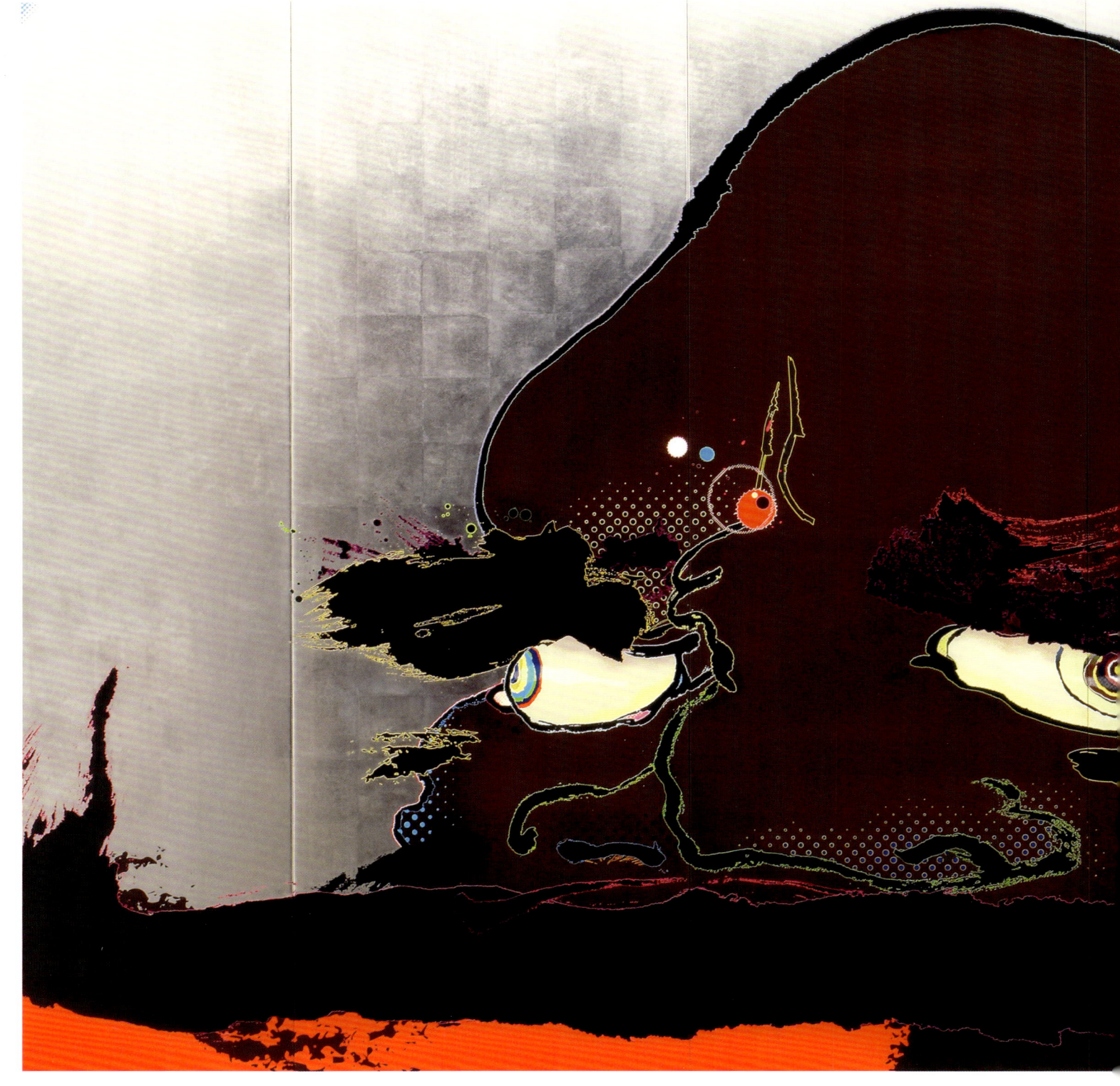

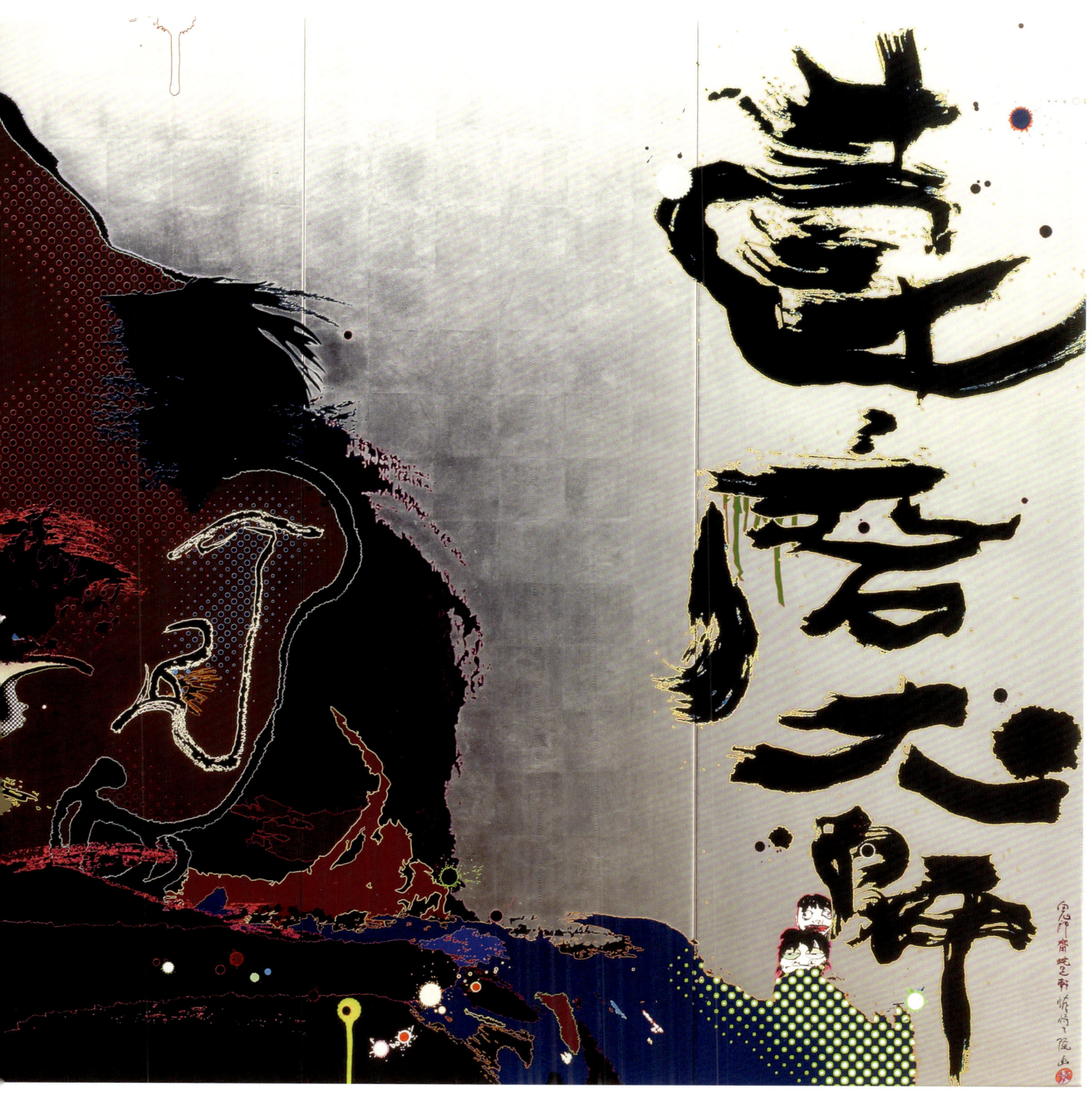

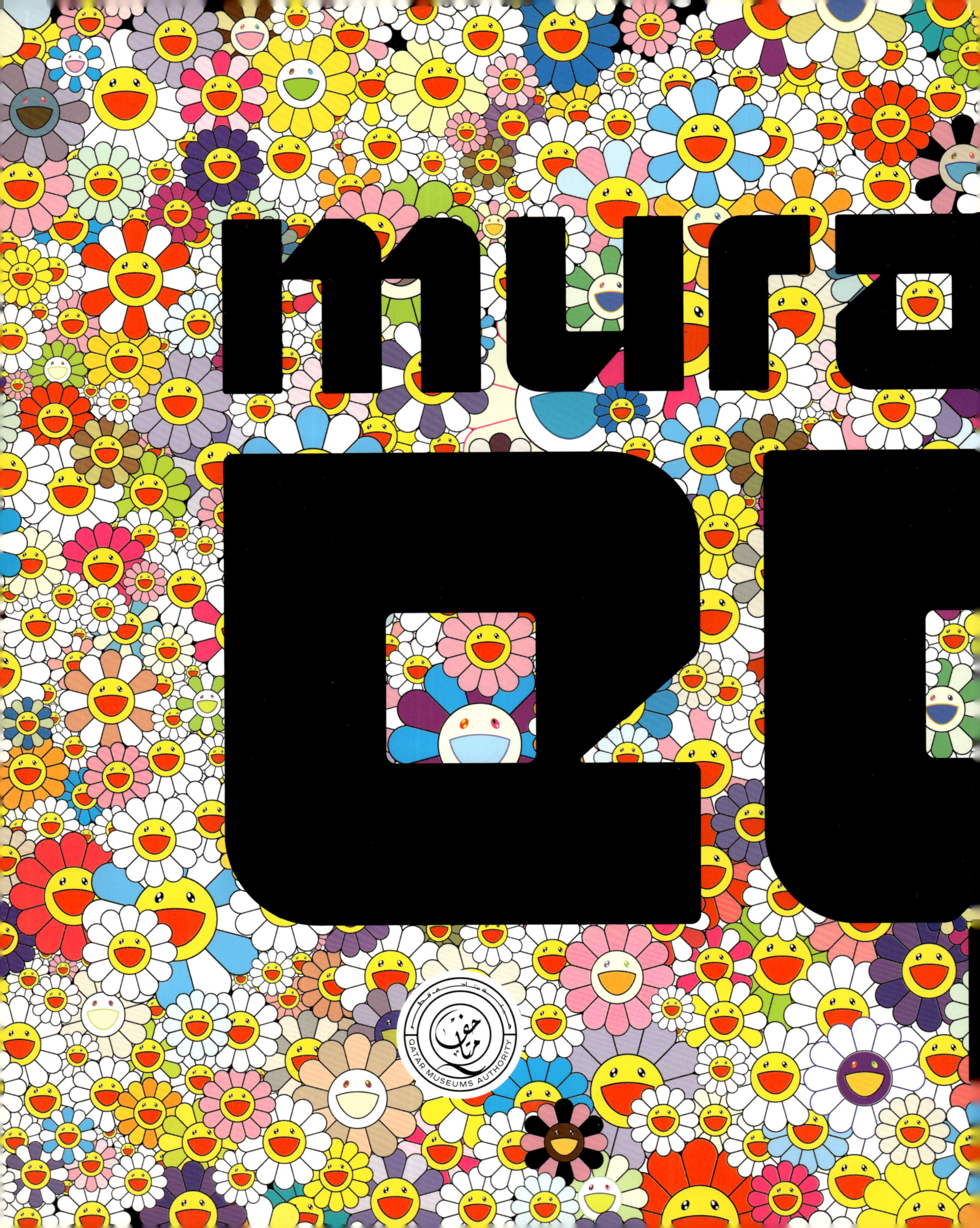

murakami

QATAR MUSEUMS AUTHORITY

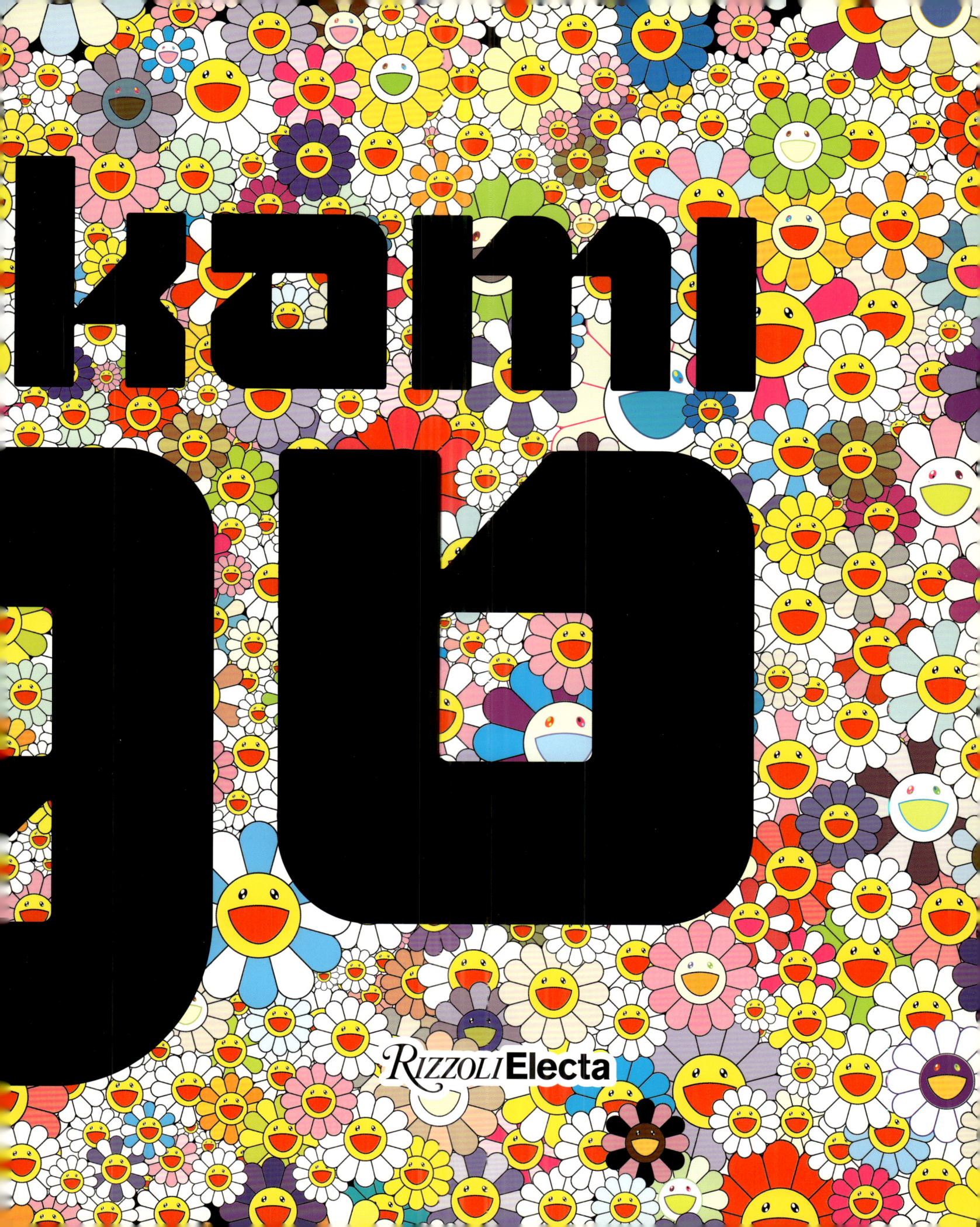

kami
DG

RIZZOLI Electa

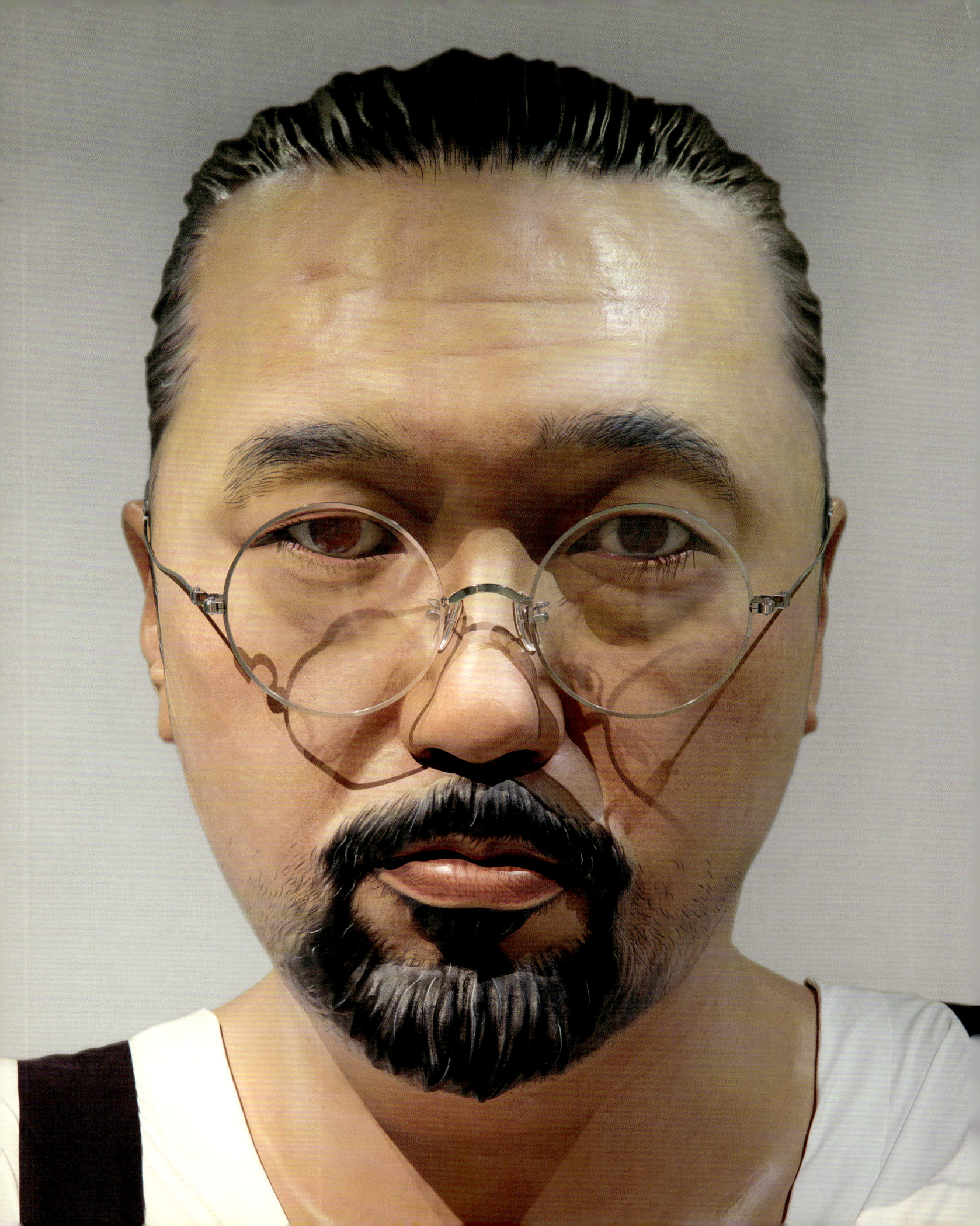

First published in the United States in 2012 by
Rizzoli Electa, a division of Rizzoli International Publications, Inc.
300 Park Avenue South
New York, NY 10010
www.rizzoliusa.com

2018 2019 2020 2021 / 10 9 8 7 6 5 4

ISBN 13: 978-0-8478-3889-9

Library of Congress Control Number: 201278395

Designed by Goto Design, New York

Color separations by ProGraphics
Printed in Italy